The International Tax Law Concept of Dividend

Series on International Taxation

VOLUME 36

Series Editors

Prof. Ruth Mason, University of Virginia School of Law
Prof. Dr Ekkehart Reimer, University of Heidelberg

Introduction & Contents

The Series on International Taxation deals with a wide variety of topics in the global tax arena. The authors include many of the field's leading experts as well as talented newcomers. Their expert views and incisive commentary has proven highly useful to practitioners and academics alike.

Objective

The volumes published in this series are aimed at offering high-quality analytical information and practical solutions for international tax practitioners.

Readership

Practitioners, academics and policy makers in international tax law.

Frequency of Publication

2-3 new volumes published each year.

The titles published in this series are listed at the end of this volume.

The International Tax Law Concept of Dividend

Second Edition

Marjaana Helminen

Published by:
Kluwer Law International B.V.
PO Box 316
2400 AH Alphen aan den Rijn
The Netherlands
Website: www.wolterskluwerlr.com

Sold and distributed in North, Central and South America by:
Wolters Kluwer Legal & Regulatory U.S.
7201 McKinney Circle
Frederick, MD 21704
United States of America
Email: customer.service@wolterskluwer.com

Sold and distributed in all other countries by:
Quadrant
Rockwood House
Haywards Heath
West Sussex
RH16 3DH
United Kingdom
Email: international-customerservice@wolterskluwer.com

Printed on acid-free paper.

ISBN 978-90-411-8394-1

e-Book: ISBN 978-90-411-8395-8
web-PDF: ISBN 978-90-411-8396-5

© 2017 Kluwer Law International BV, The Netherlands

All rights reserved. No part of this publication may be reproduced, stored in a retrieval system, or transmitted in any form or by any means, electronic, mechanical, photocopying, recording, or otherwise, without written permission from the publisher.

Permission to use this content must be obtained from the copyright owner. Please apply to: Permissions Department, Wolters Kluwer Legal & Regulatory U.S., 76 Ninth Avenue, 7th Floor, New York, NY 10011-5201, USA. Website: www.wolterskluwerlr.com

Printed in the United Kingdom.

MIX
FSC® C103993

Table of Contents

Preface		xi
List of Abbreviations		xiii

CHAPTER 1
Introduction — 1

§1.01	Subject	1
§1.02	Specific Purpose and Scope of the Study	2
§1.03	Approach and Research Methods	8
§1.04	Relevance of the Study	9
	[A] Double Taxation or Non-taxation Caused by Different Dividend Definitions	9
	[B] The Concept of Dividend and Tax Neutrality	10
§1.05	Materials	12
§1.06	Terminology	13
§1.07	Outline of the Study	15

CHAPTER 2
Tax Treatment of Inter-Corporate Cross-Border Dividends — 17

§2.01	Domestic Law Dividend Taxation Systems	17
§2.02	EU Tax Law	18
	[A] The Parent-Subsidiary Directive	18
	[B] The TFEU	19
	[1] Permanent Establishments	19
	[2] Foreign-Source Dividend of a Resident	20
	[3] Dividend Received by a Non-resident	22
§2.03	Tax Treaties	25
§2.04	A Comparison Between the Taxation of Dividend and Other Income	27

Table of Contents

CHAPTER 3
Interaction among Different Legal Systems of International Tax Law   33
§3.01 Relationship among Different Legal Systems of International Tax Law   33
    [A] Relevance of the Relationship   33
    [B] Domestic Tax Laws of Two States   33
    [C] Tax Treaties and Domestic Tax Law   34
    [D] EU Tax Law and Domestic Tax Law   36
    [E] Tax Treaties and EU Tax Law   39
§3.02 The Classification Conflicts of International Tax Law   40
    [A] Description of the Problem   40
    [B] Solutions to Classification Conflicts   44
        [1] General Solutions   44
        [2] Express Definitions in Tax Treaties   48
        [3] The Rule of Interpretation in Tax Treaties   49
        [4] Double Taxation Relief Articles   51
        [5] Mutual Agreement Procedure and Arbitration   53
        [6] Solutions in Actual Tax Treaties   54
    [C] Conclusions   56

CHAPTER 4
Different Dividend Concepts in International Tax Law   59
§4.01 The Norms Determining the Tax Law Concept of a Dividend   59
§4.02 Domestic Laws   62
§4.03 The EU Parent-Subsidiary Directive   63
§4.04 Tax Treaties   66
    [A] Introduction   66
    [B] The Model Conventions   66
    [C] Actual Tax Treaties   70
§4.05 Conclusions   71

CHAPTER 5
Dividend-Distributing Entities   75
§5.01 Introduction   75
§5.02 Domestic Laws   76
    [A] Different Forms of Doing Business   76
    [B] Entity Classification for Tax Law Purposes   77
    [C] Dividend-Distributing Entities   78
    [D] Inconsistent Classification and the Elimination of Double Taxation   78
§5.03 The EU Parent-Subsidiary Directive   79
§5.04 Tax Treaties   81
    [A] The Model Conventions   81
    [B] Actual Tax Treaties   88
§5.05 Conclusions   91

Table of Contents

CHAPTER 6
Dividend-Stripping and the Dividend-Generating Relationship ... 93
§6.01 Introduction ... 93
§6.02 The Basic Relationship ... 94
    [A] Domestic Tax Laws ... 94
    [B] The Parent-Subsidiary Directive ... 95
    [C] Tax Treaties ... 98
        [1] The Model Conventions ... 98
        [2] Actual Tax Treaties ... 99
    [D] Conclusions ... 100
§6.03 Classification of Payments under Dividend-Stripping Arrangements ... 101
    [A] Proceeds from the Transfer of Dividend Rights ... 101
        [1] Introduction ... 101
        [2] Domestic Tax Laws ... 101
        [3] The EU Parent-Subsidiary Directive ... 102
        [4] Tax Treaties ... 103
        [5] Conclusions ... 106
    [B] Substitute Payments under Equity Securities Lending Transactions ... 108
        [1] Introduction ... 108
        [2] Domestic Tax Laws ... 110
        [3] The EU Parent-Subsidiary Directive ... 111
        [4] Tax Treaties ... 112
        [5] Conclusions ... 116
    [C] Dividend Equivalent Payments from Derivative Financial Instruments ... 117
        [1] Introduction ... 117
        [2] Domestic Tax Laws ... 123
        [3] The Parent-Subsidiary Directive ... 124
        [4] Tax Treaties ... 125
        [5] Conclusions ... 127

CHAPTER 7
Fictive Distributions as a Dividend ... 129
§7.01 Classification of CFC Income ... 129
    [A] Introduction ... 129
    [B] Domestic Tax Laws ... 132
    [C] EU Law ... 132
        [1] The TFEU and the Anti-tax Avoidance Directive ... 132
        [2] The EU Parent-Subsidiary Directive ... 134
    [D] Tax Treaties ... 136
    [E] Conclusions ... 142
§7.02 Treatment of Bonus Shares ... 142
    [A] Introduction ... 142

Table of Contents

	[B] Domestic Tax Laws	143
	[C] The EU Parent-Subsidiary Directive	144
	[D] Tax Treaties	145
	[E] Conclusions	148

CHAPTER 8
Classification of Economic Benefits from Corporations to Their Shareholders in the Form of Transfer Prices — 151
§8.01 Introduction — 151
§8.02 Domestic Laws — 154
§8.03 EU Tax Law — 155
　[A] The TFEU — 155
　[B] The Parent-Subsidiary Directive — 156
§8.04 Tax Treaties — 158
§8.05 Conclusions — 163

CHAPTER 9
Classification of Return on Debt-Equity Hybrids — 165
§9.01 Introduction — 165
§9.02 General Approaches — 167
　[A] General Characteristics of Debt and Equity — 167
　[B] Domestic Tax Laws — 170
　[C] EU Law — 172
　　[1] Relevance — 172
　　[2] The P-S Directive and the Elimination of Double Taxation — 172
　　[3] The EU Directives and the Elimination of Double Non-taxation — 176
　[D] Tax Treaties — 178
　　[1] The Model Conventions — 178
　　[2] Actual Tax Treaties — 182
§9.03 Interest on Long-Term or Perpetual Debt — 184
　[A] Introduction — 184
　[B] Domestic Tax Laws — 185
　[C] The EU Parent-Subsidiary Directive — 186
　[D] Tax Treaties — 186
§9.04 Interest on Profit-Participating Debt Instruments — 188
　[A] Introduction — 188
　[B] Domestic Tax Laws — 189
　[C] The EU Parent-Subsidiary Directive — 190
　[D] Tax Treaties — 191
§9.05 Interest on Convertible Debt Instruments — 194
　[A] Introduction — 194
　[B] Domestic Tax Laws — 195
　[C] The Parent-Subsidiary Directive — 196

	[D] Tax Treaties	196
§9.06	Interest on Subordinated Debt Instruments	198
	[A] Introduction	198
	[B] Domestic Tax Laws	199
	[C] The EU Parent-Subsidiary Directive	199
	[D] Tax Treaties	200
§9.07	Classification of the Return on Preferred Shares	201
	[A] Introduction	201
	[B] Domestic Tax Laws	203
	[C] The EU Parent-Subsidiary Directive	203
	[D] Tax Treaties	205
§9.08	Conclusions	207

CHAPTER 10
Classification of Interest in Thin Capitalization Situations 209
§10.01	Introduction	209
§10.02	Non-discrimination	211
	[A] Tax Treaties	211
	[B] The TFEU	212
§10.03	The EU Parent-Subsidiary Directive	214
§10.04	Tax Treaties	217
§10.05	Conclusions	223

CHAPTER 11
Classification of Liquidation Distributions 225
§11.01	Introduction	225
§11.02	Domestic Tax Laws	227
§11.03	The EU Parent-Subsidiary Directive	228
§11.04	Tax Treaties	232
	[A] The Model Treaties	232
	[B] Actual Treaties	239
§11.05	Conclusions	240

CHAPTER 12
Concluding Remarks 241
§12.01	General	241
§12.02	Dividend-Distributing Entities	241
§12.03	Dividend-Stripping and the Dividend-Generating Relationship	243
	[A] The Basic Relationship	243
	[B] Dividend-Stripping Arrangements	244
	[1] Transfer of Dividend Rights	244
	[2] Equity Securities Lending Transactions	245
	[3] Derivative Financial Instruments	246
§12.04	Fictive Distributions	246
	[A] CFC Income	246

Table of Contents

	[B] Bonus Shares	247
§12.05	Economic Benefits in the Form of Transfer Prices	247
§12.06	Return on Debt-Equity Hybrids	248
§12.07	Thin Capitalization Interest	249
§12.08	Liquidation Distributions	249
§12.09	Final Conclusions	250

Bibliography 253

Index 281

Preface

My doctoral thesis *The Dividend Concept in International Tax Law – Dividend Payments Between Corporate Entities* was published by Kluwer in 1999. In 2000, the book was awarded the International Fiscal Association Mitchell B. Carrol Price. Almost a decade later, the publisher contacted me with an interesting proposal. Kluwer wanted to publish an updated edition of my doctoral thesis, which they considered to have become a classic. My first reaction to the publisher's idea was somewhat suspicious because I had never heard about a second edition of a doctoral thesis. After some consultation with Kluwer, I however agreed to publish a second book on the international tax law concept of dividend with Kluwer. In order to make a clear difference between the original doctoral thesis and the new book on the dividend concept, I decided, however, not to publish the new book as a second revised edition of the original, but as a separate work with a slightly different title and somewhat different scope.

The first edition of this second book, *The International Tax Law Concept of Dividend*, was published in 2010. Since then the developments in international tax law have been rapid. The Organisation for Economic Co-operation and Development (OECD) and the European Union (EU) initiatives against base erosion and profit shifting (BEPS) have had and will have a huge impact on the tax treatment of different cross-border arrangements.

This second revised edition of *The International Tax Law Concept of Dividend* follows the structure and rough outline of the original doctoral thesis. The country specific parts of the book, however, have been replaced with more general parts providing examples of the different domestic law approaches. The core of this book is in the EU Parent-Subsidiary Directive concept of profit distribution and in the model tax convention concept of dividend. This second edition includes the impact of the BEPS project on the covered issues. The relevance of the EU Anti-tax Avoidance Directive and the Multilateral Convention to Implement Tax Treaty Related Measures to Prevent Base Erosion and Profit shifting are taken into account. Also relevant new case law and new literature have been considered in this second edition.

Marjaana Helminen
Helsinki, December 2016

List of Abbreviations

AB	*Aktiebolag* (limited company, Sweden)
ABL	*Aktiebolagslag* (Act on Limited Companies, Sweden)
AG	*Aktiengesellschaft* (public limited company, Germany)
AktG	*Aktiengesetz* (Act on Public Limited Companies, Germany)
AO	*Abgabenordnung* (Fiscal Code, Germany)
Anti-Tax Avoidance Directive	Council Directive (EU) 2016/1164 of 12 July 2016 laying down rules against tax avoidance practices that directly affect the functioning of the internal market.
AStG	*Aussensteuergesetz, Gesetz über die Besteuerung bei Auslandsbeziehungen* (International Tax Act, Germany)
AvrL	*Lag om avräkning av utlandsk skatt* (Act on Foreign Tax Credit, Sweden)
BEPS	OECD/G20 Base erosion and profit shifting project
BFH	*Bundesfinanzhof* (Federal Fiscal Court, Germany)
BGB	*Bürgerliches Gesetzbuch* (Civil Code, Germany)
BMF	*Bundesministerium der Finanzen* (The Ministry of Finance, Germany)
BStBl	*Bundessteuerblatt* (Official Tax Gazette – laws, cases, etc., Germany)
CFC	Controlled foreign corporation
EC	European Community
EC Treaty	The Treaty establishing the European Community (the name of the treaty was changed to The Treaty on the Functioning of the European Union by the Treaty of Lisbon, which was signed on 13.12.2007 and which entered into force on 1.12.2009)

List of Abbreviations

EEA	European Economic Area
EFL	*Lag om ekonomiska föreningar* (Act on Economic Associations, Sweden)
EFTA	European Free Trade Association
EStG	*Einkommensteuergesetz* (Income Tax Act, Germany)
EU	European Union
EU Court	The Court of Justice of the European Union
EVL	*Laki elinkeinotulon verottamisesta* (Business Income Tax Act, Finland)
GmbH	*Gesellschaft mit beschränkter Haftung* (Limited liability company, Germany)
GmbHG	*Gesetz betreffende die Gesellschaften mit beschränkter Haftung* (Act on Limited Liability Companies, Germany)
HBL	*Lagen om handelsbolaglag och enkla bolag* (Act on Partnerships, Sweden)
HE	*Hallituksen esitys* (Government Bill, Finland)
HGB	*Handelsgesetzbuch* (Commercial Code, Germany)
IBFD	International Bureau of Fiscal Documentation
IFA	International Fiscal Association
Interest-Royalty Directive	Council Directive 2003/49/EC of 3 June 2003 on a Common System of Taxation Applicable to Interest and Royalty Payments Made between Associated Companies of Different Member States.
IRC	Internal Revenue Code (the US)
IRS	Internal Revenue Service (the US)
KapErhStG	*Gesetz über steuerliche Massnahmen bei Erhöhung des Nennkapitals aus Gesellschaftsmitteln und bei Überlassung von eigen Aktien an Arbeitnehmer, Kapitalerhöhungsteuergesetz* (Act on Tax Measures in Connection with Increases in Nominal Capital out of Company Funds and with Distribution of Stock to Employees, Germany)
KG	*Kommanditgesellschaft* (limited partnership, Germany)
KGaA	*Kommanditgesellschaft auf Aktien* (partnership limited by shares, Germany)
KHO	*Korkein hallinto-oikeus* (Supreme Administrative Court of Finland)
KL	*Kommunalskattelagen* (Municipal Tax Act, Sweden)
KM	*Komitean mietintö* (committee report, Finland)

List of Abbreviations

KStG	*Körperschaftsteuergesetz* (Corporate Income Tax Act, Germany)
KStR	*Körperschaftsteuer-Richtlinie* (Corporate Income Tax Guidelines, Germany)
KupL	*Kupongskattelag* (Withholding Tax Act, Sweden)
KVL	*Keskusverolautakunta* (Central Tax Board, Finland)
LähdeveroL	*Laki rajoitetusti verovelvollisen tulon ja varallisuuden verottamisesta* (Act on Taxation of Income and Wealth of a Person With Limited Tax Liability, Finland)
MenetelmäL	*Laki kansainvälisen kaksinkertaisen verotuksen poistamisesta* (Act on Elimination of International Double Taxation, Finland)
NSFS	*Nordiska skattevetenskapliga forskningsrädet skriftserie* (Series of publications of the Nordic Tax Scientific Research Board)
OECD	Organisation for Economic Co-operation and Development
OECD Model	Model Tax Convention on Income and Capital of the Organisation for Economic Co-operation and Development (15.7.2014)
OHG	*Offene Handelsgesellschaft* (partnership with unlimited liability, Germany)
OSK	*osuuskunta* (Cooperative Society, Finland)
Oy	*osakeyhtiö* (Limited Company, Finland)
OYL	*osakeyhtiölaki* (Companies Act, Finland)
P-S Directive	Council Directive 2011/96/EU on the common system of taxation applicable in the case of parent companies and subsidiaries of different Member States (30 November 2011)
RSV	*Riksskatteverkets rapport* (Report of the State's Tax Office, Sweden)
RFH	*Reichsfinanzhof* (Supreme Finance Court, Germany)
RÅ	*Regeringsrättens Årsbok* (Decision of the Supreme Administrative Court, Sweden)
SIL	*Lagen om statlig inkomstskatt* (National Income Tax Act, Sweden)
SijoitusrahastoL	*Sijoitusrahastolaki* (Act on Investment Funds, Finland)
SOU	*Statens offentliga utredningar* (State's public account, Sweden)

List of Abbreviations

TEU	The Treaty on European Union (TEU is used in this book to refer to the Treaty on European Union in the form as amended by the Treaty of Lisbon of 13.12.2007, which entered into force on 1.12.2009)
TFEU	The Treaty on the Functioning of the European Union (i.e., the EC Treaty as amended and renamed by the Treaty of Lisbon, which was signed on 13.12.2007 and which entered into force on 1.12.2009)
TVL	*Tuloverolaki* (Income Tax Act, Finland)
UN Model	United Nations Model Double Taxation Convention between Developed and Developing Countries (2011)
US Model	US Model Income Tax Convention (17.2.2016)
VaVM	*Valtiovarainvaliokunnan mietintö* (Report of the Finance Committee of the Parliament, Finland)
VerL	*Verotuslaki* (On 18.12.1995 repealed Taxing Act, Finland)
VeroH	*Verohallitus* (The National Board of Taxes, Finland)
VKL	*Velkakirjalaki* (The Promissory Notes Act, Finland)
VM	*Valtiovarainministeriön työryhmämuistio* (working group report of the Ministry of Finance, also Ministry of Finance in general, Finland)
VML	*Laki verotusmenettelystä* (Taxing Act, Finland)
VVL	*Varallisuusverolaki* (Wealth Tax Act, Finland)
VäliyhteisöL	*Laki ulkomaisten väliyhteisöjen osakkaiden verotuksesta* (Act on Taxation of Shareholders of Foreign Controlled Corporations, Finland)
YHL	*Laki yhtiöveron hyvityksestä* (Act on Imputation Credit, Finland)

CHAPTER 1
Introduction

§1.01 SUBJECT

Classification of corporate distributions is a major problem facing tax authorities and tax practitioners. Internationally, capital moves at a breakneck speed and the value of cross-border inter-corporate investments and finance has grown rapidly. The instruments used for finance and investment both in national and in international relations have become numerous and complex. There are many forms in which profits of a corporate entity resident in one state may be distributed to a corporate entity resident in another state. The fact that these different forms may be taxed very differently produces substantial tax planning opportunities for multinational enterprises. Due to the increasing amount and complexity of the possible inter-corporate cross-border transactions, it has become more and more difficult to keep abreast of them and to give them a name in order for the proper tax assessments to be made.

'Dividend' in its economic sense is the return on an equity investment in a corporate entity. Dividend distribution is a transaction in which corporate profits are distributed to the owners of the corporate entity without the corporate entity's expectation of receiving anything in return. As a result, the assets of the corporate entity decrease and the assets of the owners increase. A dividend distribution based upon the decision of the owners at a formally recognized meeting is the basic form of such a transaction. It is, however, only one of the forms in which corporate profits may legally be distributed to the owners of a corporate entity without any equivalent value or benefit in exchange or in which an investor may enjoy a return on an equity investment.

The question is to what extent do these other transactions, where corporate profits are transferred to the owners of the corporate entity, constitute a dividend and to what extent do they constitute some other type of income for tax purposes. From an economic perspective, it seems natural to tax all forms of return on equity investments in the same way. From a company law perspective, however, a distinction between the different possible forms may be made. It may be difficult to distinguish between a remuneration that actually constitutes a return on equity capital, and a payment from a corporate entity to its owners, that constitutes another form of a remuneration or repayment of capital.

The solutions to the classification problems are not necessarily the same for different states. The tax treatment of the different forms in which an owner may benefit from corporate profits is often different, not only in one state, but particularly in the cross-border situations where two different states are involved. The tax laws of two states may define the concept of 'dividend' differently. Therefore, in cross-border situations, classification conflicts may and do emerge. Certain transactions may be regarded as constituting a dividend in the view of the tax authorities of one state but not in the view of the tax authorities of another state. Such inconsistent classification may lead to either international double taxation or non-taxation. Therefore, it is important to draw the line between a dividend and other transactions similar in nature to a dividend, especially in cross-border situations.

This study covers different types of inter-corporate cross-border arrangements where an investor may receive a 'dividend equivalent return' directly from a corporate entity or indirectly through a third party. The issues covered will include:

- the extent to which these constitute a dividend for the purposes of the different legal systems of international tax law;
- the extent to which inconsistent income classification with respect to the covered arrangements lead or may lead to conflicts that further lead or may lead to international double taxation or non-taxation; and finally;
- whether and by what means such conflicts are or may be resolved in practice.

§1.02 SPECIFIC PURPOSE AND SCOPE OF THE STUDY

In order for proper tax assessment to be carried out, four basic determinations must be made:

(1) Who is the right tax subject?
(2) What is the tax object?
(3) What is the tax rate to be applied in connection with the tax subject and tax object?
(4) What is the amount of the tax when the tax rate is applied to the tax object?[1]

In cross-border situations, this enquiry also includes determining which state or states have taxing rights with respect to a specific tax subject and tax object, and to what extent. In cross-border interactions, the answers to these questions depend upon the different legal systems of international tax law, that is, the domestic tax law of each

---

1. *See* for these steps, for example, Tikka (1972), 30–46.

state concerned, upon any applicable tax treaty, and, with respect to the Member States of the European Union (EU), upon EU tax law.

In this study, the focus is on determining the tax object. The purpose is to determine under what conditions different cross-border arrangements produce income that is or that may be taxed as a dividend and thereby to clarify and define the concept of 'dividend' in international tax law.[2] The tax law term 'dividend' is defined with respect to different possible arrangements between parties resident in two different states. For the purposes of this study, it is irrelevant who the right tax subject is for a dividend, and what the actual tax burden is on the dividend.

In general, a dividend means a profit distribution from a corporate entity to its owners by virtue of the owner's status as such. Dividend distribution is a transaction by which the assets of the distributing corporate entity decrease and the assets of the receiving owner increase. Dividend distribution is a transfer of an economic benefit from a corporate entity to its owner for no equivalent value or benefit in exchange or, in the case that there might be some return value or benefit, it does not fully correspond to the economic benefit received.[3] This general definition of 'dividend' may be broken down further.

In order to answer the question as to what items of income qualify as a dividend, a determination must be made as to what entities qualify as dividend-distributing entities under the different legal systems of international tax law. Not all transfers of benefits from a qualifying entity to another entity constitute a dividend; a certain relationship must exist between the parties and the benefit must be transferred because of this special relationship. In addition, the question of which part of the benefit transferred is to be taxed as dividend must be answered. Finally, in order to arrive at the actual taxing consequence, it must be determined who the right tax subject is with respect to the dividend received. All these determinations must be made both in the state where the distributing entity is a resident and in the state where the income recipient is a resident. The answers to these questions depend upon domestic tax law, upon any applicable tax treaties, and, with respect to EU Member States, upon EU tax law.

Identifying the dividend-distributing entity, the dividend-generating relationship and the amount of taxable dividend determines the international tax law concept of 'dividend'. These, then, are the relevant features of this study. The questions concerning the right taxpayer of the dividend received and the actual tax rate do not, strictly speaking, determine the concept of 'dividend', but rather only give some indication of how a dividend is taxed and as whose income a dividend is recognized. These questions, therefore, are not covered by this study. The actual tax treatment of the

---

2. International tax law is a branch of tax law, traditionally considered to cover all tax provisions concerning situations involving the territory of more than one state. In other words, the term is used to refer to all tax provisions regulating the so-called cross-border situations. *See*, for example, Vogel et al. (1997), 10, Schaumburg (1998), 1–3, Helminen (2013), 29, Helminen (2016), 1, Helminen (2016a), Ch. 3 and Rohatgi (2005), 1. *See* for a discussion on the term from the time when the meaning was not yet quite clear in Bühler (1964), 3 and Knechtle (1979), 11–16.
3. *See* for these general characteristics of a dividend, for example, Sandström (1962), 3.

income that is regarded as constituting a dividend is covered in this study only to the extent that it illustrates the importance of distinguishing a dividend from other income.[4]

Questions concerning valuation or timing are not covered in this study, although these questions, to a certain extent, are meaningful in determining the concept of a dividend. Valuation problems would require a separate study even by limiting a review of them to those that arise in connection with dividend taxation. These difficult problems are widely covered in numerous studies concerning constructive dividends and transfer pricing and, therefore, are excluded from the scope of this study. For the purposes of this study, the assumption made is that the value of distributed assets, which is taken into account for tax purposes, is clear. The question concerning the moment when a dividend is paid and realized as taxable income is also not covered.

One important objective of this study is to identify and systemize the international tax law issues relating to the question of distinguishing transactions constituting a dividend from other transactions. As a result, this study systematically covers the most important issues relating to distinguishing inter-corporate dividend transactions from other inter-corporate transactions for the purposes of international tax law. By systematically studying the cases in which the line between a dividend and some other types of income is hazy, this study provides an answer to the question of what transactions constitute dividend in international tax law.

This study evaluates the question of what entities qualify as dividend-distributing entities. It considers the typical domestic law forms of business organizations in evaluating which of these forms are regarded as dividend-distributing entities for the purposes of the different legal systems of international tax law. Both incorporated and unincorporated business enterprises are discussed. Different non-business or non-profit entities are, however, beyond the scope of this study, regardless of whether they appear in a form available for business organizations.

Investment funds, as a special group of entities, are, in principle, of interest in determining what entities qualify as a dividend-distributing entity. Through an investment fund, an investor may indirectly invest in the equity capital of a dividend-distributing entity. Under the domestic tax law of different states, it varies whether investment funds themselves are treated as separate taxable entities and as such are considered to be dividend-distributing entities or whether investment funds are treated as more or less transparent entities. It follows, then, that income from investment funds may be treated in one state as a dividend and in another state as some other type of

---

4. This study excludes also the issue of beneficial ownership despite the fact that especially the availability of tax treaty benefits in the source state depends on who the beneficial owner of the dividend is. *See* for the beneficial owner concept, for example, Doernberg and van Raad (1997), 84–85 and 106, Hinnekens (1989), 359, paras 12–12.7 of the Commentary on Art. 10(2) of the OECD Model, paras 8–11 of the Commentary on Art. 11(2) of the OECD Model and paras 4–4.6 of the Commentary on Art. 12(1) of the OECD Model, OECD (1987a), 93, Vogel et al. (1997), 562–563, Reimer & Rust (2015), 816–818, International Fiscal Association (2000), Helminen (2016c), s. 3.3.3.3., Helminen (2002), 434–460, Helminen (2013), 94, Helminen (2016), 44, Helminen (2016a), Ch. 4, Todellinen omistaja, Lang et al. (2013), Ryynänen (2003), 345–366, Rohatgi (2005), 147, Du Toit (1999) and Wheeler (2005), 478–482. *See* Wheeler (2007), 17–58 about conflicts in the attribution of income to a person.

income. Because of the huge amount of other questions concerning the concept of a dividend, the question concerning investment funds has been left out of this study.[5]

A certain kind of a relationship must exist between two entities in order for a distribution between them to constitute a dividend. What is important is to determine whether a shareholder relationship is required, or whether other kinds of relationships qualify. The ownership of a dividend right may be separated from a share ownership. The question of whether the income from the alienation of such a right may constitute a dividend is addressed in this study and the discussion also includes whether substitute payments in connection with equity securities lending transactions may constitute a dividend. A similar question concerns dividend equivalent payments on derivative financial instruments.

In general, only distributed and not undistributed corporate profits are taxed as dividends. Sometimes, especially where a corporation is regarded only as a conduit, the undistributed profits of a controlled foreign corporation (CFC) may, however, be taxed as income for the shareholders. Under domestic tax law, such fictive income may be taxed as a dividend under a special CFC regime. This study does not aim at exhaustively explaining and detailing such regimes and their compatibility with tax treaties and EU tax law. Instead, this study aims at determining the extent to which undistributed profits of a corporation may be and actually are classified as a dividend because of such special regimes.

Similarly, sometimes the bonus shares issued by a corporation to its shareholders are taxed as a dividend. Dividend taxation may be possible in situations where a corporation issues new shares to the shareholders of the corporation without any equivalent value or benefit in exchange. This study evaluates the extent to which such an issue is deemed to constitute a dividend, although such an issue does not include an actual, but rather only a fictive, distribution of corporate profits to shareholders.

The purpose of this study is also to find out to what extent hidden profit distributions from a corporation to its shareholders may or do constitute a dividend under the different legal systems of international tax law. This issue relates to the problem of tax classification of benefits in the form of prices deviating from 'arm's length prices' used in transactions between a corporation and its shareholders. What is interesting, with respect to this study, is the extent to which transfers including a return value or benefit deviating from the arm's length standard may be and actually are taxed as a dividend. The starting point of the study is that the arm's length price is determined and the study only examines the extent to which dividend taxation may occur where the arm's length standard is not met.

The so-called hybrid instruments possessing characteristics of both debt and equity are important to consider when drawing the line between interest and a dividend. This study evaluates the kind of hybrid instruments, returns on which may

---

5. *See*, for example, Helminen (1999a–d) and Helminen (2000), for the tax classification of cross-border investment fund distributions and Viitala (2005) for the tax treatment of investment funds in general. *See also* the report of 9 Dec. 2009 of the OECD Committee on Fiscal Affairs on the granting of treaty benefits with respect to the income of Collective Investment Vehicles (adopted on 23 Apr. 2010).

constitute a dividend for tax purposes. Because of the vast array of hybrid instruments, each and every possible hybrid instrument cannot be covered. Instead, this study looks at certain basic forms of hybrid instruments used in most states. Certain typical equity characteristics in debt instruments and debt characteristics in equity instruments are covered to determine what characteristics make interest reclassifiable as a dividend or a dividend reclassifiable as interest for the purposes of the different legal systems of international tax law. The basic characteristics selected are the lack of a maturity date, profit participation, convertibility, subordination, the lack of voting rights and redeemability.

Thin capitalization situations are also relevant when drawing the line between interest and a dividend. What is of interest, with respect to this study, is the extent to which interest may be and actually is classified as a dividend if a state, under its domestic tax law, considers a corporation to be thinly capitalized. This study does not attempt to solve the problem of when a corporation should be considered or is considered thinly capitalized under the domestic tax law of different states. This study does not concentrate on the interesting question of tax treaty or EU law compatibility of domestic law thin capitalization regimes, but concentrates on the tax classification of interest when thin capitalization regimes are applied in conformity with EU law and tax treaties.

Finally, this study discusses the extent to which distributions made in connection with the basic forms of total or partial corporate liquidations, that is, redemption of shares, reduction of share capital or total liquidation of a corporate entity may or do constitute a dividend under the different legal systems of international tax law. The variety and amount of forms of corporate reorganizations legally possible in different countries is huge. Therefore, it is not reasonable to cover all possible corporate reorganizations, but only the three basic forms, in this study. The scope of this study excludes the question as to what extent other kinds of corporate reorganizations, such as mergers or divisions, may realize income taxed as a dividend.

The solution to the problem of determining in which state a dividend-distributing entity or a dividend recipient is regarded to be a resident has an important impact on what payments are considered a dividend. The extensive and complex problems relating to determination of the tax residence of a business entity are, however, not covered in this study. Problems relating to the fact that an entity has a dual residence or is not resident in any state are not covered. In this study, it is assumed that it is clear in which state the companies involved are resident from the perspective of both domestic tax law and tax treaties.[6]

One limitation of this study is that it only covers an inter-corporate dividend, that is, a dividend paid from an entity regarded as a separately taxable entity for tax purposes to another such entity. Situations where a dividend is paid from a corporate entity to an individual or to an entity not treated as a separately taxable entity are excluded. Entities not taxed as separate entities are covered only to the extent identifying the dividend-distributing entities.

---

6. *See*, for example, Malmgrén (2009) and Couzin (2002) about tax residence of corporate entities.

The exclusion of other than separate taxable entities from the scope of this study allows for the focus to be placed on corporate income taxation while the tax treatment and the special problems involved in the taxation of individuals and of tax transparent entities may be excluded. What remains beyond the scope of this study is the problems relating to payments, the substance of which is actually wages or pensions, paid in the form of a dividend or a dividend paid in the form of wages or pensions. This limitation is necessary in order to keep the study within reasonable limits. It also increases the coherence especially since EU tax law includes specific rules concerning only inter-corporate dividends but not dividends received by individuals.

Even though dividends paid to non-corporate recipients are excluded, both direct investment dividend and portfolio dividend are discussed. The situation arising where the dividend-receiving corporate entity has a holding or interest exceeding a certain level in the dividend-distributing company and the situation where the holding or interest is below the level are both covered.

Because it is not even possible to define the concept of a dividend universally, this study will not attempt to do so. Instead, the international tax law concept of a dividend will be evaluated with reference to bilateral and multilateral income tax treaties[7] and especially the Model Tax Convention on Income and Capital of the Organisation for Economic Co-operation and Development (OECD Model),[8] the United States Model Income Tax Convention (US Model)[9] and the United Nations Model Double Taxation Convention Between Developed and Developing Countries (UN Model).[10] Also EU tax law, and especially the dividend concept of Council Directive 2011/96/EU on the common system of taxation applicable in the case of parent companies and subsidiaries of different Member States (30 November 2011) (the P-S Directive), is looked at. The

---

7. Most income tax treaties are bilateral and there are only a few multilateral treaties. The multilateral income tax treaty among the Nordic countries (Denmark, Finland, Iceland, Norway, Sweden), signed on 23 Sep. 1996, provides for a good example of a multilateral income tax treaty. *See also* Rohatgi (2005), 75–77 about multilateral tax treaties and Andersson et al. (1991), Helminen (2013a), Helminen (2007), Helminen (2007a), Helminen (2007b) and Helminen (2007c) about the Nordic Treaty. On 24 Nov. 2016 the text of the Multilateral Convention to Implement Tax Treaty Related Measures to Prevent Base Erosion and Profit Shifting was published. The multilateral treaty that will modify the existing bilateral and multilateral treaties will have to be signed and ratified before it comes effective.
8. The first complete version of the OECD Model Convention and its official commentary is from the year 1963. This version was revised and a new Model with an official commentary was published in 1977. The present version is originally from 1992 but it has been updated on a continuous basis. All the references in this study to the OECD Model are to the 15 Jul. 2014 condensed version, if not otherwise mentioned. *See* about the development of the OECD Model, for example, the Introduction to the OECD Model paras 1–10, Vogel et al. (1997), 17–19 and Reimer & Rust (2015), 1–3.
9. The present version of the US Model is from 17 Feb. 2016. The 2016 version replaced the version form 15 Nov. 2006, which replaced the version from 20 Sep. 1996, which replaced the draft Model Income Tax Convention of 1981. *See* for the history of the US Model, Doernberg and van Raad (1997), 1. The US Model is used in this study as an example of the various model tax treaties of different countries.
10. The present version of the UN Model is from 2011 and it replaced the 2001 version, which replaced the 1980 version of the UN Model. UN has also published a manual for the negotiations of bilateral tax treaties between developed and developing countries. *See* UN (2003). *See*, for example, Coesters (2004), 4–5 and Rohatgi (2005), 66–68 for the history of the UN Model.

domestic tax law meanings of the term 'dividend' will be covered only on the basis of examples describing the different approaches applied commonly in different states.

§1.03 APPROACH AND RESEARCH METHODS

The approach of this study is primarily that of a traditional legal study. The emphasis of this study is in determining the positive law concept of a dividend. A search is made of the international tax law in effect in order to define the concept of a dividend. Items that are taxed as a dividend in accordance with the provisions of the different legal systems of international tax law determine the concept of a dividend in international tax law. For the positive tax law concept of a dividend, it is not relevant to determine what items of income are taxed as a dividend but should not be and what items of income are not taxed as a dividend but should be. This kind of consideration has relevance only *de lege ferenda*.[11]

To some extent, this study evaluates the present situation also in light of tax policy goals. Because the answers to these kinds of questions, however, always depend upon the policy goals chosen, such considerations are not central to the study. Therefore, the *de lege ferenda* considerations in this study are primarily concentrated upon identifying the points where the domestic tax laws of different states may operate unsatisfactorily or in conflict with either the EU Parent-Subsidiary Directive (P-S Directive) or tax treaties and therefore, call for amendments.

Because the scope of this study is international tax law, the starting points, as well as the solutions to the problems of the study, are the ones found in international tax law norms. The definition of the concept of the dividend is looked for primarily in the tax treaties, EU tax law and the domestic tax laws of different states. Domestic law definitions of a dividend are of interest only to the extent that the domestic law definition is simultaneously the definition for international tax law purposes. For the same reason, company law concepts are covered only to the extent that they define the possible legal forms of dividend-distributing entities and profit transfers. This study evaluates the extent to which these company law forms are determinative for tax law purposes.

The comparative method is not used in this study to clarify the domestic tax law of one single state. In other words, the definition of the term 'dividend' in one single state's domestic law is not interpreted by comparing it to the definitions in the systems of other countries.[12] The comparative method is only used in its conventional meaning, which means that the differences in domestic law definitions are used to elicit any internationally agreed-upon principles behind the definitions of the term 'dividend'. This method may also be used to identify the differences between the definitions of different states.[13] The purpose is to consider to what extent the concept of a dividend

---

11. *See*, for example, Myrsky (1997), 529–534 and Tikka (1983), 1079–1093 for the different approaches of tax law research.
12. *See* Aarnio (1988), 50 for the comparative method from this perspective.
13. *See*, for example, Bogdan (1978), for the comparative method as a method of legal study and Thuronyi (2003) and Sacchetto and Barasi (2008) for an introduction to comparative tax law.

gets an internationally agreed definition and to what extent the term gets different definitions under the international tax law of different states. It is interesting how the definitions interact in cross-border situations. A comparison between different definitions of different legal systems of international tax law is used primarily to find out the extent to which the differences may lead to conflict situations in taxation.

§1.04　RELEVANCE OF THE STUDY

[A]　Double Taxation or Non-taxation Caused by Different Dividend Definitions

Legal terms of different legal systems are not identical. The law of some states may include terms that are unknown in the law of other states. In addition, even though the same terms were used in different legal systems, the meaning of the terms may not be identical, and the legal facts that are covered by the terms may be different at least in some respects.

International tax law has to cope with interaction among several legal systems. Tax treaty terms, terms of EU tax law and terms used in different states' domestic tax law may not be the same and the same terms may have different definitions. The fact that tax terms used in different legal systems are not similar and the fact that those similar terms may be defined differently cause conflicts in cross-border relations.

'Dividend' is a term that has equivalents in different legal systems and languages. There is always an area of legal facts, which is covered by all the equivalents. In addition to this common ground, there is, however, an area of legal facts that is covered by some of the equivalents, but not all. An item of income may be taxed as a dividend in the state from which the income is paid, that is, in the source state, and not as a dividend but as some other kind of income in the state where the income is received, or vice versa. This inconsistency may lead to unintended taxation consequences.

Differences in the terms, and in the definitions of the terms under the different legal systems of international tax law, may cause either over-taxation or undertaxation. Different terms and inconsistent definitions of the same terms under two or more legal systems may unintentionally lead to both juridical international double taxation and economic international double taxation or to non-taxation. Interaction between different legal systems of international tax law may lead to situations where the same income item is taxed in two different states in the hands of one person or in two different states in the hands of two different persons. Or it may not be taxed in any state.[14] Although double taxation or non-taxation resulting from such interaction is not forbidden by customary international law, it is generally considered to be undesirable

---

14. For international double taxation and about the methods for avoiding international double taxation see, for example, Bühler (1964), 32–34, Escher (1974), 43–68 and 81–136, Auranen (1979), 271–275, Pires (1989), Vapaavuori (1991), 40–49, Suurnäkki (1992), 46–60, Helminen (1994), 14–18, Helminen (2013), 69–89, Helminen (2016), 26–45, Helminen (2016a), Ch. 4, Vogel et al. (1997), 9–10 and Reimer & Rust (2015), 12–22.

and the problem is sought to be eliminated by unilateral, bilateral and multilateral means.[15]

Over-taxation or under-taxation may be caused, among other reasons, by different definitions of the term 'dividend' under two different states' domestic tax law, and under different states' domestic tax law and under tax treaties. The problem is obvious in a non-treaty situation, but it is also a problem in tax treaty situations because the definitions of the terms used in tax treaties may themselves be unclear and may leave room for interpretation. The problem also exists because the area of legal cases covered by the term in a tax treaty may be different from the area covered by the same term used in other domestic legislation. Therefore, there is a lot of room for conflicts and interpretation. It is also possible that taxpayers purposely avoid tax by taking advantage of the differences in the definitions. Alternatively, taxing authorities may intentionally seek to reach interpretations that bring tax revenues to the state in question.

By determining the international tax law concept of a dividend, this study identifies the points at which the differences in the definitions of the term 'dividend' under the different legal systems of international tax law cause possibilities for cross-border tax planning and tax avoidance[16] or bring about the danger of over-taxation.

[B] The Concept of Dividend and Tax Neutrality

Tax neutrality is widely considered to be one of the basic principles of a good taxing system in market economies[17] because it is regarded as promoting economic efficiency.[18] Taxation should not affect the choice of economic operations, and the arguments made for a choice should be other than fiscal. A tax system that does not alter the rational choice of operating compared to a situation with no taxation is a

---

15. See Vogel et al. (1997), 12 and Reimer & Rust (2015), 14 on how only tax treaties, not customary international law, currently forbid international double taxation. Also, the elimination of double taxation required in tax treaties is only partial, and does not eliminate the problem. In addition to tax treaties, also EU law includes provisions that require the Member States to eliminate double taxation in certain situations. There is, however, no general requirement in EU law to eliminate double taxation. See, for example, Helminen (2015), 43–46 and Helminen (2014), 391–412.
16. See for definitions and the relationship between the concepts of tax planning, tax avoidance and tax evasion OECD (1987a), 16–17, Lindencrona (1976), 105–106, Bergström (1978), 19–21, Ruding Report (1992), 138 and Rädler (1994), 311. See also Tikka (1972), 26–38, Tikka (1992), 584, Bergström (1992), 597 and Hultqvist (1995), 375–386. See for tax avoidance also e.g., Vanistendael (2016), 163–172 and Murray (2013). In this study, the term tax avoidance is used as a general term, referring to any unacceptable means of avoiding tax in one state.
17. Neutrality in taxation has been a leading principle in many tax reforms. See, for example, Andersson (1995), 28. See Weisbach (2015), 635–652 for the use of neutralities in international tax policy For the principles of a good taxation system in general, see, for example, Helminen (2016a), 47–50, Wikstöm (2008), 139–161, Rohatgi (2005), 1, Aalto (1988), 8–9, Tikka (1990), at 47–49 and Kukkonen (1994), 351–356. See also Shome (1995), 3 and 20, with regard to how efficiency, equity, neutrality and administrative feasibility have been the main objectives of tax reforms carried out in most industrialized countries after the Second World War. See also Koskenkylä (1987), 1 and Ylä-Liedepohja (1992), 342.
18. See for taxation and efficiency Zee (1995), 25–29 and about the inefficiency of economy that non-neutral taxation causes in Koskenkylä (1987), 2–3.

neutral one.[19] In practice, however, taxation is in many respects non-neutral, and a completely neutral taxing system is not even possible.[20]

Neutrality is not only seen as a policy goal with respect to one state's taxation, but also as desirable in order to achieve the most efficient allocation of investment capital in a worldwide economy.[21] Tax neutrality in a global economy is, however, even more difficult to achieve than tax neutrality with respect to one state's taxation.[22]

If taxation was neutral, it would be irrelevant from a taxation perspective whether business is carried out in an incorporated or unincorporated form and whether the business is financed either by debt or by equity. The form in which investors enjoyed their return on the investment would be irrelevant. If taxation was neutral in every sense, it would be needless for taxation purposes to determine which payments are a dividend and which are not. It would make no difference how an economic transaction was labelled because, from an economic standpoint, similar transactions would be subject to similar tax burdens no matter what the form used.

The lack of tax neutrality makes it relevant to distinguish between a dividend and other income. So long as a dividend from a corporation and income from unincorporated entities are not taxed neutrally, it is relevant to draw the line between companies

---

19. *See* Tikka (1990), 47, Ylä-Liedepohja (1992), 342, Kukkonen (1994), 351-352, Lodin (1973), 29, Ståhl (1996), 90-99, Ståhl (1997), 231 and Andersson and Norrman (1987), at 5. It is, however, agreed that a taxing system as neutral as possible is a desirable object only to the extent that there are no arguments strong enough to use taxation as a method of directing economic activities. *See* Wikström (1994), 8-20 for the relationship between neutral taxation and directing taxation.
20. It is argued that taxation to some extent always affects economic decision-making, despite the lack of the purpose to direct economic activities. For example, Harris (1996), 31 recognizes that '...all taxes are non-neutral to some extent...', because '...all taxes affect in some manner the allocation of resources...'. *See also* Musgrave and Musgrave (1989), 279, Ylä-Liedepohja (1992), 346 and Vapaavuori (1991), 50. As long as there are numerous different taxes, taxable objects and taxing subjects, neutrality may be achieved only in a narrower sense, with respect to certain objects.
21. For the world economy efficiency, *see* Utz (1993), 202-203 and Sörensen (1990), 22-41, 62. In the international context, tax neutrality is usually divided into 'capital-export neutrality' and 'capital-import neutrality'. Capital-export neutrality is attained when tax factors do not affect the choice between investing at home and investing in any state abroad. It is attained when business decisions relating to location of investment are unaffected by the differences in the tax treatment in different states. Capital-import neutrality, on the other hand, is attained when all investments made in a single state are subject to an equivalent economic burden of tax irrespective of whether investors are domestic or foreign. *See* for neutrality in international context and the concepts of capital export neutrality and capital-import neutrality Rohatgi (2005), 1, Richman (1963), 5-11, Musgrave (1987), 205-207, Sörensen (1990), 26, van Raad (1986), 256-265, Faria (1995), 220-221, OECD (1991), 18 and 39-42, Vapaavuori (1991), 51-53, Viherkenttä (1991), 42-43, Ruding Report (1992), 17 and 34-37, Helminen (1994), 26-28, Saarikivi (1994), 178-183, Helminen (2016a), 47-49, Helminen (2016), 11-12, Helminen (2016a), Ch. 3 and Terra and Wattel (2012), Ch. 4.2.2. *See* for the concepts especially in connection with equity investments in Ståhl (1996), 93-114 and Ståhl (1997), 231-233.
22. As Niskakangas (1983), 185 states, so long as there are no two states with equally severe taxing system, neutrality is possible only with respect to taxation in one state. *See also* Andersson and Norrman (1987), 23. It is well known that as long as different states apply different systems of taxing companies and their shareholders and apply the systems differently to resident and non-resident persons, capital export neutrality and capital-import neutrality cannot be achieved simultaneously in dividend taxation. *See* Ståhl (1996), 111 and Terra and Wattel (2012), Ch. 4.2.2.

that are allowed to distribute a dividend and companies that are not. Similarly, so long as the taxation of debt and equity and interest and a dividend is not neutral, it is essential to draw the line between the concepts of debt and equity and the concepts of interest and a dividend. So long as the taxation of a dividend compared to the taxation of other possible forms of corporate distributions is not neutral, it is relevant to draw the line between a dividend and other means of transferring company profits to shareholders.

§1.05 MATERIALS

International tax law has become a popular field of study over the past few decades. There are a large number of comprehensive works on international taxation published in different languages. For example, the following has been used in this study: Vogel's *Klaus Vogel on Double Taxation Conventions*,[23] Schaumburg's *Internationales Steuerrecht*, Rohatgi's *Basic International Taxation, Global Tax Treaty Commentaries* edited by Vann and the works *Kansainvälinen verotus, Kansainvälinen tuloverotus* and *Finnish International Taxation* of the author of this study.

The OECD Model Convention and its official Commentary (the Commentary) are probably the most important sources of interpretation for the terms of bilateral tax treaties. The OECD Model and its Commentary have relevance, not only among OECD Member States, but also in other contexts. Most bilateral income tax conventions are based directly or indirectly on the OECD Model. The OECD Model, however, has had important impact not only upon bilateral conventions, but also upon other model conventions like the UN Model and the US Model.[24] Within certain limits, the official commentary on the OECD Model[25] has become a widely accepted guide to the interpretation and application of the provisions of the actual tax treaties in force.[26]

Because most treaties are either directly or indirectly based upon the OECD Model, the problems in this study are evaluated primarily in light of the OECD Model. The UN Model and the US Model are mentioned only where the Models deviate from the OECD Model. An important source is the Commentary on the OECD Model. In determining the tax treaty definition of the term 'dividend', central sources in this study have also been the comprehensive work of Professor Vogel's *Klaus Vogel on Double Taxation Conventions* and also the work of Professors Doernberg and van Raad entitled *The 1996 United States Model Income Tax Convention*.

The definition of 'profit distribution' of the P-S Directive governs the EU tax law concept of profit distribution. In addition, the general provisions of the Treaty on European Union (TEU) and the Treaty on the Functioning of the European Union (TFEU) also affect the taxation of dividends. The main sources on EU tax law used in

---

23. Also the fourth edition of the book edited by Reimer and Rust has been used in this revised 2017 edition.
24. For example, already the original 1980 version of the UN Model was based on the 1977 version of the OECD Model.
25. The Commentary referred to here is the official interpretations by the OECD of the OECD Model.
26. *See*, for example, Vogel et al. (1997), 43–47 for the importance of the OECD Model Convention as source of interpretation.

this study are the work of Professors Terra and Wattel called *European Tax Law*, *EU Skatterätt* of Ståhl, Österman, Hilling and Öberg, *EU Tax Law* of the author of this study and *Handbuch des Europäisches Steuer- und Abgabensrechts* edited by Birk. Worth mentioning is also Ståhl's doctoral thesis *Aktiebeskattning och fria kapitalrörelser* dealing with cross-border dividends.

Numerous articles that have appeared in different tax periodicals have been influential to this study, such as the *Bulletin for International Taxation* (formerly *Bulletin for International Fiscal Documentation*), *EC Tax Review*, *European Taxation*, *Internationales Steuerrecht*, *Intertax*, *Skattenytt*, *Svensk skattetidning*,[27] *Tax Notes International* and *Verotus*.[28] The tax periodicals have been of great importance besides the 1999 published doctoral thesis of the author of this study titled *The Dividend Concept in International Tax Law – Dividend Payments Between Corporate Entities* as there are no other comprehensive studies on the concept of a dividend.[29]

§1.06 TERMINOLOGY

In this study, the term 'domestic tax law' is used to refer to the unilateral law of each state. The term does not cover tax treaties, even though tax treaties are often made a part of a state's domestic law. When tax treaties are referred to in this study, they are expressly mentioned.

The term 'entity' is used to denote the various forms of transparent or non-transparent legal arrangements through or with which business activities are conducted. For the purposes of this study, the term 'owner' is used as a general term and refers to persons with an equity interest in an entity. The term 'partner' is used to refer specifically to an owner of a partnership entity and the term 'shareholder' is used specifically to refer to the owner of a corporate entity.

The terms 'corporation' and 'corporate entity' are used in this study to refer either to entities incorporated under company law or to entities that are taxed as separate entities. This use of the terms does not require that the state of residence of the entity treat the entity as a separate tax subject. The term is also used in situations where another state treats the entity as a separately taxable entity. The term 'company' is used in a more general way to cover corporations, unincorporated entities and entities taxed as transparent entities. 'Company' is, however, also used in a more specific way in situations where it is used in connection with tax treaties or the EU Parent-Subsidiary Directive, which expressly uses the term 'company' instead of the term 'corporation'.

The term 'inter-corporate dividend' is used to refer to a dividend paid from an entity taxed as a separate entity to another entity taxed as a separate entity. In

---

27. *Skattenytt* and *Svensk skattetidning* are Swedish language periodicals on taxation.
28. *Verotus* is a Finnish language periodical on taxation.
29. The 1990 doctoral thesis *Hybride Finanzierungen im internationalen Steuerrecht* by Lang covers the concept of the dividend in a limited sense. The dissertation deals with the problem of distinguishing debt from equity for the purposes of distinguishing between interest and the dividend for tax treaty purposes.

classification conflict situations, this term includes situations where at least one state views both entities as separately taxable entities.

Related companies, where one company holds an interest in the other company, are referred to here as 'subsidiary company, and parent company'. These terms are used as general terms referring to the relationship between the companies. The terms are not used as specific juridical or legal terms of either domestic tax law or company law or as juridical or legal terms of EU law or tax treaty law.

The terms, 'direct investment dividend' and 'portfolio dividend' are used as general terms. 'Direct investment dividend' refers to a dividend that is paid from a company to another company holding a substantial interest either in the capital or in the voting rights of the first company. 'Portfolio dividend' is used to refer to a dividend where the requirements of a direct investment dividend are not fulfilled. The terms discussed in this paragraph may acquire very different specific definitions depending upon the level of international tax law, which is implicated, that is, domestic tax law, tax treaties or EU tax law. The study will expressly mention these instances where the terms are used in a specific way.

The term 'resident of a state' is used broadly in this study and covers any person who, under the tax laws of the state of residence, is liable to be taxed by that state on the grounds of domicile, residence, place of management or other criterion of a similar nature. The term is not regarded as covering persons who are liable to be taxed in a state only because of income from sources in that state or because of capital situated in that state. The term 'non-resident' is used to refer to persons who are not liable to be taxed in the state in question for the above-mentioned reasons. From this broad definition of the term 'residence', it may follow that a person is simultaneously regarded as a resident in two or more states. This study does not deal with problems caused by such dual or multiple residence.

The term 'open dividend' is used in this study to refer specifically to distributions made in the company law form of a dividend, that is, generally a distribution based upon the decision of the shareholders' meeting. The use of the term 'open dividend' is necessary because in some states a distinction is made between the tax treatment of an open and a constructive dividend. The term 'open dividend' is used instead of the general term 'dividend' where this distinction needs to be highlighted. Similarly, when 'constructive dividend' is specifically discussed, the term 'constructive dividend' is used, although under certain tax systems the tax treatment of a constructive dividend does not, generally, differ from the treatment of an open dividend.

The concept of 'thin capitalization' is used in this study to refer to tax problems relating to the use of excessive debt finance compared with equity finance. The concept of thin capitalization is used to refer to situations where the amount of debt finance compared with the amount of equity finance indicates that the actual nature of a debt investment is closer to equity. The term 'hybrid debt' is used to refer to situations where an investment in the form of debt is, because of typical equity characteristics attached to it, closer in nature to equity. The term 'thin capitalization' is not considered to cover situations of hybrid debt.

§1.07 OUTLINE OF THE STUDY

This study is organized according to doctrinal concepts. This approach is useful for general observation and for the comparison of the similarities and differences in dividend definitions found under the different legal systems of international tax law. This study examines how the various issues are solved under domestic tax law of different states, and how EU tax law and tax treaties affect the domestic law treatment.

Chapter 2 briefly covers the typical tax treatment of cross-border dividends compared to the tax treatment of different types of other cross-border income such as interest, royalties, rentals and capital gains. The purpose of this chapter is to illustrate the relevance of income classification in cross-border situations.

Chapter 3 deals with specific problems caused by the interaction of the different legal systems of international tax law. The chapter briefly describes the relationships between the different legal systems of international tax law and discusses the problems and conflicts caused by inconsistent income classification under domestic tax law of two different states and under tax treaties.

Chapter 4 briefly covers the typical different dividend definitions found in the domestic tax laws of different states, under the EU P-S Directive and in different tax treaties. It covers the basic tax norms of each of these legal systems of international tax law that determine the tax law concept of dividend under each system.

Chapter 5 provides a fundamental analysis of the question of what forms an entity may take in order to qualify as a dividend-distributing entity for tax purposes under each of the different legal systems of international tax law. It evaluates which entities, organized under the company law of different states, qualify as such entities.

Chapter 6 evaluates what kind of a relationship is required between a dividend-distributing entity and the recipient of a distribution to constitute a dividend under the different legal systems of international tax law. This chapter evaluates whether dividend equivalent payments may be and are taxed as a dividend, even though they are not paid from a corporation to its shareholder. The study looks at situations where the right to a dividend is separated from the shares to which the dividend pertains and includes discussion on whether substitute payments in equity securities lending transactions or dividend equivalent payments on derivative financial instruments constitute a dividend.

Chapter 7 deals with special questions relating to the tax treatment of fictive distributions. This chapter evaluates the extent to which special domestic law regimes allow undistributed corporate profits of a foreign-controlled company to be classified and taxed as a dividend. It also covers a discussion of the extent to which shareholders are deemed to receive income that may be taxed as a dividend in connection with an increase of share capital.

Chapter 8 evaluates the extent to which the use of a return value or benefit deviating from the arm's length standard in different transactions between a corporation and its shareholders constitutes a dividend.

Chapter 9 evaluates the extent to which a return on different kinds of hybrid instruments is and may be taxed as a dividend. The chapter begins with a general discussion that is followed by a more thorough evaluation of the question from the perspective of certain typical characteristics of hybrid instruments. These characteristics include the lack of a maturity date, profit participation, convertibility, subordination, the lack of voting rights and the possibility of redemption.

Chapter 10 evaluates the extent to which debt is and may be reclassified as equity and interest is and may be taxed as dividend in the case of thinly capitalized companies.

Chapter 11 deals with the tax classification of liquidation proceeds. The chapter evaluates the extent to which distributions in connection with a share redemption, a reduction of share capital, or a total liquidation and dissolution of a corporation are taxed as a dividend.

Chapter 12 is a summary of the study's most important conclusions. This chapter summarizes the points where inconsistent income classification under the domestic tax law of different states may lead to unsolved classification conflicts under tax treaties. This chapter discusses also the extent to which these conflicts may lead to international double taxation or non-taxation and the possibilities of correcting the conflicts.

CHAPTER 2
Tax Treatment of Inter-Corporate Cross-Border Dividends

§2.01 DOMESTIC LAW DIVIDEND TAXATION SYSTEMS

The tax treatment of corporate entities and their shareholders, with respect to distributed profits, varies between states. Some states apply a 'classical system', where the taxation of a corporation and its shareholders is not integrated and economic double taxation is not eliminated.[1] Under a classical system, in its pure format, the distributed corporate profits are fully taxed first by the distributing corporation and the distributed amount is then fully taxed again as dividend for the shareholder. Dividends distributed to the shareholders are not regarded to be tax deductible to the distributing company. It is, however, not common to apply the classical system in its pure format even though it is clearly the simplest system available. Most states consider it necessary to alleviate economic double taxation of distributed corporate profits at least partly.

Instead of a pure classical system, most states apply a semi-classical system or a form of an 'integrated system', where economic double taxation is eliminated or alleviated at least partly by some method.[2] Domestic inter-company dividends especially may be completely or partly tax exempt even in those countries applying a classical system. Alternatively, a reduced tax rate, dividend-received deduction or a dividend imputation credit may be available. The recent trend has been to move away

---

1. Economic double taxation refers to a situation in which two different tax subjects are taxed for the same income. See, for example, Helminen (2016), 38.
2. See McLure (1979) for a comprehensive study about different integration systems compared to the classical system. See also Sato and Bird (1975), 385–395 and Norr (1982), 71–149. See Norr (1982), 41–69 and Vann (2003), 23–25 especially about arguments for and against an integrated system compared to a classical system.

from the imputation credit system to other systems eliminating economic double taxation at least partially.[3]

As a rule, the domestic law systems providing for elimination or alleviation of economic double taxation are not fully applicable in the case of cross-border dividends. Cross-border dividends, therefore, often are subject to more burdensome tax treatment compared to pure domestic dividends. Cross-border dividends may be subject to dividend withholding tax in the source state and dividend taxation (corporate taxation based on tax assessment) in the state of residence of the dividend recipient.

The domestic tax law of most states distinguishes between the tax treatment of a cross-border direct investment dividend and a portfolio dividend. The tax provisions concerning a direct investment dividend apply to an inter-company dividend in situations where the recipient has a substantial holding in either the capital or the voting rights of the dividend-distributing company. Any other dividend is taxed as a portfolio dividend.

In general, the rules concerning direct investment dividends are formed to facilitate direct investment and to eliminate or mitigate both international juridical double taxation and international economic double or multiple taxation of groups of companies. For neutrality reasons, the tax burden of an inter-company direct investment dividend is brought to correspond closely to the tax burden of the profits from permanent establishments. As a consequence, both international economic and juridical double taxation is often eliminated either by the credit or by the exemption method. The taxation of a portfolio dividend, instead, need not be in line with the taxation of entrepreneurial earnings, and, therefore, often only international juridical and not economic double taxation is eliminated.

§2.02 EU TAX LAW

[A] The Parent-Subsidiary Directive

There is no common dividend taxation system in the EU Member States, but each state applies its own system.[4] The Parent-Subsidiary Directive (P-S Directive),[5] however, limits taxation of profit distributions from subsidiaries resident in an EU Member State

---

3. *See*, for example, Terra and Wattel (2012), Ch. 4.2.3 and Vann (2003), 21–70 for different domestic law dividend taxation systems and Rohatgi (2005), 266 and International Fiscal Association (2003), for country examples of the different systems.
4. There are several studies on whether and how dividend taxation systems among the EU Member States should be harmonized. *See* Ståhl (1996), 138–165, Ståhl (1997), 228 and Iihi et al. (2003), 71–79. In 1975, a proposition was prepared for a directive of the council concerning the harmonization of systems of company taxation and on withholding taxes on a dividend (COM (75) 392 final), but the proposition was withdrawn. *See* Thömmes (1990), 106–107, Ståhl (1996), 150–155 and Iihi et al. (2003), 75–77. The problem was dealt with also in the Report of the committee of independent experts on company taxation from year 1992 often referred to as the Ruding report (1992). It is not likely that the dividend taxation systems of the EU Member States will be harmonized.
5. Council Directive 2011/96/EU on the common system of taxation applicable in the case of parent companies and subsidiaries of different Member States (30 Nov. 2011). *See* Helminen (2015), 15–180 about the directive.

to parent companies resident in another Member State. In order for the P-S Directive to apply, the parent company must hold at least 10% of the capital in the subsidiary, or, if bilaterally agreed, at least 10% of the voting rights in the subsidiary.[6] The P-S Directive, thus, only applies to direct investment dividends, and not to portfolio dividends. Also, qualifying profit distributions connected with a permanent establishment come under the scope of the P-S Directive.[7]

Article 4 of the P-S Directive requires the state of residence of a parent company to provide relief in instances of international economic and juridical double taxation of a dividend received from a subsidiary resident in another EU Member State.[8] The relief may be granted in the form of either a credit or an exemption.[9] If the credit method is applied, both direct and indirect foreign tax credits are required.[10] Article 5 of the P-S Directive prohibits any imposition of withholding tax in the state of residence of the subsidiary on profits distributed from a subsidiary to the parent company.[11] The provisions of the P-S Directive take precedence over any conflicting domestic law or tax treaty provision.[12]

[B] The TFEU

[1] Permanent Establishments

The freedom of establishment principle of the TFEU[13] has had a huge impact on the dividend taxation systems of the EU Member States. For example, the countries that apply the dividend imputation credit system are required to extend the scope of application of the imputation credit to cover in addition to resident taxpayers also non-resident taxpayers from other EU Member States if the dividend is connected with a permanent establishment in the state applying the imputation system. The credit must be made available in the case of permanent establishments even though the

---

6. See Terra and Wattel (2012), Ch. 9.3.2 and Helminen (2015), 166–167 about this holding requirement.
7. See Helminen (2015), 158–162.
8. Also, qualifying profit distributions connected with a permanent establishment are covered. See Helminen (2015), 131–134.
9. The Member States must not set any conditions that are not mentioned in the directive for a taxpayer to benefit from the elimination of double taxation. See C-138/07 *Cobelfret*.
10. See Terra and Wattel (2012), Ch. 4.2.2.5 and Helminen (2015), 171–174 about the possibility to select between the exemption method and the credit method.
11. See about the withholding tax concept of the P-S Directive C-375/98 *Epson*, C-294/99 *Athinaïki Zythopoiia*, C-58/01 *Océ van der Grinten*, C-446/04 *Test Claimants in the FII Group Litigation* and C-284/06 *Burda*. The source state is not even allowed to first withhold a tax and then refund it; a qualifying dividend must be totally exempted. See Terra and Wattel (2012), Ch. 9.6 and Helminen (2015), 170–174. The same treatment applies to profit distributions connected with permanent establishments. See Helminen (2015), 171–174. According to Art. 7, Art. 5 does not hinder the advance corporate tax or compensatory tax under the imputation systems of different Member States.
12. See, for example, Helminen (2015), 5–6 about primacy of EU law.
13. The Treaty on the Functioning of the European Union (i.e., the EC Treaty as amended and renamed by the Treaty of Lisbon, which was signed on 13 Dec. 2007 and which entered into force on 1 Dec. 2009).

taxpayer is a non-resident.[14] Because of the European Economic Area (EEA) Agreement, the same requirement applies in the case of permanent establishments of residents of the European Free Trade Association (EFTA) States.

The requirement of an equally beneficial source state tax treatment of resident dividend recipients and non-resident taxpayers with a permanent establishment in the source state also applies in the case of dividend taxation systems other than the imputation credit system. If, for example, the tax system of a Member State exempts dividends received by resident companies, the state must not tax dividends received by non-resident companies of other EU or EEA States, if the dividends are connected with a permanent establishment of the company in the state concerned.[15]

[2] Foreign-Source Dividend of a Resident

The national dividend taxation systems of the EU Member States must also comply with the TFEU in regard to situations in which the dividend is not connected with a permanent establishment. Case C-35/98 *Verkooijen* of the EU Court concerned the national tax system of the Netherlands under which dividends could be tax exempt in the case of domestic dividends but not in the case of foreign-source dividends. This system was considered to be in conflict with Directive 88/361/EEC of 24 June 1988 for the implementation of the TFEU (former EC Treaty) article on free movement of capital, even though the directive is not a tax directive.[16]

After the *Verkooijen* judgment, it was not surprising that the EU Court found in case C-319/02 *Manninen* that the dividend imputation credit system of Finland was in conflict with EU law because the imputation credit under the system was available only in the case of Finnish-source dividends but not in the case of foreign-source dividends.[17]

In the *Manninen* case, the free movement of capital principle was considered to require that Finnish-source dividends and foreign-source dividends from other EU Member States are subject to as beneficial tax treatment in Finland.[18] The imputation credit based on the national tax system of Finland had to be made available to Finnish resident taxpayers not only in the case of Finnish-source dividends but also in the case of foreign-source dividends from other EU Member States.[19] The amount of the imputation credit in the case of foreign-source dividends had to be determined on the

---

14. 270/83 *Commission v. France* (*avoir fiscal*).
15. *See* Helminen (2015), 94–95 for the impact of the TFEU freedom of establishment on the tax treatment of dividends connected with a permanent establishment.
16. *See also*, for example, Vapaavuori (2001), 460–471 and CFE (2002), 241–246 about the *Verkooijen* case.
17. *See also*, for example, Hintsanen and Pettersson (2005), 130–137 about the *Manninen* case.
18. Because of the EEA Agreement, the same requirement also applies in the case of dividends from such EEA States that are not Members of the EU.
19. *See also* C-292/04 *Meilicke* and C-262/09 *Meilicke II*.

Chapter 2: Tax Treatment of Inter-Corporate Cross-Border Dividends §2.02[B]

basis of the corporate tax paid by the foreign dividend distributor in its state of residence.[20]

After the *Manninen* case, it was somewhat unexpected that in case C-513/04 *Kerckhaert-Morres* concerning the dividend tax system of Belgium, the EU Court did not require the state of residence of the dividend recipient to give a tax credit for the dividend withholding taxes levied in the source state. The source state withholding taxes did not need to be credited when the residence state applied the same tax rate to foreign-source and domestic-source dividends. The difference compared to the *Manninen* case was that the *Kerckhaert-Morres* case did not concern a dividend imputation credit system but a foreign tax credit.[21]

Based on the judgment of the EU Court in case C-446/04, *Test Claimants in the FII Group Litigation*, it is clear that the articles of the TFEU on freedom of establishment and free movement of capital require that the state of residence of a dividend recipient subjects foreign-source dividends from other EU Member States to equally beneficial tax treatment as applies to domestic-source dividends.[22]

The tax treatment of domestic and foreign-source dividends may be different provided the treatment is equally beneficial. The corporate tax paid by the dividend-distributing company in its state of residence must be taken into account in the state of residence of the dividend recipient if the same is done in the case of domestic-source dividends or if the dividends would be tax exempt if they were domestic-source dividends. Also, a possible advance corporate tax must be taken into account.[23]

In principle, the Member States have the right to choose whether to apply the credit method or the exemption method. The credit method can be applied to foreign dividends even though the exemption method is applied to domestic dividends, provided that the credit method also provides for an indirect tax credit.[24] The credit method can be applied instead of the exemption method, provided that the tax rate applied to foreign-source dividends is not higher than the rate applied to domestic source dividends and that the tax credit is at least equal to the amount paid in the

---

20. See also C-292/04 *Meilicke* and C-262/09 *Meilicke II*. See decision KHO 2004/3360 of the Supreme Administrative Court of Finland given on the basis of the *Manninen* ruling and SK 563/2005 for Finnish legislation enacted after the *Manninen* decision for the purposes of repaying the overpaid taxes. See also, for example, Merisalo (2005), 236–252 about how the years' 1998–2004 overpaid taxes were repaid in Finland after the *Manninen* ruling. See also joined cases C-397/98 and C-410/98 *Metallgesellschaft* and *Commission* (2003) about the EU law compatibility of the systems applied under the dividend imputation systems with the purpose of safeguarding the circumstance that distributed corporate profits are taxed at least once. See also, for example, Newey (2001), 287–292 about the *Metallgesellschaft* case.
21. See also C-540/11 Levy and Sebbag.
22. The same requirement applies to a mechanism of the residence state capping the amount of direct taxes to a certain percentage. The mechanism must take into account taxes paid in other countries (e.g., source state dividend withholding taxes) in the same way that it takes into account taxes paid in the residence state. See C-375/12 *Bouanich*.
23. See also C-292/04 *Meilicke* and C-201/05 *Test Claimants in the CFC and Dividend Group Litigation* and C-406/07 *Commission v. Greece* and C-310/09 *Accor*. See, for example, English (2005), 200–214, Cadosch et al. (2006), 622–635 and Denys (2007), 221–237 about the EU law compatibility of dividend taxation systems in general.
24. The Supreme Administrative Court of Austria followed this interpretation in case VwGH, 17 Apr. 2008, 2008/15/0064.

source state, up to the limit of the tax charged in the state of residence of the dividend recipient.[25]

The credit method instead of the exemption method is accepted provided that the administrative burdens imposed on the taxpayer in order to qualify for the credit are not excessive. According to the *Haribo* case, information demanded by the national tax authority from the company receiving dividends that relates to the tax that has been charged on the profits of the dividend-distributing company is an intrinsic part of the very operation of the credit method and cannot be regarded as an excessive administrative burden.[26]

Also the reverse situation in which the exemption method is applied in a cross-border situation and the dividend imputation credit system is applied in domestic situations is in principle allowed.[27] The application of the two different systems, however, must not lead to worse treatment of the cross-border situation compared to a comparable domestic situation.[28]

In the case of dividends received from a non-Member State, beneficial tax treatment is not required if granting the benefit would require information from the state of residence of the dividend-distributing company.[29]

Based on C-436/08 and C-437/08 *Haribo*, it is in accordance with the TFEU to grant a tax benefit in the case of dividends from the EEA states outside the EU only if a comprehensive agreement for mutual assistance with regard to administrative matters exists between the countries concerned. Instead it may not be acceptable to require that an agreement on enforcement exists between the states.

[3]   Dividend Received by a Non-resident

In addition to its relevance to the tax treatment of inbound dividends, the TFEU also has significant relevance to the tax treatment in the source state of outbound dividends paid to the residents of the other EU Member States. The TFEU may limit the source state taxing rights in situations in which a non-resident dividend recipient is considered to be in a comparable situation with a resident dividend recipient.

The EU Court has held that the situation of resident dividend recipients and non-resident dividend recipients is not necessarily comparable as regards the national provisions with the objective of eliminating economic double taxation of dividends distributed by domestic companies.[30]

---

25. C-446/04 *Test Claimants in the FII Group Litigation*, paras 48 and 57, C-201/05 *Test Claimants in the CFC and Dividend Group Litigation*, para. 39, joined cases C-436/08 and C-437/08 *Haribo* C-437/08, paras 86–104 and C-310/09 *Accor*, paras 87–90.
26. C-436/08 and C-437/08 *Haribo*, para. 104.
27. C-47/12 *Kronos*, para. 67.
28. C-47/12 *Kronos*, para. 68.
29. C-201/05 *See Test Claimants in the CFC and Dividend Group Litigation*.
30. C-170/05 *Denkavit 2*, para. 34, C-540/07 *Commission v. Italy*, para. 51, C-379/05 *Amurta*, para. 37 and C-284/09 *Commission v. Germany*, para. 55. *See also*, for example, Kemmeren (2008), 4–11 and Bellingwout (2008), 124–132 about the *Amurta* case.

If, according to national tax law and the tax treaties of a Member State, however, both residents and non-residents are subject to taxes on dividends from domestic companies, the situation of a resident and a non-resident dividend recipient is comparable.[31] In such a situation, the use by the source state of its taxing rights causes the risk of economic double taxation irrespective of the tax treatment in the state of residence of the dividend recipient. In such a situation, the state of residence of the dividend-distributing company must ensure that non-resident dividend recipients are subject to the same treatment as applies to resident dividend recipients in regard to the system applied for the purposes of eliminating economic double taxation in the source state.[32]

The source state must not levy a dividend withholding tax on the dividends paid to other EU Member States if dividends paid to residents are effectively tax exempt.[33] Source state dividend withholding taxes must not be levied even where the non-resident would not have a permanent establishment in the state of residence of the dividend-paying company and even where the state of residence of the dividend recipient would apply the credit system for the purposes of eliminating international double taxation if the credit is not available.[34] Because of the freedom of establishment principle and the free movement of capital principle of the TFEU and the EEA Agreement, EU or EEA national residents of EU and EFTA States must be subject to equally beneficial tax treatment as applies to resident dividend recipients in a comparable situation.[35] If there is no agreement on information exchange between an EU Member State and an EFTA state, different treatment may, however, be accepted.[36] Even in these situations a tax benefit should be categorically denied from non-resident tax payers without giving them the possibility to show that they fulfil all the requirements concerning the benefit.[37]

---

31. C-487/08 *Commission v. Spain*, para. 51, C-374/04 *Test Claimants in Class IV of the ACT Group Litigation*, para. 68, C-540/07 *Commission v. Italy*, para. 52, C-170/05 *Denkavit 2*, para. 35, C-303/07 *Aberdeen*, para. 43, C-284/09 *Commission v. Germany*, para. 56 and C-379/05 *Amurta*, para. 38.
32. *See* C-487/08 *Commission v. Spain*, para. 52, C-374/04 *Test Claimants in Class IV of the ACT Group Litigation*, para. 70, C-540/07 *Commission v. Italy*, para. 53, C-303/07 *Aberdeen*, para. 44, C-284/09 *Commission v. Germany*, para. 57, C-384/11 *Tate & Lyle Investments*, para. 32, C-387/11 *Commission v. Belgium*, para. 50 and C-379/05 *Amurta*, para. 39.
33. *See* Commission 2003, C-487/08 *Commission v. Spain*, C-265/04 *Bouanich*, C-379/05 *Amurta*, C-170/05 *Denkavit 2*, C-374/04 *Test Claimants in Class IV of the ACT Group Litigation*, C-521/07 *Commission v. the Netherlands* and C-446/04 *Test Claimants in the FII Group Litigation*.
34. *See* Commission 2003, C-487/08 *Commission v. Spain*, C-265/04 *Bouanich*, C-379/05 *Amurta*, C-170/05 *Denkavit 2*, C-374/04 *Test Claimants in Class IV of the ACT Group Litigation*, C-521/07 *Commission v. the Netherlands* and C-446/04 *Test Claimants in the FII Group Litigation*.
35. C-170/05 *Denkavit 2*, C-379/05 *Amurta*, C-384/11 *Tate & Lyle Investments*, the joined cases C-338/11 and C-347/11 *Santander Asset Management et al.*, C-38/11 *Amorim Energia* and C-303/07 *Aberdeen Property Fininvest Alpha*. *See also* Tenore (2010a), 75–78, Helminen (2008b), 354–360, Helminen (2015), 99–102, Helminen (2008c), 354–360, Helminen (2010a), 402–408 and Wahlroos & Kuivisto (2008), 60–66 about the tax treatment of dividends paid to non-residents. *See* van Sprundel (2008), 607–618 about the Netherlands dividend withholding tax system from the perspective of the TFEU, and Pato (2008), 197–220 and Pato & Seize (2009), 114–121 about the tax treatment of investment funds from the perspective of EU law.
36. *See*, for example, C-540/07 *Commission v. Italy*.
37. C-493/09 *Commission v. Portugal*, paras 45–52.

In *Fokus Bank* (Case E-1/04), the EFTA Court held that Norway had to extend the national dividend imputation credit to non-resident dividend recipients if the credit was available to residents. This decision was based on Article 40 of the EEA Agreement, which corresponds in its relevant parts to Article 63 of the TFEU on free movement of capital.[38]

After the *Fokus Bank* case, the EU Court held in *Test Claimants in Class IV of the ACT Group Litigation* (Case C-374/04) that there is no conflict with the TFEU even though the British dividend imputation credit was available only in the case of dividends received by domestic companies but not in the case of dividends received by non-resident companies, which were not liable to tax in Great Britain (the source state).

There is no conflict with the TFEU where a Member State does not extend the right to a dividend imputation credit agreed in a bilateral tax treaty to resident companies of EU Member States that are not parties to the tax treaty.[39]

The source state does not have the right to refrain from eliminating international economic double taxation caused by taxes levied in that country in the case of non-resident dividend recipients solely because the state of residence of the dividend recipient unilaterally has chosen to apply the credit method for the purposes of eliminating international double taxation. To the extent that a non-resident dividend recipient is in a comparable situation with a resident, economic double taxation has to be eliminated in the source state to the same extent as it is eliminated in the case of resident dividend recipients.[40] A full tax credit agreed on in a bilateral tax treaty, instead, may make source state taxation of dividends paid to non-residents allowable.[41] The fact that tax treaties require a lower source state tax compared to domestic tax law treatment, instead, is not sufficient.[42]

The national dividend taxation systems of the EU Member States must comply with the basic freedoms not only in regard to the provisions with the purpose of eliminating economic double taxation on dividends but also in other respects. For example, such deductions which have a direct connection with the activities of a non-resident in the source state must be made available to the non-resident if they are available to residents in a similar situation in the source state.[43]

---

38. *See*, for example, Larking (2005), 69–77 about the *Fokus* case.
39. C-374/04 *Test Claimants in Class IV of the ACT Group Litigation*.
40. C-379/05 *Amurta*. *See* C-11/07 *Eckelkamp*, paras 68–69 and C-43/07 *Arens-Sikken*, paras 65–67 about the same principle in connection with the tax treatment of inheritances.
41. C-374/04 *Test Claimants in Class IV of the ACT Group Litigation*, para. 71, C-379/05 *Amurta*, para. 79, C-540/07 *Commission v. Italy*, para. 36, C-48/08 *Commission v. Spain*, para. 58, C-384/11 *Tate & Lyle Investments*, para. 36 joined cases C-10/14, C-14/14 and C-17/14 *Miljoen, X and Société Générale*, paras 78–80 and C-284/09 *Commission v. Germany*, paras 62–68.
42. C-184/09 *Commission v. Germany*, para. 65.
43. For example, in case C-342/10 *Commission v. Finland*, the tax treatment in Finland was found to be in conflict with the free movement of capital principle, because the non-resident pension funds receiving dividends from Finland were not entitled to the same deductions as Finnish resident pension funds in a similar situation. *See also* joined cases C-10/14, C-14/14 and C-17/14 *Miljoen, X and Société Générale*, paras 57–59. *See*, however, C-600/10 *Commission v. Germany* in which the EU Court rejected the claim with respect to the deduction of bank and transaction fees, as the Commission did not prove that the costs concerned actually occur for foreign funds.

Based on joined cases C-10/14, C-14/14 and C-17/14 *Miljoen, X and Société Générale*, the fact that a dividend withholding tax is a final tax for non-residents, whereas the withholding tax system for residents provides a mechanism for deducting or reimbursing the tax withheld, creates a forbidden restriction if this system leads to a higher final tax burden for non-residents compared to residents.[44]

§2.03 TAX TREATIES

Tax treaties include a special article regulating the tax treatment of cross-border dividends in a tax treaty situation. Most of the dividend articles of the actual bilateral or multilateral tax treaties are based on Article 10 of the OECD Model but they differ in detail. Article 10 of the OECD Model limits the taxes imposed upon the recipient of a cross-border dividend. Instead, it does not in any way affect the corporation tax levied upon the profits of the company distributing the dividend.[45]

According to Article 10(1) of the OECD Model,[46] a dividend received by a resident of one of the contracting states from a company resident in the other contracting state, may be taxed in the state of residence of the recipient. According to Article 10(2), such a dividend may also be taxed in the state of residence of the dividend-paying company, that is, in the source state, but to a limited extent.[47]

The OECD Model distinguishes between the tax treatment of a direct investment dividend and the tax treatment of a portfolio dividend. According to Article 10(2) of the Model, if the beneficial owner of a direct investment dividend is resident in the recipient's state of residence, the tax charged in the source state shall not exceed 5% of the gross amount of the dividend. This maximum rate applies if the beneficial owner is a company, other than a partnership, which directly holds at least 25% of the capital of the company paying the dividend. In all other cases, if the beneficial owner of a dividend is resident in the recipient's state of residence, the source state tax shall not exceed 15% of the gross amount of the dividend.

The dividend definitions of the UN and the US Models differ from the OECD Model as regards the limit between a direct investment dividend and a portfolio dividend. The holding requirement is different. In the UN Model, it is 10% of the capital

---

44. *See also* Helminen (2015), 99–102 about the implications of EU law on the tax treatment of dividends received by non-residents.
45. Article 10(2) of the OECD Model. The same also applies with respect to Art. 10 of the UN and the US Models. Article 10 does not, thus, in any way affect the application of the integrated domestic law systems of taxing corporations and their shareholders, such as the imputation system, but rather assumes a classical system. Some treaties include an express reference to the special domestic law dividend taxation system, such as the imputation credit system and to the way in which the system affects the application of the tax treaty dividend article. *See also* Harris (2016) about Art. 10 of the OECD Model.
46. The wording of Art. 10(1) of the OECD, the US and the UN Model are identical.
47. Article 10(2) of the 2014 version of the OECD Model specifically clarifies that para. 2 applies to dividends paid by a company which is a resident of a Contracting State. The earlier versions only used the term 'such', from which it could be concluded that it referred to the para. 1 dividends paid by a company, which is a resident of a Contracting State. The US and US Models still use only the term such.

of the company paying the dividend and in the US Model, it is 10% of aggregate vote and values of the shares of the payor company.[48]

The definition of the holding requirement for a direct investment dividend varies also among actual treaties. In the same way, the maximum tax rate allowed for the source state may differ from the rates referred to in the model conventions. Many treaties do not include any source state taxing right with respect to direct investment dividends and some treaties lack source state taxing right also with respect to portfolio dividends. The treaties between the different EU Member States especially may not give any taxing right to the source state with respect to direct investment dividends, because the P-S Directive, in any case, prevents the levying of any source state dividend withholding taxes in the case of direct investment dividends covered by the Directive.

The OECD Model grants the source state primary, but limited, taxing right when the beneficial owner of the income is resident in the recipient's state of residence.[49] The OECD Model instead grants the state of residence of the dividend recipient full taxing rights, but with the requirement that a credit be granted in accordance with Article 23A(2) or 23B for the taxes paid in accordance with Article 10 in the source state.[50]

The credit method of Article 23 of the US Model provides for an indirect credit in addition to a direct credit for a direct investment dividend. Indirect credit means that, in addition to the dividend withholding tax, also the foreign corporate income tax paid by the foreign subsidiary with respect to the profits out of which the dividend is paid is deductible from the taxes payable in the state of residence of the dividend recipient.

Instead of the credit method, many actual tax treaties provide an exemption for direct investment dividends and in the case of the credit system but both a direct and an indirect tax credit may be available. Only direct credit is usually available in the case of portfolio dividends. The method referred to in actual tax treaties for the purposes of eliminating international double taxation in the state of residence of the dividend recipient usually reflects the domestic law system of the residence state.

---

48. The US Model requires that the holding lasted for a twelve-month period ending on the date on which the entitlement to the dividend is determined. The UN Model differs from the OECD and US Models also in that it does not include a specific source state maximum tax rate but leaves the percentage to be established in bilateral negotiations.
49. See about the beneficial owner concept as a method of avoiding treaty shopping Sjöholm (1996), 385-386. See, however, Lindencrona (1994), 110 for how the beneficial owner requirement may not always be very effective in tackling treaty shopping. It depends on the state concerned on how strictly the beneficial owner requirement is interpreted and applied. See for the definition of the term, beneficial owner, as the real economic owner, Doernberg and van Raad (1997), 84-85 and 106, Hinnekens (1989), 359, paras 12-12.2 of the Commentary on Art. 10(2) of the OECD Model, para. 8 of the Commentary on Art. 11(2) of the OECD Model and para. 4 of the Commentary on Art. 12(1) of the OECD Model, OECD (1987a), 93, Vogel et al. (1997), 562-563, International Fiscal Association (2000), Helminen (2002), 434-460, Helminen (2016a), 19 and 312, Helminen (2016), 44, Ryynänen (2003), 345-366, Rohatgi (2005), 147, du Toit (1999), du Toit (2010) 500-509, Verdoner et.al. (2010) 419-429 and Wheeler (2005), 478-482.
50. Article 23A(2) and 23B of the UN Model are substantially similar to the same articles of the OECD Model. Article 23 of the US Model is comparable but not in every respect identical to Art. 23B of the OECD Model. Some treaties with developing countries also provide the so-called tax sparing credit, that is, credit for notional tax. See e.g., Vogel et al. (1997), 1248-1258 and Ekkehart & Rust (2015), 1637-1640 for the tax sparing credit.

According to Article 10(5) of the OECD Model, a state may not tax a dividend solely because a dividend is paid from income or profits derived from the state. The source of a dividend is not the state where the profits out of which the dividend is paid are generated.[51] Similarly, a state may not tax the undistributed profits of a company, which is resident in another state even though the profits consist of income or profits arising in the first state. Most actual treaties make a reference to a similar principle to that of Article 10(5) of the OECD Model. Many actual treaties, however, fail to mention that undistributed profits may not be subjected to a tax on a company's undistributed profits.

Article 10(4) of the OECD Model and the substantially similar Article 10(8) of the US Model include a special provision concerning the taxation of a dividend received by a permanent establishment. Accordingly, a dividend received by a permanent establishment is taxed under Article 7 (Business profits) in the same way as any income received by a permanent establishment. This treatment covers dividends if the holding in respect of which the dividends are paid is effectively connected with the permanent establishment. This principle is followed by most actual treaties.[52]

In conclusion, the treatment of a dividend is very similar under different treaties. There is however certain variation. The most important differences among actual treaties concern the definition of a direct investment dividend and the maximum amount of source state tax allowed. The treaties also differ from each other with respect to the method used for the elimination of double taxation. There is also other treaty specific variation[53]

§2.04 A COMPARISON BETWEEN THE TAXATION OF DIVIDEND AND OTHER INCOME

The determination of the type of income an item is to be taxed as is especially important in cross-border situations. Classification of an item of income under domestic law, for EU tax law purposes and under tax treaties, has a great impact on tax treatment. Income classification affects not only the total tax burden of the income item but also in which of the states involved the income will be taxed. The following analysis illustrates the typical tax treatment of business profits, interest, royalty payments, rental payments and capital gains in cross-border situations. This analysis gives a picture of the relevance of the classification of income as a dividend instead of as some other type of income.

---

51. *See* paras 33–35 of the Commentary on Art. 10(5) of the OECD Model. For example, some US treaties also include a reservation for such tax.
52. Article 10(4) of the UN Model still refers in addition to permanent establishments also to a fixed base, because the UN Model still has a separate article on independent personal services unlike the OECD and the US Model. *See* e.g., Sasseville & Vann (2016) for the tax treaty provisions on business profits. *See* for a fundamental study on taxation of permanent establishments: Skaar (1991). Permanent Establishment Erosion of a Tax Treaty Principle.
53. Already Art. 10 of the US Model includes other specialities, which were not mentioned here. *See also* e.g., Harris (2016) for the variation.

Corporations and their shareholders may be in a business relationship with each other. A corporation may make different payments to its shareholders for goods and services received from the shareholders. In general, such payments, unlike a dividend, constitute deductible business expenses for the paying corporation and taxable income for the recipient. According to Article 7(1) of the OECD Model, profits of an enterprise are taxable only in the state of residence of the enterprise unless the enterprise engages in business in the other state via a permanent establishment situated therein.[54] In tax treaty situations, business profits are therefore generally only taxed in the state of residence of the recipient of the business profits, unlike a dividend, which may be taxed partly in the source state and partly in the state of residence of the recipient.

Taxpayers may use different transactions, which realize business expenses and business profits, instead of a dividend in order to gain the benefit of tax deductibility and in order to avoid withholding tax in the source state. Dividend classification is, thus, generally in the interest of the source state. For the state of residence of the income recipient, the business profit classification is more advantageous. A direct investment dividend, in particular, may be used to avoid taxation in the state of residence of the income recipient.

Shareholders of a corporation and other investors may also make a debt investment in a corporation rather than an equity investment. Return on debt investment, even from a corporation to its shareholder, is taxed as interest whereas return on equity investment is taxed as a dividend. Unlike a dividend, interest is also generally regarded as a deductible expense in the taxation of the payer corporation. The possible interest deduction limitation provisions, the arm's length test and possible general anti-avoidance provisions, however, must be taken into account in tax planning based on interest deductions.[55]

In addition to the difference in tax deductibility, there is a difference in the source state tax treatment of the income recipient. Interest is often taxed as income for the recipient only in the state of residence of the recipient either because of a domestic law rule, tax treaty rule or because of an EU law requirement.

In contrast to the OECD Model, many tax treaties do not include any source state taxing right in respect of interest income and only the state of residence of the interest recipient is allowed to tax it.[56] Irrespective of the tax treaty treatment, the EU

---

54. This principle is included also in actual tax treaties.
55. See e.g., Helminen (2016c), s. 1.1.2.1 for how interest is used for cross-border tax planning purposes. See, however, Jacobs (1989), 464–471 for how the classical corporation tax system is more likely to discriminate equity finance compared to debt finance whereas in an imputation system the discrimination is not necessarily as probable. The domestic law imputations systems, however, may not apply in cross-border situations, for which there may be no difference. There has also been a trend of moving away from the dividend imputation credit system to a modification of the classical system. Only a few countries still apply the imputation credit system that used to be rather popular still in the 1990s. One important reason for this trend is the fact that the imputation credit system could not easily be adapted to the non-discrimination requirements of EU law. See Helminen (2015), 94–104 for the EU law requirements of a dividend taxation system.
56. Article 11(1) of the OECD Model gives limited taxing right to the source state. See also Helminen (2016c), Hinny (2008), 17–50 and Äimä (2009) about the tax treatment of cross-border interest of corporate entities.

Interest-Royalty Directive prevents source state withholding taxes in the case of cross-border interest payments covered by the Directive.[57] The Interest-Royalty Directive eliminates source state taxation of interest paid between associated companies of two different EU Member States when there is at least a 25% association present.[58] Dividend classification is thus often in the interest of the source state whereas interest classification is in the interest of the state of residence of the income recipient.

Corporations and their shareholders may further enter into agreements, which produce income from the corporation to the shareholder that is classified as royalties. Royalties are generally regarded as tax-deductible business expenses for the payer. Royalties are often subject to withholding tax in the source state under domestic law. However, under tax treaties, source state taxation may be hindered and royalties may only be taxed in the state of residence of the recipient.[59] Irrespective of the tax treaty treatment, the EU Interest-Royalty Directive prevents source state withholding taxes in the case of cross-border royalty payments covered by the Directive.[60] The Interest-Royalty Directive eliminates source state taxation of royalties paid between companies of two different EU Member States, when there is at least a 25% association present.[61] It is, thus, in the interest of the source state to classify an income item as a dividend, rather than as royalties. The classification as royalties is more advantageous to the state of residence of the income recipient.

A corporation may pay rent to a shareholder for the use of the property of the shareholder. Unlike dividends, rental payments are regarded as a deductible business expense. Under domestic law, rental payments made to non-residents may be subject to tax both in the source state and in the state of residence of the recipient. According to Article 6(1) of the OECD Model, income from immovable property may be taxed in the state where it is situated. According to Article 6(3), this tax treatment applies to income from direct use, letting or use in any other form of the immovable property. Under the OECD Model, any income item not dealt with in any of the special articles of the Model shall be taxed under Article 21(1) only in the state of residence of the income recipient. Rental payments from movable property are, therefore, generally only taxed in the state of residence of the recipient of the income. Dividend classification is more advantageous to the source state, whereas the other state may want to argue that an

---

57. Council Directive 2003/49/EC on a Common System of Taxation Applicable to Interest and Royalty Payments Made between Associated Companies of Different Member States (3 Jun. 2003).
58. *See* Helminen (2015), 185–205, Terra and Wattel (2012), Ch. 13 and Ståhl, Österman, Hilling and Öberg (2011), Ch. 7 for the scope of application and the tax consequences of the application of the EU Interest-Royalty Directive. Also, the general anti-discrimination provisions of the TFEU limit taxation of interest paid between residents of two different EU Member States.
59. *See* Art. 12(1) of the OECD Model. *See* e.g., Jiménez (2016) for the tax treaty provisions concerning royalties.
60. Council Directive 2003/49/EC on a Common System of Taxation Applicable to Interest and Royalty Payments Made between Associated Companies of Different Member States (3 Jun. 2003).
61. *See* Helminen (2015), 185–205, Terra and Wattel (2012), Ch. 13 and Ståhl, Österman, Hilling and Öberg (2011), Ch. 7, about the scope of application and the tax consequences of the application of the EU Interest-Royalty Directive. Also, the general anti-discrimination provisions of the TFEU limit taxation of royalties paid between residents of two different EU Member States.

income item qualifies under tax treaty articles similar to Article 6 or 21 of the OECD Model.

Shareholders may also receive income from a corporation by selling different kinds of property, including the corporation's own shares, to the corporation. Income from the sale of property generally constitutes capital gains for the recipient. Income from the sale of property is generally taxable in the state where the property is situated only with respect to income from the sale of real property. In contrast, income from movable property is generally only taxed in the state of residence of the seller. The price paid is also tax deductible for the payer, unlike a dividend. The same scheme applies under most tax treaties. According to Article 13(1) of the OECD Model, gains derived from the alienation of immovable property may be taxed in the state in which the property is situated. Instead, according to Article 13(4) of the OECD Model, gains from the alienation of movable property are generally taxed only in the state of residence of the alienor.[62] Source state taxation may, thus, be avoided by transactions that realize capital gains on movable property rather than a dividend.

Table 2.1 illustrates the typical tax treatment of interest, royalties, rental payments and capital gains as compared with a dividend.

Table 2.1 Taxation of a Dividend Compared to Other Income

	Interest	*Royalty*	*Rentals/m.p.*	*Cap. Gains/m.p.*	*Portfolio Dividend*	*Direct Inv. Dividend*
CITs	No	No	No	No	Yes	Yes
WHTs	No	No	No	No	Yes	No
CITr	Yes	Yes	Yes	Yes	Yes	No
EDTr	–	–	–	–	Direct credit	Exemption/direct and indirect credit

CITs Corporate income tax of the payer in the source state

WHTs Tax of the income recipient in the source state

CITr Tax of the income recipient in the recipient's state of residence

EDTr Elimination of double taxation in the state of residence of the income recipient with respect to the taxes paid in the source state

m.p. Movable property

Cap. Capital

direct inv. Direct investment

---

62. Article 13(5) of the US Model is substantially similar to Art. 13(4) of the OECD Model. *See* e.g., Jinya & Avella (2016) for the tax treaty provisions concerning capital gains.

Chapter 2: Tax Treatment of Inter-Corporate Cross-Border Dividends §2.04

The schedule illustrates how the major portion of tax revenue from a dividend goes to the source state whereas the major portion of the tax revenue from other types of income goes to the state of residence of the recipient. In conclusion, taxpayers may use interest, royalties, rental payments and capital gains instead of a dividend in order to avoid taxes in the source state. A direct investment dividend instead may be used to avoid taxation in the state of residence of the income recipient. Therefore, it is in the interest of the source state to classify an income item as a dividend rather than as any other type of income. In contrast, it is in the interest of the state of residence of the income recipient to classify an income item as any other type of income rather than as a dividend.

CHAPTER 3
Interaction among Different Legal Systems of International Tax Law

§3.01 RELATIONSHIP AMONG DIFFERENT LEGAL SYSTEMS OF INTERNATIONAL TAX LAW

[A] Relevance of the Relationship

The domestic tax regimes of different states, EU tax law and tax treaty law each constitute a separate *legal system*. The taxation of cross-border transactions, therefore, always involves the interaction between two or more legal systems. The rules under these different legal systems may not be consistent with each other and may conflict with each other. Also, the concepts of the different legal systems may be different, and cause conflicts. Therefore, in order to be able to tax a cross-border transaction or to determine the international tax law concept of dividend, one hurdle that must be dealt with is the interrelationship of the different legal systems in international tax law.

[B] Domestic Tax Laws of Two States

The concept of dividend may be defined in different ways under the domestic tax law of two different states. Despite the differences, each state determines according to its own domestic law what transactions constitute dividend for domestic tax law purposes. Also, in cross-border situations, each state may tax transactions without being obliged to pay any attention to the taxation regime of the other state involved. Each state may treat a cross-border transaction as constituting dividend for domestic tax law purposes only if, according to the domestic tax law of that state, the transaction constitutes dividend. As a consequence, the same income item may be treated as dividend under the tax law of one of the states but as some other type of income under the tax law of the other state. This inconsistent classification may, in turn, lead to international double taxation or non-taxation.

[C] Tax Treaties and Domestic Tax Law

Tax treaties are *international agreements having effect on or as domestic tax law* by coordinating or governing the interaction of two or more otherwise independent and autonomous tax systems.[1] Tax treaties operate through domestic tax law by limiting or modifying the application of domestic law but not by creating a new taxing right. Tax treaties set the limits of the extent to which a state is allowed to tax but actual taxation must be based on domestic tax law other than tax treaties.[2]

Tax treaties do not obligate the contracting states to amend their domestic legislation. Therefore, they may end up in conflict with other domestic tax provisions. International law, however, requires that other domestic law does not violate a binding tax treaty.[3] Therefore, under domestic law, tax treaties are, in general, given priority over other domestic tax law. The *priority of tax treaty provisions* is based either upon the principle that special rules get priority over more general law or upon the principle that a tax treaty as subsequent law prevails over earlier domestic law.[4]

---

1. The legal nature of a tax treaty simultaneously as domestic tax law and as international agreement is referred to as 'the dual nature' of double taxation conventions or the 'twofold' nature of double taxation conventions. See, for example, Becker and Würm (1988), 258, Katz (1993), 649, Lindencrona (1994), 11 and Helminen (2016), 4. Vogel and Prokisch (1993), 59, divide states into three groups depending on how tax treaties are made domestic law in each state. In the first group, tax treaties become a part of domestic law automatically without any special parliamentary approval. In the second group, tax treaties become domestic law only after a legal approval. In the third group, tax treaties have to be transformed into domestic statutes in order to get the effect of domestic legislation. See also Rohatgi (2005), 35–36, Vogel (1982), 115–117, Vogel et al. (1997), 2426 and Ekkehart & Rust (2015), 24–28 for examples of the practice in different countries.
2. This principle is often referred to as the 'golden rule of tax treaty law', or as the 'negative effect of tax treaties'. See, for example, Sandström (1949), 35, Knechtle (1979) 174, Wiman (1987), 341–342, Sundgren (1992), 284–285, Lindencrona (1994), 24, Andersson (1992), 112, Wiman (1995), 566, Vogel et al. (1997), 27–28 and 107 and Helminen (2016), 10. Some exceptional tax treaty provisions such as Art. 25 of the OECD Model concerning the mutual agreement procedure are, however, sometimes interpreted to set forth obligations that go beyond domestic law of the contracting states.
3. This requirement is based on the principle of *pacta sunt servanda* and good faith, set forth, for example, in Art. 26 of the Vienna Convention on the Law of Treaties. Furthermore, Art. 27 of the Vienna Convention bans justification of a breach of a treaty by reference to domestic law. See about the domestic law changes constituting treaty override and about the possible consequences of treaty override Vogel et al. (1997), 67–71 and Ekkehart & Rust (2015), 69–72.
4. *See* about different country practices Rohatgi (2005), 35–36, Becker and Würm (1988), 258–259, Vogel et al. (1997), 21–26, van Raad (1986), 28, Vogel and Prokisch (1993), 59–60, Niskakangas (1983), 68–69, Suurnäkki (1992), 66–68, Helminen (2016), 4, Lindencrona (1994), 24–26, Sandler (1994), 33, Debatin (1988), 727 and 729, Pöllatch (1993), 327–328, Vogel et al. (1997), 24–25, 27–28 and 71, Vogel (1982), 117, Sandler (1994), 92, Wiman (1987), 343, Doernberg and van Raad (1990), 206, Katz (1993) 615, 620–623, Langer (1980), 552–553, Hariton (1994a), 1055–1056, Scherer (1995), 13–14, Metzger (1996), 222 and Raedel and French (1995), 1602.

Tax treaty provisions are relevant only to the application of the treaty itself, but not in the interpretation and application of domestic law.[5] Tax treaty definitions of different terms must be used only to solve which of the contracting states has the taxing right and to what extent. Within the limits provided by a tax treaty, each state may use its own domestic tax law definitions to classify and tax income. As long as and to the extent that the applicable tax treaty does not prevent a state from taxing an item of income, the state may tax the income in accordance with its own domestic law.[6] Therefore, an item of income under a tax treaty may qualify as a different type of income than it would under domestic tax law.

Depending upon the relation between the scope of the tax treaty definition and the scope of the domestic law definition of the term dividend, the effects of a tax treaty are different. A tax treaty definition either may be broader than the definition of the same term in domestic legislation, or it may be narrower than the domestic law definition with respect to certain items of income. A treaty term may also be simultaneously broader, with respect to certain items of income, and narrower, with respect to certain other items of income than the domestic law definition of the same term.

When *the treaty definition is broader*, then certain income items fall under the definition of the term as set forth in the treaty article, but do not fall under the definition of the same term in domestic law.[7] In other words, for example, an item of income that does not constitute dividend for domestic law purposes qualifies as dividend for tax treaty purposes. Similarly, when *the treaty definition of the term is narrower*, certain income items do not fit under the definition of the treaty article but fit within the definition of the same term under domestic law. In other words, for example, certain items of income that are taxed as dividend under the domestic law of a state do not qualify as dividend but as some other type of income under the applicable tax treaty. It is also possible that the treaty definition is simultaneously broader with respect to the source state definition, but narrower with respect to the definition in the state of residence of the recipient of certain income items, or vice versa.

If the treaty definition of a term is broader with respect to a certain item of income than the definition of the same term in domestic law, the taxing result will not be affected. If the item of income in question may be taxed in the state according to the treaty provision, the taxing result in the state is exactly the same as if the definition is broader than or the same as the domestic law definition of that income category.[8] If the treaty definition of dividend is the same as or broader than the domestic law definition, and if the source state classifies an item of income as dividend under its domestic tax law, the item always qualifies as dividend for tax treaty purposes as well. The state may classify the income for tax treaty purposes consistently with the domestic law classification. The state taxes the income as dividend according to the domestic law rules concerning dividend to the extent that the tax treaty gives the taxing right with

---

5. Naturally if a domestic law provision refers to a specific treaty provision, the treaty provision may have relevance in interpreting the domestic law provision.
6. See e.g., Vogel et al. (1997), 224–225, Lindencrona (1994), 26 and Ståhl (1996a), 434.
7. *See also* Avery Jones (1993), 608.
8. *Ibid.*

respect to dividend to the source state. The difference between the breadth of the tax treaty definition and the domestic law definition thus does not affect the taxing result in any way.

Instead, *if the treaty definition of an income type is narrower than the domestic law definition of the term*, certain income items go under a certain income category according to domestic law, but do not fit under the definition of the same term under a tax treaty.[9] In other words, for example, domestic law dividend does not qualify as dividend but rather as some other type of income under a tax treaty. The effect of this conflict on the taxation outcome depends upon whether the treaty's treatment of the income as other type of income is either the same as the treaty's treatment of dividend, or different. *Only to the extent that the treaty gives the taxing right with respect to the other income type to a state may that state tax the income under domestic tax law.*

In conclusion, *only the fact that the tax treaty definition is narrower than the domestic law definition with respect to a certain item of income actually has a bearing upon the taxation of that item of income.* Instead, the fact that treaty definition is broader than the domestic law definition has no effect upon taxation, as the income qualifies in any case under the treaty definition. Another thing is that in such a situation, some other items of income, for example, items classified as interest under domestic law, must be taxed under the broader dividend article of a tax treaty. The same outcome would apply if the tax treaty definition of the term interest would be narrower than the domestic law definition of interest.

[D] EU Tax Law and Domestic Tax Law

EU law consists of *primary and secondary sources of law*. The primary sources of EU law include the EU founding treaties (the TEU and the TFEU),[10] which are treaties under international law. Secondary sources of EU law instead include different norms issued by the EU organs on the authorization of the founding treaties.[11]

Positive harmonization of direct taxation within the EU is based on Article 114 of the TFEU, which allows *directives* to be issued to approximate tax laws of the Member States.[12] A directive is addressed to and binding upon one or more Member States. The Member States have to achieve the result described in a specific directive by adapting it to their domestic law within a certain period of time. The provisions of a directive may become a law enforceable and directly applicable within a Member State if the

---

9. *Ibid.*
10. The TEU and the TFEU. *See*, for example, Helminen (2015), 9–12 about the founding treaties.
11. *See*, for example, Helminen (2015), 20–25, Easson (1993), 1–19, Penttilä (1996), 1–4, and Penttilä (1996a), 235–237.
12. *See*, for example, Helminen (2015), 21–24, Terra and Wattel (2012), Ch. 2.6 and Hinnekens (1994). The term positive harmonization or integration is used to refer to directives and other legal acts that approximate the tax laws of the Member States. The term negative harmonization or integration, instead, is used when referring to harmonization based on the impact of the judgments of the EU Court or, for example, on the impact of international tax competition. *See* Helminen (2016), 10.

Member State fails to implement the directive properly by a designated deadline.[13] Member States may not introduce or maintain domestic tax law concerning direct taxation, which conflicts with the TEU or the TFEU[14] or with the EU directives.[15]

Especially the *P-S Directive*[16] concerning the tax treatment of profit distributions between parent and subsidiary companies in different Member States is relevant in this study. The *Denkavit* judgment of the EU Court[17] confirmed the direct applicability of the articles of the P-S Directive, in a situation of an improper implementation of the Directive. The P-S Directive *overrides domestic law and is directly applicable to the extent that it leads to a more advantageous taxation* of a person resident in an EU Member State.

The issue of the breadth of a P-S Directive definition compared to the breadth of a domestic law definition is similar as the issue of the breadth of a tax treaty term compared to the breadth of a domestic law term, discussed above. For example, the definition of the concept of profit distribution in the P-S Directive may be broader with respect to certain items of income, and be narrower with respect to others as the definition of the same concept under the domestic tax law of the EU Member States.[18]

The relevance of the breadth factor is, however, different in the relation between EU directives and domestic tax law than between tax treaties and domestic tax law. This difference in relevance arises because of the requirement that EU directives are implemented into the domestic tax law of the Member States. Therefore, there actually should be no conflicts. Because of an incomplete implementation or an inconsistent interpretation of the P-S Directive, however, two Member States may view different items of income as qualifying as profit distributions as outlined by the P-S Directive. The conflicts that arise are, therefore, actually only conflicts between the domestic laws of two different states caused by incomplete implementation or by differences in the interpretation of the directives.[19]

---

13. *See* about the legal nature of directives, for example, Craig and De Búrca (2015), s. 7, Helminen (2015), 22–24, Penttilä (1996), 3–4 and Brokelind (1996), 900–903. *See* about the direct effect also 26/62 *van Gend & Loos*, 148/78 *Publico Ministerio v. Ratti*, and 8/81 *Becker*. *See* for more cases on this matter Helminen (2015), 8–9 and Wattel (2012), Ch. 3.5.1.
14. Especially Art. 49 of the TFEU on the freedom of establishment and Art. 63 on the free movement of capital are relevant from the perspective of dividend taxation.
15. The primacy is based on Art. 288 of the TFEU. *See*, for example, Helminen (2015), 23–24, Terra and Wattel (2012), Ch. 3.5.1, Hinnekens (1994), 160, Pieper (1995), 90–93 and Carrero (1996), 290. The principle of *primacy of EU law over any conflicting domestic* law is clearly expressed in EU Court case law. *See* 6/64 *Costa v. Enel*, 11/70 *International Handelsgesellschaft GmbH. v. Einfuhr- und Vorratstelle für Getreide und Futtermittel* and 26/62 *van Gend & Loos*.
16. Council Directive 2011/96/EU on the common system of taxation applicable in the case of parent companies and subsidiaries of different Member States (30 Nov. 2011).
17. Joined cases C-283/94, C-291/94 and C-292/94, *Denkavit, VITIC and Voormeer*. *See* about the Denkavit case also, for example, Brokelind (1996), 900–903 and in Maisto (1997), 180–189.
18. The domestic law provisions concerning dividend taxation often do not even use the term 'profit distribution' but instead the term 'dividend'.
19. A conflict between the definitions of terms of the EU directives and tax treaties is actually not a separate issue. Because EU directives are implemented into domestic law, the conflict issue goes back to the conflict between the definitions of domestic law and tax treaties. Because of possible improper implementation and because of interpretation conflicts, in practice, also the conflict between the terms of the directives and tax treaties is relevant. *See* about EU law interpretation concerning the P-S Directive also, for example, Tenore (2009), 37–44.

Two Member States may understand a term or definition of a directive differently. Therefore, with respect to the same cross-border transaction, one state may follow its own domestic law provisions implementing the directive, whereas another may not follow the implementing provisions of its own. One of the states may apply the provisions in a situation where, according to the directive, it actually would not be required to do so. Because the EU directives on direct taxes, however, only set forth the minimum requirements, such treatment does not, in any way, conflict with the directive. It is possible, however, that one of the states does not apply the implementing rules to an item of income that actually should be covered by the directive. Taxation in that state may conflict with the directive.

The P-S Directive itself does not provide for a solution to a conflict. The articles of the EU directives are, however, directly applicable if the domestic law of the Member States conflicts with the directives, that is, if domestic concepts prevent an EU directive from achieving its results. In contrast, in situations where the domestic concepts extend the scope of an EU directive on direct taxes, and offer more generous tax treatment, domestic concepts may be applied. Even though different from the concepts of the directive, these domestic law concepts, when applied, do not limit the directive from achieving its objective.[20]

The question of whether the domestic law of a Member State conflicts with a directive may be solved by the EU Court. The European Court of Justice may develop the definitions of the terms of the EU directives.[21] In practice, there are some judgments of the EU Court concerning the application of the P-S Directive.[22]

---

20. The domestic law or tax treaty norms on direct taxation that lead to more lenient tax consequences to the taxpayer than EU law requires are seldom in conflict with EU law. EU tax directives, for example, do not require a minimum corporate tax, that is, that national corporate taxes exceed a certain level. Except for certain exceptions, the Member States have the right to choose not to levy certain direct taxes, provided that the tax treatment does not amount to state aid forbidden by the TFEU. The Savings Directive, that is, Council Directive 2003/48/EC of 3 Jun. 2003 on taxation of savings income in the form of interest payments, was an exception, and provided for a minimum tax rate for certain situations. The Savings Directive was repealed from 1 Jan. 2016. In the future, the EU law provisions requiring taxation in certain specific situations, however, will most likely increase. In 2014 such a provision was included, for example, in the EU P-S Directive. *See* Art. 1 of the P-S Directive after the 2014 amendment and Helminen (2015), 6–8. Also the new Anti-tax avoidance Directive (Council Directive (EU) 2016/1164 of 12 Jul. 2016 laying down rules against tax avoidance practices that directly affect the functioning of the internal market) requires taxation in certain situations that come under the scope of the Directive.
21. It is the task of the EU Court to ensure that the law is observed in the interpretation and application of the EU founding treaties. The Court oversees that the actions of the Member States or the EU organs do not violate the founding treaties. The Court may give a judgment on whether the direct tax directives based on the authorization of the TFEU and their implementation under the domestic laws of the Member States are in accordance with the TFEU. The purpose of the judgments of the EU Court is to guarantee uniform interpretation of EU law in the Member States. *See* Helminen (2015), 393–398.
22. Interpretation of the P-S Directive was the subject in the joined cases C-283/94, C-291/94 and C-292/94 *Denkavit, VITIC and Voormeer* and in C-375/98 *EPSON Europe*, C-294/99 *Athinaïki Zythopoiia*, C-58/01 *Océ Van der Grinten*, C-27/07 *Banque Fédérative du Crédit Mutuel*, C-48/07 *Les Vergers du Vieux Tauves*, C-138/07 *Cobelfret*, C-247/08 *Gaz de Francet* and in the joined cases C-439/07 and C-499/07 *KBC Bank*.

[E] Tax Treaties and EU Tax Law

EU Member States may conclude tax treaties with each other and with third states.[23] As described above, the EU Court case law clearly indicates that EU law takes precedence over the domestic tax law of the Member States and that domestic law of the Member States must not be amended to conflict with EU law. The Member States must neither conclude nor apply tax treaties that contain provisions in conflict with EU law. *Both primary and secondary EU law take precedence in a conflict situation over both old and new tax treaties concluded between two Member States.*[24]

The situation is more complex when there is a conflict between EU law and the provisions of a tax treaty concluded between a Member State and a non-Member State. EU law applies to the Member State also in these conflict situations.[25] Article 351 of the TFEU, however, provides that *tax treaties between a Member State and a third state concluded before 1.1.1958 in the case of the old Member States and after the date of accession in the case of the new Member States are to be respected.* The Member States are, however, obligated to try to renegotiate conflicting provisions to ensure EU law compatibility.

Article 351 does not state an explicit rule for the treaties concluded after the entry into force of the EC Treaty in its original form in 1958 or after the entry into force of the accession treaties. The article must, however, be interpreted to mean that after the entry into force of the EC treaty as regards the old Member States and after the entry into force of the accession treaties as regards the new Member States, *a Member State is not allowed to conclude a tax treaty with a non-Member State, which is incompatible with EU law* without the Member State breaching its obligations under EU law.[26] Of course, *a non-Member State is not affected by either primary or secondary EU tax law.* Only the EU Member State, thus, breaches its obligations under EU law if it applies a tax treaty provision in conflict with EU law. Instead, if the Member State fails to follow a

---

23. *See* C-336/96 *Gilly,* C-307/97 *Saint-Gobain,* C-470/04 *N,* C-513/04 *Kerckhaert and Morres,* C-374/04 *Test Claimants in Class IV of the ACT Group Litigation* and C-524/04 *Test Claimants in the Thin Cap Group Litigation.* About the relationship between EU law and tax treaties *see also,* for example, O'Shea (2008), Helminen (2015), 26–35, Kemmeren (2008a), 156–158, Mattsson (2007), 221–234, Hilling (2005), 213–252, Pistone (2002), van den Hurk (2004), 17–30, Pistone (2005), 4–9 and Pistone (2007), 75–81.
24. *See,* for example, 82/72 *C.J. Walder v. Bestuur der Sociale Verzekeringsbank* and C-336/96 *Gilly,* 235/87 *Matteucci,* 286/86 *Deserbais,* C-307/97 *Saint Gobain,* C-279/93 *Schumacker* and C-265/04 *Bouanich. See also,* for example, Helminen (2015), 28–29, Panayi (2007), 130–131, Hinnekens (1994), 146, Becker and Thömmes (1991), 175, Hamaekers (1993), 26, Malherbe and Delattre (1996), 14, Penttilä (1996), 5, Penttilä (1996a), 243, Malherbe and Delattre (1996), 14, Jann (1996), 160, Schusch (1996), 164, Eicker (1998), 322 and 324, and Carrero (1996), 290.
25. It is possible that a treaty with a third state conflicts with EU law by binding the Member State to behaviour that is in violation of EU law or by authorizing the third state to behaviour that in the territory of European Union leads to a conflict with EU law. *See* examples of such situations in Vogel et al. (1997), 74.
26. *See* for this opinion Hinnekens (1994), 156–157, van Unnik and Boudesteijn (1993), 108–109, Lamg (1996), 30–32, *Tax Treaty Interpretation* (1997), 32–33 and Malherbe and Delattre (1996), 14. *See* about tax treaties between a Member State and a non-Member State also, for example, Helminen (2015), 30–33, Vanistendael (1999), 163–170, Vogel, Gutmann and Dourado (2006), 83–94, Panayi (2007), 122–126 and 129–130, Fontana (2007), 597, Pistone (2006), 243–244, Vapaavuori (2003), 23–25 and Malmgrén (2006), 356–366.

tax treaty concluded with a non-Member State, the Member State may breach its obligations under general international law with respect to the treaty partner who is not bound by EU law.[27]

The primacy of EU law over tax treaties in relation to dividend taxation means that the Member States must not apply tax treaty provisions conflicting with the P-S Directive or the TEU or the TFEU. Basically this relationship means that the Member States must not apply tax treaty provisions, which would be less favourable to the taxpayers covered by the P-S Directive than the provisions of the Directive or which would conflict with the TFEU and especially Article 49 of the TFEU on the freedom of establishment and Article 63 of the TFEU on the free movement of capital. Tax treaty provisions that are, on the other hand, more favourable to the taxpayer than the treatment based on the P-S Directive may be applied, provided that the treaty rules do not infringe upon the intended objectives of EU law.[28] The anti-avoidance provision included in Article 1 of the P-S Directive in 2014, for example, must be respected. The Directive benefits or similar benefits shall not be granted to arrangements that fall under the anti-avoidance provision.[29]

In contrast to the cross-border situations concerning two or more Member States, the tax treatment of cross-border dividends concerning a Member State and a non-Member State as such may hardly frustrate the effect of the P-S Directive.[30] The tax treatment in these situations, however, may be in conflict with the TFEU especially with the free movement of capital principle of Article 63 of the TFEU.

§3.02 THE CLASSIFICATION CONFLICTS OF INTERNATIONAL TAX LAW

[A] Description of the Problem

Before an item of income may be taxed, a determination must be made as to what type of income it constitutes under the different legal systems of international tax law. With

---

27. It may be argued that the Member State is not held to its obligations to observe a tax treaty if the non-Member State, with whom the treaty was completed was aware of the fact that the Member State was incompetent to conclude the treaty because of a fundamental rule of national law. However, it may also be argued that the non-Member State was entitled to the expectation that the EU Member State had complied with its Community obligations when concluding the tax treaty. See Hinnekens (1994), fn. 49 and Kemmeren (1997), 146–147.
28. See Tax Treaty Interpretation (1997), 32–36 and Clayson (1994), 43. It has even been discussed whether the P-S Directive prohibits EU Member States from concluding tax treaties that include provisions concerning dividend. It is, however, clear that because the scope of the P-S Directive is very limited, covering only intra-group dividend between companies of Member States, the P-S Directive may not be interpreted in this way. In fact, the P-S Directive specifically establishes the possibility of applying tax treaties simultaneously and alternatively. For example, Art. 7(2) of the P-S Directive states that 'This Directive shall not affect the application of domestic or agreement-based provisions designed to eliminate or lessen economic double taxation of dividend, in particular provisions relating to the payment of tax credits to the recipients of dividend....'.
29. See Helminen (2015), 178–180 and Weber (2016), 98–129 for the P-S Directive anti-avoidance provision.
30. See also, for example, Carrero (1996), 290.

respect to each item of income, a determination must be made as to its *tax classification* for purposes of domestic tax laws of the states involved, for purposes of EU tax law and for purposes of tax treaties.[31] Because of the independence of these different legal systems, it is possible that the same entities and income items may be differently classified for the different purposes.

Inconsistent classification under domestic tax law of two states does not, however, constitute a conflict of laws. For example, even if an item of income had been classified as dividend for tax treaty purposes or for the domestic tax law purposes of a state, it does not need to be taxed as dividend under the domestic law of the other state concerned and vice versa. Classification for domestic tax law purposes does not actually involve a conflict, but rather only *a problem of classification*. The problem of how foreign-source income or foreign entities are classified for domestic tax law purposes is actually only a *substitution problem*.[32]

Tax treaty classification involves more difficult problems. In a tax treaty situation, the manner in which the tax treaty is to be applied either to or with the domestic tax law of the contracting states in a particular situation must be determined. A determination must be made as to the definition of the treaty terms and concepts and the application of the treaty terms to economic facts.[33]

Tax treaties as independent legal systems have languages of their own.[34] Tax treaties may include terms that are unknown in other domestic law or the terms used in tax treaties may be the same as those terms used in domestic law, but they may have another definition in a tax treaty. One and the same term may have a tax treaty definition and a domestic law definition. Especially as tax treaties include legal terms that are simultaneously also terms of the contracting states' domestic law, the same term might have a different definition in each contracting state's domestic law and in a tax treaty.

The same problem applies with respect to EU tax law. Also, *EU tax law forms a separate legal system*, with separate language, concepts and definitions. Therefore, the definition of the terms used in EU tax law may differ from the definition of the same terms used in tax treaties or in the domestic tax law of the Member States.

Because the terms and language of tax treaties and domestic tax law differ from each other, the definitions of an income type under a tax treaty and under different states' domestic law are not necessarily identical. Despite these differences, tax treaty definitions must be used for tax treaty classification purposes, and domestic law definitions must be used for domestic law classification purposes. The tax treaty definition determines the type of the income for tax treaty purposes even though the income would qualify under another income category under the treaty states' domestic

---

31. Synonymously to the term, classification, is often used the term, characterization, and even the term, categorization, or, qualification.
32. The term substitution problem borrowed from private law is used in this meaning, for example, by Vogel et al. (1997), 52.
33. *See* about this nature of tax treaties interacting with domestic law Katz (1993), 625.
34. *See*, for example, Vogel and Prokisch (1993), 62, Widmer (1970), 21 and Niskakangas (1983), 72.

law. Similarly, the domestic tax law definition determines the type of income for domestic tax law purposes.

It is not always clear under what, if any, tax treaty income category an item of income qualifies. This uncertainty may lead to a situation where the two contracting states classify the item of income inconsistently also for tax treaty purposes. Such a conflict may be referred to as a *classification conflict of international tax law*.[35] This term includes both situations where the conflict leads to double taxation (i.e., a positive classification conflict) and situations where the conflict leads to double non-taxation (i.e., negative classification conflict).[36]

The concept of classification conflict of international tax law in its *broad definition* is used to refer to any inconsistent subsumption of a fact, form or term under two different legal systems of international tax law.[37] In *strict terms*, a classification conflict of international tax law, however, includes only conflicts in tax treaty classification or EU tax law classification.[38] As described above, classification for the domestic tax law purposes of two states, strictly speaking, does not include a classification conflict but only a classification problem.[39]

Classification and *interpretation* have a very close connection to each other. The problem of how a tax treaty term is understood when it is not simultaneously a legal

---

35. Often, especially in German literature, the term, qualification conflict of international tax law, referring especially to tax treaty situations, is synonymously used. *See*, for example, Gündisch (2005), 424–431 Also, the term, characterization conflict or categorization conflict, is often used for the same purpose. For example, von Poser and Gross-Naedlitz (1972), 1–2, Hannes (1992), 23 and Piltz (1993), 21–22, recognize the inexact nature and the loose usage of the terms. The term, classification conflict or characterization conflict, is better than qualification conflict in the sense that qualification conflict is actually a term of international private law. The term qualification, as used in connection with international tax law, should not be mixed with the same term used in private international law, referring to conflict of law situations. *See* about the international private law meaning Escher (1974), 74–75, Stobbe (1989), 242, von Poser and Gross-Naedlitz (1972), 3–8 and Hannes (1992), 24–28. *See* Knobbe-Keuk (1991), 306, Vogel et al. (1997), 52, Lindencrona (1972), 160–166 and Hannes (1992) 31–36 about how the term, qualification of international private law, is, however, borrowed to international tax law. In order to avoid confusion, it seems reasonable that the use of the term qualification in connection with international tax law should be very limited. Because of this possibility of confusion, the term, classification conflict, is used throughout this study instead of the term qualification conflict.
36. *See* von Poser and Gross-Naedlitz (1972), 125–127, Diehl (1978), 517–518 and Hannes (1992), 35 and 305, about the differentiation between positive and negative classification conflicts. Hannes (1992), 35 and 305 differentiates also virtual classification conflict where inconsistent classification does not have effect on the tax burden. *See*, however, von Poser and Gross-Naedlitz (1972), 118–119, for a sometimes used definition of the term, classification conflict, covering only double taxation situations. *See* Lang (2004), 73–119 about the problem of double non-taxation in general.
37. *See* von Poser and Gross-Naedlitz (1972), 20, Hannes (1992), 2, 32–33, 88–128 and 305 and Piltz (1993), 23–25, about the use of the term in the broad sense. Hannes (1992), 129–141 covers a wide range of different definitions expressed by various authors.
38. Sometimes the term classification conflict is used especially and only to refer to problems in which two treaty states would qualify a treaty term differently because the treaty term is differently used in each of the states domestic law. *See* Stobbe (1989), 243. Also Vogel gives the term a very strict meaning covering only situations where a tax treaty includes terms that are simultaneously terms of the contracting states' domestic law. *See* about this definition used especially by Vogel in Vogel (1982a), 292, Hannes (1992), 137–138 and Vogel et al. (1997), 52.
39. *See* Hannes (1992), 306.

Chapter 3: Legal Systems of International Tax Law §3.02[A]

term of a contracting state's domestic law is, strictly speaking, not a classification problem, but simply a problem of interpretation. The same applies actually also with respect to tax treaty terms that are simultaneously terms of domestic tax law, but are defined in the treaty itself. In these situations, there is no conflict on the question of which state's law to apply for the classification, in the same way as there is no conflict in a non-treaty situation. In situations described above, inconsistent taxation is instead caused by inconsistent interpretation of tax treaty terms.

In an *interpretation conflict*, although the two contracting states define a tax treaty term according to the same rules, the states end up defining the tax treaty term differently or interpret different items to be covered by the definition.[40] A classification conflict includes, in its strictest sense, only conflicts raising the question of what rules determine the definition of undefined tax treaty terms, which are simultaneously terms of each state's domestic law. A classification conflict includes the problem of what definition of several possible definitions is to be applied. Instead, interpretation involves the question of what items are included under the selected definition.[41] Classification for domestic law purposes is, thus, actually a problem of interpretation of domestic tax law. Also, classification for tax treaty purposes or for EU tax law purposes involves only partly the question of which rules are used to determine income classification and partly involves a problem of interpreting the treaty terms or the EU tax law.

Interpretation and classification, however, always have a very close connection to each other, and, may, in an actual situation, not always be clearly separate.[42] It may be argued that it is actually a question of interpreting a tax treaty when it comes to solving a classification conflict in a tax treaty situation. Actually, classification in tax treaty context is about the question of which rules are applied in interpreting tax treaties.[43] It is also clear that inconsistent interpretation of a tax treaty too may lead to classification conflict.

The fact that an item of income may be given *inconsistent taxable status in two different states* may lead to double exemption of income or to the deductibility of a certain item in one state but not to a corresponding income taxation of the item in the other state. In addition to *double non-taxation*, inconsistent classification in different states may easily lead to *international double taxation*.

---

40. *See* about this differentiation between the terms qualification and interpretation, Widmann (1985), 238. Also, for example, Escher (1974), 77–78 makes clear distinction between classification and interpretation. However, sometimes the term qualification is used loosely to refer also to interpretation problems. *See* Hannes (1992), 31–32, about how this is the case especially in older tax literature.
41. Hannes (1992), 245 and 307, differentiates between *echte* and *unechte* qualification conflicts depending on whether the conflict emerged from differences in interpretation of a tax treaty or from reasons outside the scope of a tax treaty or emerged by a different determination of facts.
42. von Poser and Gross-Naedlitz (1972), 111 uses the term, *Die mittelbaren Auslegungskonflict*, which may be translated as indirect interpretation conflict, referring to qualification conflict.
43. *See* Piltz (1993), 23 and Hannes (1992), 44. Because of the close connection the term 'interpretation' or 'classification' may not be used very exactly. *See*, for examples, on the inexact usage of these terms in von Poser and Gross-Naedlitz (1972), 112 and 120, and Debatin (1979), 439–499.

Non-taxation or double taxation is possible especially in non-treaty situations, but also in treaty situations, if the two contracting states reach an inconsistent treaty classification. If one of the states, for example, treats an item of income as dividend under the treaty between the states and the other state treats it as some other type of income, international double taxation may not be eliminated. This failure to eliminate international double taxation occurs because the states apply different rules of a tax treaty to divide taxing rights between the contracting states. In order for a tax treaty to function properly, a classification conflict should be solved in favour of one of the possibly applicable tax treaty articles. In the same way, also a classification conflict with respect to an EU Directive should be solved in order for the directive to function properly. If a term is not clearly defined in the tax *treaty or directive itself*, it must be decided whether the term is to be defined in the same way as the same term is defined in the *domestic law* of either of the states concerned or whether the term should be given an *autonomous definition*.[44]

[B] Solutions to Classification Conflicts

[1] General Solutions

Classification conflicts have to be solved by the actions of the authorities of the states concerned. There is no supranational authority that could solve tax law classification conflicts. Only the definition of the terms of the EU directives and other EU law can be interpreted also by the EU Court.[45] Basically, there are *two ways* of tackling classification problems. A *classification conflict may be totally eliminated* by finding a common classification in some way. Often, it is, however, more realistic not to eliminate the conflict itself, but *only to eliminate the unwanted effects of double taxation or double non-taxation caused by the conflict*.[46]

In a non-treaty situation between non-EU Member States, the need to solve classification problems is not as pressing as in a treaty situation. The states involved are

---

44. Tax treaty law does not, however, include such binding conflict of law rules as international private law. Tax treaty rules are not conflict of law rules, but rather only divide tax sources and taxable objects among the contracting states. The rules of international tax law and especially those of tax treaties are, thus, classification and assignment rules or distributive rules in respect to taxing right. See Debatin (1988), 728, Hannes (1992), 29–30 and 33 and Vogel et al. (1997), 26–27.
45. There are some exceptions. For example, Art. 25 of the Austria – Germany income tax treaty (2000) includes a provision on compulsory arbitration in the EU Court.
46. This is the approach of, for example, the recommended hybrid mismatch provisions of the BEPS Action 2 report and the EU Anti-tax avoidance Directive provision on hybrid mismatch arrangements. The provisions do not seek to eliminate any inconsistent classification of hybrids and the income on hybrids but instead eliminate the undesirable deduction – non-inclusion or double deduction situations caused by the mismatches. See OECD (2015) and Art. 9 of the Anti-tax Avoidance Directive. *See also* Part II of the Multilateral Convention to Implement Tax Treaty Related Measures to Prevent Base Erosion and Profit Shifting. The text of the multilateral treaty was published on 24 Nov. 2016 and will have to be signed and ratified before it will come effective.

not required to eliminate international double taxation or non-taxation.[47] In a non-treaty situation, the solutions to classification problems depend solely upon the will and unilateral actions of the states involved. Double taxation caused by the inconsistent classification of an entity or an item of income in two states may be avoided by *unilateral elimination of double taxation* in the state of residence of the income recipient, despite the inconsistent classification. This action does not, however, eliminate the classification problem itself, but only serves to limit its effects. This solution is possible also only with respect to positive classification problems but does not help with a negative classification problem, that is, in a situation of double non-taxation.[48] Unilateral domestic law provisions, however, may be used also to eliminate double non-taxation situations.

The unwanted effects of a negative classification problem may be avoided in the state of residence of the income recipient, for example, by means of different *subject-to-tax clauses*. These clauses exempt income otherwise exempted, only if it has been subject to tax in the other state.[49] Another method, and one that in practice is used even more frequently, is to use the *credit method* rather than the exemption method in the elimination of double taxation.[50] These methods may also be used, of course, in bilateral or multilateral tax treaties.[51] Both methods, however, only eliminate the effects of a classification problem but do not eliminate the problem itself.

One solution for eliminating the problem of double non-taxation caused by inconsistent classification would be to amend the domestic law provisions concerning classification unilaterally so that they refer to *foreign law classification*. Reference to foreign law classification as a decisive factor is, however, not very usual in practice. It is more usual that foreign law classification is taken into account only as one element when making the domestic law classification.[52] The undesirable tax effects caused by inconsistent classification, however, may be eliminated even though the classification itself would not be touched. The OECD/G20 BEPS Action 2 recommendations on neutralizing hybrid mismatches and the hybrid mismatch provision of the EU Anti-tax Avoidance Directive are good examples of such provisions.[53]

---

47. In the case of the EU Member States double taxation of course must be eliminated to the extent required by the P-S Directive and other EU Directives. EU law, however, does not include a general requirement to eliminate double taxation. *See* Helminen (2015), 43–52 and Helminen (2014), 391–412.
48. *See* about this problem, for example, Hannes (1992), 257.
49. *See* Hannes (1992), 261 about subject-to-tax-clauses as a solution to negative classification conflicts in tax treaties.
50. *See* Hannes (1992), 261 about this method and Lang (2004), 88–112 and Helminen (2016a), 115–120 for different methods used for coping with double non-taxation.
51. *See* e.g., Part II of the Multilateral Convention to Implement Tax Treaty Related Measures to Prevent Base Erosion and Profit Shifting. The text of the multilateral treaty was published on 24 Nov. 2016 and will have to be signed and ratified before it comes effective.
52. *See* about this practice with respect to entity classification in the chapter of this study dealing with dividend-distributing entities.
53. *See* OECD (2015) and Part II of the Multilateral Convention to Implement Tax Treaty Related Measures to Prevent Base Erosion and Profit Shifting. The text of the multilateral treaty was published on 24 Nov. 2016 and will have to be signed and ratified before it comes effective. *See also* Art. 9 of the Anti-tax avoidance Directive. The original form of the proposed hybrid mismatch provision of the Proposal for the EU Anti-tax avoidance Directive required the EU

The basic question with respect to tax treaty classification conflicts is to what extent must the state of residence of the income recipient accept the source state classification or at least give credit or exempt income in order to eliminate international double taxation. This question cannot be answered similarly with respect to all cases, but the answer clearly depends on the case concerned.[54]

In a situation where the applicable tax treaty itself fails to give any guidance to solving a classification problem *four approaches to solving the problem* are, in principle, possible. These are: [1.] *lex fori classification*, [2.] *source state classification*, [3.] *classification of the state of residence of the income recipient* and [4.] *autonomous classification*.[55] In the *lex fori* approach, each state applying the treaty, defines treaty terms according to its own domestic legislation. In this approach, each state gives a treaty term the same definition as the same term has in its own domestic legislation. The *lex fori* approach may be expressly referred to in the treaty text or the treaty states may otherwise end up using this approach.

The primary argument for the *lex fori* approach is the principle that treaty partners intended to waive their sovereignty only to the extent that the treaty text clearly evidences this waiver. Because the *lex fori* approach allows each state to define treaty terms according to its own law, each state may interpret terms in the way that is in accordance with the principle of the minimum waiver of sovereignty. However, it is also clear that this approach does not always fulfil the object of a tax treaty. The *lex fori* approach may easily lead to inconsistent classification and, therefore, to double taxation or double non-taxation. The *lex fori* approach, at its worst, may lead to a situation where tax treaty interpretation is carried out in much the same way as is the interpretation of other domestic legislation, that is, paying no attention to the treaty as a bilateral agreement with a language of its own. The *lex fori* approach, anyhow, makes a tax treaty easy to operate, because each state is allowed to apply and interpret the treaty and its terms according to its own domestic legislation, which the authorities of each state are certainly best acquainted with.[56]

In *source state classification*, tax treaty terms are defined in accordance with the law of the state where the income arises. In other words, both contracting states give to undefined treaty terms the definition that the terms have in the domestic tax law of the source state of the income. In practice, this approach makes the treaty difficult to operate for the state of residence of the income recipient, because in order to solve

---

Member States to follow the classification of another in the case of hybrid instruments and entities. *See* Art. 10 of the Proposal for a Council Directive laying down rules against tax avoidance practices that directly affect the functioning of the internal market, COM(2016) 26 final, 28.1.2016. The final version of the Anti-tax Avoidance Directive, however, does not include such a provision, but a provision that only eliminates the harmful effects of hybrid mismatches. *See* Art. 9 of the Anti-tax avoidance Directive. A provision requiring the Member States to follow the classification of another state would have gone beyond what is necessary for the functioning of the EU internal market and, thus would not have been in accordance with the EU primary law. *See* Helminen (2015a), 325–339 for the requirements for a hybrid mismatch provision to be in accordance with primary EU law.

54. *See* Avery Jones et al. (1996), 145.
55. These terms have been borrowed directly from international private law. *See* von Poser and Gross-Naedlitz (1972), 13 and Vogel et al. (1997), 54.
56. *See* about the arguments in favour and against the *lex fori* approach Vogel et al. (1997), 56–59.

classification problems, the state of residence must be aware of the domestic law of the source state. This approach, however, leads to uniform interpretation more likely than does the *lex fori* approach. Double taxation caused by classification conflict would, thus, normally be avoided.

It may be recommended that the state of residence of the income recipient follows the classification of the source state whenever the source state classification is in accordance with the treaty, or at least eliminates double taxation with respect to the income.[57] A weak point of this approach is that it does not distribute taxable events equally between the contracting states, but rather benefits the state that has a broader definition of the term in question in its own domestic law.[58] An important argument in favour of the source state approach is that a treaty is much easier for the source state to operate if the source state may independently interpret tax treaty terms according to its own law.[59]

Another possible solution is that both contracting states classify a treaty term according to the law of the state of the residence of the income recipient. The *state of residence classification* is a natural choice because according to most of the distributive provisions of tax treaties in conformity with the OECD Model, the state of residence has the primary taxing right. The residence state approach in most cases allows the state having the primary taxing right to make the classification according to its own legislation.

The state of residence approach is not, however, unproblematic. One serious problem in this approach is the possibility of dual residence. Both contracting states may claim to be the state of residence and each would make the classification according to its own law.[60] Also, the residence state approach leads to uniform classification only if both the states interpret the law of the state of residence similarly or if one of the states accepts the interpretation made by the other. It is problematic that this approach allows the state with the broadest definition to benefit most. It is also problematic for the source state to apply the treaty if it has to make the classification according to another state's legislation.[61]

Finally, it is possible that the contracting states search for a consistent classification in the context of the treaty, autonomous of the domestic law of each state. The *autonomous classification* approach considers the tax treaty to be a group of rules, which are independent of the domestic law of each state. According to this approach, a tax treaty has its own language and definitions. Because the domestic laws of different states are different, an autonomous classification sensitive to the context of a

---

57. *See The American Law Institute Federal Tax Project* (1992), 237.
58. Vogel et al. (1997), 57 and Avery Jones (1986), 79, correctly point out that states could deliberately extend the internal law definitions of the terms used in tax treaties, and take advantage of the source state approach.
59. *See* for the arguments in favour and against source state classification Vogel et al. (1997), 57–58.
60. *See* Grossmann, Klaus (1995), *Doppelt ansässige Kapitalgesellschaften im internationalen Steuerrech*, for a thorough study on the problem of corporations with dual residence.
61. *See* for the arguments in favour and against the state of residence classification Vogel et al. (1997), 58.

treaty best serves the goal of a consistent and equal interpretation and application of the treaty by both contracting states.[62]

In searching for an autonomous classification, the methods of tax treaty interpretation get relevance. One method of interpretation is the *historical method*, which involves trying to ascertain the intention of the treaty partners at the time of the signing of the treaty. Another method is one of *teleological interpretation*, which may be carried out by trying to learn the objective object and purpose of the treaty and its provisions as understood by the time of the interpretation. The approach may also be a *grammatical* one, which means that the interpretation is searched for from the term itself in its context. Finally, the approach might be a *systematic* one, which means that an interpretation is sought by looking at the system that the terms and articles of a treaty form. All these approaches may be used together to reach a consistent classification.[63]

Even if the autonomous approach is used, the two contracting states may reach different classifications. The two states might interpret a treaty term differently even though no resort is made to domestic law. A common classification will certainly be reached only if the states make the autonomous classification together.

[2] Express Definitions in Tax Treaties

The starting point in solving tax treaty classification conflicts, as also in interpreting tax treaties, is that the solution must be searched for from the treaty text itself. The clearest solution to a classification conflict is if a tax treaty expressly defines the term in question, which is the case, for example, with respect to the term dividend under the OECD Model. Then, strictly speaking, there is no classification problem because the treaty itself solves it. In other words, for tax treaty purposes, the definition of the treaty and not the definitions of the domestic law of the two contracting states must be used. The problem as to what items of income qualify under an income category that is defined in the treaty itself, therefore, is rather only a problem of interpretation.

This interpretation problem must be solved in accordance with the general rules of interpretation of tax treaties. In interpreting what the treaty definition covers, the decisive part is what the treaty partners intended the definition to mean. The interpretation of the definition is to be sought from the context of the treaty. The interpretation must be sought both from the treaty itself and from its context, such as the purpose of the treaty term.[64] It must, however, be decided to what extent domestic

---

62. For example, Lindencrona (1994), 77–78, Vogel and Prokisch (1993), 55, 62 in accordance with the opinion of the OECD and the *International Fiscal Association 1993* congress, and Vogel et al. (1997), 58 and Ekkehart & Rust (2015), 60 consider autonomous interpretation to be the best method.
63. *See* about the different methods of interpretation, for example, in Aarnio (1978), 101–103, Sainio (1976), 33–35, Lindencrona (1972), 162 and Pöllacht (1993), 331–335.
64. *See* about tax treaty interpretation, for example, in Barenfeld (2005), 23–51, Lang (2000), International Fiscal Association (1960, 1991, 1993), Avery Jones (1986), Piltz (1993), 31–32, Hannes (1992), 43–87, Vogel et al. (1997), 32–51, Helminen (2016), 23–25, Arnold (2010), 2–16, Rohatgi (2005), 38–56, Avery Jones (2016), Ekkehart & Rust (2015), 34–52 and Engelen (2004).

law of the contracting states should be used to clarify the treaty definition or to define the possibly undefined terms used in the definition. For example, the dividend definition of the OECD Model includes many undefined terms, which leave room for inconsistent interpretation and classification conflicts.

[3] The Rule of Interpretation in Tax Treaties

In practice, references in tax treaty definitions to domestic law cannot be avoided and it is unreasonable even to try to avoid them.[65] It is common that a treaty refers to the domestic law definition of a treaty term as the treaty definition. The domestic law definition may be referred to also in an article including a general rule of interpretation.[66] The reference to domestic law may also be tacit. The treaty may, for example, use a term of one of the contracting states domestic law.[67]

A classification problem is solved when a tax treaty provision clearly refers to domestic law of one of the contracting states.[68] Despite a clear reference to definitions of one of the contracting states domestic law, uniform interpretation may be achieved only if the other state is bound by the classification made by the state referred to. In any case, the incidence of both the express treaty definitions and the references to a treaty country's domestic law in tax treaties has increased.[69]

Many tax treaties include an article corresponding to *Article 3(2) of the OECD Model*. It provides a partial solution to classification problems dealing with interpretation of undefined treaty terms that are simultaneously terms of the domestic law of the contracting states.[70] Article 3(2) is a general rule compared to the special tax treaty rules of interpretation, but a special rule compared to general principles and rules of interpreting tax treaties. Special treaty definitions and references of special provisions to specific domestic law definitions take precedence over Article 3(2).[71]

See for the general methods of interpretation, for example, Aarnio (1978), 101–103, Aarnio (1988), 260–287 and Aarnio (1982), 150–162.

65. The application of a tax treaty is easier if it does not include too many definitions that would lead to meaning deviating from domestic law meanings. Reference to domestic law also promotes legal certainty. Too specific and limiting definitions of legal terms in tax treaties are not practical. This is because of the differences in domestic law of the contracting states and because of the efforts to keep tax treaties flexibly applicable over time despite continuous changes in domestic legislation. *See* Vogel and Prokisch (1993), 77.
66. For example, Art. 3(2) of the OECD Model solves the problem with respect to undefined treaty terms by reference to domestic law. *See* more closely below.
67. *See* examples of tacit reference to domestic law Vogel and Prokisch (1993), 75–76.
68. Even if a reference is made to one of the states, for example, to the state of residence, which of the states is the state of residence must be solved, and this may not be clear. *See* about the problem of corporations with dual residence in the study of Klaus Grossman (1995). *Doppelt ansässige Kapitalgesellschaften im internationalen Steuerrecht.*
69. *See* Katz (1993), 625.
70. The reference to domestic tax law and other domestic law allows ambulatory instead of static interpretation. It allows a reference to the domestic law meaning at the time the treaty is applied. *See* para. 11 of the Commentary on Art. 3 of the OECD Model. *See* about ambulatory interpretation also, for example, Vogel et al. (1997), 64–65 and Ekkehart & Rust (2015), 65–67.
71. *See* about this hierarchy Vogel et al. (1997), 209.

According to Article 3(2) of the OECD Model, an undefined treaty term shall have the meaning of the same term in the domestic law of the state that is applying the treaty, unless the context requires otherwise.[72] The definition of a term in the text of the tax treaty itself is primary and the definition of the undefined treaty terms must be looked for from the context of the treaty itself.[73] If the context, however, does not require a universal interpretation, each state applying the treaty may interpret treaty terms according to its own domestic law.[74] This approach can be explained by the fact that states usually attempt to protect their sovereignty to the greatest extent possible in respect to taxation.[75]

Article 3(2) has only limited relevance with respect to dividends, because Article 10(3) of the OECD Model includes a special definition of the term dividend and a special rule of interpretation concerning dividends. According to Article 10(3) dividend means '...[1.] income from shares...or [2. income from] other rights not being debt-claims...[3.] as well as income from other corporate rights which is subject to the same taxation treatment as income from shares by the laws of the State of which the company making the distribution is a resident'. Article 3(2) is primarily relevant to this definition only with respect to the undefined terms of the definition in the first two parts of the definition which are not covered by the special rule of interpretation of the third part referring to domestic law.

The third part of the dividend definition of Article 10(3) of the OECD Model expressly refers to the tax law of the source state. The state of residence of the income

---

72. According to the wording of the treaties that follows the US Model, a different meaning may also be found if the meaning is reached in a mutual agreement procedure. Although Art. 3(2) of the OECD Model does not literally refer to the possibility of finding a meaning to a term via mutual agreement procedure, Art. 25(3) of the OECD Model provides the possibility.
73. *See* Avery Jones et al. (1984a), 90–96, about what is regarded to be covered by the context of a treaty in addition to the treaty text itself. Any contextual meaning may not override domestic law meaning but the term, require, implies that there must be strong reasons in order for the contextual meaning to be used. *See*, for example, Déry and Ward (1993), 285. There are different opinions expressed among authors about what the relationship in Art. 3(2) is between a domestic law meaning and a contextual law meaning. *See*, for example, Vogel and Prokisch (1993), 81, Vogel et al. (1997), 209 and 213–215 and Lang (2000).
74. There is no unanimity on how the term application in Art. 3(2) of the OECD Model should be understood. Some authors are of the opinion that the term leads to source state classification instead of *lex fori* classification, because the state of residence of income recipient cannot be viewed as applying to the treaty. Others instead view Art. 3(2) to mean *lex fori* classification. In the opinion of the author of this study, solving classification problems by interpreting the term application of the Art. 3(2) narrowly, leading to source state classification is rather artificial. There are not really other arguments supporting this kind of interpretation than the need for a common interpretation. The Commentary on the OECD Model also do not suggest that the state of residence of the recipient of income should in any case accept the source state classification. It is rather accepted in the OECD Model that different classifications might be reached and, therefore, there is Art. 25 concerning mutual agreement procedure in the Model, which may be referred to in order to solve disputes between the contracting states. *See* Avery Jones et al. (1984), 50–54, Vogel and Prokisch (1993), 78–79, Avery Jones (1993), 608–610, Déry and Ward (1993), 281–284, van Raad (1996), 6, Avery Jones (1993a), 254–255, Vogel et al. (1997), 211–212 and Shannon (1989), 457 for a discussion on the different opinions on this subject.
75. The original purpose of the article was that each state is allowed to interpret undefined treaty terms by reference to each own domestic law, in order to preserve each state's sovereignty. *See Tax Treaty Interpretation* (1997), 8-20–8-21.

recipient must, thus, accept the classification in accordance with the tax law of the source state. From the wording '...as well as income from other corporate rights...' it, however, follows that to a certain extent also the third part of the definition is dependent on the interpretation of the two first autonomous parts of the dividend definition. Article 3(2) may, therefore, have relevance indirectly also in interpreting the third part of the dividend definition.

[4] Double Taxation Relief Articles

There may be no rule in a tax treaty that would require a classification conflict to be solved in favour of a certain classification. Therefore, it may be asked to what extent the state of residence of the income recipient must, despite inconsistent classification, eliminate international double taxation. In practice, double taxation relief articles of tax treaties are very differently worded. Therefore, also the answer to the question to what extent double taxation must be eliminated in a classification conflict situation depends on the treaty in question.

In general, dividend may be taxed not only in the state of residence of the income recipient but also in the source state. Instead, other income such as business income, interest, royalties and capital gains from immovable property are taxed more often only in the state of residence of the income recipient. Therefore, double taxation may emerge especially when the source state classifies an income item as dividend and the state of residence of the recipient of the income classifies the item as some other type of income. In such a situation, the state of residence of the income recipient views that there should be no source state tax that should be credited.

In contrast, in a situation where the source state does not classify an item of income as dividend and the other state classifies it as dividend, the classification conflict most often may cause only double non-taxation. Double non-taxation emerges if the state of residence of the income recipient views the income as direct investment dividend to which it applies the exemption system.[76] The double taxation problem with respect to the application of the double taxation relief provisions of tax treaties concerns situations where the source state classifies income as dividend and the state of residence of the income recipient defines it as some other type of income.

The Commentary on the OECD Model suggests that the state of residence should grant a credit for withholding taxes on dividend even though the state itself would not classify the income as dividend. This requirement applies as long as the state of residence recognizes that the source state taxed the item concerned in accordance with Article 10, that is, when it was proper for the source state to tax the income as dividend under the dividend article of the treaty.[77] This requirement seems correct at least with respect to the part of the dividend definition referring to the source state classification,

---

76. *See* International Fiscal Association (2004) about the problem of double non-taxation and about the possible solutions to the problem.
77. Paragraphs 32.1–32.3 and 68 of the Commentary on Art. 23 of the OECD Model. The issue of elimination of double taxation in a classification conflict situation is dealt with also in the OECD partnership report. *See* OECD (1999).

which actually requires the state of residence to not only eliminate double taxation, but in fact treat the income as dividend for tax treaty purposes.

The same requirement also applies, however, with respect to income that the source state views to qualify under the autonomous part of the dividend definition. This part, however, should be interpreted autonomously or in accordance with the rule of Article 3(2) of the OECD Model, in accordance with the law of the state applying the treaty. Therefore, in situations where the source state views income to qualify under the autonomous part of the dividend definition, the state of residence does not actually have to accept the classification of the source state. If, however, the source state had applied the treaty properly, the state of residence should, despite the classification conflict, eliminate double taxation with respect to the dividend withholding tax imposed in the source state.[78]

Double tax relief articles of actual treaties differ with respect to dividend. Some articles require a credit for '...income defined as dividend in Article 10...' or '...items of income dealt with in Article 10...' and some require a credit simply for 'dividend' without referring to Article 10. If there is a reference to Article 10, it must be evaluated in light of Article 10 whether the source state classification is proper. Instead, if the reference is on dividend, in general it is unclear whether the dividend article of the treaty or the law of the source state or the law of the residence state is decisive.[79]

When the reference is to Article 10, the relief must be granted, as is suggested also in the Commentaries, if the source state has properly applied Article 10. In the case in which the reference is only to dividend, but not expressly to the dividend article, it is unclear what the proper application means. The dividend definition of Article 10 applies primarily only with respect to Article 10 but not with respect to other articles. The term 'dividend' used in the relief article may, therefore, be regarded as an undefined treaty term that must be interpreted in accordance with Article 3(2) according to the law of the state applying the treaty unless the context requires otherwise.[80]

According to the opinion of the author of this study, in most cases, the context of the double taxation relief article requires the definition of the dividend article to prevail in these situations also.[81] The dividend article, in most cases, may be said to have the closest connection to the relief article, because the relief article after all concerns granting a credit with respect to the withholding tax levied in accordance with the

---

78. Based on the wording of Art. 23 of the OECD Model, a foreign tax credit should be made available, if the source state taxed the income concerned in accordance with Art. 10. *See also* para. 32.3 of the Commentary on Art. 23 of the OECD Model. Unfortunately, in practice, classification conflicts may still not be avoided. *See* para. 32.5 of the Commentary on Art. 23 of the OECD Model and, for example, Avery Jones (2001), 220–224, Vogel (2003), 41–44, Rust (2003), 45–50 and Teixeira (2009), 464–466.
79. *See* about this problem Avery Jones et al. (1996), 128 and Avery Jones et al. (1999), 104–107.
80. *See* about this interpretation also Avery Jones et al. (1999), 105.
81. *See also* Avery Jones et al. (1999), 105, which mentions that 'If the context does otherwise require, some other meaning has to be applied which is likely to be the definition in the dividend article...'. *See also* Vogel et al. (1997), 649 and 1212–1213, which, however, seems to refer rather to the situations where the relief article refers to dividends by a reference to an article number.

dividend article. Symmetry argument also promotes this interpretation.[82] Therefore, also in the case of these treaties, the state of residence should eliminate double taxation if the source state properly applies the dividend article.[83] The proper application is, however, a fact that the contracting states may not be unanimous about. Therefore, the requirement to grant relief in situations of conflicting income classification is a question that often calls for reference to a mutual agreement procedure.

Until recently, the risk of double taxation was considered to be a bigger problem than the risk of double non-taxation. The OECD Model does not eliminate double non-taxation situations caused by classification conflicts properly where the exemption method is applied by the residence state. The OECD Model does not require the residence state to deny an exemption in a situation in which the source state classifies a cross-border payment as a tax-deductible payment which a tax treaty does not allow to be taxed in the source state.[84] This problem was recognized also in the OECD/BEPS Action 2 report on hybrid mismatches. The report recommends that at least paragraph 4 of Article 23 A of the OECD Model would be included in treaties that apply the exemption method. Also an express provision could be included allowing the use of credit method instead of the exemption method with respect to dividends that are deductible in the source state.[85]

[5] *Mutual Agreement Procedure and Arbitration*

Article 3(2) of the US Model specifically mentions that the definition of domestic law may be used unless the context requires otherwise or unless competent authorities reach a common definition in a mutual agreement procedure.[86] Article 3(2) of the OECD Model, instead, does not literally refer to the possibility of finding a meaning to a term via a mutual agreement procedure. Article 25(3) of the OECD Model, however, provides for the same possibility. According to the Commentaries on this article, a mutual agreement procedure may be used in particular '...where a term has been incompletely or ambiguously defined in the Convention...' to '...complete or clarify its

---

82. The possible situations where the definition of the dividend article may not have to be used for the purposes of the relief article are the ones where the exemption method is used instead of the credit method. In such situations, where it is not the question of granting a credit with respect to the source state withholding tax, the connection to the dividend article, which is the withholding article, is weaker. *See also* Avery Jones et al. (1999), 106–108, according to which depending on the actual wording of the relief article, in some cases, the domestic law definition of the state of residence should be decisive, because the relief provision, after all, concerns taxation in that state.
83. This problem is discussed thoroughly with respect to different relief Articles in Avery Jones et al. (1996), 118–146.
84. Paragraph 4 of Art. 23 A of the OECD Model does not eliminate the problem and many treaties do not include even this Paragraph.
85. *See* OECD (2015), 147. *See also* Part II of the Multilateral Convention to Implement Tax Treaty Related Measures to Prevent Base Erosion and Profit Shifting. The text of the multilateral treaty was published on 24 Nov. 2016 and will have to be signed and ratified before it comes effective.
86. *See* about the situations when mutual agreement procedure may be used to define a term in US tax treaties e.g., Avery Jones et al. (1984), 20 and Katz (1993), 639–644.

definition in order for obviate any difficulty...'.[87] A classification conflict may, thus, be solved in a mutual agreement procedure between the competent authorities of the contracting parties.

The weakness in using a mutual agreement procedure as the solution to classification conflicts is that it may actually be used only with respect to positive classification conflicts. Mutual agreement procedure actually is helpful only in situations where the classification conflict leads to double taxation, whereas it does not provide a solution to negative classification conflicts where the classification conflict leads to double non-taxation. There is also no requirement for the contracting states to reach an agreement in mutual agreement procedure.[88]

Because of the deficits of the mutual agreement procedure in 2008, the possibility of compulsory arbitration was added to the OECD Model Convention as a way to resolve double taxation situations.[89] Unfortunately, even now only very few actual tax treaties include the possibility of compulsory arbitration.[90] In 2016, the Commission proposed an EU directive on double taxation dispute resolution mechanism with broad scope of application and including arbitration.[91] Also the Multilateral Convention to Implement Tax Treaty Related Measures to Prevent Base Erosion and Profit Shifting will improve dispute resolution.[92]

[6] Solutions in Actual Tax Treaties

In practice, it is impossible to totally prevent classification conflicts. The inclusion of specific definitions in tax treaties only limits but does not eliminate the problem. A definition is never to the extent exact that inconsistent classification or interpretation would be completely avoided. Specific rules of interpretation also do not totally prevent the possibility of conflicts. Most actual tax treaties include an express dividend definition with a reference to source state classification. At least with respect to the part of the dividend definitions that refers to the classification of the source state, the state of residence of the dividend recipient should accept the classification of the source state. This requirement applies to the extent that the state accepts that the other state has applied and interpreted the article correctly.

---

87. Paragraph 52 of the Commentary on Art. 25.
88. *See* about the functioning of the mutual agreement procedure, for example, Commentary on Art. 25 of the OECD Model, Vogel et al. (1997), 1339–1392, Ekkehart & Rust (2015), 1735–1826, Helminen (2016a), 2571–2573 and Lang and Züger (2002). The Multilateral Convention to Implement Tax Treaty Related Measures to Prevent Base Erosion and Profit Shifting, the text of which was published on 24 Nov. 2016, will improve the mutual agreement procedure and arbitration. *See* Part V of the Convention.
89. *See* Art. 25(5) of the OECD Model. *See also*, for example, Ekkehart & Rust (2015), 1808–1819, Ault and Sasseville (2009), 208–215 and de Ruiter (2008), 493–499 about Art. 25(5).
90. *See*, for example, Park-Tillinghast (2004), Groen (2002), 3–27, Züger (2001) and Züger (2002), 31–38 about arbitration provisions in tax treaties.
91. Proposal for a Council Directive on Double Taxation Dispute Resolution Mechanism in the European Union, 25.10.2016, COM(2016) 686 final.
92. The text of teh Convention was published on 24 Nov. 2016 and it will have to be signed and ratified before it will enter into force.

Most actual tax treaties also include an article similar to Article 3(2) of the OECD Model referring to the law of the state applying the treaty unless the context requires otherwise. In some treaties, the general provision of interpretation, however, is formed slightly differently. An undefined term may be referred to have the meaning of the law of the state applying the treaty if the context requires it. Under this type of treaties, common interpretation clearly is the first choice, whereas domestic law meanings may be used only if the context so requires.

The articles of the actual tax treaties with the purpose of elimination of international double taxation differ in detail from each other. Most treaties seem to use solely the term 'income' in these articles and only some refer expressly to income from dividend within the meaning of Article 10 (dividend), and some refer simply to dividend. In most classification conflict situations, the state of residence of the income recipient must, therefore, eliminate double taxation, if the dividend article is properly applied and if the taxed amount may be regarded as income. The treaties that refer to the term 'dividend', instead, raise a question as to which rules govern the interpretation of the term 'dividend'. As expressed earlier, however, the context of the relief articles should require in most cases that the definition of the dividend article prevails, although it is not expressly referred to.

Double exemption is prevented under many actual tax treaties by the application of the credit method instead of exemption method in the classification conflict situations that otherwise would lead to double non-taxation.[93] The credit method may be applied, for example, in a situation where the source state classifies an income item as dividend for tax treaty purposes but the state of residence of the income recipient views the income as some other type of income. It may be, however, unclear if the shift from the exemption method to the credit method is applicable in any case of inconsistent interpretation or whether it requires that the treaty be properly applied and that the classification conflict be real.[94] Under some treaties, the problem of double exemption is avoided by limiting the applicability of dividend exemption to situations where the profit from which the income is paid has been subject to normal corporate tax in the other state.

Many actual treaties, in the same way as the OECD Model, do not prevent the possibility of double non-taxation where the state of residence of the income recipient classifies the income as direct investment dividend and the source state as some type of income not taxed in the source state. The problem has less relevance in the case of countries with tax treaty policy that direct investment dividends are exempted both in the source state and in the state of residence of the recipient anyway. There is, however, a problem if the double exemption is combined with a deduction in the source state. Such deduction and exemption outcome caused by classification conflicts should be eliminated. For example, the P-S Directive now includes a provision that

---

93. *See also* Vogel et al. (1997), 60–61 and Vetter (1997), 649–652.
94. *See* about this problem Vogel et al. (1997), 61 and Vetter (1997), 650–651.

denies the exemption in such a situation[95] and also the OECD/G20 BEPS project proposes similar provisions.[96]

[C] Conclusions

The domestic tax laws of different states, EU tax law and tax treaties are all separate legal systems. Therefore, the same terms under these different legal systems of international tax law may have different meanings.

An item of income may be classified differently for domestic tax law purposes in the state of residence of the payer of the income and in the state of residence of the recipient of the income. One of the states may classify an item of income as dividend whereas the other state may classify it as some other type of income.

Tax treaties do not affect domestic law classification of two contracting states. Tax treaty classification must be made in accordance with the classification rules of tax treaties whereas domestic law classification must be made in accordance with the classification rules of domestic law. Therefore, it is possible that domestic law classification of a contracting state with respect to an item of income differs, both from the domestic law classification of the other contracting state and from the tax treaty classification. An item of income may be classified as dividend under domestic tax law but as some other type of income for tax treaty purposes or vice versa.

Tax treaty classification of an item of income has meaning with respect to domestic law only in the sense that it gives the limits in which taxation is allowed under domestic tax law. Actual classification conflicts, thus, do not emerge between domestic tax laws of two states or between domestic tax law of a state and tax treaties.

Two contracting states may also reach an inconsistent tax treaty classification. The state of residence of the payer may classify an item of income as dividend for tax treaty purposes, whereas the state of residence of the recipient may treat the income as some other type of income under the same treaty. Such an actual classification conflict may easily lead to international non-taxation or double taxation. Therefore, an actual classification conflict of international tax law should be solved. If unanimous classification is not reached, at least international double taxation or non-taxation caused by the problem should be eliminated.

Under tax treaties, the state of residence often has to accept dividend classification of the source state. However, to the extent that the express dividend definition of a tax treaty is unclear, a classification conflict remains unsolved unless the context requires a unanimous classification or unless unanimous classification is reached under the mutual agreement procedure. However, despite an unsolved classification conflict, the state of residence of an income recipient is required to eliminate international double taxation to the extent that the state agrees that the other state correctly applied the treaty.

---

95. Article 4(1) of the P-S Directive.
96. *See* OECD (2015). *See also* Part II of the Multilateral Convention to Implement Tax Treaty Related Measures to Prevent Base Erosion and Profit Shifting. The text of the multilateral treaty was published on 24 Nov. 2016 and will have to be signed and ratified before it comes effective.

In the same way as with respect to tax treaties, inconsistent income classification under domestic tax law of two states may also lead to inconsistent classification for the purposes of the P-S Directive. One EU Member State concerned may view an item of income as a profit distribution under the P-S Directive whereas the other may not. One of the states may, therefore, apply the domestic law rules of implementing the P-S Directive whereas the other state may not apply the implementing rules of its own. The P-S Directive does not require the states to solve such situations. Therefore, if the meaning with respect to an actual situation is not clarified by the EU Court, the conflict remains unsolved, unless the states agree on a common interpretation or unless one of the states in question unilaterally amends its interpretation. The P-S Directive, however, eliminates non-taxation situations caused by inconsistent classifications by requiring taxation of payments that are deductible in the source state.

CHAPTER 4
Different Dividend Concepts in International Tax Law

§4.01 THE NORMS DETERMINING THE TAX LAW CONCEPT OF A DIVIDEND

The term 'dividend' has many different definitions under the different legal systems of international tax law. It may be unclear whether a transaction is covered by the different dividend concepts found in a state's domestic tax law, in the P-S Directive or in a tax treaty.

The clearest situation is if the term is expressly defined for the purpose in question. However, in spite of such an express definition, it may be unclear, what transactions qualify under the definition. It is also possible that the term is used but is not defined. In these cases, it must be determined what is meant by the term for different purposes of the norms concerning the taxation of dividends. It is also possible that the term derives its meaning from company law or from economic language. Often, the meaning of the term has to be interpreted in light of various sources, namely, the context where the term is used, the case law concerning dividends and the preparatory material on the tax provisions concerning dividends.[1]

Legal norms, in general, are either regulative norms or constitutive norms.[2] Regulative norms make things ordered, forbidden or allowed, while constitutive norms determine which legal facts go under which legal concept. Because this study is concerned with the interpretation of the concept of a dividend, constitutive norms are of primary focus. Constitutive norms, with respect to the term 'dividend', are the norms that determine whether or not a transaction constitutes a dividend.

When interpreting which legal facts go under the definition of the term 'dividend', all the rules concerning a dividend are meaningful as the term derives its

---
1. *See* how a tax term may get its meaning, for example, Tikka (1972), 91–93.
2. *See* Aarnio (1988), 70–77.

meaning from the rules that are applied. The legal institution called a dividend is created by these different rules. The rules that determine who may pay a dividend, to whom a dividend may be paid, how the payment must occur, what kind of investment must be behind a dividend, what kind of income is taxed as a dividend and so on, determine the concept of a dividend. The legal institution of a dividend is actually the sum of these norms. The tax law concept of a dividend obtains its meaning through the constitutive norms concerning dividend taxation.

Constitutive norms may be formed in different ways. They may be norms, which determine a legal thing by regulating what the thing in question must do and what it must not do. On the other hand, they may be norms that determine things in the form of x = y. Further, they may be norms that determine things in the form of y applies to x. Finally, they may be norms that determine an essential and sufficient condition for the existence of a thing.[3]

Constitutive norms are, for example, the rules regulating how a dividend must be paid or a rule that prescribes that a dividend constitutes income taxed as income from capital. A constitutive norm is also, for example, a rule that prescribes that a constructive dividend is to be treated as a dividend in taxation. It may also be a rule that provides that if a company paying a share of its profits to its shareholders has labelled the payment as a dividend, then, the payment is always considered to be a dividend. If a payment is not labelled as a dividend, the payment is never considered to be a dividend, even if the substance of the payment could be considered as a dividend.

Another way to describe constitutive norms is to divide them into three main groups: competence norms, procedure norms and legal definitions or qualification norms.[4] Constitutive competence norms are the kind of norms that give rights or competence or that limit rights or competence. These rules are expressed as 'may', 'can', 'is allowed', 'has right to', 'cannot' and so on. Procedure norms, on the other hand, may be described as legal operating directions; these norms are the ones that prescribe the procedures that have to be followed in order for a legal institution to be created. Legal definitions are the rules that define legal concepts. A legal definition may appear, for example, in the form of 'In this law x means y'.[5]

A competence norm is, for example, a norm that provides that a group of shareholders that hold a certain proportion of company's shares may demand a dividend payment of a certain amount. A procedure norm is, for example, a rule that provides that a dividend payment is considered a legal dividend payment according to company law only if the payment is carried out according to the rules for dividend payment in company law. Qualification norms are, for example, norms that define the items that are regarded as a dividend in taxation.

Constitutive norms determining the meaning of the concept of dividend include both company law and tax law norms. The legal concept of dividend is based on

---

3. *See* Aarnio (1988), 73–74.
4. *See* Aarnio (1988), 75–76. Tikka (1972), 46–53 classifies legal terms as behavioural norms, qualification norms and competence norms.
5. *See* Aarnio (1988), 75–76.

Chapter 4: Different Dividend Concepts in International Tax Law §4.01

company law.[6] The dividend concept of company law reflects and organizes the different interests of a company and its owners as well as those of the creditors of the company. Company law sets the limits in which company profits may be used to satisfy the interests of the company, different shareholders and different creditors. In general, a dividend is a distribution made by a corporation to its shareholders based on the decision of the shareholders' meeting. The general term 'distribution' covers any form in which corporate assets are transferred to shareholders for no proper return value or benefit to the paying corporation.[7]

Taxes are levied on different economic transactions that are regulated by company law and other segments of law. As a general principle, it is accepted that tax law respects general principles of company law, and that there should be an adequate correspondence between tax law rules and accounting rules.[8] Many tax terms have developed from company law terms;[9] therefore, tax law terms and concepts often correspond to the same company law terms and concepts. In practice, however, tax terms often develop independently in order to meet the needs of taxation and, therefore, do not always correspond to the terms of company law. This is an inevitable consequence primarily caused by the differing objectives of company law and tax law.[10]

Tax law has to follow economic substance more closely than company law. Tax neutrality requires that all activities, which are similar in economic substance, despite the form in which the activities are carried out, be taxed similarly.[11] In order to prevent opportunities for tax avoidance, tax law must not blindly follow company law terms. Due to the closer relationship to economic substance, tax terms may receive a meaning independent of the same terms used in company law.[12] The company law form used is often disregarded in taxation in situations where the economic substance of the transaction clearly deviates from the company law form used.[13] In situations that involve the abuse of company law forms, economic substance is decisive for taxation purposes.[14]

The more complex the economic reality becomes, the more independent from company law tax law must be.[15] The meaning of the tax law concept of dividend is,

---

6. *See* Kilpi (1962), 18–19 and 25.
7. *See*, for example, Jan Andersson (1995), 306–308.
8. *See* about this principle David (1996), 10–11. The relation between company law and tax law terms has been long a widely discussed subject. *See* Kilpi (1983), 33, Kilpi (1952), 4–13, Voipio (1968), 1–3 and 88, Bergström (1978), Tikka (1972), 91–92, Vesanen (1981), 83–89 and Ryynänen (1996), 110–111 and 192–193. Also seminar B 'The influence of corporate law and accounting principles in determining taxable income' of the International Fiscal Association Congress 1996 held in Geneva tackled this problem.
9. Sometimes tax law is regarded only as an additional part of company law. *See also* Vesanen (1981), 83–89, for discussion on whether tax law terms derive from company law.
10. *See* Lodin (1973), 25, Bergström (1978), 13–14 and 83, Schlütter (1985), 216, Vesanen (1981), 84, Kilpi (1962), 28 and Kilpi (1987), 11 for this most important reason for the difference.
11. *See* for taxation and neutrality above in Ch. 1 and about form and substance in tax law e.g., Zimmer (2002), 19–67 and Knuutinen (2009).
12. *See also* Lodin (1973), 41.
13. It is also possible that tax law terms are borrowed by company law.
14. As Kilpi (1987), 10 points out, this is a characteristic and not exceptional in income taxation.
15. For example, Rosenberg (1980), 175 recognized the increasing independence of tax law.

therefore, in many respects broader than the meaning of the term under company law. In the name of tax neutrality or in order to prevent tax avoidance, not only must a dividend, in the company law sense, be classified as a dividend for tax purposes, but other kinds of transactions must be too.

Because taxation does not necessarily follow the company law forms even in a single jurisdiction, it is understandable that taxation of one state is quite independent from the company law terms and forms of another state. Tax law classification of foreign entities and foreign-source income is often made not only independent from the foreign company law classification but also from the foreign tax law classification. Due to the great variety and substance of possible company law forms in different states, taxation cannot rely on company law forms of foreign jurisdictions.[16] However, it cannot be said that company law of one state would not have any effect on the taxation of cross-border transactions in another state. The foreign company law form used determines the legal characteristics of a foreign entity or transaction. These characteristics may have an effect in determining the tax law classification of the entity or transaction in another state.[17]

The meaning of the tax law concept of dividend depends on the rules determining whether an item of income is taxed as a dividend or not. The positive tax law concept of dividend derives its meaning from what is taxed as a dividend. For the purposes of the positive law concept of a dividend, it is irrelevant whether any income that is not taxed as a dividend should be taxed as a dividend because of its company law form or economic substance or for other reasons. Nor is it meaningful whether certain items of income taxed as a dividend should not be taxed as a dividend but rather as some other type of income. These kinds of considerations have meaning only *de lege ferenda* and with respect to determining how positive law norms should be interpreted.

§4.02 DOMESTIC LAWS

It varies state by state, whether the tax law term 'dividend' is expressly defined in domestic statutory tax law or whether the definition of the term is based on case law. It seems that the domestic tax law of most states does not include an exhaustive express definition of dividend. The tax laws somehow assume that it is known what dividend is, without having to define it. The tax laws may then only mention in regard to certain specific borderline situations whether the situation produces income taxed as dividend or at least in the same way as dividend.

Also, the extent to which tax law terms follow company law terms and their definitions varies. For example, the US federal tax laws cannot follow company law terms and definitions very closely because the company law provisions concerning profit distribution from a corporation to its shareholders vary from state to state. In this type of a federal state, company law classification cannot be properly used for tax law

---

16. *See* Schlütter (1985), 218.
17. It is of course possible that the tax laws of a certain state specifically give the legal or tax classification of another state decisive relevance in a certain specific situation.

classification, but tax law classification must be independent from company law classification.[18]

In other states, like in Sweden, the connection between tax law and company law has traditionally been much closer.[19] The starting point has been that the tax term 'dividend' has the same meaning as the same term under company law.[20] In practice, however, even in these countries the meaning of the tax law term 'dividend' differs from the company law term of dividend. Even in these countries, if the form used does not conform to the substance, the substance of a legal transaction may be decisive in taxation, even though the form had been accepted for company law purposes. Company law forms may be disregarded through tax law interpretation or on the basis of specific tax avoidance provisions.

Basically in all countries, the tax law concept of dividend is, in some respects, broader and, in other respects, narrower than the concept of company law. What is a lawful dividend under company law is not necessarily a dividend for corporate tax purposes, and what is an unlawful dividend from a company law perspective may be taxed as a dividend. It is possible that a distribution made in the form of a dividend is not taxed as a dividend and a distribution made in some other form is taxed as a dividend.

The tax law definition of the term 'dividend' varies state by state. In addition to a common ground, there are a number of such borderline cases, which fall under the tax provisions concerning dividends in some states but under some other tax provisions in other states. It varies, for example, whether a repayment of capital constitutes a dividend, when a hybrid instrument creates dividends, whether liquidation distributions constitute dividends, whether a constructive dividend is considered to be a dividend, and so on.

Even in one state the same item of income may be treated as dividend for the purposes of certain domestic tax provisions but as some other type of income for the purposes of other domestic tax provisions. The same item of income may be treated as dividend, for example, when paid to a non-resident but not when paid to a resident taxpayer. Because of this variation, it is clear that there is a huge risk of conflicts in cross-border situations.

§4.03 THE EU PARENT-SUBSIDIARY DIRECTIVE

The second EU company law directive, the so-called Capital Directive,[21] dealing with public companies, sets limitations on the company law rules concerning profit

---

18. *See also* Lodin (1973), 50.
19. *See* for the principle Gäverth (1996), 591.
20. *See*, for example, Sandström (1962), 23–24, Grosskopf (1993), 109, Grosskopf et al. (1997), 154 and Helminen (1999), 76–78 for the relationship of the company law term 'dividend' and tax law term 'dividend' in Sweden.
21. Directive 2012/30/EU of the European Parliament and of the Council of 25 Oct. 2012 on coordination of safeguards which, for the protection of the interests of members and others, are required by Member States of companies within the meaning of the second paragraph of Art. 54 of the Treaty on the Functioning of the European Union, in respect of the formation of public

distributions made by public companies of EU Member States. It follows from Article 17(4) of the Directive that the term 'distribution' as used in the Directive means in particular the payment of dividends and of interest relating to shares.

The only provisions of EU tax law that concern specifically dividends are the rules of the P-S Directive. The meaning of the concept 'profit distribution' in the P-S Directive is clearly broader, in some respects, and is narrower, in other respects, than the meaning of the same concept in the Capital Directive. The Capital Directive cannot be used to interpret the concept of profit distribution in the P-S Directive.

The P-S Directive sets both subjective and objective requirements that have to be fulfilled in order for the P-S Directive to apply. The subjective requirements are: first, the distributions must be made between corporations organized in certain legal forms, which are expressly mentioned in the Directive;[22] second, the distributing and recipient corporations must have fiscal residence in different EU Member States;[23] and, third, the corporations must be subject to one of the corporation taxes listed in the P-S Directive.[24] Also, distributions received by permanent establishment of qualifying companies may come under the scope of the Directive.[25] The objective requirements are: that distributions of corporate profits are made by a subsidiary to a parent company that holds a minimum of 10% of the subsidiary's capital or voting rights;[26] and, that the distribution are made by virtue of the parent company's association with the subsidiary, for motives or causes different from a liquidation of the company.[27]

A definition of 'dividend' was contained in the Proposal for a Directive of the Council Concerning the Harmonization of Systems of Company Taxation and of Withholding Taxes on Dividends (the Proposal).[28] Dividend was defined in Article 2(1), as:

> [T]hat part of the profits of any corporation of a Member State, other than a corporation in liquidation, distributed by it by virtue of a proper decision of its competent authorities and divided among its members in proportion to their rights as members of the corporation; distributions of bonus shares are not regarded as dividend within the meaning of the present directive.

According to Article 7 of the Proposal, however, the directive would have been applicable to any distribution that is regarded as a dividend distribution under the law of the source state.

---

limited liability companies and the maintenance and alteration of their capital, with a view to making such safeguards equivalent.
22. The corporations must each carry one of the legal forms listed in the annex of the Directive. Arts 1 and 2(a)(i) of the Directive. See for the qualifying entities below in the chapter concerning dividend-distributing entities and Helminen (2015), 162–165.
23. Articles 1 and 2(a)(ii) of the Directive. See also Helminen (2015), 162–165. In the case of distributions connected with a permanent establishment situated in another Member State, the companies may be from the same Member State. See Helminen (2015), 165.
24. Articles 1 and 2(a)(iii) of the Directive. See also Helminen (2015), 162–165.
25. Articles 1 and 2(b) of the Directive. See also Helminen (2015), 165–166.
26. Article 3 of the Directive. See also Helminen (2015), 166–167.
27. Article 4 of the Directive. See also Helminen (2015), 167–169.
28. Submitted to the Council by the Commission 23 Jul. 1975, COM (75) 392 final, withdrawn by decision of the Commission of 18 Apr. 1990.

Chapter 4: Different Dividend Concepts in International Tax Law §4.03

The P-S Directive does not use the term 'dividend' but uses the expression 'distribution of profits' or 'distributed profits'. These expressions are included in Articles 1, 4 and 5 of the P-S Directive. According to Article 1 of the P-S Directive, this concept covers both the distributions of profits received by companies and paid by companies, as long as the distribution occurs between qualifying companies. Also, distributions received by or made to a qualifying permanent establishment of a qualifying company come under the scope of the Directive. According to Article 4, distributions of corporate profits by a subsidiary to the parent company or its permanent establishment, by virtue of the companies' association with each other, are covered as long as the subsidiary is not liquidated.

The P-S Directive itself does not define the concepts of the distribution of profits or distributed profits. Nor does it refer to the domestic law of either state involved in the way that the Proposal does. It seems, therefore, that the concept of the distribution of profits must be given an autonomous meaning independent of domestic law definitions or tax treaty definitions. This autonomous meaning cannot, however, be totally independent of domestic law meanings. After all, it is a matter of the taxation of domestic law distributions of different states.[29] The definition has to be partly worked out with reference to each state's domestic law.[30] This interpretation is in line with the objective of the P-S Directive expressed in its preamble to eliminate the disadvantage of taxation, which is more burdensome in cross-border relations than in domestic relations. This objective requires that economic double taxation should be avoided in all the same situations where it is avoided in domestic relations. However, interpretation based solely on domestic law is not possible because the concept of the distribution of profits may be given a different meaning in different EU Member States.

In general, the term 'distribution of profits' is understood to have a somewhat broader meaning than the term 'dividend'.[31] In company law, the term 'distribution of profits' is often used to mean any distribution of company profits no matter who the recipient is. The term, therefore, also includes distributions to persons other than shareholders.[32] In general, a distribution of profits to shareholders includes such transactions between a company and its shareholders, by which the assets of the company are decreased and the assets of the shareholder increased. A distribution of company profits from a company to its shareholders includes, in addition to a dividend, other gratuitous transfers to shareholders based on a shareholder relationship.

The concept of the distribution of profits must be given quite a broad meaning also in the case of the P-S Directive. One reason for this interpretation is that the term 'dividend' could have been used in the P-S Directive, if it had been intended for the

---

29. Also, for example, Hinnekens (1995), 219 mentions a reference to domestic law, especially because Art. 10 of the OECD Model refers to domestic law.
30. *See* Farmer and Lyal (1994), 272-273, which points out that the interpretation should not be left wholly to national law.
31. *See* for the relationship of the term 'distribution of profits' and the term 'dividend' de Hosson (1990), 433 and Sommerhalder (1996), 93-94.
32. For this difference, *see* Myrsky (1988), 259. Interestingly enough in accounting the term 'profit distribution' is traditionally regarded to include taxes and interest payments in addition to dividends. *See*, for example, Mannio (1997), 27-29. In taxation, interest does not, however, constitute a profit distribution.

meaning to be narrow. A broad meaning is also in line with the objective of the P-S Directive to avoid economic double taxation of profits, which a parent company receives from its subsidiaries.[33] This objective is not expressly mentioned in the P-S Directive in its adopted form, but, instead, it actually only requires that the taxation of cross-border situations be made as advantageous as the taxation of domestic relations. However, a broad meaning is required in order for the P-S Directive to cover all situations where economic double taxation is alleviated under the domestic law of the different Member States.

In conclusion, the concept of profit distribution should cover any kind of transfers of benefits from a qualifying corporate entity to another qualifying corporate entity for no equivalent value or benefit in exchange, '...by virtue of the parent company's association with its subsidiary...'. This definition should apply to the extent that an item is not expressly excluded in the P-S Directive and to the extent that the transfer is such that, in principle, it could be subject to economic double taxation.

§4.04 TAX TREATIES

[A] Introduction

Tax treaties are generally organized into different income types to which different rules apply. Usually, dividend constitutes a separate income type. The income types of tax treaties may not and, in fact, in many cases, do not resemble the types or schedules of income in the domestic tax law of different states. Nor does the definition of dividend for tax treaty purposes necessarily correspond to the definition of dividend for domestic law purposes. A tax treaty definition of an income type is independent from the domestic law definitions of the same income type.[34]

The formulation of the definition of dividend differs from treaty to treaty. The approaches of different tax treaties vary from very general definitions to definitions including a long list of specific examples constituting a dividend. Many definitions also refer to the domestic law definition of the contracting parties. The dividend definitions of tax treaties determine with binding effect whether or not certain items of income qualify as a dividend for tax treaty purposes both with respect to the source state and with respect to the state of residence of the income recipient.

[B] The Model Conventions

Article 10 of the OECD Model, the US Model and the UN Model concern division of taxing rights in regard to dividends. According to Article 10(3) of the OECD Model and the UN Model:

---

33. This objective was already clearly expressed in the general part of the explanatory memorandum of the Proposal for a Council Directive concerning the common system of taxation applicable in the case of parent companies and subsidiaries of different Member States, submitted by the Commission to the Council on 16 Jan. 1969, COM (69) 6 final.
34. Obviously treaty definitions may refer to domestic law concepts.

[t]he term dividend as used in this Article means:
(1) income from shares, 'jouissance' shares or 'jouissance' rights, mining shares, founders' shares; or
(2) [income from] other rights, not being debt-claims, participating in profits;
(3) as well as income from other corporate rights which is subject to the same taxation treatment as income from shares by the laws of the State of which the company making the distribution is a resident.

According to Article 10(7) of the US Model:

For purposes of this Article, the term dividend means:
(1) income from shares; or
(2) [income from] other rights, not being debt-claims, participating in profits;
(3) as well as income that is subjected to the same taxation treatment as income from shares under the laws of the State of which the company making the distribution is a resident.

The term does not include distributions that are treated as gain under the laws of the Contracting State of which the company making the distribution is resident.

The definition of the OECD, UN and US Models is the meaning of the term 'dividend' only for the purposes of Article 10 of the Conventions. The term 'dividend' for the purposes of the other articles of the Models may get a meaning different from the meaning of the term under Article 10. In principle, a different meaning may apply for the purposes of Article 23 of the Models concerning the elimination of double taxation. In practice, however, the context of Article 23 should, in most cases, require that the dividend definition be the same as in Article 10.[35]

The dividend definitions of the models consist of three parts. The first two parts define the term 'dividend' autonomously. These parts must be interpreted according to the general rule of Article 3(2) of the Models, referring to the law of the state applying the treaty if the context does not require otherwise. The third part of the definitions refers to the definition of the tax law of the source state.

The first part of the definitions enumerates certain corporate rights, the income from which is a dividend. A profit distribution on the expressly enumerated corporate rights is a dividend for tax treaty purposes, irrespective of domestic law classification. The first part of the dividend definition of the OECD Model and the UN Model covers income from shares, *jouissance* shares, *jouissance* rights, mining shares and founders' shares. The first part of the definition of the US Model, on the other hand, only includes income from shares. There is, however, not a very substantial difference between the definitions, because the rights listed expressly in the definition of the OECD Model generally qualify as dividend under the other parts of the US Model.[36] In all of the

---

35. The 1996 version of the US Model differed from the present form of the Model and from the UN and the OECD Models in the way that the dividend definition of Art. 10 was referred to define the term dividend for all purposes of the Convention. In practice, the difference should not have much relevance, because the context of the other treaty articles, in most cases, requires that the dividend definition is the same as in Art. 10. *See* Hattingh (2009), 509–517, Harris (1999/2000), 1–224 and Harris (2016) for the history and development of the dividend definition of the dividend article of the OECD Model.
36. *See* Doernberg and van Raad (1997), 89 and Vogel et al. (1997), 648.

Models, the list of special rights generating income to be considered as a dividend for treaty purposes is only a list of examples and does not exclude items that are not enumerated.[37]

The second part of the dividend definitions of the OECD, the UN and the US Model are all similar. The second part of the definitions covers income from other rights, not being debt-claims, participating in profits. According to the Commentaries, the second part of the dividend definition of Article 10(3) of the OECD Model, '...assimilates to shares all securities issued by companies which carry a right to participate in the companies' profits without being debt-claims...'.[38] These second parts clearly are connected to the first parts. Corporate rights that are not expressly enumerated may qualify under this general definition of the second part of the dividend definition as long as these corporate rights are not debt-claims and as long as they participate in profits. From this connection of the two first parts of the definitions, it follows that the items expressly enumerated in the first part must also be income from rights, not being debt-claims, participating in profits.[39]

The third part of the dividend definitions of the OECD and the UN Model covers income from any *other corporate right*, not covered under the first two parts, which is subject to the same taxation treatment as income from shares by the laws of the state of which the company making the distribution is a resident. From the wording '...as well as other corporate rights...', in this third part of the definition, it is clear that there is also a connection between the autonomous parts, that is, the first and second parts, of the definition and this third part of the definition. From this wording, it must be concluded that the rights in the autonomous parts must also be corporate rights in order for them to qualify under the definition. Because the third part clearly also must include items other than those items qualifying under the second part of the definition, restrictions of the second part with respect to debt-claims and profit participation cannot refer to the third part.[40] However, the difference is not very substantial because income from corporate rights, in general, is not income from debt-claims and corporate rights, in general, participate in profits.[41]

The third part of the definition of the US Model covers any other income that is subject to the same taxation treatment as income from shares under the laws of the state of which the company making the distribution is a resident. The definition of the US Model is somewhat broader than the definition in the OECD and the UN Models because it covers any income taxed in the same way as income from shares in the state

---

37. *See* paras 23 and 24 of the Commentary on Art. 10 of the OECD Model.
38. Paragraph 24 of the Commentary on Art. 10 of the OECD Model.
39. *See* for this connection between the parts of the definition Vogel et al. (1997), 649 and 655. *See* for the structure of the dividend definition of the OECD Model also Hattingh (2009), 517–518.
40. *See* for this connection Vogel et al. (1997), 649.
41. *See* Avery Jones et al. (2009), 19–23 for the history of the phrase 'other corporate rights' used in the third part of the dividend definition. *See* for more details about the interpretation of the term 'corporate right' below in Ch. 9 s. §9.02[D] of this study.

Chapter 4: Different Dividend Concepts in International Tax Law   §4.04[B]

in which the company making the distribution is a resident, whereas the other Models only cover income from corporate rights.[42]

The autonomous parts of the US Model definition do not seem to require that the income be from corporate rights. In addition, the third part of the definition of the US Model also seems to cover income from debt-claims and income from rights not participating in profits so long as the state of residence of the company making the distribution treats such income as a dividend. However, from the Technical Explanation to the 2006 version of the US Model,[43] it may be concluded that the dividend definition of the US Models is also meant to only cover income from corporate rights under its autonomous parts.[44] It may also be concluded that only income from rights that are treated as equity, at least under the tax law of the source state, qualifies under the third part of the definition. Debt-claims would only be covered to the extent they are reclassified as equity in the source state.[45]

The reference to source state classification under the Models does not mean that such items of income that are not taxed as a dividend according to the law of the source state cannot qualify as a dividend for tax treaty purposes. The reference to the law of the source state only means that at least such items of income that are a dividend according to the law of the source state are to also be treated as a dividend for tax treaty purposes. It does not mean that other items of income could not be treated as a dividend. Other items of income, although not expressly enumerated as examples, may be classified as a dividend for tax treaty purposes under the second part of the dividend definition.

The reference to domestic law under the third part of the definitions is clearly secondary, with respect to the autonomous parts of the dividend definitions. In other words, if a transaction fits under the autonomous part of the dividend definition, domestic law does not affect the classification. Only if a transaction does not fit under the autonomous part must the question of whether the transaction should be treated as a dividend under the third part of the definition in accordance with domestic law be considered.

To the extent that an item of income qualifies under the autonomous parts of the dividend definitions, both contracting states must classify the income as a dividend for treaty purposes despite the domestic law classification of each state. If an item of income does not qualify under the autonomous parts, the source state classification may become the treaty classification to the extent that the item qualifies under the third

---

42. On the other hand, the definition of the US Model is narrower that teh definition of teh OECD and the UN Models in the respect that it specifically excludes distributions treated as gains under the laws of the state of which the company making the distribution is a resident.
43. United States Model Technical Explanation Accompanying the United States Model Income Tax Convention of 15 Nov. 2006.
44. 'The term includes income from shares, or other corporate rights, that are not treated as debt under the law of the source State, that participate in the profits of the company....' Para. 166 of the Technical Explanation.
45. 'Finally, a payment denominated as interest that is made by thinly capitalized corporation may be treated as a dividend to the extent that the debt is recharacterized as equity under the laws of the source State....' Para. 167 of the Technical Explanation.

part of the dividend definition. In such a situation, the state of residence of the income recipient must accept the source state classification.

[C] Actual Tax Treaties

Actual tax treaties include a dividend definition in the article concerning division of taxing rights in regard to dividends in the same way as the Models do. The dividend definitions largely follow the definitions in the Models, but differ in detail. The dividend definitions define the term 'dividend' for the purposes of the whole convention or only for the purposes of the dividend article. If dividend is defined only for the purposes of the dividend article, it is possible that for other purposes, the term gets a meaning different from the dividend article meaning. However, in practice, the context of other treaty articles, in most cases, should require that the same definition also be used for other purposes of the treaty.

Many treaties only mention income from shares expressly in the autonomous parts of their dividend definitions whereas some treaties include a longer list of expressly enumerated corporate rights. For example, share certificates in cooperative societies, *jouissance* shares, *jouissance* rights, mining shares and founders' shares may be mentioned.

The dividend definition of most actual treaties also includes a part similar to the second part of the dividend definitions of the Models. The definitions include income from '…other rights, not being debt-claims, participating in profits…'. The definition of the treaties, which do not include this express reference, however, is not necessarily narrower than the definitions of the other treaties. The difference is that under the other treaties income from rights participating in profits are taxed as a dividend so long as the right is not a debt-claim, no matter how the income is taxed in the contracting states. Under the treaties that lack the express reference, such income, if it is not income from the expressly enumerated rights, may only qualify if it is taxed in the source state in the same way as income from shares is taxed.

Most actual tax treaties also include a reference to the domestic tax law of the source state. Many actual treaties follow the OECD Model and only cover other income from corporate rights so long as it is taxed in the same way as income from shares in the source state is taxed. The treaties of many countries, however, include a broader definition and include income from any other rights without a requirement of the right being a corporate right. However, if interpreted in accordance with the Technical Explanations of the US 2006 Model, the definition of these treaties also only covers such rights that are reclassified as equity in the source state. The definitions of some treaties are clearly broader. They may cover any income from a company that is taxed in the source state in the same way as income from shares is taxed.[46]

---

46. The formulations lacking a reference to the term 'corporate right' are understood by the fact that they avoid the interpretative problems concerning the term 'corporate right'. *See* Avery Jones et al. (2009), 30–31, for examples of such treaties which lack a reference to a corporate right and for examples of the different wordings used in these treaties. *See* Ch. 9 s. §9.02[D] for the interpretation of the term 'corporate right'.

Most of the dividend definitions of actual tax treaties also include some additional clarification of what items are covered by the term 'dividend'. For example, income under a sleeping partnership (i.e., *stille Gesellschaft*), partiary loans (i.e., *partiarisches Darlehen*) or profit obligations (i.e., *Gewinnobligation*), and distributions on certificates of an investment trust or fund may be covered. The items that are expressly mentioned as a dividend, without any reference to their tax treatment in the contracting states, qualify as a dividend for tax treaty purposes although not taxed as a dividend under domestic law.[47]

§4.05 CONCLUSIONS

Despite having great similarity, the definitions of the term 'dividend' as used in the different legal systems of international tax law, clearly differ on many points. Different items of income may be treated as a dividend under the domestic law of different states, under the P-S Directive and under tax treaties. In cross-border relations, the differences in dividend concepts may lead to classification conflicts. These classification conflicts arise because it is not clear what the exact meaning of the concept of dividend is in these different legal systems of international tax law.

The statutory tax laws of only certain states include an express definition of the term 'dividend'. The definition of the domestic tax law term 'dividend' of the other states must be interpreted with the help of the domestic law tax provisions concerning the taxation of a dividend and court cases concerning these provisions. The P-S Directive also lacks a definition clarifying what items of income qualify whereas tax treaties include a definition of the term. However, the tax treaty definitions also leave a lot of room for interpretation. The definitions include many undefined terms and, in the end, these definitions refer to the domestic tax law of the contracting states.

Another problem in determining what items of income are taxed as a dividend in cross-border situations stems from the different usage of the terms 'profit distribution' and 'dividend' under the different legal systems of international tax law, and the relationship between these terms. Under the company law of different states, the term 'profit distribution' is often used instead of the term 'dividend'. Even if the tax law concept of dividend is based on the company law concept of profit distribution, the company law concepts and the tax law concepts differ in many respects. On some points, the tax law concepts of a dividend are broader, and, on some points, narrower than similar company law concepts.

The tax law concepts of dividend have developed to meet the different needs of taxation, taking into account both the company law form of a distribution and the economic substance of the transaction. The company law concept of profit distribution and the company law form, in general, have very limited relevance when defining the meaning of the tax law concept of dividend. The company law classification is not always decisive. Although from a company law perspective, a distribution would be illegal, it may be taxed as dividend.

---

47. *See also* e.g., Harris (2016) for treaty variation in regard to the dividend definition.

The domestic tax laws of the different states also refer to both profit distribution and a dividend. The term 'profit distribution' is generally broader than the term 'dividend'. Under the domestic tax laws of many states, however, many items that do not strictly speaking qualify as dividends are taxed in the same way as dividends. These items may include, for example, different types of constructive dividend distributions. For different tax law purposes, the items covered may be different.

The P-S Directive uses the term 'distribution of profits' instead of the term 'dividend'. Following the usage of the terms 'dividend' and 'distribution of profits' in the different EU Member States, the P-S Directive should cover not only distributions paid in the form of a dividend but also a wide range of other items of income. Because different items of income may be taxed as a dividend under the different Member States' domestic tax law, the meaning of the concept distribution of profits under the P-S Directive may not be derived directly from the different domestic law concepts. The concept should be assigned an autonomous P-S Directive meaning. Because the Member States must implement the P-S Directive into their individual domestic tax law, each state actually ascribes its own meaning to the P-S Directive term 'profit distribution' through its own domestic tax law. The domestic law implementation may, however, be in conflict with the actual autonomous P-S Directive meaning.

The tax law provisions of each Member State implementing the P-S Directive may lead to a conflict with the P-S Directive. Such conflict may arise because the implementing laws in the different Member States may not provide a special definition of the terms 'profit distribution' or 'dividend' for the purposes of the situations covered by the P-S Directive. The tax law provisions of the Member States' domestic laws implementing the P-S Directive use the general domestic law definitions, which may be narrower than the P-S Directive meaning of the terms.[48]

Tax treaties use the term 'dividend' instead of the term 'profit distribution'. Following the general usage of the terms, it seems that the tax treaty meaning of the term 'dividend' is narrower than the term 'profit distribution' under the P-S Directive. It is, however, also possible that the tax treaty term 'dividend' is broader than the P-S Directive term 'profit distribution' because the express definition of the term 'dividend' in different treaties may expressly include many kinds of items of income that normally would not be considered to be dividend. Under many tax treaties, any income that is taxed in the source state in the same way as income from shares is taxed as a dividend. The treaties, in general, cover not only the domestic law dividend, but also any other income that is taxed in the same way as a dividend is taxed in the source state. The tax treaty term 'dividend' may get quite a broad meaning.[49] With respect to tax treaties, it is important to determine to what extent the state of residence of the income recipient must accept the source state classification in situations where the two states tax different items of income in the same way that they tax income from shares.

---

48. *See also*, for example, Ryynänen (1997), 35 about the problem.
49. Paragraph 15 of the Commentary on Art. 10(2) of the OECD Model uses the phrase '...dividend, i.e. distributions of profits to shareholders...'. The term 'dividend' is thus clearly used in quite a broad sense also in the Model.

In conclusion, the meaning of the term 'dividend' under the domestic law of different states, under the P-S Directive and under the different tax treaties varies. It cannot be said, in a general way, which one of the meanings is broader and which one is narrower compared to another even though the term 'profit distribution', in general, is broader than the term 'dividend'. Each of the meanings differs and may, in some respects, be broader, and, in other respects, be narrower than another. The different concepts may lead to conflict with each other in different situations.

CHAPTER 5
Dividend-Distributing Entities

§5.01 INTRODUCTION

The fiscal status of each economic actor must be determined for tax purposes. Entity or subject classification is a prerequisite for income classification. Each possible form of doing business must be analysed as to whether or not it constitutes a tax subject separate from its owners. In general, only separate tax subjects, but not transparent entities, qualify as dividend-distributing entities.

A fiscally transparent or pass-through entity is not taxable per se, but its profits are taxed as income for the owners of the entity, whether or not such profits are actually distributed to the owners.[1] A non-transparent entity is a separate tax subject and is taxed per se.[2] Profits of a non-transparent entity are, in general, not taxed as income for the owners of the entity until they are actually distributed to the owners. Distributed profits of a non-transparent entity may be subject to economic double taxation because they are first taxed by the distributing entity and then as income for the owners of the entity.

In cross-border situations, not only must the tax status of domestic law entities be determined, but also the tax status of various possible foreign law entities. In cross-border situations, it is possible that the state of residence of an entity and the state of residence of the owners of the entity classify the entity differently for tax purposes. One state may view the entity as a transparent entity whereas the other may view it as a separate tax subject. Such entities that are classified differently under the domestic tax law of two different states are commonly referred to as hybrid entities.

The state of residence of a profit-distributing entity classifies the profit distribution as a dividend only if the distributing entity is regarded as a dividend-distributing

---

1. Tax transparency may in practice apply to different extents. Le Gall (1995), 662–663, for example, differentiates total tax transparency, tax transparency limited to tax payment and intermediate tax transparency. *See* for a definition of the term 'transparent' also van Raad (1988), 21–22.
2. *See* for a definition of the term 'non-transparent' van Raad (1988), 22.

entity. Similarly, the state of residence of the recipient of the distribution taxes the distribution as a dividend only if the state regards the foreign entity as a dividend-distributing entity. As a consequence of this relation between entity classification and income classification, entity classification conflicts are likely to lead to income classification conflicts. Inconsistent entity classification, under the domestic law of different states, may easily lead to international non-taxation or double taxation.[3]

Entity classification is a prerequisite for income classification, not only for domestic tax law purposes, but also for tax treaty purposes. For tax treaty purposes, it must be determined whether an entity qualifies as an entity subject to treaty benefits. If it does qualify, then it must be further determined whether the entity qualifies as a dividend-distributing entity under the treaty.

Although domestic law classification and tax treaty classification are, in principle, separate and independent from each other, inconsistent entity classification under domestic law may also lead to classification conflict in the application of a tax treaty. One of the contracting states may consider that a treaty between two states is not applicable with respect to an entity because it does not qualify as an entity subject to treaty benefits, whereas the other state may apply the treaty. Although both states may view the entity as qualifying for treaty benefits, one of the states may view it as a dividend-distributing entity whereas the other may not. In such a situation, the two states may consider the distributions from the entity to fall under two different treaty articles. Such different treatment may again lead to non-taxation or double taxation.

§5.02 DOMESTIC LAWS

[A] Different Forms of Doing Business

The domestic law entity forms available for conducting business vary state by state. The domestic laws of most countries recognize certain capital company forms, partnership forms and cooperative societies. These may include, for example, public and private companies limited by shares and general and limited partnerships. Despite many similarities, the legal characteristics of the different entity forms vary country by country depending on the domestic law concerned. The legal systems of some countries include also entity forms that are completely unknown under the legal systems of some other countries. As an example of such entity forms, the common law trusts or the German silent partnerships may be mentioned. The variation in the legal characteristics of the entity forms available for business means a challenge to entity classification for tax law purposes.[4]

---

3. *See* for the possibilities of using hybrid entities for international tax planning, for example, Rohatgi (2007), 102–105, Barenfeld (2005), 130–144, Lamers and Stevens (2004), 155–164, Tobin and Seto (1994), 315–320, Harvey, Burke and Shapiro (1995), 1609–1618, and Readel and French (1995), 1597.
4. *See*, for example, Barenfeld (2005), 56–67 for the development of different entity forms in different countries, and, for example, Avery Jones et al. (2009), 13–14 for examples of the entity forms of different countries.

[B] Entity Classification for Tax Law Purposes

For domestic tax law purposes, each country must determine how to classify foreign entity forms whether or not similar entity forms are recognized by company law of the state concerned. For domestic tax law purposes, it must be determined whether a foreign entity qualifies as a transparent or as a non-transparent entity.

Besides transparent and non-transparent entities, the domestic tax laws of different states may recognize certain other groups of entities that must be separated for tax purposes. For example, for the US tax purposes it must be determined whether an entity qualifies as a transparent partnership, as a non-transparent corporation or as a trust, which is treated as a separately taxable entity with respect to accumulated income but as a conduit when income is distributed.

It varies among states whether there are specific statutory tax provisions on how foreign entities should be classified for tax purposes or whether entity classification is based on tax practice and case law. Based on specific provisions or on case law, different countries have adopted different approaches on how the tax status of a foreign entity is determined.

The tax laws of certain countries include express lists of the characteristics of an entity that must be looked at when classifying a foreign entity for domestic tax law purposes. The domestic tax laws of other countries may only mention that foreign entities that are similar to certain domestic entity forms get the same tax status as the corresponding domestic law entities (similarity approach). This similarity approach seems to be most commonly used.[5] Some states, such as the US, allow many foreign entities to elect their tax law classification (elective approach)[6] and some states classify all foreign business entities in the same way as either transparent or non-transparent (fixed approach).[7]

In most countries, the company law classification of a foreign entity is not decisive for tax purposes. Also, the tax law classification of the state under which laws an entity is formed is considered to be decisive only in some countries. Often, the tax classification of the state of organization is taken into account only as one characteristic among others when determining the tax classification for the purposes of other countries.

The characteristics that are commonly looked at when determining the tax law status of a foreign entity on the basis of the similarity approach include, for example, whether the entity is a legal person, whether limited liability exists, whether free transferability of interests exists, whether there are associates, whether there is an

---

5. *See* OECD (1999), 9.
6. *See*, for example, Rohatgi (2007), 102–105 and Barenfeld (2005), 119–123 for the US check-the-box system.
7. *See*, for example, Barenfeld (2005), 108–125, Avery Jones et al. (2002), 288–320, Rohatgi (2002), 557–561, Selig (2003) and Lang & Staringer (2014), 34–39 for the different approaches in entity classification.

objective to carry on a business for profit and to divide the gains therefrom, whether there is continuity of life and whether there is centralization of management.[8]

The more typical the characteristics of a corporation rather than those of a partnership are present, the more probable it is that an entity is classified as a separately taxable entity for tax purposes. On the other hand, the more typical the characteristics of a partnership are present, the more probable it is that an entity is classified as a transparent entity for tax purposes.[9]

Because of the differences among the domestic law entity forms of different states and because of the different domestic tax law approaches in entity classification, classification conflicts occur very easily. The same entity may be classified differently for the tax purposes of the state of its organization and for the tax purposes of other states. Entity classification conflicts are less probable in the case of typical corporation or partnership forms but the likeliness of an entity classification conflict increases in the case of other entity forms. The elective approach and the fixed approach especially lead very easily to a classification conflict even in the case of typical corporation and partnership forms.

[C] Dividend-Distributing Entities

The domestic law tax treatment of each state determines whether or not an entity qualifies as a dividend-distributing entity for domestic tax law purposes in that state. Under the domestic tax law of most states, only entities classified as separately taxable corporate entities under the domestic law of the state concerned qualify as dividend-distributing entities. It depends on the entity classification approach applied, which entities qualify as dividend-distributing entities. Therefore, inconsistent entity classification under the domestic tax laws of two states very easily leads to inconsistent income classification under the domestic tax laws of the two states.

[D] Inconsistent Classification and the Elimination of Double Taxation

Commonly, the state of residence of the owners of a transparent foreign entity eliminates international double taxation with respect to both the foreign taxes paid by the foreign entity and the foreign taxes paid by the owners. If the credit system is applied, both the foreign taxes paid by the foreign entity and the foreign taxes paid by the owners are creditable in the taxation of the owners. Some states, however, accept a foreign tax credit in the case of foreign transparent entities only in respect of those foreign taxes paid by the owners themselves.

---

8. *See also* e.g., Lang & Staringer (2014), 36–37 for the typical characteristics relevant in the comparability test in different jurisdictions.
9. *See* for examples of different country practices International Fiscal Association (2014), Herrmann (2003), 42–44, Snel and Mas (2003), 367–377, Inland Revenue (1999), 627, Avery Jones et al. (2002), 288–320, Inland Revenue (2000), 809–812 and Helminen (1999), 94–98, 101–104, 107–109 and 112–113 and the references there.

The owners of a separately taxable foreign entity especially are usually eligible only to elimination of international double taxation with respect to the foreign taxes paid by themselves. Only juridical but not economical double taxation may be eliminated in the case of non-transparent entities. Indirect tax credit may be available in the case of direct investment corporate owners of a non-transparent entity.

The entity classification in the state of residence of the foreign entity as a transparent or as a non-transparent entity is decisive when determining whether only foreign taxes paid by the owners, or also foreign taxes paid by the foreign entity are creditable in the state of residence of the owners. Entity classification conflicts may lead to uneliminated double taxation especially in the case of such states that do not give a tax credit for the taxes paid by a foreign entity considered to be transparent in that state but as a non-transparent entity in its state of organization.

§5.03 THE EU PARENT-SUBSIDIARY DIRECTIVE

In order to qualify for the benefits provided by the P-S Directive, an entity must be a '...company of a Member State...'.[10] The entity must take one of the forms listed in the annex to the P-S Directive and it must be considered to be a resident in a Member State according to the tax laws of that Member State, and be subject to the corporate tax of the state '...without the possibility of an option or of being exempt...'.[11]

Private and public companies limited by shares of different Member States typically come under the scope of application of the P-S Directive.[12] European Companies (*Societas Europaea*– SE) and European Cooperative Societies (*Societas Cooperatia Europaea* – SCE) also come under the scope of the directive.[13] Otherwise, it depends on the Member State concerned, which entity forms are covered.

In the case of some Member States, the Annex to the P-S Directive expressly includes a list of all the national entity forms covered. These lists are exhaustive.[14] For example, national cooperative society forms may be included in the list of some Member States but not in the list of all Member States.[15] National partnership forms are

---

10. Article 1 of the P-S Directive.
11. Article 2 of the P-S Directive. It must not be treated as resident outside the EU for the purposes of any treaty entered into between a Member State and a third state. *See* Helminen (2015), 162–165, Terra and Wattel (2012), Ch. 9.3.1, Tenore (2010), 224–225 and Tumpel (1996), 188–199 about the company concept of the P-S Directive. It is not completely clear what is meant by the phrase 'subject to tax without the possibility of being exempt'. The phrase is, however, widely considered to mean a subjective obligation to pay tax. A solely objective obligation to pay tax is not considered to qualify, but the company must be effectively taxed. If an entity is regarded as a separately taxable entity, but is effectively exempted from tax, the entity does not qualify under the P-S Directive. Low taxes, however, qualify. *See* Helminen (2015), 162–165, Terra and Wattel (2012), Ch. 9.3.1, Fibbe (2006), 99–102, de Hosson (1990a), 429 and Vanistendael (1992), 603 about the interpretation of the phrase 'subject to tax without the possibility of being exempt'.
12. *See* the Annex I to the P-S Directive.
13. *See* para. a. of Part A of Annex I to the P-S Directive.
14. C-247/08 *Gaz de France*, para. 32.
15. Because of the freedom of establishment principle of the TFEU, it is possible that tax benefits similar to the benefits based on the P-S Directive must be made available also to entity forms not

usually not included in the list and in most situations they would fall outside the scope of the directive because they are not separately taxable entities.

Some Member States have not included an express list of all possible national entity forms in the Annex to the directive but they have determined broadly that all national company forms incorporated under the law of the state concerned come under the scope of the directive provided that the other two criteria set forth in Article 2 of the P-S Directive are met.[16]

This type of a broad formulation is practical because it is less probable that this formulation leads to a treatment in conflict with the freedom of establishment principle than the formulation including a list of the different national entity forms covered. It is possible that an express list of national entity forms excludes an entity, which is to the extent similar to the entity forms covered that the entity must be subject to the tax benefits similar to the benefits of the P-S Directive in order for its tax treatment not to be in conflict with the freedom of establishment principle.[17] However, a broad and general determination of the entities covered may be problematic in the way that it may lead to a conflict if the state of residence of the subsidiary and the state of residence of the parent company interpret the term 'company' differently.[18]

Even if a company would take one of the entity forms covered by the P-S Directive, it comes under the scope of the directive only if it is subject to one of the taxes listed in the directive (or to any other tax that may be substituted for any of the expressly mentioned taxes) without the possibility of an option or of being exempt. Tax-exempt entities do not come under the scope of the directive even if they would take a form covered by the directive. Entities that can choose whether to be treated as an exempt entity or not also fall outside the scope of the directive.

Different partnership forms that are not treated as separately taxable entities also fall outside the scope of the P-S Directive. However, hybrid entity forms that are treated as a separately taxable entity in one Member State but as a transparent entity in another Member State may come under the scope of the directive. The state of residence of the parent company is required to eliminate both economic and juridical double taxation even though it would treat the subsidiary as a transparent entity and would therefore see no profit distribution.[19]

The P-S Directive does not set any limit for the required tax but companies established in low-tax states also come under the scope of the directive. It is somewhat

---

covered by the list included in the Annex to the P-S Directive. *See* C-303/07 *Aberdeen Property Fininvest Alpha* and C-247/08 *Gaz de France*, para. 60.

16. In the Proposal for a Council Directive amending Directive 90/435/EEC of 23 Jul. 1990 on the common system of taxation applicable in the case of parent companies and subsidiaries of different Member States, COM (93) 293, submitted by the Commission on 26 Jul. 1993, it was suggested that the P-S Directive should be amended to include all enterprises that are subject to corporate tax and that engage in cross-border activities. This proposal, however, did not lead to an amendment of the P-S Directive.
17. *See* C-303/07 *Aberdeen Property Fininvest Alpha*.
18. *See also* Helminen (2015), 162–165, Terra and Wattel (2012), Ch. 9.3.1, Maisto (2004), 171–173 and Fibbe (2006), 96–99 for the entity forms covered by the P-S Directive.
19. Article 4(2) of the P-S Directive. *See*, for example, Russo (2006), 479–480 for the application of the P-S Directive in the case of hybrid entities.

unclear, however, as to what extent partially tax-exempt entities come under the scope of application of the directive.[20]

Because the P-S Directive only sets minimum requirements to the Member States, the Member States are free to include entities not covered by the P-S Directive to their domestic law implementing rules and to extend similar benefit based on the P-S Directive benefits to cover other entities also. Under the domestic law implementation provisions, the P-S Directive benefits may be extended to cover, for example, cooperative societies that are considered to be dividend-distributing entities under domestic law but that are not covered by the P-S Directive. Similar benefits may also be based on a bilateral tax treaty between the states concerned.

§5.04 TAX TREATIES

[A] The Model Conventions

According to Article 1 of the OECD Model, the Convention only applies to *resident persons*.[21] In order for a tax treaty to apply to an entity, that entity must be both a person and a resident in at least one of the contracting states.

According to Article 3(1)(a) of the OECD Model, the term '*person*' includes individuals, companies and '...any other body of persons...'.[22] According to the Commentary, the term should be understood in a very broad sense, including '...any entity which, although not incorporated, is treated as a body corporate for tax purposes...'.[23] The definition of the term 'person' in Article 3(1)(a) of the US Model, also specifically includes estates, trusts and partnerships, in addition to individuals, companies and any body of persons. The difference between the OECD Model and the US Model is, however, not very substantial because estates, trusts and partnerships are also covered by the OECD Model, if not as companies, then, as '...any other body of persons...'.[24]

---

20. *See*, for example, Fibbe (2006), 99–102 about this problem.
21. This requirement is also included in Art. 1 of the UN Model and in Art. 1 of the US Model. The US Model, however, expressly mentions that the requirement applies 'except as otherwise provided in the Convention...'. *See* para. 1 of the Commentary on Art. 1 of the OECD Model.
22. Article 3 of the UN Model is similar to Art. 3 of the OECD Model.
23. Paragraph 2 of the Commentary on Art. 3. *See also* e.g., Le Gall (1995), 666 and Vogel et al. (1997), 173 for this broad definition.
24. From the wording of Art. 3(1)(a) of the US Model, '...an estate, a trust, a partnership...and any other body of persons...', essentially follows that estates, trusts and partnerships are bodies of persons. Also, for example, Doernberg and Van Raad (1997), 25 is of the opinion that the term 'person' in the OECD Model also covers estates, trusts and partnerships as bodies of persons. According to para. 1 of the Commentary on Art. 3 of the OECD Model, the definition in Art. 3(1)(a) is not exhaustive and should be understood in a very broad sense. Since the amendments of the Commentary on the OECD Model based on the OECD 1999 partnership report, also the Commentary on the OECD Model expressly mention that partnerships are persons either because they are companies or because they are other bodies of persons. *See* para. 2 of the Commentary on Art. 3 of the OECD Model. *See also* Barenfeld (2005), 150–151, Schaffner (2000), 219 and Lang (2000a), 33.

The term *'resident'* is defined in Article 4(1) of the OECD, the UN and the US Models, as '…any person who, under the laws of that State, is *liable to tax* therein…'.[25] In order for an entity to qualify for tax treaty benefits, it must be liable to tax with respect to its worldwide income as a separate tax subject in at least one of the contracting states. Therefore, in general, only entities considered as separate entities for tax purposes, but not transparent entities, qualify for tax treaty benefits. If an entity falls under the general corporate tax liability, most states consider that it is immaterial if the entity is for some reason exempt from the payment of corporate tax.[26]

According to Article 10(1) of the OECD Model, Article 10 applies only to '…dividend paid by a company which is a resident…'. Furthermore, according to Article 10(3) of the OECD Model, the term 'dividend' in respect of that article '…means income from shares…or other rights, not being debt-claims, participating in profits, as well as income from other *corporate rights* which is subjected to the same taxation treatment as income from shares by the laws of the State of which the company making the distribution is a resident…'.[27] As a result, it is clear that the dividend concept of Article 10 of the OECD Model only covers payments made by an entity that qualifies as a *company* under the treaty. Also, paragraphs 1, 2 and 7 of Article 10 of the US Model require that a dividend be paid by an entity that qualifies as a company.[28]

From the definition in Article 3(1)(a) of the OECD Model, it follows that *a company always qualifies as a person*. As long as an entity qualifies as a resident

---

25. The term 'residence' does not cover situations in which the entity is liable to tax only with respect to income from sources in that state. *See* Art. 4(1) of the Models.
26. If a person is not a resident of a contracting state, the treaty may have relevance to the person generally only because of certain special provisions concerning nationals of the contracting states, provided that the person is a national of one of the states. Such a provision may be, for example, the non-discrimination article of the treaty concerned. *See also*, for example, paras 8.5–8.7 of the Commentary on Art. 4 of the OECD Model, OECD (1999), 15, Lang (2000), 35–38, Barenfeld (2005), 152–176, Resch (2009), 124, Helminen (2016a), 149 and Helminen (2016b),189–192 for the interpretation of the requirement of being 'liable to tax'.
27. Similar definitions are included in Art. 10 of the UN Model.
28. Even though para. 5 of Art. 10 of the 2006 version of the US Model did not use the term company but only referred to the payer, it was clear that also for the purposes of the US 2006 Model only dividends paid by companies qualified under Art. 10 because paras 1 and 2 required that the payer was a company. The 1996 version of the US Model was unclear on this point, because it did not specifically require a dividend to be paid by an entity that is a company. According to Arts 10(1), 10(2) and 10(5) of the US Model, a dividend paid by any resident qualified as a dividend under Art. 10 of the treaty. It, therefore, seemed to follow that a dividend-distributing entity under the US Model did not have to be a company. The purpose of the US Model, as may be interpreted from the Technical Explanation to the 1996 version of the US Model, however, seemed to narrow the scope of eligible entities to companies. The Technical Explanation specified that the dividend definition included income from '…other *corporate rights* that are not treated as debt under the law of the source state, that participate in the profits of the *company*…' in addition to income from shares. The Technical Explanation further mentions that the term 'dividend' includes '…income that is subjected to the same tax treatment as income from shares by the law of the state of source…'. *See* Art. 10, paras 146 and 147 of the Technical Explanation to the 1996 US Model and Doernberg and van Raad (1997), 88. With respect to the actual treaties that follow the US 1996 Model, the interpretation depends on whether the contracting states accept this interpretation or not. If the treaty partner does not accept the US interpretation of the Technical Explanation, the other contracting party may very well interpret the autonomous part of the dividend definition to include income that is not paid by a company. *See* Helminen (1999), 129 about the practical relevance of the unclear wording under the US 1996 Model.

company, it also qualifies as a resident person. Therefore, the term, 'company' rather than the term, 'person' is of primary importance with respect to dividend taxation.

The term *company* is defined in Article 3(1)(b) of the OECD Model as '...any body corporate or any entity which is treated as a body corporate for tax purposes...'. This definition applies for the purposes of the Convention only if the context does not require otherwise.[29] In principle, the meaning of the term 'company' for the purposes of the dividend article might thus diverge from the meaning of the term in Article 3(1)(b). In practice, however, there should be no divergence because in the Commentary it is said that the definition of Article 3(1)(b) '...is drafted with special regard to the Article on dividend...'.[30] According to the Commentary on Article 10(3), the '...notion of dividend basically concerns distributions by companies within the meaning of subparagraph (b) of paragraph 1 of Article 3...'.[31]

The concept *corporate rights* is not expressly defined in the Model. However, a similar concept, 'body corporate', is used to define the term 'company' and the concept 'corporate rights' in Article 10(3) of the OECD Model defining the term 'dividend'. Therefore, so long as an entity qualifies as a company it is also an entity that may issue corporate rights.[32] As a result, the term 'corporate rights' is actually not relevant in distinguishing dividend-distributing entities from other entities, but rather only in distinguishing between different kinds of investments in a company.[33]

The term *company* covers any body corporate, that is, any entity that is regarded as an independent legal person with general legal capacity under the legal system of a contracting state.[34] Treatment as a separate tax subject is not required. This conclusion must be made from the wording of Article 3(1)(b), including references to both a body corporate and any entity treated as a body corporate for tax purposes. Any legal person may, thus, qualify as a company.[35]

Because the OECD Model Convention, according to Article 1 of the OECD Model, applies only to *residents* that, according to Article 4, are persons that are liable to tax in

---

29. Substantially similar definitions are included in the UN and US Models. *See* Doernberg and van Raad (1997), 2, for how the Technical Explanation as a unilateral document is not part of the treaty context, if not accepted by the treaty partner by the time of completing the actual treaty.
30. Paragraph 3 of the Commentary on Art. 3 of the OECD Model.
31. Paragraph 24 of the Commentary on Art. 10 of the OECD Model.
32. This connection is especially clear in the Finnish and German language translations of the OECD Model that use the term, *yhtiöosuuksista*, or *Gesellschaftsanteilen*, that correspond to the term 'company units' rather than the term 'corporate right'. *See also* Avery Jones et al. (2009), 23, for how the use of different languages can lead to different interpretations concerning the term 'corporate' and the term 'body corporate'.
33. *See* Avery Jones et al. (2009), 14–19, for examples of corporate rights in the companies of different countries. Because the term 'corporate right' in the dividend definition of Art. 10(3) of the OECD Model is used primarily to distinguish dividend constituting equity investments from other investments, the term is not discussed further here but in the chapter below concerning distinction between debt and equity.
34. *See* Vogel et al. (1997), 171–172 and Ekkehart & Rust (2015), 186. *See also* Tenore (2010), 222–224 about the term 'company' of the OECD Model.
35. This interpretation is, especially, clear in the Finnish, Swedish or German language versions of the OECD Model that use the terms, *oikeushenkilö, juridisk person* or *juristische Personen*, that may be translated as 'legal person' rather than 'body corporate'. *See also* Avery Jones et al. (2009), 7–9 who consider that the relevance of the tax treatment is restricted to the second part of the definition of the term company.

a contracting state, not all legal persons qualify as companies for the purposes of tax treaty protection. In general, if a company is not considered to be a separately taxable entity liable to tax with respect to its worldwide income, at least in one of the contracting states, the entity does not qualify for treaty benefits, even though it is a company.[36]

In addition to legal persons, Article 3(1)(b) defines, as a company, any other *entity treated as a body corporate for tax purposes*. Unlike Article 3(1)(b) of the OECD Model, Article 3(1)(b) of the US Model expressly mentions that the reference is to the law of the state in which the entity is resident.[37] According to paragraph 3 of the Commentary on Article 3(1) of the OECD Model, the term 'company' also covers any taxable unit, which is treated as a body corporate '…according to the tax laws of the Contracting State in which it is a resident…'.[38] The OECD and the US Models, thus, do not differ in substance.[39] For the purposes of both the Models, the term 'company' covers any entity, whether or not a legal person, that is treated as a legal person for tax purposes in the state where the entity is resident.[40] Such an entity is any entity treated as a separate tax subject in one of the contracting states.[41] The US Model, however, is clearer in referring expressly to the state of residence treatment unlike the OECD Model that refers to the state of residence treatment only in the Commentary.

In conclusion, under the Models, not only does a legal person qualify as a company but also any entity treated as a separate tax subject liable to tax in one of the contracting states. The other contracting state must then accept the corporate classification.

A legal person that is not taxed as a body corporate, even though it is a company, qualifies for tax treaty benefits only if it is a resident in at least one of the contracting

---

36. For this reason, the reference to a body corporate in the definition of the term company is unnecessary and could be deleted. This suggestion is also made, for example, by Avery Jones et al. (2009), 44.
37. Article 3(1)(b) of the 2006 version of the US Model still referred to the state in which the entity is organized.
38. The same paragraph of the 2010 version of the OECD Model still referred to the state of organization instead of the state of residence. The state of organization should refer to the state under the commercial law of which the entity is organized. This may, of course, be a state other than the state of residence of the same entity for tax treaty purposes as determined in accordance with Art. 4 of the Models.
39. For clarity reasons, it would, however, be recommendable that also the OECD Model and actual treaties would make an express reference to the state the law of which is decisive. Inconsistent interpretation and application of tax treaties would be better avoided if an express reference would be included. *See*, for example, Avery Jones et al. (2009), 11–12, who consider that because the wording of the OECD Model contained no reference to a contracting state, the Commentaries should most appropriately be viewed as illustrating the common case in which the entity is organized under the laws of a contracting state and is also a resident there and not as limiting the definition.
40. This is especially clear in the Finnish, Swedish and German language versions of the OECD Model that use the terms, *oikeushenkilönä, såsom juridisk person*, or *wie juristische Personen*, which may be translated as 'legal person' rather than 'body corporate'. *See also* Resch (2009), 123 for this interpretation.
41. van Raad (1988), 34–35, also points out that the reference to body corporate must cover both entities that are regarded and those that are not regarded as legal entities for company law purposes. Whether the entity is taxed as a non-transparent entity is decisive.

states because it is liable to tax in that state with respect to its worldwide income. If a company is not taxed in the state of its organization as a separate tax subject, it does not qualify for treaty benefits unless it is liable to tax in the other contracting state. In situations where the entity is not a resident in the state of its organization for tax treaty purposes, it is the treatment in the other contracting state that determines the entity's entitlement to treaty benefits.

According to paragraphs 1, 2 and 3 of Article 10 of the OECD Model, only resident companies qualify as dividend-distributing entities. Thus, any entity that is taxed as a body corporate, that is, as a separately taxable subject in a contracting state, qualifies as a dividend-distributing entity under the Model.

An entity that is not treated as a separately taxable entity in the state of its organization, may qualify as a dividend-distributing entity only if it is taxed as a separately taxable entity with respect to its worldwide income in the other contracting state.[42] In this case, the distribution from the entity may qualify as a dividend under Article 10 of the Model only if the distribution is made to a person resident in the state where the entity is organized. In such a situation, the distributing entity is a resident of the other state and Article 10 of the Model only applies with respect to distributions from a resident of one contracting state to a resident of the other contracting state.[43]

The above interpretation does not conflict, but rather, in most cases, is in accordance with Article 10(3) of the OECD Model. Article 10(3), after all, defines a dividend as '...income from other corporate rights which is subjected to the same taxation treatment...by the laws of the state of which the company making the distribution is resident...'. This interpretation is also in accordance with paragraph 27 of the Commentary on Article 10(3) of the Model. According to this paragraph, a partnership does not qualify as a dividend-distributing entity unless it is treated as a separate tax subject in the state of its effective management.

According to Article 3(1)(b), as interpreted in accordance with the Commentary, the status of an entity as a company is determined with reference to the law of the state of its residence. In order for the treaty to apply to the company at all, and, in order for the company to qualify as a dividend-distributing entity under the dividend article, a company must be a resident. If an entity is treated as a separately taxable entity in the state of its organization, and the other state does not claim to be the state of residence of the entity because its effective management is not situated there, the entity is a resident in the state of organization. In such a situation, the entity qualifies as a dividend-distributing company because the state of its organization, which is simultaneously the state of residence, treats the entity as such. In such a situation, it is immaterial how the other contracting state views the entity.

According to Article 4(3), in a dual-residence situation, that is, where both contracting states claim the right to tax the entity as a resident, the state of residence is

---

42. This interpretation follows from the Commentary on Art. 3(1)(b) of the OECD Model.
43. For these situations, it is very understandable that the reference in the Commentary on Art. 3(1)(b) of the OECD Model was changed from the state of organization to the stat of residence. Avery Jones et al. (2009), 44 suggested this change already before it was made to the Commentary.

the state of effective management.[44] In a dual-residence situation, it is immaterial whether the classification of the state of organization or the state of residence is used to determine the company status. In such a situation, both states tax the entity as a separate tax subject, and the entity, therefore, qualifies as a company in both states.[45]

If the state of organization of an entity treats the entity as a transparent entity, the treaty only applies to the entity if the entity is liable to tax in the other contracting state, because otherwise it cannot be a resident. In practice, the other state may claim to have the taxing right in situations where the effective management of the entity is situated in the other state. In such a case, it is actually the treatment in the other state that determines whether a distribution from such an entity may qualify as a dividend. The treaty between these two states may apply to a distribution from the entity only if the recipient of the distribution is a resident in the state of organization of the entity. In other cases, it is not the treaty between the first two states but the treaty between the other state and the state of residence of the recipient that is applicable and that must be applied to determine the status of the entity.[46]

Where the recipient is a resident of the state of organization of the entity, a problem may actually emerge only if the entity is not a legal person. If the entity is a legal person, it is a resident company and a dividend-distributing entity in the other state, although it is taxed as a transparent entity in the first state. Only if the entity is not a legal person, a problem may emerge if the state of organization classification is followed. The tax treatment in the state of organization suggests that the entity does not qualify as a dividend-distributing entity and the treatment in the state of residence of the distributing entity suggests that the entity is a dividend-distributing entity. This situation is the only one where there seems to be a real problem and where it makes a difference whether the state of organization treatment or the state of residence treatment is followed. If Article 3(1)(b) would be interpreted as referring to an

---

44. The OECD/G20 BEPS Action 2 on hybrid mismatches deals also with the tax treaty dual-residence tie-brake rule. Accordingly Art. 4(3) of the OECD Model will be amended to refer to the mutual agreement procedure as a solution to the dual residence conflicts instead of always solving the conflict in favour of the state of the effective management. See OECD (2015), 137. Article 4(4) of the US Model goes even further in ensuring that dual residence companies are not used unduly to claim treaty benefits. According to Art. 4(4) a dual resident company is not considered to be a resident of either state for purposes of claiming treaty benefits. Article 4 of the Multilateral Convention to Implement Tax Treaty Related Measures to Prevent Base Erosion and Profit Shifting also refers to the mutual agreement and mentions that in the absence of such agreement the person concerned shall not be entitled to any relief or exemption under the applicable tax treaties. The text of the Convention was published on 24 Nov. 2016 and it will have to be signed and ratified before it will enter into force.
45. In a dual-residence situation, the distributing entity is a person liable to tax in the state in which the effective management is situated and resident in that state for tax treaty purposes. If this is not the state where the entity is organized, the state of organization is not important with respect to the treatment of a dividend paid by the entity, unless the dividend recipient is resident in that state. Taxation of a dividend distributed by the entity in such a situation actually involves only the state of residence of the dividend-distributing entity and the state of residence of the dividend recipient, and not the state of organization of the entity. Therefore, there is no point in classifying an entity in accordance with the law of the state of its organization where the state of residence of the entity is another state for tax treaty purposes.
46. If the recipients are residents in the same state where the entity is resident, the determination is of course made purely in accordance with domestic law of the state.

interpretation in accordance with the tax law of the state of organization, and Article 10(3) in accordance with the state of residence, the treaty would refer to two different states. Therefore, the reference of the Commentary on Article 3(1)(b) to the state of residence makes sense.

However, there would actually be no conflict between the classification in accordance with the tax treatment in the state of organization and paragraph 27 of the Commentary on Article 10(3). Paragraph 27 only states that a distribution from a partnership is not a dividend unless the state of residence treats the entity as a separate tax subject. It does not state that in such a case the distribution must be treated as a dividend. The entity classification in the state of organization, from which it follows that the distribution is not a dividend, could also be followed in this case.

This interpretation would not be in conflict with Article 10(3) of the OECD Model, referring to the classification of the state of residence. The requirement that a dividend must be paid by a company and the definition in Article 10(3) of what kind of income paid by a company qualifies as a dividend are separate and independent from each other. Article 10(3) is, of course, dependent upon the company requirement in the way that the items enumerated in Article 10(3) are taxed as a dividend only if they are paid by a company. In contrast, the company definition is not dependent upon Article 10(3). Therefore, the reference to the state of residence of the dividend-distributing entity in Article 10(3) has no relevance with respect to the company definition.

The above interpretation should be followed especially if the wording of Article 3(1)(b) of a treaty defining the term 'company' expressly referred to the tax treatment in the state of organization. It may be argued that, because the wording of Article 3(1)(b) fails to refer expressly to the tax treatment in the state of organization, in this situation the context may require that the tax treatment in the state of residence of the company be decisive. It is somewhat peculiar, however, that the decisive classification should be the one made by a state which, in any case, is concerned with the distribution only if the recipient of the distribution is one of its residents.

In conclusion, it must be said that the OECD Model is unclear about the situation described above. It is uncertain whether the status of an entity as a dividend-distributing company should be determined in accordance with the tax treatment in the state of organization of the entity or the state of residence of the entity. Only the Commentary on Article 3 clarifies that the treatment in the state of residence is decisive. It is also important to note that until the 2010 version of the OECD Model, the Commentary still referred to the state of organization treatment instead of the state of residence treatment. Luckily this unclearness has real relevance only in those situations where the entity is not a legal person and is treated as a transparent entity in the state of organization of the entity and is treated as a separate tax subject in the other contracting state.

In this situation, the contracting states may each define the term 'company' according to the tax treatment of each respective state. Either interpretation seems to be in accordance with the Model because the Model is unclear, and also the Commentary has been unclear, in this respect. This ambiguity may lead to an income classification conflict, which, in turn, may lead to double taxation. Double taxation occurs if the state of organization as the state of residence of the income recipient does not eliminate the double taxation with respect to the dividend withholding tax possibly imposed in the source state. But because both states correctly applied the treaty, neither one may be required to eliminate the double taxation. Thus, a conflict emerges, which should be solved by mutual agreement procedure. In order to avoid conflicts, the OECD Model and actual treaties should refer expressly to the state of residence treatment in Article 3(1)(b) itself and not only in the Commentary.

[B] Actual Tax Treaties

Most actual tax treaties follow the OECD Model in respect to the fact that only *resident companies* qualify as dividend-distributing entities.[47] The residence, for the purposes of most actual treaties, is defined following Article 4 of the OECD Model. Normally, only an entity that is taxed as a separate subject with respect to its worldwide income in at least one of the contracting states qualifies as a resident and as a dividend-distributing entity for tax treaty purposes. Entities classified in both of the contracting states as a separate tax subject qualify as dividend-distributing entities.[48] In contrast, entities that are classified in both of the contracting states as transparent entities do not qualify as dividend-distributing entities.

Entities taxed as transparent entities qualify as residents only under some exceptional treaties. A number of actual treaties include special provisions concerning the residence of partnerships or trusts. For example, according to many US treaties the term 'resident' applies in the case of income derived or paid by a partnership, estate or trust only to the extent that the income derived by such partnership, estate or trust is subject to tax in that state as the income of a resident, either in its hands or in the hands of its partners or beneficiaries. Instead, according to the Nordic multilateral treaty,[49] a body of persons is a resident in a state only to the extent that its income is taxed in a way corresponding to the taxation treatment of a person resident in that state. Also, the rules of some treaties concerning dual-residence situations of legal persons differ from the Models. For example, the mutual agreement procedure may be referred to as a means for solving the conflict.[50]

The term *company* is defined under most treaties as any body corporate or any entity that is treated as a body corporate for tax purposes. Most of these treaties follow the Models and include as companies legal persons whether or not they are taxed as separate subjects and also other entities if taxed as separate subjects. Some treaties, however, include only an entity treated as a body corporate for tax purposes. Under

---

47. Some treaties include in addition to resident companies, certain other expressly mentioned entity forms. For example, many German treaties include expressly German silent partnerships and investment funds.
48. Of course, it is required that in a dual-residence situation, the state of residence of the dividend-distributing entity be considered to be one of the states and the state of residence of the dividend recipient the other of the contracting states.
49. *See*, for example, Andersson et al. (1991), Helminen (2013a) and Helminen (2007–2007c) about the Nordic Treaty.
50. This will also be the approach of teh OECD Model in the future. *See* OECD (2015), 137.

these treaties, the company law status of an entity is irrelevant. The decisive factor is the treatment as a separate taxable entity.

Most treaties do not expressly state what state's law is decisive in determining whether an entity is a body corporate or an entity taxed as a body corporate. Following the interpretation of the Models, the applicable law in these cases should be the law of the state of residence of an entity. An express reference to the state the law of which is decisive, however, would be clearer and would better avoid inconsistent interpretations in different states.

Inconsistent entity classification in the contracting states is likely to lead to income classification problems in the case of many actual treaties. Conflicts may arise in situations where one of the states classifies an entity as a separate tax subject, whereas the other classifies the entity as a transparent entity. If a legal person is classified as a separate tax subject in the state where the entity is organized, but as a transparent entity in the other state, the entity qualifies as a dividend-distributing entity under most treaties despite the conflict. This classification is due to the fact that under most treaties a legal person qualifies as a company despite its tax treatment. Because the company is taxed in one of the states as a separate subject, it is also a resident.

In such a situation, the other state has to accept the entity classification of the state of organization and has to treat distributions from the entity under the applicable treaty as a dividend. The state must eliminate double taxation with respect to the dividend following the rules of the treaty concerning the elimination of double taxation.[51] In this situation, inconsistent entity classification under the domestic tax law of the contracting states does not lead to a treaty conflict, but is solved in favour of the classification of the state of organization which is the state residence of the entity.

If the state of organization of the legal person treats the entity as a transparent entity and the other state treats it as a separate tax subject, the treaty between these two states normally applies to distributions from the entity only if the recipient of the distribution is a resident in the state of organization of the distributing entity. The entity is not a resident in the state of its organization but only in the other state, and a dividend under the treaty must be paid from a resident of one contracting state to a resident of the other contracting state. Only if the recipient of the distribution is a resident in the state of organization does the distribution qualify as a dividend under the treaty between the state of organization and the other state because the entity is a resident company in the other state. In such a situation, despite the classification in the state of organization of the distributing entity, the state of residence of the recipient of the distribution should eliminate double taxation following the dividend treatment of the other state. This requirement follows from the fact that a legal person qualifies as a company despite the treatment in the state of organization.

If the distributing entity is not a legal person and is taxed as a separate subject in the state of its organization and as a transparent entity in the other state, the entity

---

51. Of course, it is possible that the other state does not view the entity as a legal person, and, therefore, does not view it as a company and not as a dividend-distributing entity. This is, however, not a very likely possibility as it is natural that the legal personality is determined in accordance with the law of the state of organization of an entity.

qualifies as a dividend-distributing company under normal treaties despite the treatment in the other state. The entity qualifies as a resident company because it is taxed separately in the state of organization. The taxation in the state of organization should be determinative with respect to the meaning of the term 'company'. However, even if this interpretation is not accepted, the distribution from the entity qualifies as dividend because the state of organization is simultaneously the state of residence. The outcome is the same if the status of the entity as a company is determined either in accordance with the law of the state of organization of the entity, or in accordance with the law of the state of residence of the entity.

Only if the other state does not deem either approach to be correct, but deems that it should be able to determine the status of the entity independently, in accordance with its own tax law, does an actual income classification conflict emerge. Such an interpretation is, however, not very likely. At least if the general view is followed, the other state should accept the classification of the state of organization and residence of the entity. The other state should also eliminate double taxation with respect to the distribution as the state of residence of the recipient of the distribution following the rules of the treaty concerning the elimination of double taxation with respect to a dividend.

In the rare situation where the distributing entity is not a legal person and is not treated as a separate tax subject in the state of its organization, but is treated as a separate tax subject in the other state, an actual classification conflict may emerge. If the status of the entity as a company is determined in accordance with the tax treatment in the state of organization, the entity does not qualify as a dividend-distributing entity. However, because the state of residence of the entity is the other state, that state may view that the status of the entity should be determined in accordance with its classification. The state, thus, views the entity as one of its resident companies. This situation may lead to an actual classification conflict.

However, even in this case, the distribution may qualify as a dividend under the treaty only if the recipient of the dividend is a resident in the state of organization of the entity. Otherwise the treaty between the states is not applicable at all to the distribution. In this situation, an actual conflict that leads to inconsistent income classification emerges. Despite the inconsistent classification, the state of residence of the recipient of the distribution should eliminate the double taxation with respect to the distribution, in accordance with the rules of the applicable treaty concerning a dividend, because the other state has also correctly applied the treaty.[52]

The treaties, under which only entities taxed as bodies corporate qualify as companies, function slightly differently. The difference in comparison with the other treaties is that a body corporate not taxed as a body corporate does not qualify as a company. In practice, however, this difference has no major relevance because, under the other treaties, a body corporate may also qualify as a resident company and as a dividend-distributing entity only if it is taxed as a separately taxable entity in at least one of the contracting states. The only difference arises in the situation where the state

---

52. This suggestion is in accordance with the Commentary on Art. 23 of the OECD Model at para. 68. *See also* Avery Jones et al. (1996), 119 and 127–128.

of organization of a legal person treats the entity as a transparent entity and the other state taxes it as a separately taxable entity. This situation does not deviate from the otherwise similar situation where the entity is not a legal person.

§5.05 CONCLUSIONS

The domestic law treatment of each state determines whether or not an entity qualifies as a dividend-distributing entity for domestic tax law purposes. The tax treaty classification only determines how the tax treaty limits the taxing power of domestic tax law, but does not affect the domestic tax law classification.

Under the domestic tax law of most states, only entities classified as separately taxable corporations qualify as dividend-distributing entities. Inconsistent entity classification under the domestic tax law of two states is likely especially in the situations where the US or a country with a similar entity classification system is involved. The US legal system includes entity forms unknown in the legal systems of many other states and the US applies the elective approach to entity classification.

As a rule, inconsistent entity classification leads to inconsistent income classification. Inconsistent income classification under the domestic tax law of two contracting states, in turn, may lead to income classification conflicts under tax treaties. Tax treaties, however, usually solve such conflicts. For tax treaty purposes, the state of residence of an income recipient usually has to accept the corporate treatment of the state of residence of an entity and the dividend treatment that follows from it.

An actual unsolved classification conflict is possible in a situation where the state of organization of an entity is one of the contracting states and the state of residence of the entity for tax treaty purposes is the other contracting state. A classification conflict is possible if the owners of the entity are residents in the same state as the state of organization and if the other state taxes the entity as a resident because the effective management of the entity is in that state. With respect to such situations, tax treaties are unclear about which state's tax treatment is decisive for treaty purposes. The tax treaties do not state whether the classification of the state of organization of an entity or the state of residence of the entity governs. Either interpretation can be considered as a correct application of the treaty. Therefore, one of the contracting states may treat the same income as a dividend while the other may not.

In a conflict situation where the state of organization of the entity is simultaneously the state of residence of the income recipient, the state might not eliminate double taxation with respect to taxes paid to the other state on a distribution. In order for the state of organization to be able to eliminate double taxation, either it should leave the income untaxed at the time of its realization or it should refund a certain portion of the taxes paid at the time of the realization upon the actual distribution of the income. Tax treaties are not clear about whether, despite the existence of a conflict, the other state must eliminate double taxation. It is suggested, however, that double taxation be eliminated in the state of residence of the income recipient because the other state correctly applied the treaty.[53]

In order to avoid the actual classification conflicts described above, tax treaties should expressly state which state's tax treatment is decisive in determining the status of an entity as a dividend-distributing entity. A reference to this issue in the Commentary to the OECD Model is not sufficient. The best solution would be that the treatment in the state of residence of an entity is decisive with respect to a dividend. The definition of the term 'company' with respect to a dividend, including a body corporate and entities taxed as bodies corporate, only serves to confuse. For the purposes of a dividend, the clearest formulation would be the one that refers only to an entity taxed as a body corporate. Accordingly, it should be expressly stated that an entity may qualify as a dividend-distributing entity only if it is treated as a separately taxable entity in the state that is the state of residence of the entity for purposes of the treaty.

In practice, entity classification only rarely can lead to situations where international double taxation would not be eliminated to the extent required by tax treaties as interpreted in the way explained above. In fact, in many cases, inconsistent classification under the domestic tax law of two contracting states leads to a situation where the states eliminate double taxation more extensively than is required by a treaty. In a situation of inconsistent entity classification, the state of residence of the owners of a foreign entity may eliminate double taxation with respect to both the foreign taxes paid by the foreign entity and the foreign taxes paid by the owners, although the applicable treaty would require a credit only with respect to the taxes paid by the owners.

---

53. This suggestion is in accordance with the Commentary on Art. 23 of the OECD Model at para. 68. *See also* Avery Jones et al. (1996), 199 and 127–128.

CHAPTER 6
Dividend-Stripping and the Dividend-Generating Relationship

§6.01 INTRODUCTION

A dividend is a profit distribution based on a shareholder relationship. Only a benefit from a separately taxable corporate entity to one of its shareholders in its capacity as such constitutes a dividend. Ordinarily, the shareholder of a corporate entity is the legal recipient of a dividend distribution and is also liable for tax on the dividend.

For tax reasons, it may be advantageous in cross-border situations to receive the economic benefit of a dividend not in the form of a dividend, but in some other form of income. Taxpayers may, for example, enter into arrangements where the legal recipient of the dividend is a resident in the same state where the dividend-distributing company is a resident, but where the economic benefit of the dividend is ultimately realized by a non-resident in the form of another type of income or gain. Such arrangements, where a third party, instead of the actual equity investor, receives the dividend from a corporate entity and transfers the economic benefit of the dividend to the actual investor in a form other than a dividend, are referred to as dividend stripping.

Dividend stripping includes any artificial arrangement, involving a third party, by which a non-resident may receive foreign-source receipts not subject to withholding tax instead of foreign-source dividend normally subject to withholding tax.[1] Alternatively, dividend-stripping arrangements may be used so that non-residents can gain the full benefits of the economic double taxation eliminating systems of domestic tax law that may not be available to non-residents. Such arrangements may also be used to gain access to the most advantageous tax treaty or to the benefits of the P-S Directive.

---

1. Dividend stripping is not an exact legal term, but is used loosely to include different arrangements of avoiding dividend taxation or taking advantage of beneficial dividend taxation not otherwise available. *See also*, for example, Bippus (1994), 948 and 952 and Gäbel (1994), 15 for the term.

Dividend stripping is possible for a shareholder, for example, by transferring the mere right to receive a future dividend without an accompanying transfer of the underlying stock. The alienor receives a dividend equivalent payment in the form of the proceeds from the alienation, even though the legal owner of the actual dividend is the alienee. Therefore, it is necessary to determine whether the dividend paid on the shares is taxed as the income of the shareholder or as the income of the holder of the dividend right.

This question concerns the determination of the proper tax subject for the distributed dividend and may be solved in accordance with the principles concerning the assignment of income. The question is, however, beyond the scope of this study, because strictly speaking it does not concern the issue of whether there is a dividend. It rather concerns the issue of as whose income the dividend is taxed.[2] With respect to this study, the more interesting question is the extent to which the proceeds from the alienation of the dividend right constitute the kind of income to the alienor, that is or that may be taxed as a dividend under the different legal systems of international tax law.

In addition to the separation of a dividend right from shares, a shareholder may, for example, sell shares prior to a dividend distribution and may buy them back again after the distribution for a price including the amount equivalent to the lost dividend distribution. Alternatively, the shareholder may lend the shares for the period of time during which a dividend distribution is made to another person and may enjoy an amount equivalent to the dividend distribution in the form of a borrow fee. These situations allow the economic benefit of a dividend ultimately realized by a person who was not the formal shareholder at the time of the distribution. The question that arises is the extent to which substitute dividend payment under equity securities lending transactions are and may be treated as a dividend under the different legal systems of international tax law.

The so-called derivative financial instruments may be used to receive dividend equivalent payments by a person that is not a shareholder, and that may never have been a shareholder. The extent to which dividend equivalent payments on synthetic equity may be and actually are treated as dividend under the different legal systems of international tax law is interesting.

§6.02 THE BASIC RELATIONSHIP

[A] Domestic Tax Laws

The relationship that is required in order for a payment or a benefit to constitute dividend for domestic tax law purposes depends on the domestic tax law provisions of the country concerned. Generally, a dividend is considered to be a return on the kind

---

2. In cross-border situations, the question as to who is the right tax subject for a dividend has relevance, for example, in determining which tax treaty is applicable to the transaction. The determination of the right tax subject may also have an effect on the tax treaty classification of the income.

of investment that generates a shareholder relationship between the investor and the corporation in which the investment is made. In general, dividend taxation also requires that the person that receives income from a corporation be a shareholder in the distributing corporation and that the payment be based on the shareholder relationship. This basic requirement is clearly expressed under the domestic tax laws of many countries. It is basically required that a dividend be paid from a corporation to one of its shareholders in its capacity as such. Dividend requires a transfer of a benefit from a corporation to one of its shareholders in the shareholder's capacity as such.

Despite the shareholder relationship requirement, benefits from a corporation to another person that is in close relationship to the shareholder may also be taxed as a dividend of the shareholder, if the benefit is transferred because of the shareholder relationship. Many countries tax any transfer of a benefit for no equivalent value or benefit in exchange between corporations under common control either as a dividend or as a constructive dividend in the hands of the common shareholder of the two corporations. Dividend taxation is possible, although no direct benefit is passed to the shareholder. In such a situation, it is assumed that one of the corporations first distributed the amount to the common shareholder that then made a contribution to the other corporation's capital.

In the case of EU Member Countries, the TFEU non-discrimination rules and especially the basic freedoms must be respected and cross-border situations must be treated as beneficially as domestic situations. Different income classification in domestic situations and in cross-border situations must not lead to more burdensome tax treatment of the cross-border situation. Sometimes, however, different treatment may be justified. The need to guarantee balanced allocation of taxing rights or the need to prevent wholly artificial tax avoidance arrangements may be accepted as justifications for a different treatment.[3]

[B] The Parent-Subsidiary Directive

The P-S Directive applies to distributions of profits by a subsidiary to its parent company.[4] According to Article 3 of the P-S Directive, a company may qualify as a parent company if it '…has a minimum holding of 10 per cent in the capital of a company…' that is then the subsidiary. If two states bilaterally agree, the criterion of a capital holding may be replaced by a holding of voting rights. The P-S Directive, thus, requires a shareholder relationship.[5]

---

3. *See*, for example, C-182/08, *Glaxo Wellcome* concerning a dividend-stripping arrangement.
4. Articles 1, 4 and 5 of the P-S Directive.
5. Because the term capital is broader than the term share capital, it is clear that a holding in capital of entities the interest in which is not represented by shares, also qualifies. The list of companies covered by the P-S Directive includes, for example, cooperative societies of many countries. It is not completely clear which items of capital in a company qualify when determining the required holding. According to Thömmes (1992), 35 the interpretation of Art. 10 of the OECD Model may be referred to in this interpretation. However, the uncertainty remains unless the European Court of Justice will clarify the term.

The P-S Directive does not state whether the holding must be direct or whether indirect holdings also qualify. Because of the lack of reference to indirect holdings in the P-S Directive, it should be interpreted restrictively. It may not be required that Member States grant P-S Directive benefits if the holding requirement is met only through an indirect holding.[6] The concept 'holding in capital' also excludes mere holdings of shares in usufruct. According to the EU Court, the term 'holding in capital' refers to a legal relation between the parent company and the subsidiary company and does not cover a situation in which a parent company has transferred its legal relationship with its subsidiary to a third party.[7]

According to Article 4 of the P-S Directive, in order for the article to apply, a distribution must be made to a parent company '…by virtue of its association with its subsidiary…'.[8] This phrase is unclear as to whether it means that only distributions that are made by virtue of the parent company's participation in the share capital of the subsidiary qualify or whether another kind of association between the parent company and the subsidiary is also acceptable. It seems that a capital holding is required because the term 'association' is used directly in connection with the terms 'parent company' and 'subsidiary' that are defined in Article 3 by reference to a holding of a company's capital.[9] However, if two Member States have replaced the requirement of a holding of capital with a requirement of a holding of voting rights by means of bilateral agreement, then an association based on the fact of a company having voting rights in another company should qualify.

Article 5 of the P-S Directive requires that profits distributed by a subsidiary to a parent company shall be exempt from source state withholding tax where the latter holds a minimum of 10% of the capital of the subsidiary. Article 5 does not mention, in the way that Article 4 does, that the distribution must be made by virtue of the association between the parent company and the subsidiary. However, the same requirement should also apply with respect to Article 5. The requirement that a distribution is made by virtue of shareholder relationship follows, in practice, from the term 'distributed profits'. The express reference in Article 4 must be only clarifying in its nature.[10]

In conclusion, the P-S Directive concerns distributions between companies where the recipient holds a certain amount of capital or voting rights in the distributing company. The distribution must be made by virtue of a holding either of capital or of voting rights in the distributing company.

---

6. This interpretation is also suggested by Thömmes (1992), 35. *See also* Helminen (2015), 166.
7. C-48/07 *Les Vergers du Vieux Tauves*. *See also* Helminen (2015), 166. *See also* Peeters and Ven de Vijver (2009), 147–156 about the case. Because of the basic freedoms of the TFEU, the treatment of cross-border situations, however, must not be worse than the treatment of domestic situations even if the case concerned would not come under the scope of the P-S Directive.
8. Article 4 of the P-S Directive.
9. Vanistendael (1992), 604 is of the opinion that the P-S Directive covers any distribution based on entitlement as a shareholder.
10. *See* for this interpretation also e.g., Thömmes (1992), 12.

Under the domestic law of many states, an economic benefit from a company to a person close to the shareholder may also be taxed as a dividend. A benefit transferred between two subsidiaries of a common parent company may be taxed as a dividend for the common parent company. This practice raises the question of whether P-S Directive benefits have to be granted in situations where a payment is made between two subsidiary companies resident in one Member State with a common parent company in another Member State. The P-S Directive, however, expressly requires a dividend to be paid from a subsidiary to its parent company by virtue of the association between the companies. Strictly interpreted, distributions between two subsidiary companies of a common parent, thus, may not qualify under the P-S Directive. As a consequence, the P-S Directive does not seem to hinder the state of residence of the subsidiaries from taxing the benefit transferred from one of the subsidiaries to the other subsidiary.

However, under domestic law, where such a benefit is taxed as a dividend, it is actually assumed that the distribution is made first to the common parent company of the subsidiaries. From the point of view of the state that taxes such income as a dividend, there is a fictive profit distribution from a subsidiary to its parent company, made by virtue of the subsidiary's association with the parent company. Thus, P-S Directive benefits must be available if the term 'profit distribution' is interpreted as including fictive profit distributions.

The wording of the P-S Directive does not expressly include fictive distributions. However, despite this omission, the P-S Directive may be interpreted as applying to situations where the domestic tax law of a Member State subjects a fictive distribution to taxation, as if an actual distribution had been made.[11] From the fictive dividend treatment under domestic law, it logically follows that the state also treats the fictive distribution as a distribution with respect to the P-S Directive. There are no grounds for the state to tax the amount that it deems to be a dividend from a subsidiary to its parent company because the state could not tax the amount if the benefit had actually been distributed as a dividend from the subsidiary to the parent company. The benefit may not be viewed as having been transferred in order to avoid dividend taxation.

If the holding requirement is fulfilled between the distributing subsidiary and the parent company, the P-S Directive hinders the state of residence of the distributing company from imposing dividend withholding tax with respect to the fictive dividend. If the state of residence of the parent company deems that the parent company has received a constructive dividend, it should also exempt the fictive income or at least eliminate double taxation with respect to the income, in accordance with the requirements of the P-S Directive.

---

11. *See* for this interpretation also Scherer (1995), 226 with respect to undistributed profits deemed to be distributed.

[C] Tax Treaties

[1] The Model Conventions

Only income from corporate rights constitutes a dividend within the meaning of Article 10 of the OECD or the US Models. In the OECD Model, the requirement of corporate rights follows directly from the wording of the definition. A dividend is '...income from shares...or other rights...as well as income from other corporate rights...'. From the phrase '...or other rights...', it also follows that shares must be rights and it follows from the phrase '...as well as income from other corporate rights...' that other rights and shares must be corporate rights as well.[12]

With respect to the US Model, the corporate rights requirement does not follow directly from the wording of the treaty, but it can be interpreted from the Technical Explanations of the US 2006 Model. According to the Technical Explanations, the dividend definition includes, in addition to income from shares, income from '...other corporate rights that are not treated as debt under the law of the source states...'. A dividend includes '...income that is subjected to the same tax treatment as income from shares by the laws of the state of source...'.[13] Therefore, at least under the autonomous parts of the dividend definition of the US Model, income must be from corporate rights. Instead, the wording '...as well as income...' in the third part of the dividend definition of the US Model seems to include any income that is taxed as income from shares in the source state. For the purposes of the US Model, it is enough that the source state views the income as '...a return on an equity investment in a corporation...',[14] whereas the OECD Model requires autonomous classification of the term 'corporate right'.

From the fact that a dividend must be income from corporate rights, it follows that, generally, only income that is received because of a person's position as a shareholder or because of a comparable relationship to a company qualifies as a dividend.[15] According to the Commentary on the OECD Model, the term 'dividend' generally means distributions of profits to the shareholders of a company as a return on the capital that the shareholders have made available to the company as its shareholders.[16]

The dividend definitions of the Model Conventions do not require the dividend to be paid to a shareholder. It is enough that the dividend be paid because of a shareholder relationship. According to the Commentary, under certain conditions, a dividend may be constituted by benefits to which a holding in a company confers entitlement that are

---

12. *See* for this requirement also Vogel et al. (1997), 649.
13. Technical Explanations, Art. 10(5) of the 2006 US Model.
14. Technical Explanations, Art. 10(5) of the 2006 US Model. *See also* Doernberg and Van Raad (1997), 88 concerning the 1996 US Model. Because the relevant wording in the 2016, 2006 and the 1996 Model and the technical explanations of the 2006 and the 1996 Model are the same, the interpretation also should be the same.
15. For example, Vogel et al. (1997), 650, interprets the corporate rights requirement to include that the income is paid because of shareholder relationship. Hattingh (2009), 518 on the other hand interprets that the term income in the dividend definition of the OECD Model 'suggests a share in the yield of capital risked as an investment in a company'.
16. Paragraphs 1 and 3 of the Commentary on Art. 10 of the OECD Model.

available to persons that are not shareholders within the meaning of company law. Dividend classification is possible in a case of concealed holdings, that is, if the legal relations between a person and the company are assimilated to a holding in a company, because the persons receiving the benefits are closely connected with a shareholder of the company. Distribution, by virtue of a holding in a company, may be taxed as a dividend if it is paid to a company belonging to the same group as the shareholder company does.[17]

[2]   Actual Tax Treaties

The dividend definition of most treaties follows the OECD Model. Under these treaties, income not expressly defined as a dividend under the treaties qualifies as a dividend only if it is paid on an equity investment in a company. The income does not, however, have to be paid to a shareholder, so long as the income is paid on an ownership interest in the paying company.

There are, however, a number of treaties that differ from the OECD Model. Many treaties, especially the ones with the US, define dividend as '… income from shares,…, or other rights (not being debt claims) participating in profits, as well as other income derived from other rights that is subject to the same taxation treatment as income from shares by the laws of the contracting state of which the company making the distribution is a resident…'. The starting point is that a dividend is a distribution based on an equity investment in a company. However, if the source state treats any other income paid by a company on other rights in the same manner as income on equity investment, that income also qualifies as a dividend under these treaties. There is no special requirement of the recipient being a shareholder, and thus distributions from companies to other persons also qualify as a dividend to the extent that they are paid by virtue of a qualifying investment.

Some US treaties define dividend slightly differently as:

> [I]ncome from shares or other rights, not being debt-claims, participating in profits, as well as income from other corporate rights which is subjected to the same taxation treatment as income from shares by the laws of the state of which the company making the distribution is a resident, and income from arrangements, including debt obligations, carrying the right to participate in profits, to the extent so characterized under the laws of the contracting state in which the income arises.

The starting point also under these treaties is that a dividend is a distribution based on an equity investment in a company. However, income on debt-claims also qualifies as a dividend if the income is from arrangements participating in profits and the source state treats the income as a dividend. These treaties do not include a special requirement that a dividend must be paid to a shareholder. Thus, distributions from a

---

17. Paragraph 29 of the Commentary on Art. 10 of the OECD Model. *See*, however, for example decision 15649 36 Droit Fiscal 39 (1984), 1092, of the Supreme Administrative Court of France from 27 Jul. 1984, in which the court considered that a payment in excess of the arm's length price did not qualify as dividend for tax treaty purposes because the payment was not made in a shareholder relationship.

company to any persons qualify as a dividend so long as the distribution is made by virtue of a qualifying investment in the distributing company.

Under some treaties, like the Nordic multilateral treaty, dividend is defined as:

> [I]ncome from shares...or other rights, not being debt-claims, participating in profits, as well as other income from a company, that is subjected to the same taxation treatment as income from shares by the laws of the State of which the company making the distribution is a resident.[18]

Under these treaties, the starting point is that a dividend is income from corporate rights. However, any other income paid by a company that is taxed in the source state in the same way as a dividend also qualifies as a dividend. These treaties do not set any requirement that the recipient must be a shareholder. To the extent that income is paid from a company on a qualifying investment or that any other income is paid from a company that is taxed as a dividend in the source state, the income also qualifies as a dividend if paid to a person that is not a shareholder.

In conclusion, under most actual treaties it is not only income to a shareholder, which constitutes a dividend, but also income to persons other than shareholders. Under most treaties a dividend must, however, be based on a shareholder relationship. Income from corporate rights qualifies as a dividend under all treaties. Most treaties also cover other income, so long as it is treated as a dividend in the source state. The treaties, which contain the broadest definitions, cover any income treated in the source state in the same way as a dividend is treated. Some treaties cover income from any rights that is treated in the source state in the same way as a dividend and some treaties cover income from any arrangement carrying the right to participate in profits. Only the treaties that closely follow the OECD Model require that a dividend always be income from corporate rights.

In conclusion, most tax treaties grant the state of residence of an income-distributing company a great deal of discretion to determine in accordance with its domestic tax law whether the relationship between the company and the income recipient is such that the income constitutes a dividend. The state of residence of the income recipient must accept the dividend classification of the source state even though the state, under its own domestic tax law, would not regard the relationship as that required for a dividend-constituting relationship. Because the status of an entity as a company is also determined in accordance with the tax classification of the state of residence of the entity, the power of the source state classification is evident.

[D] Conclusions

The dividend concept of domestic tax laws, the P-S Directive and tax treaties all cover income paid by a company to its shareholder because of the shareholder relationship. It depends on the domestic tax law provisions of the country concerned to what extent

---

18. Article 10(6) of the Nordic Treaty. This is the translation of the author of this study from the Finnish language version of the treaty. *See also* Helminen (2013a), 241–245 for the dividend definition of the Nordic Treaty.

and in what situations also payments made to persons other than shareholders and payments made on other than equity investments constitute dividends for the domestic tax law purposes of the country concerned.

The P-S Directive expressly covers only payments from a subsidiary to its parent company made because of the shareholder relationship between the payer and the recipient. The shareholder relationship must be based on capital or voting rights depending on the country concerned. Fictive distributions are covered if the state concerned considers them to be made in a qualifying relationship.

The dividend definitions of the tax treaties that follow the OECD Model cover only income from corporate rights. The recipient of a dividend, however, does not have to be a shareholder. Many other treaties include a broader dividend definition and may also cover other income, which is treated in the same way as dividend for tax purposes in the source state.

§6.03 CLASSIFICATION OF PAYMENTS UNDER DIVIDEND-STRIPPING ARRANGEMENTS

[A] Proceeds from the Transfer of Dividend Rights

[1] Introduction

A shareholder may transfer the mere right to receive a future dividend without an accompanying transfer of the underlying stock, or may transfer the stock but retain the mere right to a dividend. Such transfers allow the alienor to receive dividend equivalent income in the form of proceeds from the alienation instead of an actual dividend. In cross-border relations, the separation of the ownership of the right to a dividend from the ownership of shares may, thus, be used to convert a cross-border dividend into some other type of income. Because of this possibility of avoiding dividend taxation, it may be asked whether and to what extent the proceeds from the alienation of a dividend right separate from the shares to which the right belongs, may be and actually are taxed as a dividend under the different legal systems of international tax law.

[2] Domestic Tax Laws

The company laws of most states do not prohibit separating the ownership of shares and dividend rights on the shares. Company laws of many states allow parties to enter into agreements establishing who is entitled to a dividend. Therefore, in principle, cross-border dividend stripping is possible in many countries.

Despite dividend stripping, income must be taxed as income for the person that actually earned it. In many countries, the assignment of income is based on a principle according to which fruits may not be attributed to a tree different from the one on which they grew. The principle that a dividend is income of the shareholder may follow also directly from the dividend definition of the domestic tax law in different states. The tax law of many states includes special rules that prevent a non-resident from avoiding dividend taxation by transferring dividend rights separately from shares to a resident person. Because of either the general principles or the specific provisions, a shareholder may not avoid dividend taxation by transferring the right to a dividend and retaining the shares to which the right belongs.

Many countries do not have special tax provisions for classifying the gain from the alienation of dividend rights separately from the shares as a dividend. Such special provisions are not considered to be necessary, because based on the basic tax law principles the shareholder is taxed for a dividend even though the shareholder had alienated the dividend right to another person. Many countries apply their general anti-avoidance provisions to tax the proceeds from the alienation of dividend rights as a dividend if the transfer constitutes an abusive use of legal forms.

Some countries have included special provisions under their tax law based on which the proceeds from the alienation of dividend rights without the shares to which they belong are taxed in the same way as dividends. In these countries, non-resident shareholders may not avoid source state dividend withholding tax by transferring the right to a dividend to a resident.

In conclusion, a non-resident shareholder is often not able to avoid the source state taxes by transferring a dividend right to a resident person, while retaining the shares. Based on general or special provisions of many countries, a dividend in such a situation may be taxed as income for the non-resident despite the transfer. Even in the countries in which such treatment does not apply, the proceeds from the alienation may be treated as a dividend.

[3]   The EU Parent-Subsidiary Directive

In situations where a shareholder qualifies as a parent company of a subsidiary resident in another EU Member State, as defined in the P-S Directive, there is no advantage in converting a dividend into capital gain in order to avoid dividend withholding tax. If the relationship between the shareholder and the company and the distribution between them are such as required in the P-S Directive, there is no dividend taxation in any case.

In situations where the P-S Directive is inapplicable, the taxpayers may attempt to take advantage of the benefits of the P-S Directive. A non-qualifying shareholder may transfer the mere rights to receive a dividend to a person that is entitled to P-S Directive benefits, while the former retains the shares. Such a transfer, however, does not make the P-S Directive applicable. The P-S Directive clearly requires that a distribution be made from a qualifying subsidiary to a qualifying parent company by virtue of its association with the subsidiary. Even if the holder of the dividend right was a qualifying parent company because of its association with the distributing subsidiary, the dividend that is based solely on the dividend right is not based on a recognized parent-subsidiary relationship. The dividend received on the grounds of a mere dividend right is not paid by virtue of the recipient parent company's association with the subsidiary, but rather on grounds of the association between the subsidiary and the shareholder that transferred the dividend right.

P-S Directive benefits are also not available with respect to the proceeds paid for the alienation of a dividend right by a shareholder of a company to another person. The P-S Directive is not applicable even though there would be a qualifying parent-subsidiary relationship between the transferee and the transferor of the dividend right. The amount paid for the alienation of the dividend right is not paid by virtue of the association between the two companies, but by virtue of the alienation of the right. The P-S Directive may be applicable with respect to the proceeds from an alienation of a dividend right only if the proceeds are paid between qualifying companies in a qualifying relationship, and only to the extent that the amount of the payments differs from the arm's length standard, and, therefore, constitutes a constructive dividend.

In conclusion, the benefits of the P-S Directive cannot be exploited by a person otherwise not entitled to the benefits by transferring dividend rights separately from the shares to which the rights belong. The proceeds from such a transaction do not qualify for P-S Directive benefits.

[4] Tax Treaties

A dividend, as defined under the Model treaties, is income from corporate rights paid by a company. Therefore, income paid by a company to a person that is not a shareholder, merely based on a dividend right, does not seem to qualify as a dividend within the meaning of the Model treaties. A dividend right is not a corporate right because it does not grant the general rights of a shareholder to the dividend right holder, but only grants the right to make a claim for payment of a dividend declared in a specific year. A dividend right does not generally entitle the holder to participate either in the profits or in the liquidation proceeds of a company. Therefore, a dividend paid to a mere holder of a dividend right seems to qualify as a dividend under the Models only if the holder receives the dividend on the grounds of the person's present or former status as a shareholder.[19]

Under the OECD Model, the requirement of a corporate right must be interpreted autonomously even with respect to the part of the dividend definition referring to source state classification. Therefore, the fact that the state of residence of the distributing company taxes the distribution under domestic law as a dividend does not make the income qualify as a dividend for treaty purposes. Instead, under the US Model, any income that is taxed the same way as a dividend in the source state is taxed qualifies as a dividend. Therefore, under the US Model, so long as the state of residence of the paying company treats the distribution as a dividend under domestic law, the income also qualifies as a dividend.

However, it may be argued, with respect to the OECD Model, that although the recipient of a dividend is not the shareholder, the income is income from shares paid to a person other than the shareholder. The OECD Model does not require that a

---

19. *See* Vogel et al. (1997), 653.

dividend is received by a shareholder, but only that it is income from shares. It may be argued that dividend received by a holder of a mere dividend right is actually paid by virtue of the shareholding of the shareholder, and, therefore, is a dividend as income from shares. However, the shareholder is not the beneficial owner of such a dividend but the holder of the dividend right is the beneficial owner instead. Therefore, if the phrase 'income from shares' is broadly interpreted, income on dividend rights also seems to qualify as a dividend under the OECD Model. In the opinion of some authors, dividend treatment, however, requires that the income recipient has been a shareholder at least at a certain point prior to the distribution so that the distribution may be said to be made by virtue of a shareholding.[20] Either one of the classifications seems to be a correct application of the treaty.

In a dividend-stripping situation, where the dividend right holder is a resident in the same state where the distributing company is a resident, there is, actually, no difference with respect to the taxing result whether the distribution is classified as other income or as a dividend for the purposes of a tax treaty following the OECD Model. In both cases, the state of residence of the income recipient, that is the same state as the state of residence of the distributing company, may tax the income.

Tax treaties do not include a special provision concerning the proceeds from the alienation of dividend rights separately from the shares to which they belong. The proceeds from such alienation must be taxed according to the general rules concerning the alienation of movable property under an article based on Article 13 of the OECD Model as capital gains. The capital gain treatment means that the state of residence of the alienor alone has the right to tax the income.

The proceeds from the alienation by a shareholder of dividend rights, alienated separately from the shares to which they belong, do not qualify as a dividend under Article 10 of the OECD Model. The company that issued the shares to which the alienated dividend rights belong does not pay the income, and the income received is clearly not income from shares or from other corporate rights, but rather it is income from the alienation of a right. Even though the payer was a company, the income from the alienation is not income from shares but is clearly income from the alienation of movable property. The proceeds from the alienation of a dividend right may only qualify as a dividend if paid between qualifying companies on the basis of a qualifying relationship to the extent that the amount of the payments differ from arm's length prices and, therefore, constitute a constructive dividend.

Under the US Model, any income, which is taxed in the source state in the same way as income from shares is taxed, qualifies as a dividend. Therefore, if the state of residence of the person that purchased the dividend right treats the income paid for such alienation as a dividend, the income also qualifies as a dividend under the US Model. The capital gains article of the Model does not prohibit such treatment. According to the Technical Explanation to the US 2006 Model, gains from shares are taxed under Article 13, but only '...to the extent such income is not otherwise characterized as income taxable under another Article (e.g., Article 10 (Dividends) ...

---

20. *Ibid.*

'.[21] The same principle should apply with respect to the alienation of dividend rights. Although the state of residence of the alienor would view the income as capital gains, it must eliminate double taxation with respect to the withholding tax imposed in the source state in accordance with the dividend article.

Under some actual treaties, income paid by a company from shares or other rights participating in profits or income from other rights taxed in the same way as income from shares is taxed in the state of residence of the distributing company qualifies as a dividend. For the purposes of some other treaties, the term 'dividend' is defined to include income from shares paid by a company or any income paid by a company if the state of residence of the payer taxes such income in the same way as it taxes income from shares. Under the Nordic multilateral treaty, income paid by a company from shares or other rights participating in profits qualifies as a dividend. In addition, any income paid by a company treated in the source state the same way as a dividend is treated qualifies as a dividend.[22]

Under these treaties differing from the OECD Model, it is clear that a dividend paid by a company to a holder of a dividend right that is not a shareholder qualifies as a dividend, at least if taxed as a dividend in the state of residence of the distributing company. Because the treaties do not require that a dividend be income from corporate rights, income from any right qualifies so long as it is paid by a company.

It may even be argued that income from a dividend right qualifies as a dividend under the autonomous part of the definition including income from other rights participating in profits. The opinion of the author of this study is, however, that because a mere dividend right does not produce a general right to corporate profits, it may not be the kind of profit-participating right intended by the treaty. Dividend treatment under the autonomous part of the dividend definition actually requires the broad interpretation described above, including the treatment as income from shares.

In conclusion, income from a dividend right may be taxed either as a dividend or as other income, but if the source state taxes such income as a dividend, it always qualifies as a dividend, with the effect that the other state has to accept the treatment and has to eliminate double taxation accordingly. It is actually immaterial whether income from dividend rights may be interpreted as qualifying under the autonomous part of the definition. The state of residence of the income recipient may tax it anyway, and, in any case, where the source state, under domestic law, treats the income as a dividend, the other state must accept the source state's classification and eliminate double taxation accordingly.

The proceeds from the alienation of a dividend right, instead, do not qualify as a dividend under these treaties differing from the OECD Model. Income from the alienation of a dividend right is not income from a right but income from the alienation of a right. Therefore, the income may only be taxed in the state of residence of the recipient of the income in accordance with the capital gains article. The source state

---

21. The Technical Explanation to Art. 13(6) of the US 2006 Model.
22. Paragraphs 1 and 6 of Art. 10 of the Nordic Treaty. *See also* Helminen (2013a), 241–245 for the dividend definition of the Nordic Treaty.

must not tax such income, although under its domestic tax law, such proceeds would be treated as a dividend.

For the purposes of many actual tax treaties, only income from a company qualifies as a dividend. A dividend must also be income from shares. Income from other corporate rights, however, qualifies if the state of residence of the company paying the income treats the income in the same way as income from shares. In addition, the definition may cover income from any arrangements containing the right to participate in profits to the extent so characterized under the laws of the contracting state. The formulation may alternatively include that income from shares paid by a company qualifies as a dividend and that income from other corporate rights qualifies, if, in the state of residence of the payer company, the income is treated in the same way as income from shares.

Under these treaties, a dividend paid to a dividend right holder, which is not a shareholder, may be treated as a dividend only if the broad interpretation described above is followed. A dividend right is not a share or other corporate right and it is also not an arrangement carrying the right to participate in profits. A dividend right gives a right to participate in dividend distributions, but does not give a general right to participate in company profits.

The proceeds from the alienation of a dividend right may qualify under these treaties as a dividend, but only if it is income from a right or income from an arrangement carrying the right to participate in profits, treated as a dividend under the domestic law of the source state. The proceeds from the alienation of dividend rights clearly do not constitute such income, but, at most, constitute income from the alienation of such rights. Therefore, the proceeds from an alienation of a dividend right do not qualify as a dividend but as income from the alienation of moveable property under the treaties. The proceeds from the alienation of a dividend right may only be taxed in the state of residence of the alienor. Therefore, although the source state would treat such proceeds as a dividend under its domestic law, the treaties do not allow taxation in the source state.

[5] **Conclusions**

The tax benefits of dividend stripping, in the form of a transfer of dividend rights by a shareholder retaining the shares, are effectively eliminated under the domestic tax laws of many countries. The states either tax the shareholder for the dividend actually paid to the holder of the dividend right or tax the proceeds from the alienation of the dividend right as a dividend. Under domestic law, the proceeds from the alienation of dividend rights, thus, may or may not be taxed as a dividend depending upon the approach.

The fact that different approaches are applied may lead to a situation where in the state of residence of the alienor of the dividend right and in the state of residence of the purchaser of such a right, the proceeds from the alienation are classified inconsistently. One of the states may treat such proceeds as a dividend and the other may treat the proceeds under the domestic tax law system concerning the alienation of property.

Such inconsistency should not, however, lead to unsolved classification conflicts under tax treaties.

The proceeds from the alienation of dividend rights, separate from the shares to which they belong, do not qualify as a dividend but as capital gains under most tax treaties. Such proceeds are not income from shares or from other corporate rights, but rather income from the alienation of a right. Despite the dividend classification of the source state, the proceeds may, therefore, only be taxed in the state of residence of the alienor. Only under some treaties may the proceeds from the alienation of dividend rights be treated as a dividend. Also, under these treaties, dividend treatment is possible usually only to the extent that the income is paid by a company and is treated as a dividend in the source state. In such a situation, the state of residence of the alienor must eliminate double taxation in accordance with the tax treaty rules concerning a dividend.

In practice, many treaties distort the domestic law approach, which treats the proceeds from the alienation of a dividend right as a dividend. Because tax treaties hinder source state taxes with respect to the proceeds from the alienation of dividend rights, dividend withholding tax may be avoided by transferring a dividend right to a resident of the same state in which the company where the transferor is a shareholder is a resident.

It may be argued, however, that the separation of dividend rights from shares is an arrangement with the sole purpose of avoiding dividend withholding tax. Therefore, it may be argued that dividend withholding tax may be imposed in spite of a treaty.

The extent to which domestic anti-avoidance provisions may be applied in a tax treaty situation is not perfectly clear in cases where the applicable treaty does not expressly refer to such provisions.[23] The threshold for the application of domestic anti-avoidance provisions to deny treaty benefits, in any case, should be high because tax treaties bind the contracting states. The OECD correctly mentions that, in the light of Articles 26 and 27 of the Vienna Convention on the Law of Treaties, tax treaty provisions prevail over domestic anti-avoidance provisions. If the application of a domestic anti-abuse rule has the effect of allowing a contracting state to tax income that the state is not allowed to tax under the provisions of the applicable tax treaty, the application of the domestic law provision would conflict with the treaty and thus cannot be applied.[24] The OECD acknowledges that it would be preferable to include an anti-avoidance provisions in tax treaties themself in order to secure the possibility of attacking tax avoidance arrangements in tax treaty situations.[25]

Many authors, however, seem to be of the opinion that, normally, the application of domestic anti-avoidance provisions is allowed to deny tax treaty benefits even though the tax treaty concerned does not mention such provisions.[26] For example,

---

23. See e.g., Helminen (2016d), 260–263 and Krever (2016), 14–16.
24. See OECD (2014), Public Discussion Draft, BEPS Action 6: Preventing the Granting of Treaty Benefits in Inappropriate Circumstances, 14 Mar. 2014 – 9 Apr. 2014, footnote 12.
25. Id., p. 22.
26. See paras 9.1–9.4 and 22.1–22.2 of the Commentary on Art. 1 of the OECD Model; and International Fiscal Association (1994a), 11 and 12 and OECD (1987a), 70, VM 1994:13 14, Theisen and Wenz (1996), 202.

where the form of an arrangement is disregarded and replaced with another on the basis of a domestic anti-avoidance provision for domestic tax law purposes, the tax treaty benefits available are also considered to depend on this true nature of the transaction.

The Commentary on the OECD Model also mentions that tax treaty benefits should not be available where obtaining tax benefits is the main purpose of a transaction or an arrangement and the tax benefit in the circumstances would be contrary to the object and purpose of the relevant provisions.[27]

There is an agreement that a general anti-avoidance provision based on the principal purposes of transactions or arrangements (principal purpose test) will be included in the OECD Model as a result of the OECD/G20 BEPS project.[28] Under that rule, if one of the principal purposes of transactions or arrangements is to obtain treaty benefits, these benefits will be denied unless it is established that granting these benefits is in accordance with the object and purpose of the provisions of the treaty.[29]

The application of domestic anti-avoidance provisions increases the risk of such double taxation that can be considered to be in conflict with the purpose of tax treaties. The state of residence of the alienor of a dividend right may not accept the classification of the other state based on a domestic law anti-avoidance provision, and, therefore, does not eliminate double taxation with respect to the withholding tax imposed by the other state.

Because of the above-mentioned problems caused by the approach treating the proceeds from the alienation of a dividend right as a dividend, such an approach is not recommendable. Dividend stripping, in the form of the transfer of dividend rights separately from shares, may better be avoided by taxing a dividend as the income of the shareholder even though the dividend right would be transferred to another person. The approach, under which a dividend is taxed as the income of the shareholder that has transferred dividend rights to another person, functions best in purely domestic situations and also in both treaty and non-treaty cross-border situations.

[B] Substitute Payments under Equity Securities Lending Transactions

[1] Introduction

The legal forms of a sale, an exchange or a lending of shares may be used for several transactions that actually neutralize each other. Shares of a company may be transferred with the knowledge of the parties that the same or similar shares will at some point in the future be returned to the original owner. Such transactions change the owner of shares only temporarily. By means of such transactions, a non-resident

---

27. Paragraph 9.5 of the Commentary on Art. 1 of the OECD Model.
28. *See* OECD (2015), 54–68. *See also* Part III of the Multilateral Convention to Implement Tax Treaty Related Measures to Prevent Base Erosion and Profit Shifting. The text of the Convention was published on 24 November and it will have to be signed and ratified before it will enter into force.
29. *See* OECD (2015), 54–68.

shareholder may convert a foreign-source dividend into a type of income not subject to withholding tax and may take advantage of a foreign law dividend taxation system, the advantages of which would not be otherwise available.

In a transfer of company shares, it is necessary to determine whether the dividend on the transferred shares is taxed as the income of the transferor or the transferee. This question of the right tax subject, however, is beyond the scope of this study. With respect to this study, the tax classification of the payments made by the transferee to the transferor as consideration for the dividend, instead, is relevant. The question is to what extent may such dividend equivalent payments in connection with different equity securities lending transactions be and actually are classified as a dividend for purposes of the different legal systems of international tax law.

Two basic structures of equity securities lending transactions may be distinguished, that is, the securities loan and the securities repurchase transaction. An equity securities loan means the transfer of title to certain equity securities from a lender to a borrower for a fee where the borrower is obliged to return securities of like kind and quantity to the lender after a certain period of time.[30] A securities loan is a loan of securities combined with a collateral of cash from the borrower to the lender, equal to the value of the lent stock.[31] Under such an arrangement, the borrower pays the lender substitute payments, that is, amounts equal to the dividend that the borrower received during the loan period.[32] In contrast, the lender makes periodic payments to the borrower equal to a market-rate interest on the collateral.[33]

The other basic form of securities lending transactions is the share repurchase transaction. In a repurchase transaction, securities are sold at one time for payment of the full value of the securities, and bought back at a later point, often after a dividend distribution, for another payment of the full value of the securities combined with an amount that reflects the time value of the money. The original owner is also compensated for the dividend received by the purchaser during the time span of the arrangement.[34]

---

30. *See*, for example, Daniels (1993), 1-2.
31. *See*, for example, Hariton (1994a), 1051.
32. *See* Gareis et al. (1993), 132 and Avi-Yonah and Swartz (1997), 790. Sometimes, substitute payments are also referred to as 'in lieu of payments' or as 'a manufactured dividend'. *See* Fink, Ferraro and Mann (1994a), 51 and Daniels (1993), 9.
33. In practice, a securities lending transaction usually involves, in addition to the lender and the borrower, an agent between the two, who has a securities lending programme established to facilitate such transactions. Securities loans, either in standardized or non-standardized form, have become more and more popular. *See* for the rapid growth in the area in the early nineties Cordner (1992), 2. Equity securities loans are used especially to hinder disturbance situations in stock trading. By equity securities loans in time stock transfers may be secured. To the equity investor, equity securities loans bring some additional returns on the investment. Instead the borrower may, for example, search for additional voting rights, for the loan period. The basic interest often is to benefit from the changes in the market value of the shares. *See* for these and other non-tax reasons for the use of equity security loans, for example, HE 218/1997, Cordner (1992), 3, May and Fox (1992), 37, Penn (1993), 927, Ikkala et al. (1997), 359 and Keinonen (1998), 157.
34. A repurchase transaction may be carried out either through the stock exchange in standardized form or bilaterally between two persons. *See*, for example, Bippus (1994), 949-952. A sale and repurchase transaction may also be combined with, for example, options in order to avoid

Securities lending transactions allow the lender or the seller/repurchaser to gain, as a return on an equity investment, dividend equivalent payments, but in the form of payments that may not be subject to tax in the source state.

Because of the nature of securities lending transactions, it may be asked whether the different transfers in such arrangements should be viewed separately from each other or should the different transfers be viewed as a whole. With respect to dividend equivalent payments, the separate transaction approach[35] would mean that the payments would not constitute a dividend but rather some other kind of income. Dividend classification is not possible because the payment is not made on the equity investment on the grounds of a shareholder relationship from a corporation to its shareholder. If this approach is followed, only payments deviating from arm's length prices may be taxed as a constructive dividend if the economic benefit moves from a corporation to its shareholder.

In the linked approach,[36] dividend equivalent payments may be taxed as a dividend. The securities lending arrangement, as a whole, produces a relationship, which is comparable to a dividend-constituting relationship. One possible approach to deal with dividend equivalent payments is the so-called look-through approach. Under this approach, substitute payments may be taxed as a dividend even though the amount of the payment would be at arm's length because the classification of the payment is made following the underlying transaction.[37]

[2] Domestic Tax Laws

In many countries, there are no special rules determining the right taxpayer for the dividend with respect to securities lending transactions, but the general principles of assignment of income are applied. It follows from the general principles that a dividend that has already been declared before a share transfer is taxed as the income of the person that owned the shares at the time that the dividend-distribution decision was made. Only a dividend declared after a transfer may be taxed as the income of the new owner. The borrower or buyer is regarded as being the owner of the shares during the time span of the arrangements if the shares are not transferred further. Therefore,

---

    exchange rate risks. *See* Bippus (1994), 950–951. In the basic form of a repurchase transaction, the buyer of the securities is obliged to retransfer the equivalent securities (full repurchase transaction), but sometimes the buyer is not obligated but only entitled to retransfer the securities (limited repurchase transaction). *See* Mettenheimer (1991), 12. Among other non-tax reasons, repurchase transactions are often used in order to receive short-term finance, to gain additional income on capital or to hinder disturbance situations in share trading. *See* HE 218/1997 and Keinonen (1998), 159–160. The same result as through the sale and repurchase of shares against cash may be achieved through an exchange and re-exchange of shares on which dividend is distributed and other shares, or other exchange and re-exchange transactions. *See* Bippus (1994), 950–952. Because these are actually only modifications of the basic buy and repurchase transactions against cash, these are not discussed further in this study.

35. *See* Plambeck et al. (1995), 667, which refers to this approach as the 'separate transaction principle'.
36. *See* Plambeck et al. (1995), 668.
37. *See* for the different approaches Warren (1993), 474–477, Plambeck et al. (1995), 667–668 and Weisbach (1995), 492, 507–519 and 526–538.

dividend received during the time span of the arrangement is taxable income for the borrower or buyer.

Even in the countries that do not have specific provisions concerning securities lending transactions, it is possible that in a clear tax avoidance situation, the seller or lender is taxed for a dividend instead of the buyer or borrower. This treatment may be based on the general anti-avoidance rules. Some countries, instead, have specific provisions determining the tax subject of the dividend payments made in the course of a securities lending transaction.

It varies whether countries treat substitute payments made under securities lending transactions as dividends or as some other type of taxable or non-taxable income. The classification and the tax treatment of the substitute payments may be based on specific provisions or on general principles of domestic tax law. Dividend withholding tax may be avoided in those countries that do not classify substitute payments as dividends. Based on anti-avoidance provisions, it is, however, possible that source state tax is levied even in those countries where the dividend classification does not apply. Source state withholding tax may be levied if the securities lending transaction was made in order to avoid dividend tax.

[3] The EU Parent-Subsidiary Directive

The P-S Directive applies to distributions from a qualifying subsidiary to a qualifying parent company, made by virtue of the association between the companies.[38] The P-S Directive benefits are available to the borrower or buyer in securities lending transactions to the extent that the borrower or buyer is a qualifying company resident in an EU Member State that is distinct from the one where the distributing company is a resident. Excluding certain cases involving a dual-residence conflict or a permanent establishment, the P-S Directive benefits are not available if the borrower or buyer is a resident in the same state as the distributing company.[39]

Article 3(2) of the P-S Directive allows Member States to deny the Directive benefits if a 10% holding is not maintained for an uninterrupted period of at least two years. This requirement allows the Member States to hinder taxpayers from benefiting from the P-S Directive through artificial arrangements in situations where the P-S Directive benefits should actually not be available.[40] Thus, in situations where a company purchases and then, shortly after a distribution, alienates shares that constitute the required participation, the P-S Directive benefits may be denied.

The P-S Directive is inapplicable to substitute dividend payments. The borrower or the buyer in securities lending transactions is not necessarily a company, and even

---

38. Articles 1–5 of the P-S Directive.
39. A dual-residence conflict situation or a situation in which the distribution is connected with a permanent establishment in another Member State may come under the scope of the P-S Directive even though strictly speaking the two companies would be from the same Member State. *See* Helminen (2015), 164 about these situations.
40. *See* Helminen (2015), 167 about the two-year holding period and joined cases C-283/94, C-291/94 and C-292/94 *Denkavit* on the interpretation of the P-S Directive article concerning the two-year period.

if it was, a parent-subsidiary relationship does not necessarily exist between the lender and borrower or the seller and buyer. Even if such relationship did exist, substitute dividend payments are not paid on the grounds of a parent-subsidiary relationship. Rather, the payment is made because of the contractual relationship between the two persons. A substitute dividend, thus, does not qualify for the benefits of the P-S Directive.

A substitute dividend may qualify for the benefits of the P-S Directive only if paid between two qualifying companies in a qualifying relationship to the extent that the amount of the payment deviates from an arm's length price and, therefore, constitutes a constructive dividend. The P-S Directive, generally, does not hinder the imposition of withholding tax on substitute dividend payments even though paid between companies resident in two different EU Member States. Neither does it hinder the state of residence of the recipient of such payments from taxing such payments.

In practice, the Member States, which do not treat a substitute dividend as a dividend under domestic law, do not apply the domestic law rules implementing the P-S Directive to a substitute dividend. Instead, many Member States, which treat a substitute dividend as a dividend, apply their domestic law implementing rules of the P-S Directive also to the substitute payments. There is, however, no requirement to extend the P-S Directive benefits unilaterally to substitute payments. It is also important to note that the P-S Directive benefits must not be made available to deductible payments.[41]

[4] Tax Treaties

A substitute dividend may qualify under tax treaties as business profits under an article similar to Article 7 of the OECD Model or it may qualify as other income, under an article similar to the other income article in Article 21 of the OECD Model. The payments qualify as business profits where the lender trades securities in the course of its regular business. The payments qualify as other income in situations where the securities lending transaction does not constitute business activity but, rather, only investment activity, and where a substitute dividend does not qualify under any other article of the applicable treaty. Because Article 10 of the OECD Model takes precedence over other income type articles, if substitute dividend payments qualify as a dividend under Article 10, the payments must be taxed in accordance with Article 10, instead of the other articles.

From the dividend definition of Article 10(3) of the OECD Model, it follows that a dividend must be income from corporate rights. The recipient of substitute dividend payments is not, strictly speaking, a shareholder and the substitute payments do not derive from corporate rights, but, instead, are based on a lending contract. Therefore, although substitute payments are determined by following the amount of a dividend distributed on the transferred shares, a substitute payment, in and of itself, is not

---

41. Article 4(1)(a) of the P-S Directive. This prohibition concerns the treatment in the state of the parent company or the permanent establishment with which the dividend is connected.

income from corporate rights. A substitute dividend may, therefore, qualify as a dividend under the OECD Model, generally, only if paid between qualifying companies in a qualifying relationship to the extent that the amount of the payments differs from an arm's length price and, therefore, constitutes a constructive dividend.

With respect to situations where substitute payments are treated as a dividend under the domestic tax law of the payer, some authors are of the opinion that a substitute dividend should also qualify as a dividend under tax treaties.[42] This interpretation is, however, only true with respect to the treaties following the US Model, the wording of which does not refer to corporate rights. The wording of the dividend definition of the OECD Model requires a dividend to be income from corporate rights. Because a substitute dividend is not income from corporate rights, it does not qualify as a dividend under the OECD Model, even though it is taxed as a dividend in the state of residence of the payer.

Securities lending transactions are often used in order to avoid dividend withholding tax, which, in the absence of the arrangement, would be imposed. The domestic law rules that treat substitute dividend payments as a dividend may, therefore, be viewed as anti-avoidance rules. It, thus, may be argued that domestic law classification should also be respected for tax treaty purposes, at least if a tax treaty includes an express reference to domestic anti-avoidance provisions.[43] This argument, however, is weak with respect to dividend-stripping situations where the actual distributing company and the share purchaser or borrower are residents in the same state, because, in such situations, the state is allowed to tax the domestic dividend in any case.

The tax treaty treatment of a substitute dividend as income that may be taxed only in the state of residence of the recipient does not hinder the source state from treating such income as a substitute dividend for domestic law purposes. The tax treaty treatment only hinders the state from subjecting the recipient of the substitute dividend to dividend withholding tax. Thus, the taxing right in the state of residence of the distributing company may be satisfactorily safeguarded even though the substitute dividend would not be treated as a dividend under a tax treaty. The same argument applies with respect to situations where the borrower or purchaser is a resident in a third state. Then, the state of residence of the distributing company may impose a withholding tax on the distribution made to the third state.

If the state of residence of the actual dividend-distributing entity wants to subject the non-resident person to tax, it seems more logical to argue that, based on the substance-over-form principle or based on anti-avoidance principles, the non-resident lender or seller of shares is the actual recipient of the dividend. This approach does not require changing the classification of the substitute dividend. The state deems a distribution to have been made from the distributing company to the non-resident

---

42. *See* e.g., Hariton (1994a), 1056.
43. *See* for the relationship between domestic anti-avoidance provisions and tax treaties, Ch. 6 s. §6.03[A][5].

lender or seller instead of to the resident borrower or purchaser. This fictive distribution is income from corporate rights and, therefore, qualifies as a dividend under a tax treaty.

This approach, however, requires respect for the domestic substance-over-form or the anti-avoidance principles for tax treaty purposes. The approach should, thus, be allowed at least with respect to treaties that expressly allow the use of domestic anti-avoidance provisions. This approach, however, easily leads to double taxation. The state of residence of the recipient of the fictive income may not eliminate double taxation with respect to the withholding tax imposed in the state of residence of the distributing company because, in its view, there has been no fictive distribution.

The dividend definition of Article 10(3) of the OECD Model, if strictly interpreted, does not cover substitute dividend payments. In order to avoid classification conflicts, it is suggested that substitute dividend payments not be taxed as a dividend under tax treaties, which follow the wording of the OECD Model. If two contracting states wish to treat a substitute dividend as a dividend for tax treaty purposes, such treatment should be expressly mentioned in a tax treaty.

If substitute dividend payments are expressly mentioned as a dividend in a dividend article of an actual tax treaty, they may be taxed as a dividend even though they are not paid by a company. If substitute dividend payments are expressly mentioned in a dividend article which otherwise follows Article 10 of the OECD Model, the context of the article may be said to require a definition deviating from the definition of Article 3(1)(b) of the term 'company'. The best solution would be to expressly state that such payments are treated as a dividend whether or not paid by a company if the intention is to include a substitute dividend paid by any person.

Another possibility is to use wording in line with Article 10(7) of the US Model, instead of the wording of the dividend article of the OECD Model. The wording of the US Model may be interpreted as including substitute dividend payments on securities lending contracts to the extent that such payments are taxed as a dividend in the state of residence of the borrower or purchaser. It is suggested, however, that if it is intended that the substitute dividend be treated as a dividend, it should be indicated expressly.

Under many actual treaties, only income from a company qualifies as a dividend. A dividend must also be income from shares. Income from other corporate rights qualifies if the state of residence of the company paying the income treats the income the same way as income from shares. In addition, the dividend definition covers income from any arrangements carrying the right to participate in profits to the extent so characterized under the laws of the contracting state. Under some other treaties, instead, income from shares paid by a company qualifies as a dividend. Income from other corporate rights also qualifies as a dividend if, in the state of residence of the payer company, the income is treated the same way as income from shares.

A substitute dividend does not qualify under any part of the above definitions even though it is paid by a company. It is neither income from corporate rights, nor income from an arrangement participating in profits. The fact that the amount of the payment depends on the amount of the dividend paid by another company does not make a share-lending agreement an arrangement participating in profits. Therefore, even though the countries would treat a substitute dividend as a dividend under their domestic laws, it does not qualify as such under these treaties. Dividend withholding tax, thus, must not be imposed on a substitute dividend. The treaties do not otherwise hinder the treatment of a substitute dividend as a dividend for domestic law purposes.

The dividend definition of some actual treaties include income from shares paid by a company or any income paid by a company if the state of residence of the payer taxes such income the same way as income from shares. The dividend definition of the Nordic multilateral treaty includes income from shares or other rights participating in profits paid by a company qualifies as a dividend. In addition, any income paid by a company treated in the source state the same way as a dividend is covered by the dividend definition.

Because under these treaties the reference to domestic law treatment does not require a dividend to be income from corporate rights, a substitute dividend qualifies as a dividend under these treaties as long as it is paid by a company and treated in the same way as a dividend in the state of residence of the payer company. The source state is allowed to impose withholding tax on a substitute dividend if the payer is a company.

It, however, would be somewhat peculiar to impose withholding tax on a substitute dividend paid by companies, but not on a substitute dividend paid by other persons. Such treatment would be peculiar especially because under many treaties the imposition of withholding tax is not possible with respect to a direct investment dividend. Withholding tax, thus, could only be imposed with respect to a substitute dividend paid by a company to an individual or to a company that does not fulfil the direct investment holding requirement. Withholding taxation could, therefore, rather easily be avoided anyway. Different treatment of individuals and companies as the borrower or the purchaser of shares, under a securities lending transaction, also distorts competition between the individuals and the companies operating in the business. Therefore, the countries should not impose withholding tax on substitute dividend even in those cases allowed by the treaties.

The most problematic treaties with respect to the substitute dividends are the ones in which the dividend definition covers income paid by a company from shares or from other rights participating in profits and income from other rights taxed the same way as income from shares in the state of residence of the distributing company. A substitute dividend is not income from shares or income from other rights participating in profits. It may qualify as a dividend only if it is income from other rights taxed in the state of residence of the payer the same way as income from shares is taxed. This raises the question of whether a substitute dividend is income from a right. It may be argued that this kind of right is not the kind meant by the treaty because the payment of a substitute dividend may only be based on an agreement between the lender and borrower. In many cases, a substitute dividend is, however, clearly income from a right and should, therefore, be taxed as a dividend under the treaty if taxed as a dividend in the source state.

It follows from the requirement that a dividend is paid from a company that, in any case, a substitute dividend may qualify as a dividend under these treaties only if the borrower or purchaser of shares is a company. In any case, if the source state levies a withholding tax, it may also be asked whether the other country must eliminate double taxation as the state of residence of the recipient of a substitute dividend with respect to the dividend withholding tax imposed. It seems that the elimination cannot be required because it is unclear whether a substitute dividend may be regarded as income from a right at all and whether it therefore was in accordance with the tax treaty to levy withholding tax.

[5] Conclusions

The classification of a substitute dividend payment for the purposes of the domestic tax law of different states varies. Some states treat a substitute dividend as a dividend, whereas some states do not classify a substitute dividend as a dividend. Differing domestic law classifications of a substitute dividend may lead to inconsistent classification in cross-border situations.

The P-S Directive does not require the exemption of a substitute dividend because it is not paid on the grounds of a parent company's association with its subsidiary. However, under domestic laws the benefits similar to the P-S Directive benefits may be extended to substitute dividends.

Tax treaties are different with respect to the classification of a substitute dividend but most treaties require that a dividend is income paid by a company. This requirement hinders the classification of a substitute dividend as a dividend if the payer is not a company. Under many treaties, a substitute dividend does not qualify as a dividend because a substitute dividend is not income from corporate rights or income from an arrangement participating in profits. Actual unsolved classification conflicts, thus, usually do not emerge.

The tax treaty treatment does not, however, hinder the states from treating a substitute dividend as a dividend under their domestic laws, but only hinders the states, in their capacity as source state, from subjecting the recipient of such income to tax. Domestic law classifications should not lead to actual classification conflicts provided that each of the states agree that a substitute dividend is neither income from corporate rights nor income from arrangements participating in profits. If the source state interprets this aspect of the treaty differently and imposes dividend withholding tax, it is difficult to require that double taxation be eliminated with respect to this withholding tax. The interpretation of the source state is not a proper application of the treaty.

Under some treaties, a substitute dividend may be classified as a dividend if it is regarded as being income from a right taxed in the same way as income from shares in the source state. Because there may be differences of opinion on the subject of whether a substitute dividend is income from a right, actual classification conflicts may emerge. Due to this uncertainty, the state of residence of the recipient of a substitute dividend may not eliminate double taxation with respect to possible withholding tax imposed in the source state. The residence state may consider that the treaty is not properly applied in the source state.

Under some treaties, a substitute dividend may be treated as a dividend if so classified in the source state. Actual classification conflicts should not emerge under these treaties. If the source state imposes a withholding tax on a substitute dividend

[C] Dividend Equivalent Payments from Derivative Financial Instruments

[1] Introduction

Financial instruments may be categorized as basic or primary instruments and derivatives. The basic instruments cover various debt and equity instruments, whereas derivatives include '...rights and obligations to transfer or exchange specified cash flows at a predetermined time in the future...'.[44] A derivative instrument is a contractual right that derives its value from the value of something else, such as a debt security, equity, commodity or a specified index.[45] Under a derivative financial instrument, the payment rights and obligations of the parties derive from the value of an underlying cash or physical market or from particular financial indices.[46]

An essential difference between basic financial instruments and derivative financial instruments is that derivative financial instruments do not generally require the payment of capital other than the payment of a premium at the time the contract is entered into. Unlike basic debt and equity securities, derivatives generally do not involve a return on an initial investment.[47]

Because a dividend, in general, is a payment on an equity investment, derivative financial instruments do not directly generate a dividend. Derivative financial instruments, generally, are therefore beyond the scope of this study.[48] Income from derivative financial instruments may be regarded as constituting a dividend only in situations where derivative financial instruments are used in order to avoid dividend taxation. An interest rate swap, for example, may be used to replace interest that otherwise would have been subject to thin capitalization rules under which the interest would have been reclassified as a dividend.[49]

Derivative financial instruments are interesting with respect to this study in the sense that they may be used to produce synthetic equity and dividend equivalent

---

44. *See*, for example, Lyons (1996), 1195. Derivatives are, generally, used to manage the risks of future contingencies. *See* Reinhold (1992), 1186, for the risk transfer as the thematic link joining notional principal contracts. Financial instruments may be categorized by their functions as price risk transferring instruments, credit risk transferring instruments, liquidity enhancing instruments, credit generating instruments or equity generating instruments. *See* OECD (1994), 8.
45. OECD (1994), 8 and OECD (1997), 598.
46. *See* Plambeck (1995), 661. In this respect, securities lending arrangements are also derivative instruments.
47. OECD (1997), 598. As noted in OECD (1994), 36, the dividing line between basic financial instruments and financial derivatives is not completely clear.
48. For comprehensive coverage of taxation of derivative financial instruments, *see* OECD (1994) or International Fiscal Association (1995).
49. *See* for tax avoidance in the means of derivative financial instruments OECD (1994), 13 and Keinonen (1995), 180.

payments. Derivative financial instruments may be used to produce income that very closely resembles a return on equity in its economic substance. The question may be asked as to what extent dividend equivalent payments may be and actually are taxed as a dividend under the different legal systems of international tax law.

The term 'derivative financial instrument' covers option contracts, forward contracts, future contracts, swap contracts, caps, floors, collars and other similar instruments.[50] The basic forms of derivative instruments are options and forwards. An option is an agreement that confers upon the buyer the right to buy or sell a specific quantity of an underlying stock at a specific price on a specified future date or during an agreed time period, but does not obligate the buyer to do so.[51] The option to buy is generally referred to as a call option and the option to sell as a put option. A forward is a contractual obligation to buy or sell a specific amount of the underlying stock or other commodity on a specific future date at a set price. A future is a standardized form of a forward contract traded on organized exchanges.[52]

The term 'notional principal contract' is often used to refer to a series of option or forward contracts. Notional principal contracts include swaps, caps, floors and collars, whereby one or more parties agree to make periodic payments reflecting the value of a specific variable index applied to an agreed-upon notional principal amount.[53] Swaps, generally, are a series of forwards. Swaps require parties to make and receive payments unconditionally. A swap is an agreement of exchanges of cash streams based on notional principal amounts and specified indices. An equity swap includes exchanges of payments based on the value of a specific stock or an equity index.[54]

Caps are merely a series of options. Caps are contracts whereby a seller makes periodic payments equal to the product of a notional principal amount and any excess of a specified index over the agreed level. The buyer pays a premium or makes a series of fixed periodic payments for the contract. A cap is a form of an interest rate guarantee whereby a borrower may limit the cost of variable rate loans by an agreed formula.[55]

Floors are merely a series of options. A floor is a form of an interest rate guarantee contract whereby a seller makes periodic payments equal to the product of a notional principal amount and any amount by which a specified index falls below a specific level. The buyer pays a single premium or makes a series of fixed periodic payments for the contract. By using floors, the lender may guard against a fall in interest rates. A floor is, thus, actually the reverse of a cap.[56]

---

50. *See also* e.g., Weidmann (2015), 7–11 for different types of derivatives.
51. The term 'underlying' means the reference point for computing the payments under a derivative financial instrument. *See* Plambeck et al. (1995), 661. *See* for options Keinonen (1995), 169, Plambeck et al. (1995), 663, OECD (1994), 19, RSV Rapport 1996:1 23 and Avi-Yonah and Swartz (1997), 794.
52. *See* OECD (1994), 108, Plambeck et al. (1995), 661–662, RSV Rapport 1996:1 23 and Avi-Yonah and Swartz (1997), 794 and 796.
53. *See* for the term 'notional principal contract' Avi-Yonah and Swartz (1997), 787 and Plambeck et al. (1995), 665.
54. Swaps are designed to exploit the different rating in different financial markets of two counterparts with complementary needs. *See* for swaps OECD (1994), 111 and RSV Rapport 1996:1 23–24.
55. OECD (1994), 107.
56. *Ibid.*, 108.

Chapter 6: Dividend-Stripping and the Dividend-Generating Relationship §6.03[C]

Collars, generally, are interest rate guarantees combining a cap and a floor agreement. In a collar agreement, a party purchases a cap and sells a floor, or purchases a floor and sells a cap. It protects two parties against changes in interest rates. If the interest rate is above the collar, one of the parties must make payments under the cap. If the rate is below the collar, the other party makes payments under the floor.[57]

Generally, with notional principal contracts, three types of income are received. These are periodic payments, non-periodic payments and termination payments.[58] These payments do not, as such, constitute a dividend. Income from derivative financial instruments is not income from corporate rights paid by a company to one of its shareholders. Derivative instruments may, however, be used to produce a situation economically similar to an equity investment but producing dividend equivalent income instead of an actual dividend. Derivatives may be used to receive dividend equivalent return without an actual investment in shares.

Derivative contracts that replicate the behaviour of shares of one or more issuers may be referred to as equity derivatives,[59] or as synthetic equity. Equity derivatives may produce a dividend equivalent income. Economic equivalents to a dividend may be received, for example, by buying a buy-option and by selling a sell-option.[60] Derivative financial instruments may also be used to swap dividend-paying stocks for a right to receive payments measured by the dividend paid on such stock.[61] By means of such arrangements, a non-resident may gain an economic benefit corresponding to the value of the dividend distributed on the shares of a corporation. The person may receive a return economically equivalent to the dividend on the shares of the company, but may avoid dividend withholding tax.[62]

The creation of synthetic equity is based on the deconstruction of financial instruments into different components of value. For example, because the bondholder has the right to receive principal and interest, a bond, economically equals principal plus interest or $B = P + I$. A stockholder has an equity or principal investment and the right to a dividend, equity, equals principal plus dividend or $E = P + D$. The buyer under a forward contract has the right to receive property and the obligation to pay the purchase price. Between the contract date and the forward date, the buyer has the use of its money, and the seller receives a dividend from the property. The forward price gives the buyer the benefit of the expected dividend and the burden of the implicit interest. A forward, therefore, represents dividend minus interest or $F = D - I$. Similarly, call options and put options may be expressed in the form of an equation with interest and dividend.[63] From these equations, it can be seen that forwards may be used to convert equity to debt and debt to equity. A bond may be created by selling equity forward, because $E - F = (P + D) - (D - I) = P + I = B$, whereas equity may

---

57. See ibid., 107. See also Plambeck et al. (1995), 665–667, for the operating of swaps, caps, floors and collars.
58. See Avi-Yonah and Swartz (1997), 788.
59. See Sheppard (1992), 119.
60. See for synthetic equity in the form of buy and sell options Keinonen (1998), 156 and 164.
61. See Avi-Yonah and Swartz (1997), 789.
62. See for the use of swaps for dividend stripping Bippus (1994), 951.
63. See May (1996), 1626–1627 and May (1997), 24–26.

be created by buying debt and a forward, because B + F = (P + I) + (D − I) = P + D = E.[64]

By means of a synthetic investment equivalent to equity, the return may be received as interest instead of as a dividend. For example, if a foreign investor would like to invest in the stock of a corporation, it may buy a bond and enter into a cash-settled forward contract to buy shares of the company on the maturity date of the bond. The investor gets a return on the investment economically similar to a stock investment in the form of interest instead of a dividend.[65] Therefore, in addition to many non-tax reasons, which would make synthetic instruments interesting, the instruments may also be used for tax avoidance purposes.[66]

The same economic outcome that may be achieved by the use of traditional instruments may also be achieved by synthetic instruments, but often with a lower tax burden. Source state withholding tax may be avoided by creating cash flows economically equivalent to income otherwise taxable. In cross-border relations, equity derivatives may be used for dividend stripping. If a non-resident person owns shares in a company, it is generally liable for the source state withholding tax on the dividend it receives on the shares. Derivative financial instruments may, therefore, be used in order to receive dividend equivalent payments reflecting the value of the actual dividend, but without any dividend withholding tax.[67]

A basic example of an instrument that may be used to produce dividend equivalent payments is an equity swap. They are often used to avoid dividend withholding tax.[68] In an equity swap, two parties agree to exchange a series of payments based on two separate indices. One of the parties makes periodic payments for a specified period of time. These payments are based on any increase in the value of a specified share index, a group of shares, or a single share, and the dividend on the shares and calculated as if a hypothetical principal amount had been invested in the shares comprising the index. The other party makes periodic payments based on a specified variable rate of interest and on any decrease in the value of the share index calculated with regard to the hypothetical principal amount.[69]

Equity swaps may be used as alternatives to repurchase contracts and securities loans to produce dividend equivalent income. A shareholder (S) of a corporation may

---

64. Forward contracts may be created synthetically, which produces further opportunities to convert debt to equity or equity to debt. For example, a forward contract = call option − put option. *See* May (1996), 1627 and Plambeck et al. (1995), 669–670, for different synthetics.
65. This example is a very simple one, but the same outcome may be received by different very complex equations. *See* for other more complex examples also involving call options, put options and swaps May (1996), 1628–1633 and May (1997), 27-2. *See also*, for examples of synthetic debt May (1997), 29–31.
66. Non-tax reasons for the use of derivative instruments to produce synthetic equity may be, for example, the avoidance of the cost of holding equity, the need to temporarily alter the mix of a portfolio of debt securities with equity returns, the attempt to speculate on price increases in the share markets or the avoidance of the limitations in foreign share holding. *See* Penn (1993), 921 for these and other non-tax reasons for creating synthetic equity.
67. *See* Sheppard (1992), 119 and Bippus (1994), 951.
68. *See* Sheppard (1992), 119, for how the use of equity swaps has become even more popular than the use of securities lending transactions for this purpose.
69. *See* Fink, Ferraro and Mann (1994a), 54 and Penn (1993), 917–918 and 919.

Chapter 6: Dividend-Stripping and the Dividend-Generating Relationship §6.03[C]

sell shares to another person (P2) for cash, using a third person (P3) as a broker, and entering into an equity swap with the third person (P3). Under the agreement, the other person (P2) makes a payment to the original shareholder (S) equal to an increase in the value of the shares, and the shareholder (S) makes a payment to the other person (P2) equal to a decrease in the value of the shares. The other person (P2) makes payments equal to the amount of the dividend paid on the shares to the original shareholder (S) and the original shareholder (S) makes payments reflecting the market rate of interest on the notional principal value equal to the value of the shares. Upon the termination of the contract, the original shareholder (S) will purchase shares of the same corporation using a third person (P3) again as a broker.[70]

Alternatively, dividend equivalent payments may be received in a compound swap. In such an arrangement, one person (A) holds certain stock and agrees to make dividend equivalent payments on the stock to another person (B), whereas the other person (B) holds other stock and agrees to make dividend equivalent payments on the other stock to the first person (A). In addition, a payment representing the net appreciation or depreciation on the two stocks will be made on the maturity date.[71]

The possibility of replicating any desired economic outcome by combining together new financial instruments and traditional instruments is a challenge for the tax legislator, the tax authorities and tax courts. They must solve how to classify income from synthetic instruments. Should a mix of a bond and a forward contract be treated according to its components as a bond and a forward contract or should the mix be characterized as equity because its economic substance is closer to equity? Should a return on the mix of the bond and the forward contract be characterized as a dividend?[72] Should the investor that uses synthetic equity be taxed like an equity investor because the investor's objective was to replicate an equity investment?[73]

Although a synthetic equity instrument may lead to a basic economic position similar to an actual equity investment, the instruments are not the same. It is clear that the payments that issue from equity swaps or from other synthetic equity are not an actual dividend. The recipient of dividend equivalent payments is not a shareholder in a dividend-distributing corporation and does not possess any of the typical shareholder rights. The synthetic instruments only create rights or claims of a party to a contract whereas only actual equity may create the legal position of a shareholder. An equity derivative investor does not put any capital into the shares of the corporation, the shareholding of which the derivative is replicating. A synthetic equity investment does not produce, for example, voting rights, liquidation privileges or other characteristics of share ownership. The holder of an equity swap does not own any corporate rights,

---

70. *See* for similar examples Schenk (1995), 597 and Bippus (1994), 951.
71. *Ibid.*
72. The problem is even more complex with respect to situations involving a mix of several basic and derivative instruments. Due to the limited scope of this study, only the situation of a bond attached with a forward contract as an economic equivalent of equity is discussed. The same principles apply to more complex situations. However, the more complex the mix of instruments, the harder it is to see the connection to equity. Therefore, the more complex the mix, the less realistic it is to characterize the mix as equity.
73. The problem with very complex instrument mixes is that it is often difficult to see the whole that the mix represents.

but only the amount of the return on the instrument is determined in accordance with the dividend paid on a certain stock.[74]

The risks of a holder of synthetic equity are different from those of a shareholder. The credit risks of a synthetic equity investment and an actual equity investment are also different. A synthetic equity instrument involves market risks because market changes may alter economic relationships. A synthetic equity instrument always involves greater legal risks because the legal classification or even the legal validity of a complex mix of instruments is unclear and may be different in different countries.[75] The tax advantages of receiving income not classified as a dividend in taxation, however, often leads to the choice of synthetic equity over actual equity, despite other disadvantages.[76]

Due to the nature of synthetic equity, it is questionable whether a derivative instrument used for the production of dividend equivalent payments may be viewed as a separate unit or as part of the underlying transaction or any other related transaction. In order to truly understand the economic substance of payments from derivative financial instruments, the instrument may have to be either segregated into its economic components or integrated with other instruments.

With respect to dividend equivalent payments, the separate transaction approach[77] would mean that the payments on derivatives do not constitute a dividend but some other kind of income. The payment is not made by a corporation to one of its shareholders on an equity investment on the grounds of a shareholder relationship. If this approach is followed, only payments that are not at arm's length may be taxed as a constructive dividend when the benefit is realized by the shareholder. In the bifurcation approach, instruments are split into underlying economic components and taxed accordingly. Bifurcation may also be referred to as the disaggregation approach. This approach means that if, for example, a forward represents interest and a dividend, the dividend component should be taxed as a dividend.

In the linked approach,[78] dividend equivalent payments may be taxed as a dividend because the arrangement as a whole produces a relationship that is comparable to a dividend-producing one. Separate transactions may be aggregated together and taxed as a unit if the separate transactions are economic components that together represent a dividend. This approach may also be referred to as the integration approach or the aggregation approach. One possible approach to deal with payments on derivative instruments that mimic dividend payments on stock is the so-called look-through approach. Payments on a derivative instrument could be classified according

---

74. *See* for these differences Schenk (1995), 598.
75. *See* for these differences Sheppard (1992), 121, Penn (1993), 918, 119 and 925, May (1996), 1633–1634 and May (1997), 31–32.
76. *See* Avi-Yonah and Swartz (1997), 789.
77. For example, in Plambeck et al. (1995), 667, this approach is referred to as the 'separate transaction principle'.
78. For example, Plambeck et al. (1995), 668 refers to this approach as the 'linked approach'.

to the return produced by the instrument to which the payment on the derivative economically corresponds.[79]

All the approaches involve difficulties. In the bifurcation approach, the valuation of the component parts may be difficult in practice and in the integration approach, the identification of the transactions that need to be integrated may be difficult.[80] The more complex the instruments used and the larger the number of instruments combined together, the more difficult is the taxation of the financial instruments. Basing the taxation of the return on synthetic instruments on the bifurcation approach is, in practice, almost impossible. The more complex the equation, the more difficult it is to divide the synthetic instrument into components, and then to tax the components separately.[81]

The integration approach is also difficult in practice. It seems unrealistic to combine various transactions in order to have a recognizable whole, and to tax the investors as if they had directly made the transaction as a whole.[82] A more realistic approach would be to tackle the problem with respect to the synthetic arrangements between related parties.[83] In practice, the separate transaction approach is the easiest to follow, but it easily leads to situations where economic equivalents are taxed differently.[84]

[2] Domestic Tax Laws

The tax treatment of derivative instruments may be very different in different countries. It varies whether there are specific provisions on derivatives or whether the treatment depends on general rules and principles of tax law. In most countries, a derivative instrument is generally recognized as a separate property right for tax purposes. It is, however, possible that a synthetic instrument, which combines a derivative instrument and an underlying physical instrument, may be treated as a whole. In tax avoidance situations, the form used may be ignored and the taxation may be carried out in line with the transaction that was mimicked.

---

79. *See* for the different approaches to tax derivative financial instruments Warren (1993), 474–477, Plambeck et al. (1995), 667–668 and Weisbach (1995), 492 and 507–519 and 526–538.
80. *See* for these two approaches, for example, Neighbour (1997), 934–935. For the practice with respect to these approaches in the United States, *see* Kau (1990), 1005–1007.
81. For example, Warren (1993), 477 points out that the approach '…involves a considerable administrative burden…'. Plambeck et al. (1995), 690 is also against the bifurcation approach because it produces uncertainty in taxation. Also, in the resolution of the International Fiscal Association on taxation of derivative financial instruments the complexity and uncertainty with respect to this approach is recognized. *See* International Fiscal Association (1995a), 82.
82. Warren (1993), 477 points out that the approach in the same way as the bifurcation approach 'involves a considerable administrative burden'. *See* for arguments for and against the integration approach and the bifurcation approach, Weisbach (1995), 493–494 and 521–526 and Strand (1995), 545–569.
83. This possibility is pointed out in May (1997), 33 and May (1996), 1635.
84. In the resolution of the International Fiscal Association on taxation of derivative financial instruments, both the separate transaction approach and the integration approach are viewed as acceptable. *See* International Fiscal Association (1995a), 81.

Dividend equivalent payments on derivative financial instruments ordinarily do not qualify as a dividend. Under the domestic law of many countries, dividend is considered to be a distribution of property made by a corporation to its shareholders out of the corporation's earnings and profits. In order for the dividend equivalent payment to qualify as a dividend, it should be a profit distribution and the recipient should be a shareholder of the distributing corporation. The distribution should affect the capital structure of the corporation and be a profit distribution on the recipient's investment in the corporation. Dividend classification does not apply because dividend equivalent payments on derivative financial instruments are not income paid by a corporation to its shareholders in their capacity as such.

In most countries, dividend equivalent payments on derivative financial instruments may be taxed as a dividend only if paid by a corporation to its shareholders to the extent that such payments differ from the arm's length standard. The part of a payment that does not differ from an arm's length payment may be treated as dividend in these countries only if the anti-avoidance provisions of the state concerned are applied. The number of states that would treat dividend equivalent payments on derivatives as dividend in other situations is limited. Non-resident investors may, thus, often avoid the source state dividend withholding tax by using synthetic equity. The OECD/G20 BEPS project, however, may lead to more limitations on the tax benefits based on the use of derivatives. The OECD, for example, proposes that hybrid mismatch situations related to financial instruments (including derivatives) and leading to a tax deduction combined with non-inclusion of income would be eliminated by specific hybrid mismatch rules.[85]

[3] The Parent-Subsidiary Directive

The P-S Directive applies to distributions from a qualifying subsidiary to a qualifying parent company, made by virtue of the association between the companies.[86] Therefore, the P-S Directive is not applicable with respect to dividend equivalent payments on equity derivatives. A qualifying parent-subsidiary relationship does not necessarily exist between the payer and the recipient of payments on equity derivatives. Even if such a relationship did exist, dividend equivalent payments are not paid on the grounds of the parent-subsidiary relationship, but, rather, due to the contractual relationship between the two persons. The fact that the amount of the payments depends on the dividend distributions of a company that is not a party to the contract does not mean that the payments are made by virtue of the parent-subsidiary relationship between the contracting parties. And in any case, the P-S Directive prevents the Directive benefits from deductible payments.[87]

---

85. *See* OECD (2015). *See also* Part II of the Multilateral Convention to Implement Tax Treaty Related Measures to Prevent Base Erosion and Profit Shifting. The text of the Convention was published on 24 November and it will have to be signed and ratified before it will enter into force.
86. Articles 1–5 of the P-S Directive.
87. Article 4(1)(a) of the P-S Directive.

Dividend equivalent payments may qualify for the benefits of the P-S Directive only if paid between qualifying companies in a qualifying relationship to the extent that the payment differs from an arm's length payment and constitutes a constructive dividend.

[4] Tax Treaties

The Model treaties do not include special rules concerning the treatment of derivative financial instruments. Income from derivative financial instruments may qualify under the Models either as business profits under Article 7 or as other income under Article 21. To the extent that the income is related to a trade or business, the income may qualify as business profits, and, in other situations, as other income.[88] Often, income from derivative financial instruments also constitutes capital gains within the meaning of Article 13 of the OECD Model or the other Models, because it is income from the alienation of property. This classification applies especially with respect to termination payments. Article 10 of the OECD Model, however, takes precedence over all the other income type articles. If income from derivative financial instruments qualifies as a dividend under Article 10, the payments must be taxed in accordance with Article 10 instead of the other articles.

Article 10(3) of the OECD Model requires that a dividend be income from corporate rights, which is income paid because of an equity investment in the distributing company. Derivative financial instruments are not corporate rights. Although the amount of dividend equivalent payments on equity derivatives is determined in accordance with actual dividend distributions, prices of shares or other indices derived from them, dividend equivalent payments on equity derivatives are not income from corporate rights. Although derivative financial instruments may be used to produce synthetic equity, dividend equivalent payments are not paid on an actual corporate right, but are based on a contractual relationship. Synthetic equity is not a share or other corporate right meant by the dividend article of the OECD Model, namely, Article 10(3).

Under the OECD Model, dividend equivalent payments from equity derivatives may qualify as a dividend only if paid between qualifying companies in a qualifying relationship to the extent that the amount of the payments differs from the arm's length standard and, therefore, constitutes a constructive dividend.[89]

With respect to situations in which dividend equivalent payments are treated as a dividend under the domestic tax law of the payer of such payments, some authors are of the opinion that the payments may also qualify as a dividend under tax treaties.[90] This interpretation seems to be correct in regard to the US Model. Article 10(5) does not

---

88. *See* the Technical Explanation 1996, Art. 7, para. 103 and Art. 21, para. 274 and the Technical Explanation 2006, Art. 21, para. 296.
89. *See* para. 7 of the Commentary on Art. 21 of the OECD Model according to which the countries may add a separate paragraph to Art. 21 clarifying the treatment of non-arm's length payments in relation to derivative financial instruments.
90. *See* for this opinion, for example, Doernberg and van Raad (1997), 2 and Penn (1993), 933.

require, autonomously interpreted, that the income, taxed in the source state in the same way as a dividend is taxed, to be income from corporate rights.[91] In order to avoid classification conflicts, it is suggested, however, that such payments are expressly mentioned in a tax treaty's dividend article if the contracting states intends to tax the payments as a dividend.

Equity derivatives may be used in order to avoid dividend withholding tax. Therefore, it may be argued that the domestic law classification should also be respected for tax treaty purposes, at least if a tax treaty includes an express reference to domestic anti-avoidance provisions. With respect to synthetic equity, however, it is difficult to claim that the equity derivative is used in order to avoid dividend taxation. Derivative contracts do not even necessarily involve an amount of capital that could have been invested in the shares of a company producing the dividend on which the amount of dividend equivalent payments is based.

It cannot be argued that the recipient of payments under an equity derivative contract would actually be a shareholder in the dividend-distributing company, the distributions of which the dividend equivalent payments mimic. Neither party to a derivative contract necessarily is or has ever been a shareholder in the company. Therefore, the treatment of dividend equivalent payments from equity derivatives as a dividend is generally not possible.

Under many actual treaties, income from shares paid by a company qualifies as a dividend. Income from other corporate rights also qualifies as a dividend, if, in the state of residence of the payer company, the income is treated the same way as income from shares is treated. Under many other treaties, only income from a company qualifies as a dividend. A dividend must also be income from shares. Income from other corporate rights qualifies if the state of residence of the company paying the income treats the income in the same way as it does income from shares. In addition, the dividend definitions may cover income from any arrangements carrying the right to participate in profits to the extent so characterized under the laws of the contracting state.

Dividend equivalent payments do not qualify as a dividend under these treaties, even though one of the states would treat such payments as a dividend. Dividend equivalent payments are neither income from corporate rights, nor income from an arrangement participating in profits. The fact that the amount of dividend equivalent payments may depend on the dividend distributions of a third party does not make the contract a corporate right or a profit-participating right.

Under some treaties, income paid by a company from shares or from other rights participating in profits qualifies as a dividend. Income from other rights taxed in the same way as income from shares in the state of residence of the distributing company also qualifies as a dividend. Dividend equivalent payments are clearly not income from shares or income from other rights participating in profits. Dividend equivalent payments, thus, may only qualify as a dividend if they are income from other rights taxed in the state of residence of the payer the same way as income from shares is

---

91. *See* Ch. 6 s. §6.02[C].

taxed. Dividend equivalent payments from equity derivatives may be treated as a dividend under these treaties to the extent that the state of residence of the payer treats the income as a dividend. Dividend equivalent payments may, however, qualify as a dividend under these treaties, in any case, only if the payer is a company.

Because most countries do not treat dividend equivalent payments on derivatives as a dividend, the issue of dividend classification under the treaties is moot. In exceptional situations where the states would treat dividend equivalent payments as a dividend, for example, based on domestic law anti-avoidance rules or principles, the classification in the state of the payer would also have to be respected for tax treaty purposes so long as the payer is a company.

Under some treaties, income from shares paid by a company qualifies as a dividend. Any income paid by a company also qualifies as a dividend if the state of residence of the payer taxes the income the same way as it taxes income from shares. Under the Nordic multilateral treaty, income paid by a company from shares or from other rights participating in profits qualifies as a dividend. In addition, any income paid by a company qualifies as a dividend if treated in the source state in the same way as a dividend is treated.[92] Under these treaties, dividend equivalent payments may be taxed as a dividend so long as they are paid by a company and treated as a dividend in the state of residence of the payer. However, because most states do not treat dividend equivalent payments as a dividend under domestic law, such payments do not normally qualify as a dividend under the treaties.

[5] Conclusions

Neither domestic laws nor tax treaties are very well equipped to address the complicated issues raised by derivative financial instruments. Non-residents may easily avoid source state withholding taxation by the use of synthetic equity investments instead of real equity investments. Taxes may be avoided by choosing a specific form of derivative transaction that produces the desired economic result.

It is rare that synthetic instruments are treated as a whole or are divided into economic components, but in most countries derivative instruments are treated as separate property rights. Therefore, it is rare that dividend equivalent payments on derivative instruments are treated as a dividend for tax purposes. Classification conflicts involving the question of dividend classification are not common.

Because of the non-dividend treatment, taxpayers may avoid dividend withholding tax by using synthetic equity. In most countries, dividend taxation is possible only if the payments made between corporations and their shareholders deviate from arm's length prices. In other cases, dividend taxation is unlikely even though, in theory, it may be possible based upon domestic law anti-avoidance principles and provisions.

Most tax treaties do not include special rules concerning equity derivatives. Because of the domestic law treatment, dividend equivalent payments on equity

---

92. Article 10(1) and (6) of the Nordic Treaty. *See also* Helminen (2013a), 241–245 for the dividend definition of the Nordic Treaty.

derivatives are usually not treated as a dividend under tax treaties. Classification conflicts involving the issue of dividend classification are rare. The treaties that do not require that a dividend be income from corporate rights allow dividend treatment if a dividend equivalent payment is made by a company and is treated in the state of residence of the company as a dividend is treated.

Derivative financial instruments are essential in modern finance and, therefore, the present treatment seems well argued. Because equity derivatives are used for many reasons other than for tax avoidance, the general treatment of income from equity derivatives as a dividend does not seem reasonable. The formation of such a specific provision covering only situations of avoidance of dividend taxation is, in practice, difficult. The general taxation of dividend equivalent payments on equity derivatives as a dividend could, to an unreasonable extent, distort the efficient use of equity derivatives. Therefore, there seems to be no reason to change the present domestic law approaches. Dividend equivalent payments on equity derivatives should be classified as a dividend only in exceptional cases of clear tax avoidance or based on domestic law rules and principles concerning transfers deviating from the arm's length standard and tax avoidance. In the case of hybrid mismatches leading to double benefits such as a deductible payment without a corresponding inclusion to taxable income of the recipient, there may be good reasons, however, to eliminate the double benefit. Adoption of the OECD/G20 BEPS project recommendations will function in this way.[93]

---

93. See OECD (2015). See also Part II of the Multilateral Convention to Implement Tax Treaty Related Measures to Prevent Base Erosion and Profit Shifting. The text of the Convention was published on 24 November and it will have to be signed and ratified before it will enter into force.

CHAPTER 7
Fictive Distributions as a Dividend

§7.01 CLASSIFICATION OF CFC INCOME

[A] Introduction

For company law purposes, corporations are generally regarded as separate legal persons.[1] From an economic perspective, however, a corporation and its shareholders may form a unit. The parent company may freely decide whether one of its subsidiaries makes a profit distribution. Therefore, from an economic perspective, the income of a corporation may be the income of its owners. Sometimes a corporation may only be a dummy. The corporation seemingly conducts economic operations, but is actually owned and controlled by a person who gains benefits from the operations.[2]

The tax treatment of a corporation is based on the separate entity theory. As a rule, a corporation is taxed as an entity separate from its owners.[3] Even corporations in a group of companies are taxed as separate subjects rather than the group being taxed as a unit.[4] The owners of corporations are not subject to tax on the income of the corporations until the income is distributed to the owners or until the owners sell

---

1. *See* for this separate entity theory of corporations, for example, Goode (1951), 9–13 and Harris (1996), 42–43. *See,* however, Harris (1996), 48–49, Brocker and Grapatin (1997), 65–78, Henn and Alexander (1983), 130, af Schultén (1984), 99–102, KM 1992: 32 362–364, Stohlmeier (1993), 135–137, Brocker and Grapatin (1997), 37–61 and 80–81, Rodhe (1984), 15–16, Rodhe (1984a), 486–489, Villa (1997), 378–379, Huttunen (1996), 36, Kuortti (1997), 168–169 and Toivanen (1995), 284 for company law cases disregarding the corporate entity.
2. *See* for the single entity theory e.g., Goode (1951), 13–22, Voipio (1971), 80 and Harris (1996), 44.
3. *See* for the separate entity theory e.g., Kilpi (1962), 1–3 and Harris (1996), 49. *See also* Goode (1952), 5 for the possible approaches.
4. The separate entity approach in its purest form leads to the so-called classical system of taxing corporations and their shareholders. *See* in contrast for the unity theory of corporations e.g., Bühler (1964), 99–101, Kilpi (1952), 304, Voipio (1971), 80 and Tikka (1972), 269. The fact that in many states taxation of corporations and shareholders is integrated at least to a certain extent indicates that, despite the starting point of the separate entity approach, a corporation and its

shares in the corporation. In cross-border situations, a state may only tax the undistributed profits of a resident corporation but not the undistributed profits of a non-resident corporation, even if resident persons would own the non-resident corporation.[5] This treatment allows taxpayers to enjoy tax deferral by positioning a corporation in a low tax jurisdiction and, thus, sheltering the income.[6] The owners of the corporation generally do not have to pay tax in their state of residence on the income collected in the foreign corporation until the income is repatriated. If the income is not repatriated, tax in the owner's state of residence may be totally avoided.[7]

The possibility to defer or totally avoid taxation in the state of residence of a taxpayer violates the capital-export neutrality principle.[8] A legal person pays less tax if it operates through a foreign corporation than if it operated directly in the foreign state or in its state of residence. If the possibility of tax deferral is not restricted in any way, taxpayers may avoid tax in the state of residence. Investments in low tax jurisdictions may be favoured. Because of these problems many states limit tax deferral by some means.

Tax avoidance through foreign entities may be tackled in many ways.[9] Many states have enacted special regimes that allow the undistributed income of a foreign corporation to be attributed to the resident owners for tax purposes even though the foreign entity is regarded as a separate entity.[10] The number of countries introducing such measures, referred to as CFC regimes, most likely, will increase in the future. The OECD/G20 BEPS action 3 recommends the introduction of CFC regimes[11] and the EU Anti-Tax Avoidance Directive requires the EU Member Countries to introduce a CFC regime.

---

shareholders are at least to a certain extent viewed as a unit. In taxation, corporations may, because of economic unity, be regarded as a part of a group. *See* e.g., Wikström (1987), 162 and Helminen (1992), 4-6.

5. This principle is expressed, for example, in Art. 7(1) of the OECD Model. A state may tax the business profits of a foreign entity only if the foreign entity has a permanent establishment in the other state. For permanent establishments, *see* Skaar (1991).
6. *See* for this problem, for example, VM 1994:13 1, OECD (1987a), 24-24 and Wenehed (2000), 19-25.
7. This tax planning strategy may be referred to as primary sheltering. Changing the character of income to a type that is exempt or taxed more advantageously may be referred to as secondary sheltering. *See* OECD (1987a), 25 and 62. The term 'conduit company' is often used to refer to constructions with the primary objective of re-channelling income from foreign sources and gaining tax advantages in the original state of source of the sheltered income. The term 'base company' is used to refer to situations of minimization of tax in the state of residence of the final owners. *See* OECD (1987a), 60 and 89-90. *See also*, for example, Dahlberg (2000), 32-36 for the different strategies.
8. *See* Ch. 1 s. §1.04[B] at fn. 21 for a definition of capital-export neutrality.
9. The use of foreign entities may be made disadvantageous by a broad definition of the term 'residence' by regarding the foreign company as a resident, or by deeming the foreign company to have a permanent establishment in the state of residence of the final owners of the company. Strict transfer pricing rules complicate the use of foreign corporations. General tax avoidance rules and principles may be used to disregard the corporate form of foreign entities. *See* for the different measures OECD (1987a), 29-36, 64-66 and 95-101.
10. *See* examples of such states International Fiscal Association (2013), Rohatgi (2007), 185-214, Lang et al. (2004), Wenehed (2000), 39-49, Vapaavuori (1996b), 205 and VM 1994:13 3.
11. *See* OECD (2015b).

Chapter 7: Fictive Distributions as a Dividend §7.01[A]

CFC regimes are significant to this study with respect to the classification of the attributed undistributed income. The foreign entity considered to be a CFC generally qualifies as a dividend-distributing entity because it is a separately taxable entity. However, there is no actual distribution. Despite this omission, CFC regimes may deem a distribution to have taken place. This study examines the extent to which such a fictive distribution may be and actually is treated as a dividend under the different legal systems of international tax law.

The taxation of the shareholders of a foreign separately taxable entity for the undistributed income may be based on different theoretical assumptions. The taxation of the resident shareholder may be based on the assumption that the sheltered income was actually realized in the hands of the shareholder. The foreign-based company may be disregarded as a corporate entity or the activities of the company may be regarded as the activities of the shareholder and attributed to the shareholder on a look-through basis.[12]

The logical result of disregarding a corporate entity is that the entity does not qualify as a dividend-distributing entity because only separately taxable entities qualify as such. In line with the tax treatment of transparent entities, attributed income should logically be taxed in the hands of the shareholders in accordance with its original classification. This approach leads to a situation similar to an entity classification conflict situation, where the resident state of the entity classifies the entity as separate but the residing state of the owners classifies it as transparent.

The taxation of the shareholder may also be based solely on the assumption that the income is economically at the shareholder's disposal.[13] The foreign corporation is not necessarily totally disregarded, but certain income of the foreign entity may be taxed in the hands of the shareholders. The taxation of the undistributed income of the foreign entity in the hands of a shareholder may be based on the fact that even though the formal owner of income is a foreign corporation, the economic owner of the income is actually the shareholder. Certain activity and certain income of a company may be regarded as the activity or income of its owners.

Income sheltered in a foreign entity may also be deemed to be distributed to the resident shareholders. This approach, referred to as the fictive distribution approach,[14] raises the question of whether such fictive distribution qualifies as a dividend for purposes of the different legal systems of international tax law. The fictive distribution approach does not require that the foreign corporation be disregarded in taxation. Even though there is no actual profit distribution from the foreign company to the resident shareholders, taxation may be based on a fictive distribution.

The fictive distribution approach differs from the look-through approach in that the separate tax subjectivity of the foreign company is taken into account. This

---

12. OECD (1987a), 66 refers to this approach as the 'piercing the veil' approach. *See also*, for example, Wenehed (2000), 63–80, OECD (2015b), 63 and Rust (2008), 493–494 for different theoretical approaches.
13. OECD (1987a), 66.
14. The term 'fictive dividend' is used in OECD (1987a), 66 and the term 'deemed dividend' is used in OECD (2015b), 63 and in Dahlberg – Wiman (2013), 39.

131

approach thus leads to a tax situation comparable to the taxation of actual distributions. A fictive distribution is taxed even though it has not yet been actually realized. It is, therefore, logical to classify the income attributed to the shareholder as a dividend.

[B] Domestic Tax Laws

The domestic tax laws of many, but not all, states include a special CFC regime or other provisions under which the undistributed income of a foreign corporation may be currently taxed in the hands of the resident shareholders.[15] The formulation of the CFC regimes and the scope of application of the regimes vary in detail. The regimes vary also in the domestic tax law classification of the CFC income. Some countries apply the fictive dividend approach whereas others apply the look-through approach or something in between. Usually only those countries that apply the fictive dividend approach consider CFC income to constitute dividend for tax purposes. The countries applying the look-through approach normally see a dividend only if the original type of the income received by the foreign company was dividend.

[C] EU Law

[1] The TFEU and the Anti-tax Avoidance Directive

The EU Anti-Tax Avoidance Directive lays down a minimum standard for the CFC regimes that each EU Member State must include in its domestic legislation.[16] Already before the issuance of the Directive the domestic tax laws of many EU Member States included a CFC regime. These domestic law CFC regimes of the EU Member States may not exclude other EU Member States from their scope. Often the domestic law CFC regimes apply to the owners of corporations resident in other EU Member States. This broad applicability has raised the question of the TFEU compatibility of these regimes that apply only in cross-border situations and therefore may mean a restriction on the TFEU basic freedoms.[17] The EU Anti-Tax Avoidance Directive, however, requires each EU Member States to include a CFC regime in each domestic tax laws and to apply the CFC regime under certain conditions also in intra-EU situations.[18] Despite this requirement, the domestic law CFC regimes and their application must comply with the TFEU.

---

15. See Eicke (2009), 293–302, Rohatgi (2007), 185–214, International Fiscal Association (2013), Lang et al. (2004) and Wenehed (2000), 39–49 for country examples.
16. See Arts 7 and 8 of the EU Anti-tax Avoidance Directive.
17. For the lively discussion on the compatibility of CFC regimes with EU law, see, for example, Helminen (2015), 142–145, Bouzoraa and Douvier (1997), 104, Vapaavuori (1998), 52–53, Kanervo (2001), 308–312, Kanervo (2001a), 423–427, Arnold and Dibout (2001), 81–88, Wenehed (2000), 93–127, Andersson (2000), 207–216, Carlberg (2000), 217–234, Lang (2002), 374–379, Vapaavuori (2002), 363–370, Dahlberg (2000), 308–313, Juusela and Walden (2002), 75–76, Helminen (2004), 214–218, Helminen (2004a), 36–38, Helminen (2005), 117–123, Schönfeld and Lieber (2006), 96–100, Whitehead (2007a), 176–183, Fontana (2006), 259–267, Fontana (2006a), 317–334, Turner (2007), 23–47, Fortuin (2007), 145–146, Rust (2008), 496–498 and Sivonen (2005), 76–81.
18. See Arts 7 and 8 of the EU Anti-tax Avoidance Directive.

§7.01[C]

In case C-196/04 *Cadbury Schweppes* concerning the UK CFC regime, the EU Court held that the application of a CFC regime may be in conflict with the freedom of establishment principle of the TFEU.[19]

The application of the national CFC regimes in the case of companies established in other EU Member States is not justified merely because of the beneficial tax treatment available in the state of establishment. EU nationals have the right to establish freely in the Member State with the most beneficial tax system.[20] Loss of tax revenue is not a reason that could justify the application of a national CFC regime in conflict with the freedom of establishment principle of the TFEU.[21] An EU Member State does not have the right to take away the benefit relating to low taxes levied in another Member State to a company established there by levying higher taxes on the owners of the company.[22]

The application of national CFC regimes that apply only in cross-border situations is acceptable in the case of companies established in other EU Member States only to the extent that the application only concerns wholly artificial arrangements with the purpose of circumventing the taxes that normally would be payable in the state of residence of the owners of the company.[23]

The application of national CFC regimes that apply only in cross-border situations is not acceptable in the case of companies established in another Member State if, based on objective factors that are ascertainable by third parties, it is shown that despite the existence of tax motives, the arrangement concerned corresponds to economic reality. The arrangement corresponds to economic reality if the company is factually established in its state of establishment and conducts genuine economic activities there.[24] It is in accordance with the TFEU to oblige the taxpayers to show that the establishment in a low-tax state is genuine, provided that this obligation does not lead to an extensive administrative burden.[25]

---

19. *See also*, for example, Schönfeld (2004), 441–452, Kanervo (2006), 542–546, Liede and Kuivisto (2006), 90–93, Bezzina et al. (2006), 206–212, Rainer et al. (2006), 636–638, Meussen (2007), 13–18, Ronfeld (2007), 45–48, Schnitger (2006), 151–155, Whitehead (2007), 1–16 and O'Shea (2007), 13–33 about the *Cadbury Schweppes* case. Before the judgment was given in *Cadbury Schweppes*, the Supreme Administrative Court of Finland, without referring the case to the EC, held that there was no conflict with the CFC regime of Finland and the TFEU. *See* decision KHO 2002/596 of the Supreme Administrative Court of Finland. The decision of the Supreme Administrative Court of Finland was highly criticized particularly because the Court did not refer the case to the EU Court. After the *Cadbury Schweppes* judgment, it is clear that the Supreme Administrative Court should have taken the TFEU into better account in its decision. *See also* Helminen (2003), 40–41 about the decision of the Supreme Administrative Court of Finland.
20. C-196/04 *Cadbury Schweppes*, paras 36–37. *See also*, for example, C-364/01 *Barbier*, C-212/97 *Centros* and C-167/01 *Inspire Art*.
21. *See*, for example, C-136/00 *Danner* and C-422/01 *Skandia and Ramstedt*.
22. *See*, for example, 270/83 *Commission v. France* (*avoir fiscal*), C-294/97 *Eurowings* and C-422/01 *Skandia and Ramstedt*.
23. C-196/04 *Cadbury Schweppes* and C-201/05 *The Test Claimants in the CFC and Dividend Group Litigation*. *See also*, for example, C-264/96 *ICI*. *See*, for example, Carlberg (2000), 219–220 about the *ICI* case. *See also* C-324/00 *Lankhorst-Hohorst*, C-9/02 *De Lasteyrie du Saillant* and C-446/03 *Marks & Spencer*.
24. C-196/04 *Cadbury Schweppes* and C-201/05 *The Test Claimants in the CFC and Dividend Group Litigation*.
25. C-201/05 *The Test Claimants in the CFC and Dividend Group Litigation*.

Taxpayers must have the right to show that there are other business reasons than just tax reasons for the establishment in a low-tax state, that the establishment abroad is genuine and that genuine economic activities are conducted there. Minimizing taxes must not be the primary, or one of the primary, motives.[26]

The EU Anti-tax Avoidance Directive provisions concerning CFC regimes seek to take the TFEU requirements into account. According to Article 7 of the Directive the requirement to include CFC income in the tax base of a parent company does not concern income from genuine arrangements[27] and 'shall not apply where the controlled foreign company carries on a substantive economic activity supported by staff, equipment, assets and premises, as evidenced by relevant facts and circumstances...'.[28]

In conclusion, the scope of application of the domestic law CFC regimes is very limited in intra-EU situations because of the TFEU freedom of establishment.

[2] The EU Parent-Subsidiary Directive

Because the TFEU allows the application of the domestic CFC regimes in the case of subsidiaries of other Member States only in the case of wholly artificial tax avoidance arrangements, the relevance of the impact of the P-S Directive on the taxation of CFC income is rather limited. It must be determined, however, whether in the tax avoidance situations in which the TFEU allows CFC taxation, the CFC income constitutes a profit distribution, which cannot be taxed because of the P-S Directive despite tax avoidance.

The P-S Directive generally prohibits the taxation of a direct investment dividend. If a fictive CFC distribution qualifies as a distribution under the P-S Directive, the P-S Directive generally hinders the taxation of CFC income in a direct investment relationship. In many cases, because the CFC regimes are especially designed to deal with CFCs, a direct investment relationship does exist.

The P-S Directive applies to the distribution of profits from a subsidiary to its parent company by virtue of the association between the companies. The P-S Directive does not concern the taxation of undistributed corporate profits, except in the case of hybrid subsidiaries. Therefore, it may be argued that the P-S Directive does not, in any way, deal with the taxation of CFC income that actually concerns the taxation of undistributed corporate profits. However, because under the domestic law of a Member State CFC income may be viewed as a fictive distribution, from the point of view of this state, it is not a question of the taxation of undistributed profits, rather, it is a question of the taxation of distributed profits.

---

26. C-196/04 *Cadbury Schweppes*. See Maisto and Pistone (2008), 503–513 and Maisto and Pistone (2008a), 554–570 for an example of an EU law compatible CFC regime.
27. See Art. 7 of the Anti-tax Avoidance Directive. According to the Directive '... an arrangement or a series thereof shall be regarded as non-genuine to the extent that the entity or permanent establishment would not own the assets or would not have undertaken the risks which generate all, or part of, its income if it were not controlled by a company where the significant people functions, which are relevant to those assets and risks, are carried out and are instrumental in generating the controlled company's income...'.
28. Article 7 of the Anti-tax Avoidance Directive.

The wording of the P-S Directive does not expressly include or exclude fictive distributions. However, the P-S Directive may be interpreted as applying to situations where the domestic tax law of a Member State subjects a fictive distribution to taxation as if an actual distribution had been made.[29] This interpretation is possible at least with respect to the domestic law regimes based on the fictive distribution approach. In a direct investment dividend relationship, the fictive distribution should then be exempt from tax or be subject to direct and indirect foreign tax credit in accordance with the P-S Directive.

If the domestic law CFC regime is not based on the fictive distribution approach, but rather is based on disregarding the foreign corporate entity, the question of the applicability of the P-S Directive becomes more problematic. With respect to such an approach, there is no distribution deemed to exist to which the P-S Directive could apply. The P-S Directive, however, requires the elimination of juridical and economic double taxation also in the case of hybrid subsidiaries treated as separate subjects in the state of residence of the subsidiary but as transparent entities in the state of residence of the parent company. Article 4(2) of P-S Directive requires the state of residence that taxes the parent company on the parent's share of the profits of the hybrid subsidiary as and when the profits arise to eliminate both economic and juridical double taxation.

The domestic CFC regimes that are based on disregarding the foreign corporate entity come very close to a conflict concerning any hybrid entity, which is treated as a separate tax subject in its state of residence but as a transparent entity in the state of residence of its owners. It may, thus, be argued that Article 4(2) requires economic and juridical double taxation to be eliminated by the state of residence of the parent company that applies the CFC regime. According to the Proposal for the directive that amended the P-S Directive to cover hybrid entities, the special provision of Article 4(2), however, does not cover taxation based on a CFC regime.[30] Therefore, it seems on the basis of the Proposal that the CFC regimes based on disregarding the foreign subsidiary may be applied even though the CFC regime would not provide for the elimination of economic double taxation in the state of residence of the parent company. It is, thus, difficult to argue that the tax treatment based on the CFC regimes based on the look-through approach would be limited by the P-S Directive.

The outcome that the P-S Directive would require economic and juridical double taxation to be eliminated in the case of the CFC regimes based on the fictive distribution approach but not in the case of the CFC regimes based on the look-through approach seems peculiar. It seems that it cannot be the purpose of the P-S Directive to cover one type of CFC regimes but not the other. It must, thus, be considered whether the fact that the national CFC regimes of the Member States can be applied in the case of subsidiaries of other EU Member States basically only in tax avoidance situations, has

---

29. *See* for this interpretation, for example, Scherer (1995), 226. However, de Hosson (1990), 427 argues that the P-S Directive does not apply because it only concerns distributed profits.
30. *See* para. 5 of the Proposal for a Council Directive amending Directive 90/435/EEC on the Common system of taxation applicable in the case of parent companies and subsidiaries of different Member States COM (2003) 462 final, Russo (2006), 479 and Helminen (2015), 174.

an effect on the applicability of the P-S Directive benefits in regard to the CFC income deemed to have been distributed on the basis of a CFC regime.

Article 1(2) of the P-S Directive includes a general anti-avoidance provision. According to the provision the Member States shall not grant the directive benefits to an arrangement or a series of arrangements which, having been put into place for the main purpose or one of the main purposes of obtaining a tax advantage that defeats the object of the directive, are not genuine having regard to all relevant facts and circumstances.[31] An arrangement or a series of arrangements are not regarded as genuine to the extent that they are not put into place for valid commercial reasons which reflect economic reality.[32] The Member States are not allowed to grant the directive benefits in situations covered by the anti-avoidance provision. It may be said that the object of the P-S Directive is not to exempt CFC income deemed to be distributed to a parent company where the subsidiary is a part of a wholly artificial tax avoidance arrangement.

Now that also the Anti-Tax Avoidance Directive requires the Member States to apply a CFC regime in intra-EU situations in the case of non-genuine arrangements or to the extent that the CFC subsidiary does not conduct substantive economic activity,[33] it would be peculiar if the P-S Directive prevented taxing the CFC income in such situations. It may thus be concluded that in the situations that the Anti-tax Avoidance Directive requires the Member States to include CFC income in the tax base of a parent company and provided that the taxation of the CFC income is in accordance with the TFEU freedom of establishment, the Member States should not grant the P-S Directive benefits. The Member States should not grant the P-S Directive benefits in these situations even if they apply the fictive distribution approach and consider CFC income to constitute dividend for domestic tax law purposes and therefore also as a profit distribution for the purposes of the P-S Directive.

[D] Tax Treaties

The majority opinion seems to be that domestic law anti-avoidance provisions may be applied in tax treaty situations even though the use of such provisions was not referred to in a tax treaty.[34] The majority seems to believe that tax treaties do not affect domestic law CFC regimes.[35] The OECD also accepts that attribution of the income of a foreign corporation to the owners is not contrary to the OECD Model if the foreign company acted as a mere intermediary, an agent, a fiduciary or a nominee of the owners.[36]

---

31. Article 1(2) of the P-S Directive.
32. Article 1(3) of the P-S Directive.
33. Article 7 of the Anti-tax Avoidance Directive.
34. See para. 22.1 of the Commentary on Art. 1 of the OECD Model. See also, for example, Gäverth (1998), 240. See, for the applicability of domestic law anti-avoidance provisions with respect to tax treaties, above in Ch. 6 s. §6.03[A][5] of this study.
35. See para. 23 of the Commentary on Art. 1 of the OECD Model, para. 14 of the Commentary on Art. 7 of the OECD Model, para. 13 of the Commentary on Art. 7 of the OECD Model as it read before 22 Jul. 2010 and para. 37 of the Commentary on Art. 10 of the OECD Model.
36. This opinion was expressed already in OECD (1987a), 70.

However, CFC regimes may be regarded as conflicting with the spirit of tax treaties if the regimes are applied not only in tax avoidance situations, but also with respect to either foreign companies engaged in active business or to companies in high tax jurisdictions.[37] It is clear that anti-avoidance provisions may be applied in situations where a tax treaty expressly refers to such rules. Therefore, many tax treaties include a special provision expressly stating that the application of the domestic law CFC regimes of the contracting states is allowed.

CFC regimes that are based on the fictive dividend approach do not disregard the foreign entity but recognize it as a separately taxable entity and only deem a distribution to exist. The foreign entity, thus, clearly qualifies as a resident company for tax treaty purposes, because both the state of residence of the entity and the state of residence of the owners of the entity treat the entity as a separately taxable entity. The treaty between the state of organization or residence of the foreign company and the state of residence of the owners is, thus, applicable in determining whether the fictive dividend taxation is in accordance with the treaty.[38] Both the states also recognize the entity as a dividend-distributing entity. Therefore, it is clear that the dividend article of the treaty must be applied to an actual distribution from the entity to the owners. Instead, it is unclear whether the treaty allows the state of residence of the owners of a separately taxable company to tax the undistributed profits of the company and what type of income the treaty considers such a fictive distribution as constituting.

According to Article 7(1) of the OECD Model, '...the profits of an enterprise of a contracting state shall be taxable only in that state unless the enterprise carries on business in the other contracting state through a permanent establishment situated therein...'.[39] Therefore, CFC regimes may be considered to be contrary to Article 7(1), unless the controlled foreign company has a permanent establishment in the state of residence of the owners of the company.[40]

CFC regimes, however, do not subject the non-resident company to taxation but rather only tax resident shareholders of the foreign company for the foreign company's profits. Article 7 arguably does not limit such taxation, because Article 7(1) only forbids the taxation of the profits of a non-resident company, but does not hinder the taxation of the resident owners.[41] However, even though the CFC regime subjects the resident shareholders to tax, but not the foreign corporation, the state taxes the profits of a non-resident corporation, which may be considered to in conflict with Article 7.[42] According to the Commentary on Article 7 of the OECD Model Article 7(1), however,

---

37. *See* OECD (1987a), 72 and para. 26 of the Commentary on Art. 1 of the OECD Model, which recommend that CFC regimes should not be applied in such situations.
38. It is possible that the place of effective management of the foreign entity is situated in the same state where the owners of the entity are residents. In such a situation, the entity may be resident of the state of the owners of the entity for tax treaty purposes. It is, therefore, actually a question of a domestic situation where the state of residence of the owners and of the entity that is the same state may tax both the entity and the owners in accordance with domestic law rules.
39. An identical provision is included in Art. 7(1) of the UN Model and in Art. 7(1) of the US Model.
40. *See*, for example, Oliver (1995), 556 and the decision of the French Conseil d'Etat of 28 Jun. 2002 in case 232276.
41. *See*, for example, Schwarz and Fischer-Zernin (1992), 49.
42. *See* for this view Sandler (1994), 70 and Bouzoraa and Douvier (1997), 104.

does not limit the application of domestic law CFC regimes because the tax levied on the resident owners of the foreign company does not reduce the profits of the foreign company and may not, therefore, be said to have been levied on the profits of the foreign company.[43] Especially with respect to the fictive dividend approach, it may be argued that the state does not tax the profits of the company but taxes a distribution, even though only a fictive one, and Article 7, therefore, does not forbid such taxation.

Article 7(1) does not apply to distributions that qualify under Article 10 of the OECD Model. If a fictive distribution qualifies under Article 10 of the OECD Model, Article 7(1) does not hinder the taxation. According to the Commentary on the OECD Model, it is not clear whether the fictive dividend should be taxed as a dividend under Article 10 or as other income under Article 21.[44] This comment indicates that, according to the OECD, the taxation of the fictive dividend is generally allowable and that the fictive dividend may also constitute a dividend. Also, the majority of the OECD states take the view that CFC regimes based on the fictive dividend approach are generally in accordance with tax treaties, if not extended to real industrial or commercial activities or to companies subject to a normal level of taxation.[45]

Under Article 10 of the OECD Model, income from shares paid by a company is treated as a dividend. Income from other corporate rights paid by a company also qualifies as a dividend, if the source state taxes the income the same way as income from shares. The part of the dividend definition referring to the source state classification is not, however, relevant with respect to the classification of CFC income because the source state does not recognize any cross-border income in such a situation. The fact that the income is not classified as a dividend or as any other type of income in the source state does not, however, hinder the income from qualifying under the autonomous part of the dividend definition as a dividend.[46] The fictive dividend must be income from shares paid by a company in order to qualify as a dividend for tax treaty purposes.

There is no doubt that the attributed amount is from shares. Instead, it may be asked whether fictive income is income at all, because there is no actual economic benefit realized by the shareholder. Article 10(3) fails to define the term 'income' and whether it covers fictive income. Applying the rule of Article 3(2), the term should be interpreted by reference to the law of the state applying the treaty if the context does not otherwise require. With respect to CFC income, the state of residence of the owner of the foreign-controlled corporation is the state applying the treaty. Therefore, if the context does not require a different interpretation, the interpretation of the term by this state is decisive. With respect to CFC income, the context may not require another

---

43. Paragraph 14 of the Commentary on Art. 7 of the OECD Model and para. 13 of the Commentary on Art. 7 of the OECD Model as it read before 22 Jul. 2010.
44. Paragraph 38 of the Commentary on Art. 10 of the OECD Model.
45. This opinion was expressed already in OECD (1987a), 71 para. 45.
46. The reference to the law of the source state includes that such items of income that are a dividend according to the law of the source state are to be treated as a dividend for tax treaty purposes. It does not include that other items of income could not be treated as a dividend. Other items of income may qualify as a dividend for tax treaty purposes under the autonomous part of the dividend definition. *See also* Vogel et al. (1997), 680–681.

interpretation because the source state in this situation does not even apply the treaty. Especially if it is a question of tax avoidance, the context should not require another interpretation. Because the state of residence of the owners deems income to exist, the income, thus, also qualifies as income for the purposes of the treaty.

It must, however, be asked whether the income is paid by a company. According to the Commentaries, the term 'paid' has a very broad meaning, covering any '…fulfillment of the obligation to put funds at the disposal of the shareholder in the manner required by contract or by custom…'.[47] The Commentaries do not answer the question of whether the fictive dividend may be regarded as paid because there are actually no funds put at the disposal of the shareholder, such a transaction being only deemed to exist. The term 'paid' is not defined in the OECD Model, and, therefore, it must also be interpreted in line with Article 3(2) in accordance with the law of the state applying the treaty. Fictive income, thus, qualifies as a dividend paid by a company if the state of residence of the owners treats it as such.[48] The fictive distribution approach, therefore, allows the state of residence of the owners of the foreign-controlled corporation to treat the fictive distribution as a dividend under tax treaties.[49]

If a state treats CFC income as a dividend, and even though it would also qualify as a dividend under the applicable tax treaty, the state may not necessarily be allowed to tax the income. The article of the applicable treaty concerning elimination of double taxation may require that the state exempt a direct investment dividend. If the state treats the fictive distribution as a dividend, and if the foreign company and the recipient company are in a direct investment relationship, the income may not be taxed even though treated as a dividend. It would be peculiar to treat the fictive distribution as a dividend but fail to apply the rules concerning the elimination of double taxation concerning dividend.

If a treaty refers to the exemption method in regard to direct investment dividends, it may be more advantageous for a state to argue that the fictive distribution is not a dividend but that it qualifies under Article 21 of the OECD Model as other income. Then treaties do not normally prohibit the taxation in the state of residence of the shareholder. According to the opinion of the author of this study, if the state treats the item as a dividend under domestic law, it is not logical, however, to argue that it does not qualify as a dividend but as other income under tax treaties. Even if the state does not tax the income as a dividend under domestic law but as some other type of income, dividend treatment under tax treaties seems proper. The state clearly deems that the item is income and the item is clearly from shares.

The argument that the state may make in order to not treat the item as a dividend under a tax treaty is that the item is not paid in the way required by the dividend article. This argument, however, is peculiar because it seems logical that if income is deemed

---

47. Paragraph 7 of the Commentary on Art. 10 of the OECD Model. *See* for the meaning of the term 'paid' also for example Harris (2016), s. 2.1.2.2.2. and Helminen (2016c), s. 2.1.1.2.5.
48. *See*, however, Wattel and Marres (2003), 66–79, who consider that fictive income is not paid and therefore does not qualify as dividend but as other income under tax treaties.
49. Also Simontacchi (2007), 266–274 and Hattingh (2009), 521 considers that the term 'paid' should not be given a substantial role so as to restrict the treaty application when an item falls under the dividend definition.

to exist, then it should also be deemed to be paid. Therefore, according to the opinion of the author of this study, if the domestic law CFC regime is based on the fictive distribution approach, the income should be treated as a dividend and not as other income under tax treaties. According to the Commentary on the OECD Model, it is, however, unclear whether CFC income must be treated as a dividend or as other income.[50]

According to Article 10(5), '[w]here a company which is a resident of a contracting state derives profits or income from the other contracting state, that other state may not...subject the company's undistributed profits to a tax on the company's undistributed profits...'. Article 10(5) prohibits the taxation of undistributed profits. However, the article only covers the taxation of the company in the source state and, therefore, does not prohibit the taxation of undistributed profits in the state of residence of the shareholders of a company.[51] Article 10(5), therefore, does not prohibit the taxation of undistributed profits of a foreign company in the hands of resident shareholders.[52]

The tax treaty classification as a dividend means that, in principle, the special tax regimes of tax treaties concerning a direct investment dividend should also apply with respect to CFC income. A fictive distribution may, therefore, have to be exempted under the tax treaty method article. However, under some treaties, the exemption method with respect to a direct investment dividend only applies with respect to income derived from active or productive enterprises, and, otherwise, the credit method is applicable. Under these treaties, CFC taxation is possible even though the CFC income would be considered to constitute dividend for tax treaty purposes.[53] It may also be argued that even if a CFC regime would not be specifically mentioned in a tax treaty, it is an anti-avoidance provision which can be applied irrespective of tax treaties. States, thus, may consider it to be allowable to tax CFC income deemed constituting a dividend irrespective of a treaty method article referring to the exemption method in regard to direct investment dividends.

CFC regimes based on the fictive dividend approach also raise the question of how to treat an actual dividend distribution if undistributed profits are already taxed in the hands of the shareholder. Because the foreign company qualifies as a dividend-distributing entity, an actual distribution from it qualifies as a dividend under the treaty between the state of residence of the company and the state of residence of the recipient. The state of residence of the distributing company may, therefore, be allowed to impose a withholding tax on the distribution. However, double taxation may result

---

50. Paragraph 38 of the Commentary on Art. 10 of the OECD Model. *See also* Wattel and Marres (2003), 66–79, who consider that fictive income is not paid and therefore does not qualify as dividend but as other income under tax treaties.
51. Paragraph 37 of the Commentary on Art. 10 of the OECD Model. *See also* OECD (1987a), 72 and Tax Treaty Interpretation (1997), 55-2.
52. According to para. 170 of the Technical Explanation to Art. 10(7) of the 2006 US Model that is substantially similar to Art. 10(5) of the OECD Model, the article does not hinder the application of domestic law CFC regimes.
53. *See* Baranowski (1996), 416 and Sandler (1994), 93.

because the same income is already taxed in the hands of the shareholder as CFC income.

The state of residence of the shareholder is required to eliminate double taxation with respect to the withholding tax. The actual dividend, however, is not taxed in the state of residence of the shareholder and there is no tax against which the foreign withholding tax could be credited. If the credit is not granted, the purpose of the treaty, however, is frustrated because double taxation is not eliminated. Therefore, it is suggested that credit be granted even though no tax is paid at the time of the actual distribution. A refund of taxes or a carry forward of the unused credit should be allowed.[54]

The relationship of tax treaties to regimes that disregard the foreign corporate entity and that are based on the look-through approach is somewhat different. With respect to such regimes, it is actually a question of an entity classification conflict. The state of residence of the entity regards the entity as a separately taxable entity and the state of residence of its owners as a transparent entity. However, as discussed above in Chapter 5, an entity qualifies as a resident company of a state for tax treaty purposes as long as it is treated as such in that state. Therefore, the treaty between the states must be applied to determine what items of income from the entity may be taxed in the state of residence of the owners of the entity.

Taxation under a CFC regime based on the look-through approach clearly includes the taxation of undistributed profits of an enterprise because a distribution is not deemed to exist even under domestic law. The look-through approach raises the question of compatibility with Article 7 of the OECD Model. It may, however, be argued that Article 7 does not hinder the taxation of the owners but only hinders the taxation of the entity. Especially because domestic general anti-avoidance rules are widely regarded to be in accordance with the OECD Model, Article 7 should not prohibit CFC taxation. However, even if the taxation of CFC income were allowed, CFC income may not qualify as a dividend for tax treaty purposes. There is no income paid by a company and neither of the contracting states even deems that such a payment exists.[55]

This approach also raises the question of the elimination of double taxation at the time of the actual dividend distribution. Because the foreign company qualifies as a dividend-distributing entity for tax treaty purposes, the state of residence may be entitled to impose withholding tax in accordance with the dividend article. Even though the state of residence of the shareholders does not tax the actual distribution, double taxation emerges with respect to the taxed CFC income. In the same way as for the fictive dividend approach, the state should, therefore, grant a credit at least for the withholding tax imposed against the taxes on CFC income.

---

54. This suggestion is made in para. 39 of the Commentary on Art. 10 of the OECD Model. *See also* OECD (1987a), 73.
55. Dividend treatment is possible if, because of domestic law anti-avoidance provisions, the treaty between the original source state and the state of residence of the owners is viewed to be applicable, instead of the treaty between the state of residence of the foreign company and the state of residence of the owners of the company. Then a dividend paid from the original source state would qualify as a dividend under the treaty.

[E] **Conclusions**

The domestic tax laws of many states include a special CFC regime aimed at taxing undistributed profits of a foreign-controlled company in the hands of the resident shareholders of the company. In relations between two EU Member States, the applicability of the regimes, however, is very limited.

The domestic law regimes are based either on the fictive distribution approach or the look-through approach or something in between. It varies state by state whether attributed CFC income is treated as dividend or as some other type of income for the domestic tax law purposes.

Despite similarities, the taxation of CFC income under a domestic regime always leads to a conflict situation. CFC regimes, after all, either tax fictive distributions from a company to its owners when the state of residence of the company does not see any distribution, or treat an entity as a more or less transparent entity even though the state of its organization treats the entity as a separately taxable entity.

CFC taxation may lead to international double taxation if an actual distribution from the company is taxed in addition to the CFC income. Most domestic law CFC regimes, however, refrain from taxing actual distributions to the extent covered by the fictive distribution. Therefore, usually CFC regimes only cause undesirable double taxation with respect to the withholding tax imposed on an actual distribution in the source state.

The P-S Directive and tax treaties may limit CFC taxation in situations where there is a qualifying holding between the company and its owners. The P-S Directive and tax treaties may hinder the taxation of CFC income based on the deemed dividend approach with respect to a direct investment dividend relationship. It is, however, possible to argue, that even though a CFC regime deems a dividend, the CFC regime is an anti-avoidance provision, which may be applied irrespective of tax treaties and irrespective of the P-S Directive.

§7.02 TREATMENT OF BONUS SHARES

[A] **Introduction**

In addition to a cash dividend, shareholders may receive a stock dividend, that is, bonus shares from a corporation in connection with an increase in the corporation's nominal capital. In an issue of bonus shares, the shareholders receive new shares for no consideration or for a consideration not corresponding to the value of the new stock. The nominal value of existing shares may also be increased without any additional investment from the shareholders.[56]

These forms of increasing the nominal value of the share capital of a corporation do not actually realize income for the shareholder because these transactions do not

---

56. *See* for different means by which shareholders may benefit from corporate profits Franks, Broyles and Carleton (1985), 404–405 and Kilpi (1962), 81–121.

Chapter 7: Fictive Distributions as a Dividend §7.02[B]

include a transfer of economic benefit from a company to its shareholders. No assets are transferred from the corporation to the shareholders. The amount of corporate assets is not changed. Even in connection with the issue of bonus shares, company assets are simply divided into more shares than before. Similarly, increasing the value of all existing shares for no consideration has no effect at all on the position of the shareholders in the company.

By disposing of bonus shares or shares with increased nominal value, a shareholder may realize actual income. A shared feature of an issue of bonus shares and a dividend distribution is that both transactions involve a distribution of the reserves of a corporation to shareholders for no return value or benefit. By selling bonus shares, shareholders may realize income as if they had received a dividend. Bonus shares may, therefore, be used to avoid dividend taxation. The essential difference with a dividend is that even though the shareholder is regarded as having received an economic benefit from the company, if the shareholder realizes the corresponding income, the shareholder essentially simultaneously relinquishes a part of its share in the company. After a dividend distribution, the proportionate share of the shareholder in the company remains unchanged.[57]

Bonus shares may be viewed in two basic ways in taxation because of the differences and similarities compared to a dividend.[58] First, the issue of bonus shares may be regarded as not including any distribution of company assets to the shareholders because the assets remain in the company. The alternative view is that bonus shares, because of their similarities to a dividend, constitute a combination of two transactions. In the first transaction, the company is deemed to have distributed assets to its shareholders, and in the second transaction, the shareholders are deemed to have reinvested the assets back into the company's stock. The latter approach, thus, includes dividend taxation. It is the extent to which bonus shares are treated as constituting a dividend distribution from a corporation to its shareholders under the different legal systems of international tax law that is relevant to this study.

[B]   Domestic Tax Laws

It varies country by country whether and in what situations bonus shares are regarded as realizing a dividend to the shareholder for domestic tax purposes. In many countries, a stock dividend is not considered an increase in the wealth of the shareholders, but rather only a transfer into share capital of profits that could otherwise have been used for a dividend distribution. Bonus shares are not regarded as constituting a distribution but only as a possibility to retain the shareholders' proportionate position in the company. Even if bonus shares are issued in such a way that the proportionate position of the shareholders in the company is changed, a transfer of benefit from one shareholder to another is deemed to have occurred rather than a transfer of benefit from a company to one of its shareholders.

---

57. *See* for this difference Kilpi (1962), 108–110.
58. *See* for the two approaches Kilpi (1962), 106–107.

Even though bonus shares would not be considered to constitute dividend to the shareholders in all situations, certain countries consider dividend taxation to apply in special situations. It is usual to tax bonus shares as dividends if the bonus issue changes the shareholders' proportionate interests in the issuing company.

Dividend taxation may apply also in a situation in which the distribution by a corporation of its own stock is payable either in stock or property at the election of any of the shareholders. Dividend treatment may apply also if the stock distribution is a disproportionate distribution, that is, if the distribution results in the receipt of money or other property by some shareholders and in an increase in the proportionate interests of other shareholders in the assets or earnings and profits of the corporation. Dividend treatment may apply also with respect to a stock distribution, which results in the receipt of preferred shares by some common shareholders and the receipt of common shares by other common shareholders.

The tax treatment may depend also on the assets from which the capital is raised. If the capital is raised from company profits, the issuance of bonus shares is often regarded as a distribution from the company to its shareholders, with an immediate reinvestment of the distributed assets. If the capital is raised from the assets of the company's reserves, bonus shares may not constitute a dividend.

[C] The EU Parent-Subsidiary Directive

The P-S Directive concerns distributions of profits from a subsidiary to its parent company by virtue of the association between the companies. The P-S Directive, however, fails to define what is meant by the term 'profit distribution'. A definition of the term 'dividend' was contained in the Proposal for a Directive of the Council concerning the Harmonization of Systems of Company and of Withholding Taxes on Dividend (the Proposal).[59]

In the Proposal, the term 'dividend' was defined in Article 2(1). Accordingly, a dividend is:

> [T]hat part of the profits of any corporation of a Member State, other than a corporation in liquidation, distributed by it by virtue of a proper decision of its competent authorities and divided among its members in proportion to their rights as members of the corporation; distributions of bonus shares are not regarded as a dividend within the meaning of the present directive.

Bonus shares were, thus, excluded from the scope of the Proposal. However, according to Article 7 of the Proposal, the Directive is applicable to any distribution that is regarded as a dividend distribution under the law of the source state. To the extent that the source state would have treated bonus shares as a dividend, the bonus shares would have also qualified under the Proposal after all.

The P-S Directive does not include a similar exclusion of bonus shares, but covers any transfers that constitute the distribution of profits from a subsidiary to its parent company, by virtue of the association between the companies. Because bonus shares

---

59. COM (75) 392 final of 23 Jul. 1975.

are clearly issued to the shareholders by virtue of the association between the companies, bonus shares must be covered if they constitute a profit distribution.[60]

The domestic tax laws of some EU Member States are based on the assumption that bonus shares do not include any transfer of profits from a company to its shareholders. Even if bonus shares are issued in such a way that the proportionate position of the shareholders in the company is changed, a transfer of benefit from one shareholder to another is deemed to have occurred rather than a transfer of benefit from a company to one of its shareholders. The domestic tax laws of some other Member States, instead, are based on the assumption that bonus shares constitute a distribution of profits from a company to its shareholders. Thus, it is clear that the EU Member States do not agree on whether or not bonus shares constitute a profit distribution.

The question of the applicability of the P-S Directive with respect to bonus shares really only concerns those states that regard bonus shares as constituting a dividend distribution or some other type of taxable income. The other states generally fulfil the requirements of the P-S Directive anyway, as they do not view the issue of bonus shares as a taxable transfer. The question with respect to the P-S Directive is actually whether the states that tax bonus shares as a dividend or other income must grant the benefits of the P-S Directive with respect to bonus shares between qualifying companies.

The wording of the P-S Directive does not expressly include or exclude fictive distributions. However, the Directive may be interpreted as applying to situations where the domestic tax law of a Member State subjects a fictive distribution to taxation as if an actual distribution had been made.[61] If a state under its domestic tax law treats bonus shares as a dividend, it may not reasonably argue that a bonus share is not the type of distribution of profit meant by the P-S Directive. Such a claim is not logical, especially because the term 'profit distribution' is generally understood to be broader than the term 'dividend'.

As a consequence, a Member State that treat bonus shares as dividend under its domestic law, should apply also its domestic law rules implementing the P-S Directive to bonus shares. This view can be supported by the fact that the purpose of the P-S Directive is to eliminate economic double taxation in cross-border situations to the same extent as it is eliminated in purely domestic situations. If the state applies the domestic law system for the elimination of economic double taxation to domestic bonus shares in domestic situations, the P-S directive benefits should be available to bonus shares in cross-border situations that fall under the scope of the P-S Directive.

[D]   Tax Treaties

Tax treaties do not expressly mention bonus shares. Therefore, it is unclear how the taxing right is divided under tax treaties with respect to bonus shares. Income from shares paid by a company qualifies as a dividend under the Model Conventions. Under

---

60. Also Vanistendael (1992), 604 recognizes that bonus shares are covered to the extent that they constitute profit distributions.
61. *See* for this interpretation, for example, Scherer (1995), 226.

the OECD Model, income from other corporate rights paid by a company qualifies as a dividend to the extent that the source state treats such income as a dividend. The US Model provides that any income paid by a company qualifies if it is treated in the source state as a dividend. If bonus shares do not qualify under these definitions, their tax treatment depends on Article 21 of the Models on other income. This classification would mean under the treaties following the models, that only the state of residence of the shareholder but not the state of residence of the issuing company could tax bonus shares.

There is no doubt that, if bonus shares constitute income paid by a company, this income is from shares. Bonus shares are, after all, issued to the shareholders of a company because of the shareholder relationship. Therefore, the tax treaty treatment of bonus shares should actually be evaluated by reference to the autonomous part of the dividend definition. It may, however, be asked, whether bonus shares constitute income at all because there is actually no income realized by the shareholder.

Especially if bonus shares are issued to all shareholders in proportion to their shareholding in the issuing company, there is no economic benefit actually realized by the shareholders. Also, in a situation where the issue of bonus shares is not proportionate, there is actually no benefit issued by a company to the shareholders, but there is a change in the position among the shareholders in the company. Bonus shares may, therefore, actually realize income for a shareholder only if a shareholder sells the right to bonus shares or sells the new shares. Bonus shares are sometimes regarded as not constituting income under domestic tax law, and other times, they are deemed as constituting income paid by a company to its shareholders. The contracting states do not necessarily agree on whether bonus shares constitute income.

Article 10(3) of the OECD Model fails to define what is meant by the term 'income' and whether it covers fictive income. Applying the rule of Article 3(2), the term should, therefore, be interpreted by reference to the law of the state applying the treaty if the context does not otherwise require.

The term 'income' is mentioned three times in the dividend definition of Article 10(3). It appears once in the autonomous part of the dividend definition in the phrase '...income from shares...', and twice in the part of the definition that refers to source state classification, in the phrase '...income from other corporate rights which is subject to the same taxation treatment as income from shares...'. This fact raises the question, should the term be interpreted similarly for the purposes of the whole definition, or might it be interpreted differently with respect to the autonomous part and the part of the dividend definition referring to source state classification?[62]

The wording of Article 10(3) seems to require that the term 'income' be given an autonomous interpretation for purposes of the whole definition. The phrase 'as well as' seems to require that only such amounts that qualify as income under the autonomous parts of the definition qualify as income under the third part of the definition.

---

62. The problem of interpreting the term, income, is recognized for example in Maisto and van den Bruinhorst (1993), 290–291. Vogel et al. (1997), 649 suggests that the term 'receipts' instead of the term 'income' should be used in the definition in order that the article is not so open to interpretation.

Therefore, the term 'income' should be interpreted autonomously for purposes of the whole definition.

It does not seem reasonable, however, to interpret the term 'income' according to different rules of interpretation than the rest of the phrase '...income from other corporate rights...subjected to the same taxation treatment as income from shares by the laws of the state of which the company making the distribution is a resident...'. Such an interpretation would lead to a peculiar outcome because the state of residence could nullify the source state classification of income from other corporate rights by giving the term 'income' an interpretation differing from that of the source state. This result certainly cannot have been the anticipated goal of the article. Further, this interpretation would not be in accordance with the Commentary on the OECD Model, according to which '...benefits in money or money's worth, such as bonus shares...' qualify as a dividend so long as the source state treats such benefits as a dividend.[63] The context could be said to require that, at least for the purposes of the third part of the definition, the term 'income' also be interpreted in accordance with the law of the source state. The state of residence of the recipient of the benefit must then accept the source state interpretation.

Article 3(2) allows for the interpretation of an undefined treaty article in accordance with the law of the state applying the treaty. However, the context with respect to the autonomous part of the dividend definition seems to require source state classification with respect to bonus shares. Bonus shares, after all, are benefits from shares. Therefore, bonus shares should actually be evaluated under the first part of the dividend definition and not under the third part of the definition concerning income from other corporate rights. Thus, the opinion of the Commentaries according to which bonus shares qualify as a dividend as long as the source state treats them as a dividend actually requires that source state interpretation is also followed with respect to the autonomous part of the dividend definition.

In conclusion, the term 'income' must be interpreted with respect to bonus shares in accordance with the law of the source state for the purposes of the whole dividend definition of Article 10(3). Even though the undefined term of income is interpreted in accordance with the rule of Article 3(2), the context may be said to require that the source state interpretation of the term 'income' be made treaty law for the purposes of the whole definition. The state of residence of the person receiving the benefit should accept the source state classification.[64]

With respect to bonus shares, it must also be asked whether they are paid in the way required by Article 10 of the OECD Model. Because the term 'paid' is not defined in the Model, it must also be interpreted according to Article 3(2) in accordance with

---

63. Paragraph 28 of the Commentary on Art. 10 of the OECD Model.
64. Vogel et al. (1997), 649–650, also suggests source state classification with respect to the term 'income' in its entirety. Vogel, however, does not defend this interpretation with the requirements of Art. 3(2). Instead, Vogel is of the opinion that the source state approach, although it must be applied, in fact leads to some extent to conflict with the wording of Art. 10(3). According to the opinion of the author of this study, there is, however, no conflict. The term income in the phrase 'income from shares', must be interpreted according to the rules of Art. 3(2) as the wording of Art. 10(3) demands, but the context requires source state classification.

the law of the state applying the treaty, unless the context otherwise requires. According to the Commentaries, the term 'paid' has a very broad meaning because the concept of payment means '...the fulfillment of the obligation to put funds at the disposal of the shareholder in the manner required by contract or by custom...'.[65] Therefore, processes that in form would not appear to constitute a dividend payment are included if the substance of the process is similar to a payment. The term includes any form of satisfying the shareholder's claim to receiving the dividend. Accordingly, the term 'payment' includes the provision of any advantage from a corporation to the shareholder so long as the advantage otherwise qualifies as a dividend.[66]

In conclusion, bonus shares qualify under Article 10 of the OECD Model as a dividend so long as the state of residence of the company issuing the bonus shares treats the bonus shares as a dividend.[67] The source state classification is, therefore, for tax treaty purposes binding on the state of residence of the person receiving bonus shares. The other state must eliminate double taxation with respect to the amount in accordance with the treaty rules concerning a dividend if the source state treats bonus shares as a dividend. On the other hand, if the source state does not treat bonus shares as a dividend, bonus shares do not qualify as a dividend for tax treaty purposes either, even though bonus shares would be treated as a dividend under the domestic tax law of the other state. In such a situation, bonus shares should be treated as other income under Article 21 despite the domestic law treatment in the other state. Many times this treatment is actually more advantageous to the other state because Article 21 grants it an undivided taxing right.

[E] Conclusions

In conclusion, bonus shares are treated differently under the domestic tax law of the different states. According to the domestic law of some countries, bonus shares are taxed as a dividend. Bonus shares are regarded as constituting a dividend distribution and an immediate reinvestment of the income back to the company.

In some other countries, the issuance of bonus shares does not constitute a dividend or any other type of taxable income for the shareholders. Taxable income is regarded as having been realized only if the shareholder alienates its right to new shares or later alienates the new shares. This income is, however, not taxed as a dividend but rather as any income from the alienation of shares. Many states, however, consider that bonus shares constitute dividend, if the bonus shares are issued in such a way that the proportionate interests of shareholders are changed.

The P-S Directive does not exclude bonus shares or any fictive distributions from the scope of the Directive. It covers all profit distributions from a subsidiary to its

---

65. Paragraph 7 of the Commentary on Art. 10 of the OECD Model.
66. *See also* for this interpretation Vogel et al. (1997), 587-588. *See also* Simontacchi (2007), 66-79 and Hattingh (2009), 521, who consider that the term 'paid' should not be given a substantial role so as to restrict the treaty application when an item falls under the dividend definition.
67. For example, Vogel et al. (1997), 679 interprets the Model to require source state classification with respect to bonus shares.

parent company by virtue of the association between the companies. To the extent that a Member State treats bonus shares as a dividend or as some other type of taxable income under its domestic tax law, it should also grant the benefits of the P-S Directive to bonus shares to the extent that bonus shares are issued by a qualifying subsidiary to a qualifying parent company.

Under the tax treaties, bonus shares qualify as a dividend so long as the source state treats them as taxable income. If the source state treats bonus shares as taxable dividend income, bonus shares qualify as a dividend for tax treaty purposes.

The fact that some states classify bonus shares as a dividend and some do not does not usually lead to income classification conflicts, which would produce double taxation. In situations where a state does not classify bonus shares as a dividend, it usually does not treat bonus shares as taxable income at all. Bonus shares are either subject to dividend treatment in both of the states or they are treated as a dividend in one of the states and not taxed at all in the other state. Bonus shares may also be left totally untaxed. Such treatment, however, is not a problem if bonus shares are left untaxed in pure domestic situations also.

CHAPTER 8
Classification of Economic Benefits from Corporations to Their Shareholders in the Form of Transfer Prices

§8.01 INTRODUCTION

Corporations and their shareholders are regarded, both for company law and for tax law purposes, as separate subjects. The separate entity approach also concerns parent companies and subsidiaries in a group of companies. Parent companies and subsidiaries may provide goods or services to each other or may make rental or financial agreements with each other. In general, such intra-group transactions are recognized for tax purposes. The prices at which a corporation transfers physical goods and intangible property or provides services to an associated corporation, that is, the so-called transfer prices,[1] constitute taxable income and deductible expenses to the corporations in the same way as to extra-group parties.

In transactions between corporations and their shareholders and between parent companies and subsidiaries, prices, conditions and forms used for the transactions do not necessarily correspond to the prices, conditions and forms that would have been used if the corporations had acted as independent enterprises operating in open markets. Intra-group transactions may be used to shift profits from one corporation to another and from one tax jurisdiction to another. Therefore, transfer pricing may be used to minimize the total tax burden of a group of companies or to avoid dividend taxation.[2]

Because of the problem described above, in order to be recognized as such in taxation, transfers between two related parties must be carried out for prices and

---

1. The term 'transfer pricing' covers setting of prices on all types of transactions between related parties. See OECD (2010), Preface, para. 11.
2. See for non-tax reasons for transfer pricing e.g., Wiman (1987), 16–18.

conditions that would have been agreed upon between two independent actors in a perfect market. In other words, the arm's length principle must be followed.[3] Article 9(1) of the OECD Model is the authoritative statement of the arm's length principle.[4] It allows taxation to be based on arm's length amounts no matter what the actual amounts are.[5] Articles 11(6) and 12(4) of the OECD Model concerning the classification of excessive interest and royalties are based on the same principle.

The EU Arbitration Convention, which provides a special procedure for the elimination of the economic double taxation caused by transfer-pricing adjustments, is also based on the arm's length principle.[6] Similarly, the domestic tax law of most countries includes a rule substantially similar to Article 9(1) of the OECD Model, which allows transfer-pricing adjustments of intra-group transactions based on the arm's length principle.[7]

Business transactions carried out at abnormal prices may include hidden profit distributions from a corporation to its shareholders. A benefit is transferred from a corporation to its shareholders if either the subsidiary has paid the parent company a price exceeding the arm's length price or if the parent company has paid its subsidiary a price below the arm's length price. In both situations, the profits of the shareholder end up higher and the profits of the corporation end up lower than in a similar transaction between independent parties. Such transactions raise the question of dividend classification.

In the first situation, the profit allocation rules allow the state of residence of the subsidiary to deny a deduction for a payment with respect to the portion exceeding the arm's length price. In the alternative situation, the state of residence of the subsidiary may include in the profits of the subsidiary the amount by which the payment, which is actually received, is below the arm's length price in addition to the amount actually received.

These situations raise the question of whether, in addition to the upward profit adjustment, the benefit transferred from the subsidiary to the parent company may be or actually is taxed as a constructive dividend in the state of residence of the subsidiary. The question that then emerges is whether that state may, or actually does, treat the benefit as an item subject to source state dividend withholding tax. The issue then arises of whether the state of residence of the recipient of the benefit must accept the possible dividend classification in the state of residence of the subsidiary and must

---

3. *See* for this definition of arm's length price, for example, Wiman (1987), 18-19, Arvidsson (1990), 21 and Niskakangas (1991), 35.
4. *See* OECD (2010), Ch. 1, para. 1.6. and VM 1995:10 51. Arts 9(1) of the UN and US Models are substantially similar to Art. 9(1) of the OECD Model.
5. *See also* e.g., Ryynänen (1996b), 470 for how Art. 9(1) allows taxation of fictive income.
6. The multilateral convention, on the elimination of double taxation in connection with the adjustment of profits of associated enterprises (90/463/EEC) was concluded in 1990 among the EU Member States. *See*, for example, Killius (1990a), 439-440 and Schelpe (1995), 68-70 for the history of the Convention, Killius (1990), 54-57, Helminen (2015), 292-297 and Terra and Wattel (2012), Ch. 11 for the scope of the Convention and Killius (1990), 59-64 and 443-446, Matikkala (1992), 168-172, Helminen (2015), 299-316, Terra and Wattel (2012), Ch. 11 and Heyvaert (1997), 1863-1864 for the procedure provided by the Convention.
7. *See* Rohatgi (2007), 252-253 and 256-274 for examples of country practices.

eliminate double taxation with respect to the withholding tax imposed in the other state.

The upward profit adjustment with respect to the subsidiary does not often include that economic benefit transferred to the parent company is actually also returned to the subsidiary, or is returned from the shareholder to the corporation or that the profits of the shareholder are adjusted downwards (correlative adjustment). For tax purposes, the question of how to handle the economic benefit received by a shareholder, which is not necessarily returned, must be resolved. Where the transferred profits are returned, it must be considered whether the return constitutes another taxable transfer or only a cancellation of the first transfer. The question is whether possible dividend taxation may be avoided by actually returning the economic benefit from the shareholder to the corporation.

There are also two basic situations in which the advantage of transfer-pricing shifts from a parent company to its subsidiary. Either the amount paid by a subsidiary to its parent company is below the arm's length price, or the parent company pays an amount to the subsidiary exceeding the arm's length price. In these situations, the state of residence of the parent company may require the profits of the parent company to be adjusted upwards. The advantage transferred from the parent company to the subsidiary is not relevant as such because it has not been shifted in a dividend relationship. If the transferred amount, however, is actually returned from the subsidiary to the parent company because of the profit adjustment, it may be asked whether this return is classified as a dividend. The state of residence of the recipient of the transfer may view the return as a new transfer from a subsidiary to the parent for no consideration and, therefore, as a dividend. The state of residence of the subsidiary making the return may also view it in the same way.[8]

The relevant question is to what extent the economic benefit transferred from a corporation to its shareholders in the form of transfer prices that deviate from the arm's length price may be and actually is taxed as a dividend under the different legal systems of international tax law. The tax effect of the return of such a benefit is also relevant. This issue involves the extent to which a return of benefit transferred from a shareholder to its corporation in the form of transfer prices constitutes a dividend as a payment from a corporation to its shareholder. For the purpose of this study, it is, however, considered to be clear what the arm's length price is. The only issue that will be discussed is the proper classification of the portion of a transfer price that deviates from the arm's length price.[9]

---

8. *See also*, for example, Taixeira (2009), 452–453 for the different situations that may constitute a hidden dividend distribution.
9. The arm's length principle of tax treaties and domestic tax law of different states and the methods of determining the arm's length price are widely studied. *See*, for example, OECD (1979), OECD (1984), OECD (2010), Bullen (2010), Wittendorff (2016), Petruzzi (2016), Isomaa-Myllymäki (2016), International Fiscal Association (1992), Wiman (1987), Arvidsson (1990) and Ryynänen (1996). The methods for finding an arm's length price are discussed in the OECD reports of 1979, 1984 and 1995, which has been continuously updated. *See* OECD (1979), OECD (1984) and OECD (2010). *See also* Vogel et al. (1997), 528–539 and the literature referred to, Niskakangas (1991), 35–36, Saunders (1989), 252–254, Arvidsson (1990), 66, Theisen and Wenz (1996), 131–134, Baranowski (1996), 278–300 and Blumenberg (1997), 1804–1808. Transfer pricing and the arm's

§8.02 DOMESTIC LAWS

Generally dividend is considered to be a distribution from a corporation to its shareholders with respect to its stock. Distributions must be paid to the shareholder in its capacity as a shareholder and not for any other reason. Under most states' tax law a dividend, however, is not required to be declared at the shareholders' meeting or to be paid in the form of a dividend. Constructive distributions also qualify as a dividend for tax purposes. Many states consider that the tax law concept of a dividend includes any economic benefit transferred from a corporation to one of its shareholders in its capacity as such, for which the shareholder does not give equivalent value in exchange. Some states however treat open dividends partly differently than constructive dividends for tax purposes.

Transfer-pricing adjustments and dividend treatment is based on special domestic law transfer-pricing adjustment provisions and the tax law provisions concerning dividends and constructive dividends. If profits from a resident subsidiary company have been transferred in the form of transfer prices to a non-resident parent company, the profits of the resident subsidiary are adjusted upwards in accordance with by the amount differing from the arm's length price. This amount is also considered to constitute a dividend distribution to the non-resident parent company. The source state dividend withholding tax based on domestic tax law provisions usually applies to this amount.

Dividend treatment applies in many states also if profits are transferred in the form of transfer prices from one subsidiary to another subsidiary of a common parent company. The resident subsidiary is considered to have paid a dividend to the parent company and the parent company is considered to have made a capital investment in the non-resident subsidiary. If the parent company is a non-resident, dividend withholding tax must be paid.

In a situation where a resident parent company returns a payment to a foreign subsidiary because of a profit adjustment in the foreign state, the return does not usually allow the resident shareholder to deduct the repayment of the distribution. There are, however, exceptions to this treatment.

If profits are transferred in the form of transfer prices from a resident parent company to a foreign subsidiary, the amount does not constitute a dividend. Because in this situation, the profits of the resident parent company are adjusted upwards, the classification of the possible return of the transferred amount from the non-resident subsidiary must be solved. As the return is paid by a subsidiary to the parent company, it may be considered to constitute a dividend.

Some states allow the return to be made free of tax. The actual return is not considered a dividend or any kind of taxable income of the parent company. Many states, however, see a separate transfer and a dividend distribution.

---

length principle are dealt with also in the OECD BEPS Actions 8–10 and 13. *See* OECD (2015c) and OECD (2015d). *See* Jan Andersson (1995), 388–429 for determining an acceptable transfer price for company law purposes.

In the obverse situation, where a resident subsidiary makes a return payment to a foreign parent company because of a profit adjustment in the foreign state, many states treat the payment as a dividend because it is a payment from a subsidiary to its parent company. Dividend withholding tax is imposed on this type of return, if allowed by a tax treaty. Some states, however, do not see a dividend and may not tax the transfer.

In conclusion, the tax treatment of economic benefits transferred from a corporation to one of its shareholders in the form of transfer prices varies under the domestic laws of different states.[10] Most countries tax economic benefits transferred from a corporation to one of its shareholders in the form of transfer prices as a constructive dividend under domestic law. There may, however, be certain differences in the ways an open dividend and a constructive dividend are treated. Most states do not consider that a return of a constructive dividend eliminates dividend taxation and many states see a return payment from a subsidiary to its parent company constituting a constructive dividend distribution.

§8.03   EU TAX LAW

[A]   The TFEU

The domestic law provisions of many EU Member States requiring the arm's length principle to be followed concern only cross-border situations. Cross-border situations, thus, may be subject to more burdensome tax treatment compared to similar domestic situations. The application of the domestic law profit adjustment provisions, thus, may be in conflict with the freedom of establishment principle of the TFEU.

According to the EU Court, the domestic law profit adjustment provisions of the EU Member States, however, comply with the TFEU freedom of establishment principle provided that certain conditions are met.[11] According to the EU Court, the objective of preventing tax avoidance together with that of preserving the balanced allocation of the power to impose taxes between the Member States justifies the worse treatment of cross-border situations as compared to domestic situations.[12] Different treatment is justified provided that the treatment does not go beyond what is necessary.

According to the EU Court, the domestic law transfer-pricing adjustment provisions based on the arm's length principle do not go beyond what is necessary if the following conditions are met. The provisions must provide for a consideration of objective and verifiable elements in order to determine whether a transaction represents an artificial arrangement entered into for tax reasons. On each occasion on which there is a suspicion that a transaction does not follow the arm's length principle, the taxpayer must be given an opportunity, without being subjected to undue administrative constraints, to provide evidence of any commercial justification that there may have been for that transaction. If it is found that the arm's length principle is not

---

10. *See,* for example, Taixeira (2009), 456–457 and Rohatgi (2007), 252–253 and 256–274.
11. C-311/08 *Société de Gestion Industrielle (SGI)*.
12. *Ibid.*, para. 69.

followed, the corrective tax measure must be confined to the part that exceeds the arm's length amount.[13]

[B] The Parent-Subsidiary Directive

Even though the domestic law transfer-pricing adjustment provisions would be in accordance with the TFEU, the P-S Directive limits the possibility of dividend taxation if the benefits from a subsidiary to its parent company fall under the scope of application of the Directive.

The P-S Directive applies to distributions of profits by a subsidiary to its parent company by virtue of the association between the companies. It covers not only a dividend but any profit distribution[14] from a qualifying subsidiary to a qualifying parent company, by virtue of the association between the two. Because the P-S Directive does not define the term 'profit distribution', it is not perfectly clear what items are included. Due to the broad term 'profit distribution' the P-S Directive must cover all transfers of economic benefits in the form of transfer prices from a qualifying subsidiary to a qualifying parent company by virtue of the association between the companies. Constructive distributions must be covered even though the text of the P-S Directive does not provide for this expressly.[15] If the P-S Directive was intended to only cover open dividend distributions, the narrower term 'dividend' should have been used instead of the term 'profit distribution'.

This interpretation is also supported by the Interest-Royalty Directive.[16] According to Article 4(2) of the Interest-Royalty Directive, the amount of interest or royalties paid between associated parties that exceeds the arm's length price does not constitute interest or royalties for the purposes of the Directive. The Interest-Royalty Directive does not, however, make any reference to how the amount that does not qualify as interest or royalty under the Directive should be classified. Because the marginal amount, however, does not qualify either as interest or as royalties, it may be treated as a dividend in the same way as the marginal amounts referred to in Articles 11(6) and 12(4) of the OECD Model.[17] To the extent that these marginal amounts are treated as a dividend, they should also qualify as profit distributions under the P-S Directive.

It is sometimes argued that a constructive dividend is not covered by the P-S Directive. This argument is supported by the claims that the sums treated as a

---

13. *See* C-311/08 *Société de Gestion Industrielle (SGI)*, paras 71–72. *See also* C-524/04 *Test Claimants in the Thin Cap Group Litigation*, para. 82, and C-201/05 *Test Claimants in the CFC and Dividend Group Litigation*, para. 84.
14. Except for liquidation distributions with respect to taxation in the state of residence of the parent company, *see* Arts 4 and 5 of the P-S Directive. *See*, for liquidation distributions, below in Ch. 11.
15. *See* for this interpretation, for example, Förster and Schollmeier (1995), 864, Ryynänen (1996), 436 and Ryynänen (1997), 35.
16. Council Directive of 3 Jun. 2003 on a common system of taxation applicable to interest and royalty payments made between associated companies of different Member States (2003/49/EC). *See also* Proposal for a council directive on a common system of taxation applicable to interest and royalty payments made between associated companies of different Member States (COM (98) 67 final) (submitted by the Commission on 6 Mar. 1998).
17. *See*, for excessive interest and royalties under tax treaties, below in Ch. 8 s. §8.04.

constructive dividend in one state are not necessarily regarded as a constructive dividend in the other state. It is also argued that it is the EU Arbitration Convention and not the P-S Directive that is specifically aimed at coping with the double taxation caused by transfer-pricing adjustments.[18] These arguments, however, are weak.

The fact that two states may not agree on whether a profit distribution exists or not does not change the fact that the state that views a distribution as existing must grant P-S Directive benefits with respect to the distribution. The application of the Arbitration Convention also does not mean that the economic benefit transferred from a subsidiary to its parent company is actually returned. A profit transfer from a corporation to one of its shareholders may still exist. Because the P-S Directive hinders the taxation of distributions of profits, this constructive profit distribution should remain untaxed if transferred between qualifying companies.

The P-S Directive does not apply to profit distributions from a parent company to its subsidiary, and therefore, it is not applicable in situations where transfer pricing is used to transfer economic benefit from a parent company to its subsidiary. In these situations, only the Arbitration Convention is applicable. Sometimes, however, the benefit is returned from the subsidiary to the parent company because of an upward profit adjustment with respect to the parent company. Should this event occur, it triggers the question of whether the P-S Directive hinders the taxation of the return. The return, after all, includes a transfer of an economic benefit from a subsidiary to its parent company. The return is also clearly made by virtue of the subsidiary's association with the parent company. Therefore, the P-S Directive must be applicable with respect to these return payments. As a result, even if either of the states treated the return as a taxable constructive dividend instead of a tax-free repayment of capital, the states must leave the return payment untaxed. The P-S Directive hinders the taxation of the return payment if it is made between qualifying companies.

Under the domestic law of different states, both an economic benefit from a company directly to the shareholder and an economic benefit from a subsidiary to another subsidiary of a common parent company may be taxed as a dividend. Therefore, it may be asked whether P-S Directive benefits have to be granted in situations, for example, in which a payment is made between two subsidiary companies resident in one Member State with a common parent company in another Member State. The P-S Directive, however, expressly requires that a dividend be paid from a subsidiary to its parent company by virtue of the association between the companies. Strictly interpreted, distributions between two subsidiary companies with a common parent company may not qualify for P-S Directive benefits. The P-S Directive, thus, does not seem to hinder the state of residence of the subsidiaries from taxing the benefit transferred from one of the subsidiaries to another subsidiary.

Under domestic law, where such a benefit is taxed as a dividend, it is deemed that the distribution is actually made first to the common parent company of the subsidiaries. The state considers that there is a fictive profit distribution from a subsidiary to its parent company made by virtue of the subsidiary's association with the parent

---

18. *See*, for example, Vaanistendael (1992), 604–605.

company. From the point of view of the state that taxes such income as a dividend, there is a distribution of profits from a subsidiary to its parent company. P-S Directive benefits must, therefore, be available if the term 'profit distribution' is interpreted to include fictive profit distributions as well.

The wording of the P-S Directive does not expressly include fictive distributions. However, the P-S Directive may be interpreted to apply to such situations where the domestic tax law of a Member State subjects a fictive distribution to taxation as if an actual distribution had been made.[19] From the fictive dividend treatment under domestic law, it logically follows that the state also treats a fictive distribution as a distribution with respect to the P-S Directive. There are no grounds for the state to tax the fictive distribution that it deems to be a dividend from a subsidiary to its parent company if it could not have taxed an actual dividend distribution from the subsidiary to the parent company as a dividend. In such a situation, the fictive distribution did not occur in order to avoid dividend taxation.

If the holding requirement is fulfilled between the distributing subsidiary and the parent company, the P-S Directive hinders the state of residence of the distributing company from imposing dividend withholding tax with respect to the fictive dividend. Also, the state of residence of the parent company, if it deems that the parent company has received the constructive dividend, should exempt the fictive income or at least should eliminate any economic double taxation with respect to the income in accordance with the requirements of the P-S Directive. If there is no qualifying relationship between the distributing subsidiary and the parent company, the P-S Directive does not hinder dividend taxation.

It is also important to note that the P-S Directive does not allow the state of residence of the parent company to exempt a distribution of profits which is deductible by the payer subsidiary. If the profits are tax deductible by the subsidiary, the state of residence of the parent company shall tax the distribution in accordance with its domestic law irrespective of the payment's classification.[20]

§8.04 TAX TREATIES

Articles 9, 11(6) and 12(4) of the OECD Model[21] are all based on the arm's length principle. Article 9 is a general rule concerning any price deviating from an arm's length price used in transactions between associated enterprises. Article 9(1) allows tax authorities to include in the profits of an enterprise the profits that would have accrued to an enterprise but have not because of the imposition of special conditions in the commercial or financial relations between two associated enterprises.

Article 9(1) does not, however, give any guidance on how the amount that deviates from the arm's length price and the adjusted profits are actually to be taxed. It only states that the adjusted profits may be '...taxed accordingly...'. No answers to

---

19. See for a similar interpretation Scherer (1995), 226 with respect to undistributed profits deemed to be distributed.
20. Article 4(1)(a) of the P-S Directive.
21. The US and UN Models include similar articles.

§8.04

the classification questions are provided by Article 9(1), which only gives the arm's length principle as a standard for determining the amount of profits that are to be regarded as income of each associated entity. Neither does Article 9(2) of the OECD Model forbid or require the dividend treatment of the economic benefit to be transferred from a corporation to its shareholders in the form of transfer prices.[22] Therefore, the classification and actual taxation of the portions of the receipts below or above the arm's length price in transactions between associated enterprises depends on the other articles of the applicable treaty and on domestic law.

Articles 11(6) and 12(4) only state that the portion of interest or royalties that exceeds the arm's length price because of a special relationship between the payer and the beneficial owner of the income does not constitute interest or royalties for tax treaty purposes. The provisions leave unanswered the classification issue in these situations, and do not deal with classification in other situations at all. The articles only state that '...the excess part of the payments shall remain taxable according to the laws of each contracting state, due regard being had to the other provisions of the Convention...'.

Each state may solve, in accordance with its own domestic tax law, how the excess amount of interest or royalties or any amount deviating from the arm's length price is classified for domestic law purposes. Domestic law classification is, however, not necessarily decisive for tax treaty purposes. The phrase '...due regard being had to the other provisions of the Convention...' requires that the treaty article under which the excessive amount is taxed must be resolved by the general rules of tax treaty classification. The domestic law classification may only govern for tax treaty purposes if Article 3(2) or Article 10(3) requires or allows the domestic law classification to become treaty law. According to the Commentary on Article 11(6) and Article 12(4):

> [T]he exact nature of such excess will need to be ascertained according to the circumstances of each case, in order to determine the category of income in which it should be classified for the purposes of applying the provisions of the tax laws of the states concerned and the provisions of the Convention.[23]

According to the Commentaries, it is also possible that the domestic laws of each state might oblige the states to apply different articles of the Convention.[24] Therefore, it may be thought that tax treaty classification could actually be made according to each state's own domestic legislation. The same conclusion may be drawn from the fact that the general rule of Article 3(2) allows classification in accordance with the domestic law of each state applying the treaty, unless the context of the treaty requires otherwise. Because it is clear that international double taxation should be eliminated also in cases of excessive royalties and interest, inconsistent classification by the two

---

22. *See* para. 9 of the Commentary on Art. 9(2) of the OECD Model according to which '... nothing in paragraph 2 prevents such secondary adjustments from being made where they are permitted under the domestic law of Contracting States'. *See also* OECD (2010), para. 4.69, according to which Art. 9(2) of the OECD Model neither forbids nor requires tax administrations to make secondary adjustments.
23. Paragraph 35 of the Commentary on Art. 11 of the OECD Model and para. 25 of the Commentary on Art. 12 of the OECD Model.
24. Paragraph 36 of the Commentary on Art. 11 of the OECD Model and para. 26 of the Commentary on Art. 12 of the OECD Model.

states is not quite in line with the purpose of tax treaties. Therefore, according to the Commentaries, such a conflict in classification should be resolved by a mutual agreement procedure.[25] It is also clear that if the amount qualifies as a dividend under the domestic law of the source state and, therefore, as a dividend under tax treaties, the other state must accept the dividend treatment for tax treaty purposes.

An economic benefit transferred from a corporation to one of its shareholders in the form of transfer prices may qualify as a dividend under Article 10 of the OECD Model only if it is income paid by a company. It must be income from shares or other rights, not being debt-claims, participating in profits, or income from other corporate rights taxed the same way as income from shares in the state of residence of the payer. Under domestic law, benefits transferred from a corporation to one of its shareholders by virtue of the shareholder relationship are taxed as a constructive dividend. Therefore, benefits taxed as a constructive dividend under domestic law generally are from a company and from shares.

The arm's length portion of transfer prices is made on the grounds of a contractual relationship between the corporation and one of its shareholders, but the amount by which the transfer price differs from the arm's length price is made on the grounds of the shareholder relationship between the persons. Therefore, the benefit is actually from shares even though it seems to be from a contract. The benefit is from shares, if the arm's length price would have been paid instead of the amount actually paid, if a shareholder relationship between the parties had not existed. The fact that the transfer price is actually interest, royalties or a sales price does not change the fact that the portion deviating from the arm's length price is income from shares if the difference derives from the shareholder relationship.[26]

Economic benefit transferred between two subsidiaries of a common parent company in the form of transfer prices may constitute income from shares. The benefit may actually be transferred because of the shareholder relationship between the subsidiaries and the parent company. According to the Commentaries, even though benefits to which a holding in a company confer entitlement are made available to persons that are not shareholders within the meaning of company law, they may sometimes constitute a dividend. Dividend classification is possible in the case of concealed holdings, that is, if the legal relations between such non-shareholding persons and the company are assimilated to a holding in a company if the persons receiving the benefits are closely connected with a shareholder of the company. Distribution by virtue of a holding in a company may, therefore, also be taxed as a dividend if it is paid to a company belonging to the same group to which the shareholder company belongs.[27]

---

25. *Ibid.*
26. *See,* for example, Niskakangas (1983), 351 for how the excessive part of royalties may constitute a dividend.
27. Paragraph 29 of the Commentary on Art. 10 of the OECD Model. *See,* however, decision 15649 36 Droit Fiscal 39 (1984), 1092, of the Supreme Administrative Court of France from 27 Jul. 1984, in which the court considered that a payment in excess of the arm's length price did not qualify as dividend for tax treaty purposes because the payment was not made in a shareholder relationship.

Chapter 8: Classification of Economic Benefits from Corporations §8.04

Dividend treatment under Article 10(3) requires that the economic benefit transferred from a corporation to one of its shareholders in the form of transfer prices constitutes income. Because a transfer-pricing benefit does not necessarily include an excessive payment but may also be in the form of a payment below the arm's length price, it must be asked whether the transfer constitutes income. Because the term 'income' is not defined in any article of the Model, it has to be interpreted in accordance with the general rule of Article 3(2) of the Model. The term must be given a contextual meaning if the context so requires and otherwise it may be given the meaning of the term under the domestic law of the state applying the treaty.

The wording of Article 10(3) seems to require that the term 'income' be given an autonomous interpretation for the purposes of the whole definition.[28] The context, however, may be said to require that the term 'income' be interpreted in accordance with the law of the source state for the purpose of the whole dividend definition with respect to a constructive dividend the same way as with bonus shares.[29] A constructive dividend, after all, is generally a benefit from shares. Therefore, a constructive dividend should be evaluated under the first part of the dividend definition and not under the third part of the definition concerning income from other corporate rights. Thus, the opinion of the Commentaries, according to which a constructive dividend qualifies as a dividend as long as the source state treats it as a dividend, actually requires that the source state interpretation is also followed with respect to the autonomous part of the dividend definition.[30]

With respect to a constructive dividend, it must also be asked whether it is paid in the way required by Article 10 of the OECD Model because, strictly speaking, no payment necessarily occurs. The benefit may also be in the form of consideration below the arm's length price. The term 'paid' is an undefined treaty term that must be interpreted in accordance with Article 3(2). As discussed above in connection with bonus shares,[31] the term must be interpreted to include any form of satisfying the shareholder's claim to receiving the dividend. Accordingly, the term 'payment' includes the provision of any economic benefit from a corporation to the shareholder so long as the benefit otherwise qualifies as a dividend.[32]

In conclusion, economic benefits from a corporation to one of its shareholders in the form of transfer prices, qualify under Article 10 of the OECD Model as a dividend

---

28. *See* the discussion in connection with bonus shares in Ch. 7 s. §7.02[D].
29. *See* Ch. 7 s. §7.02[D].
30. *See also*, for this interpretation, Vogel et al. (1997), 649–650. Vogel does not, however, defend this interpretation with the requirements of Art. 3(2). According to Vogel, the source state approach leads to conflict with the wording of Art. 10(3). According to the opinion of the author of this study, there is, however, actually no conflict, because the term income in the phrase '...income from shares...' must be interpreted according to the rules of Art. 3(2) as the wording of Art. 10(3) demands, but the context requires source state classification. Also, according to the Technical Explanation of the 2006 US Model, Art. 10, para. 166, a constructive dividend, which results from a non-arm's length transaction between a corporation and a related party, is a dividend under the 2006 US Model.
31. *See* Ch. 7 s. §7.02[D].
32. *See* for this interpretation also Vogel et al. (1997), 587–588 and Wattel and Marres (2003), 66–68 who consider a constructive dividend to be paid in the way required for dividend classification for tax treaty purposes.

so long as the state of residence of the constructive dividend-distributing entity classifies the constructive dividend as a dividend.[33] This interpretation is reasonable in practice because, generally, it is in the interests of the state from which the benefit is transferred abroad, to tax the income as a dividend, and not in the interests of the other state. Therefore, if the classification of the other state were to be decisive, that state could effectively hinder taxation in the source state.

The same interpretation should apply with respect to all benefits from a corporation to one of its shareholders in the form of transfer prices. Some may argue that Articles 11(6) and 12(4) of the OECD Model allow the state of residence of the recipient of excessive interest or royalties to make its own classification. This argument may be made because of the phrase '...according to the laws of each contracting state...' of Articles 11(6) and 12(4) of the OECD Model.[34] However, in situations where excessive interest or royalties are paid from a corporation to one of its shareholders, the dividend classification of the source state should be accepted. This interpretation is in accordance with the Commentaries according to which benefits, such as a constructive dividend, qualify as a dividend under the OECD Model so long as the source state treats the benefits as a dividend.[35] The reference in Articles 11(6) and 12(4) to the laws of each contracting state also includes that due regard must be had to the other provisions of the convention. Therefore, the reference to domestic law does not actually include more than the treatment under domestic law, whereas the limits for taxation under domestic law must be derived from the provisions of the convention.

Source state classification with respect to transfer-pricing benefits from a corporation to one of its shareholders means that so long as the state of residence treats such benefit as a constructive dividend, the other state must also treat the amount as a dividend under the applicable treaty. The other state must eliminate double taxation with respect to the amount in accordance with the treaty rules concerning a dividend.[36] This requirement only concerns, of course, the amount that the other state agrees to be the difference between the amount actually paid and the arm's length amount. If the other state does not consider that there is a deviation between the transfer price used and the arm's length price, that state does not have to accept the classification as a dividend. Therefore, the fact that the other state should accept the dividend classification of the source state does not have very much relevance in practice. In order for the states to reach an agreement with respect to the arm's length price, a mutual agreement procedure is often needed.

Because a constructive dividend generally qualifies as a dividend under the OECD Model, the actual return payment from a subsidiary to its parent company of a

---

33. *See* for this interpretation also Teixeira (2009), 461. Teixeira, however, recognizes that the tax administrations of certain countries consider that constructive dividends qualify as dividends for tax treaty purposes only if they are dividends for the company law purposes of the source state. Otherwise, they are considered to be other income qualifying under an article based on Art. 21 of the OECD Model.
34. *See* for this conclusion Piltz (1995), 119–120 and Portner (1996), 26.
35. Paragraph 28 of the Commentary on Art. 10 of the OECD Model.
36. In practice, however, states often do not consider that such an obligation exists. *See* Höhn (1982), 141–142 and Piltz (1995), 120.

benefit transferred from a parent company to the subsidiary also qualifies as a dividend. Such a payment qualifies as income paid by a company and as income from shares. Therefore, to the extent that the state of residence of the subsidiary views the repayment as a constructive dividend subject to withholding tax under domestic law instead of as a repayment of capital, it may impose withholding tax in accordance with the tax treaty's dividend article. If the other state views the return as a taxable transfer, it must at least eliminate the double taxation with respect to the withholding tax imposed in the source state.

The dividend definitions of the dividend articles of most actual tax treaties are similar to Article 10 of the OECD Model on the points relevant to the taxation of economic benefits from a corporation to one of its shareholders in the form of transfer prices. Under these treaties, these benefits should be treated as a dividend so long as the source state treats them as a dividend. The state of residence of the recipient of these benefits should, in these situations, eliminate double taxation in accordance with the rules of the applicable treaty concerning a dividend provided the state agrees that the transfer price actually deviates from the arm's length price.

§8.05 CONCLUSIONS

In practice, double taxation is often caused by the fact that two states have different opinions on what the arm's length price is in transactions between related parties. Even though the states, in principle, would agree on the classification of economic benefits transferred from a corporation to its shareholder in the form of transfer prices, in practice, double taxation is often not avoided.

Many, but not all countries, tax economic benefits transferred from a corporation to one of its shareholders in the form of transfer prices as a constructive dividend under domestic law. The treatment in different countries may be different. There may be certain differences in the ways an open dividend and a constructive dividend are treated. Most states do not consider that a return of a constructive dividend eliminates dividend taxation.

In most countries, it is considered that a benefit from a corporation to one of its shareholders in the form of transfer prices generally qualifies as a dividend both for the purposes of the P-S Directive and for the purposes of tax treaties. Therefore, with respect to benefits transferred in direct investment relations between companies resident in different EU Member States, the source state does not impose withholding tax even though the benefit is treated as a dividend.

Despite the fact that most states generally agree that a constructive dividend qualifies as a dividend under tax treaties, in practice, double taxation may not be avoided. Because it is only in the interests of the source state to argue that there is a benefit transferred from it to another state in the form of transfer prices, the other state does not necessarily recognize this benefit. Therefore, the state of residence of the recipient of such a benefit may not eliminate double taxation with respect to the taxes imposed in the source state, even though the source state, in principle, has correctly applied the treaty. The same problem applies with respect to the P-S Directive. The reason for this problem is that the state of residence of the recipient of a benefit may consider that there is no deviation from the arm's length price. In such a situation, neither the tax treaties nor the P-S Directive requires that the state eliminate double taxation. Therefore, the parties may have to resort to either the mutual agreement procedure, tax treaty arbitration or the Arbitration Convention to solve the issue.

CHAPTER 9
Classification of Return on Debt-Equity Hybrids

§9.01 INTRODUCTION

There are a number of forms that corporate financing may take within the bounds of company and contract law. The basic forms of finance are equity and debt. Return on a debt investment is interest, whereas generally, only a return on an equity investment that constitutes a shareholder relationship may be a dividend. Most states treat debt and equity, and interest and dividends differently for tax purposes.[1] The tax treatment of debt and equity is not neutral, even though economically both debt and equity investments in a company have the same function, that is, to enable the company to generate profits. Because the tax treatment of equity finance and debt finance is not neutral, tax implications have a substantial impact on finance decisions.

Generally, debt finance tends to be favoured over equity finance in taxation.[2] The total tax burden on debt finance is often lower than it is on equity finance.[3] Therefore, corporations tend to prefer debt finance in order to minimize the total tax burden on corporate finance. A dividend is normally not deductible from the paying corporation's taxable profits, whereas interest reduces the corporation's taxable profits. The main portion of tax revenue from interest is usually realized by the state to which interest is paid, whereas the main portion of tax revenue from a dividend is realized by the state from which a dividend is paid. Source state interest withholding tax is also often lower

---

1. *See*, for example, Plitz (1996), 87 and Rohatgi (2005), 264–272.
2. *See* OECD (1991), Ch. 4. *See* e.g., Sommerhalder (1996), 82 and Rohatgi (2005), 264–272, generally for tax consequences of equity or debt.
3. In a situation with a very low rate of corporation tax and an exemption for a dividend received, the total tax burden on equity may be lower than that of debt. *See*, for example, Jacobs (1996), 26 for facts that affect whether debt or equity finance is favoured in taxation.

than the source state dividend withholding tax.[4] Debt finance may, therefore, be used to reduce tax in the source state. The lack of tax neutrality between equity and debt financing creates possibilities for tax planning and requires debt and equity, and interest and dividends to be distinguished for tax purposes.

Debt and equity instruments are often economically substitutable for one another. From an investor's point of view, it may be irrelevant whether an investment is made in the form of debt or equity. Corporations may also be financed with the so-called mixed or hybrid financial instruments that possess features of both equity instruments and debt instruments, or which may be converted from one type to the other.[5] Such debt-equity hybrids[6] include corporate shares attached with conditions that make the shares, from an economic point of view, closer to debt, and loan contracts attached with conditions that make the loan in its economic substance closer to an equity investment.

Hybrid instruments are often formed by adding certain elements of equity instruments to debt instruments. Interest on a loan contract may depend on company profits, the loan may be subordinated compared to other debt, it may be convertible to corporate shares or it may be perpetual. The return and risks of a debt investment may be made economically closer to the return and risks of an equity investment. On the other hand, a share investment may be attached with a fixed return, or the shares may be redeemable. Therefore, sometimes a debtor-creditor relationship may, in its economic substance, be very close to a shareholder relationship and vice versa.

For various legal, economic and commercial reasons, companies use mixed financing forms to combine the advantages of both equity and debt. A hybrid may allow an investor to share in the earnings and growth of a corporation in the way that a shareholder is allowed to, while allowing the investor to cut its exposure or possible loss in the way normally possible only for lenders. Debt-equity hybrids are often used, for example, to lower the cost of debt capital, to make debt instruments more attractive to investors or to attract equity investors. Debt financing is often favoured in contrast

---

4. It is often in the interests of the source state to prevent excessive debt finance. *See*, for example, Äimä (2009), 158–168, Vapaavuori (1996a), 527, Essers et al. (1994), 167–170 and Arnold (1994), 512, for the differences in the taxation of debt and equity. *See* Raedel and French (1995), 1594, for tax arguments for different capital mixes.
5. The term 'hybrid instrument' or 'mixed instrument' is used to refer to any kinds of financial instruments that have characteristics of more than one type of financial instrument. *See*, for example, OECD (1994), 7–8, Piltz (1995a), 125, Bureau Francis Lefebvre, Loyens & Volkmaars, Oppenhoff & Rädler (1996), 8, Duncan (2000), 22 and Rohatgi (2007), 105–106. Sometimes the term 'mezzanine financing' is used to refer to instruments with both debt and equity characteristics. *See* Wood (1995), 39. Hybrid financial instruments form a group of complex financial instruments, or innovative or new financial instruments that also include other kinds of complex financial instruments, such as derivative financial instruments. *See*, for complex financial instruments, Hariton (1988), 731–788 and OECD (1994). *See also*, for the terms, Lyons (1996), 1195 and Neighbour (1997), 931. The term 'financial instrument' covers both the terms 'financing instruments' and 'investment instruments'. The difference between these two terms is that the former is from the perspective of the financing corporation whereas the latter is from the perspective of the investor. *See*, for these two terms, for example David (1996), 3 and 8 and Mannio (1997), 245. *See* for the terminology related to hybrid financial instruments also e.g., Bärsch (2012), 9–12.
6. The term 'debt-equity hybrid' is used, for example, in Hariton (1988), 732.

to equity financing because the granting and repaying of loans is often more flexible, additional debt finance does not affect shareholding structure, debt does not take part in entrepreneurial risks and debt is in a better position in a company liquidation than equity. Equity providers usually also expect a higher yield than debt providers as compensation for the higher risk. The objective may be to attain the security of equity finance but the tax treatment of debt finance.[7]

So long as the distinctions between debt and equity and between interest and dividend are maintained in taxation, the classification of each instrument and the return on it must be determined.[8] However, because of the mixed characteristics, the classification of hybrid instruments and the payments related to them is not always clear and there is a danger of inconsistent classification.[9] One state may treat a certain financial transaction as a loan whereas another state may treat it simultaneously as an equity contribution. A return on a hybrid instrument may also be treated as a dividend in one state and as interest in another. This asymmetry may be exploited in international tax planning or in international tax avoidance.[10]

The relevant issue for this study is the extent to which the interest on hybrid debt may be and actually is treated as a dividend under the different legal systems of international tax law. The extent to which dividend treatment may be and actually is denied for a dividend on hybrid equity is also of interest.

§9.02 GENERAL APPROACHES

[A] General Characteristics of Debt and Equity

The distinction between interest and a dividend in taxation is based on the distinction between debt and equity or on the distinction between a debtor-creditor relationship and a shareholder relationship. In order to determine whether certain income from a corporation constitutes interest or a dividend for tax purposes, it must be determined whether the investment on which the income is paid as return is debt or equity.

The starting point is that the legal form of an investment is respected for tax purposes as well.[11] Tax classification and company law classification of a hybrid may not, however, be the same because the objective of the distinction of debt from equity

---

7. *See* Piltz (1995a), 126, Keinonen (1995a), 237, Raineri and Engle (1996), 1716, Hariton (1994), 501, Korge (1996), 753 and Bureau Francis Lefebvre, Loyens & Volkmaars, Oppenhoff & Rädler (1996), 8–9, Äimä (2009), 137–142 and Rohatgi (2007), 111, for arguments for the use of hybrid financing.
8. It may be asked whether the differentiation between debt and equity should be eliminated in taxation. Ryynänen (1996), 429 recognizes that taxation of interest and a dividend should be more neutral. Similarly, Brown recognizes in Lyons (1996), 1196 that '…opportunities for arbitrage will always be present until a tax system is adopted that removes the difference between debt and equity…'. *See* Schön (2012), 490–502 for reasons to keep or abolish the distinction between debt and equity for tax purposes.
9. *See* Andersson (1995), 26, for this uncertainty.
10. *See*, for example, OECD (2015). OECD (1994), 101–102, Solway and Bothamley (1995), 1680–1681, Raedel and French (1995), 1596–1597, Rohatgi (2005), 111 and Helminen (2016a), 365–367, for the use of hybrid instruments for tax planning in cross-border situations.
11. *See* Arnold (1994), 498, Essers et al. (1994), 171 and Jackson (1990), 319.

is different for tax purposes and for company law purposes. Because the taxation of debt and equity is not neutral, in distinguishing between debt and equity and between interest and dividends, it is not necessarily the company law form, but the actual economic substance that may be determinative.[12] The possibility of using hybrid instruments with mixed characteristics for tax avoidance purposes requires a new way of looking at the economic nature of the instruments and the returns on the instruments. Therefore, for tax purposes, the typical legal and economic characteristics of debt and equity need to be examined.[13]

The fundamental difference between a pure debt investment and a pure equity investment is that the relationship between a debtor and a creditor is based on a loan contract, whereas the shareholder relationship is based on company law. Another primary difference between a typical debt and a typical equity investment is the requirement of repayment. A creditor has a right to a refund at the end of the fixed time period. A shareholder, on the other hand, is not entitled to any refund during the lifetime of the company, that is, before the winding up of the company. An equity investment is, thus, perpetual in its nature, whereas a debt investment is only temporary. In a company liquidation, the rights of equity investors are subordinated to the rights of the debt investors. All creditors must be satisfied before the equity investors may have a share in the proceeds.

Another difference is that a creditor is entitled to a fixed payment of return on the investment even if the debtor corporation had not earned benefits in contrast to a shareholder who is entitled to a return on the investment only if the company makes a decision to distribute profits. The exact amount of interest may not be known in advance, but at least the formula according to which the return is calculated will be. Interest is, generally, a fixed amount of return agreed upon in a loan contract, whereas the amount of a dividend distribution is based on a decision of a shareholders' meeting. The potential for interest is limited, whereas the potential for a dividend is unlimited. A shareholder is also entitled to liquidation proceeds. Everything that is left after all the creditors have been satisfied is shared by the equity investors. The unlimited return potential compensates for the higher risk of equity as compared to debt. A shareholder is also generally entitled to direct control of the company unlike creditors.

A debt investment is very close to equity in its economic substance if a debt contract includes conditions that allow the investor to participate in the issuer company's profits and risks. A loan may be perpetual and the repayment of a loan may be subordinated to other loans in the case of insolvency. Interest on a loan may depend on company profits and a loan may participate in hidden reserves and in the liquidation proceeds of the debtor company. A loan may also be convertible into the debtor company's shares. The fact that the debt-to-equity ratio of the debtor company is significantly higher than in other companies in the same industry may indicate that a

---

12. *See* Hariton (1994), 521 and Ryynänen (1996), 394 for the relevance of economic substance in tax classification.
13. *See,* for example, Villa (1997), 42, 94, 115 and 134, Lawrence (1990), 118, Collado and Rey (1993), 110, Essers et al. (1994), 170, Ryynänen (1996), 387–390, Engle and Raineri (1996), 774 and Raineri and Engle (1996), 1716, for typical equity and debt characteristics.

creditor also shares in the risk of the debtor company.[14] Similarly, an equity investment may be very close to debt from an economic perspective. The investment may not be perpetual because the shares are redeemable. The investment may not carry voting rights. Therefore, all characteristics of an instrument must be evaluated in order to determine whether an investment is closer to debt or equity in its true nature.

Debt-equity hybrids may be placed on an imaginary line depending on the debt and equity characteristics involved. At one end of this line, there is a pure loan with fixed interest and, at the other end, there is a pure equity investment with a shareholder position with all its rights attached including the right to a dividend. Next to the pure debt, there is a loan, the interest on which is not fixed but is dependent upon the profits of the company. Next to the pure equity investment, there is an investment in capital stock, which does not carry a voting right but carries a preferential right to a dividend.[15] Depending on how much of either typical debt or equity characteristics are included in an instrument, the closer it may be to either the pure debt or pure equity. The tax classification of an instrument may also depend on whether the instrument includes more debt or more equity characteristics.

From an economic point of view, there is little reason for the distinction between the tax treatment of debt and equity. Both equity and debt are claims upon the assets of a corporation and both are acquired in exchange for capital. A shareholder loan especially may be distinguished from equity with reference to company law or tax law, but from an economic point of view, they are similar to each other.[16] From an economic point of view, there is not much difference between the return on debt and the return on equity, that is, between interest and a dividend. Both interest and a dividend are, by their economic nature, remuneration to the investor for the use of the invested capital. Shareholders of a widely held corporation are, from an economic point of view, in a very similar position to the lenders of a widely held corporation. In contrast, shareholder lenders in a closely held corporation may attain, by means of a loan contract, a position similar to a shareholding.

The only actual difference, from an economic point of view, between debt and equity is the variability of the returns. The distinction should, therefore, be made according to the risk that is involved. A shareholder's intention is to bear the risk of the enterprise, whereas a creditor does not have the intention to assume such a risk. In principle, a creditor bears a smaller risk than an equity holder that a return on the investment will not be paid and that the investment will not be paid back.[17] Because the return on equity depends on company profits and on a distribution decision and because the remuneration of the investment is subordinate to creditors' claims, equity generally bears a higher risk than debt.[18]

---

14. *See* OECD (1979), 87, Collado and Rey (1993), 111, Hariton (1994), 503, King (1995), 159 and Piltz (1996), 102.
15. This illustration is used by Kilpi (1962), 11.
16. *See* for this point Kilpi (1962), 222 and Ryynänen (1996), 108.
17. *See* Ryynänen (1996), 389, for how it is not an absolute fact that a creditor always bears a smaller risk than an equity investor does. However, in relations between equity investors and creditors of one single company, this fact is true.
18. *See* for this distinction Hariton (1988), 775.

The economic difference in the risks of debt and equity is based primarily on legislation. In many situations, the distinctions between debt and equity, and interest and dividends cannot be supported by economic arguments. The distinction, therefore, would not be necessary for tax purposes. However, if a distinction is made, the risk involved in an instrument should be evaluated in determining the classification.[19] The distinction should be made by considering the whole of the instrument, and not its characteristics separately.[20]

Concentrating on the economic substance instead of the legal form is in line with the principle of tax neutrality. In order for a tax system to be neutral, economically equivalent instruments should be taxed in the same way. The form in which an investment is made should not make a difference in taxation to the extent that the instruments are economically equivalent. It should not be possible to avoid taxation through the use of instruments that are economically similar to instruments subject to tax. Therefore, the more equity characteristics that are included in a debt investment and vice versa, the more reason there is to tax the debt as equity or equity as debt. The problem is determining what level of equivalency is required to exist between two instruments in order for similar taxation to be required. A hybrid debt instrument may be largely economically equivalent to an actual investment in the share capital of a company, but it is never identical, no matter how many equity characteristics are involved.

[B] Domestic Tax Laws

In most countries, a corporation may decide relatively freely on how the corporation is financed. Shareholders of a corporation may make pure equity, pure debt or different hybrid investments in the corporation. The classification of an instrument may, however, differ depending on whether it is classified for company law, accounting or tax purposes.

In most countries, the form alone is not decisive in the tax classification of a hybrid instrument. The doctrine of substance-over-form has a strong tradition in many countries. Transactions may be taxed in accordance with their economic and legal substance rather than according to their form. Therefore, in many countries, hybrid instruments and returns on them are evaluated in accordance with their actual economic and legal substance. Interest on debt hybrids may be treated as a dividend if the substance of the instrument is closer to equity and the substance of the interest is closer to a dividend.

Even though the substance of an instrument may be decisive for tax purposes, it is not common that countries bifurcate an instrument into an equity part and a debt part for tax purposes. In most countries, a hybrid instrument is to be classified either as debt or equity for tax purposes.

---

19. *See* Hariton (1988), 775 and Ryynänen (1996), 108 for this suggestion.
20. *See* OECD (1979), 88–89 for this suggestion.

Often the likelihood of reclassification is greater in the case of debt from related parties compared to third-party debt. The general domestic anti-avoidance provisions may be applied to reclassify hybrid debt as equity if the form of debt is used instead of the form of equity in order to avoid taxes.

The domestic laws of some countries expressly mention which hybrid instruments constitute debt and which constitute equity for tax purposes. Even in these countries, the lists defining the classification of hybrids, however, are usually not exhaustive.

The domestic tax law of many countries does not include such express provisions mentioning which hybrids constitute debt and which constitute equity for tax purposes. The definition of a shareholder compared to a debt investor is often based on case law.

The domestic tax laws of different countries may include lists of the factors that are taken into account when determining the classification of a hybrid. Similar factors may be taken into account for classification purposes based on case law. These factors may include, for example:[21]

- whether there is interest deviating from the arm's length price;
- whether there is proportionality among the shareholders;
- whether profit-dependent interest or profit participation exist;
- the presence or absence of an unconditional promise on the part of the issuer to pay a certain sum on demand at a fixed maturity date that is in the reasonably foreseeable future;
- possession by the holder of the right to enforce the payment of principal and interest;
- the right of holders to participate in the management of the issuer;
- the identity between the holders of the instruments and the shareholders of the issuer;
- the label placed on the instruments by the parties;
- whether the instruments are intended to be treated as debt or equity for non-tax purposes;
- the certainty of the return or the risk involved;
- whether there is a fixed rate of interest;
- the source for the payments required by the instrument;
- the voting power of the holder;
- the status of the holder as equal or inferior to regular corporate creditors;
- whether the instrument is subordinated to or preferred over other indebtedness;
- whether the instrument is convertible into the stock of the corporation;
- thin capitalization or the debt-to-equity ratio of the corporation; and
- the ability of the corporation to obtain loans from outside sources.

---

21. *See*, for example, Robertson and Burckel (1988), 785–787, Benson and McKenna (1994), 311, Benson and McKenna (1994a), 466–467, Kempler (1996), 51–53, Engle and Raineri (1996), 773 and Raineri and Engle (1996), 1723, Mittelstadt and Corrigan (1990), 4, Sommerhalder (1996), 88 and McCarthy (1997) for the different characteristics.

It depends on the country concerned which of the characters are looked at. Usually, the classification chosen by the parties is not binding on the tax authorities. In most countries, the whole of the characters instead of a single character is decisive. In most countries, the determination of whether an instrument constitutes debt or equity for tax purposes requires a case-by-case approach where the different equity and debt characteristics are evaluated.

Most countries do not consider the classification in the other country concerned as decisive. Many countries, however, consider the classification in the other country as one characteristic that may be looked at among the other characters that are looked at when determining the classification.[22]

[C] EU Law

[1] Relevance

Nothing in EU law, in principle, hinders the classification of hybrid instruments in accordance with their economic substance rather than in accordance with their form for tax purposes. EU law does not affect the domestic tax law classification of interest as a dividend or a dividend as interest. The resulting tax treatment, however, must comply with the TFEU basic freedoms,[23] the provisions of the EU Anti-Tax Avoidance Directive, the Interest-Royalties Directive and the P-S Directive. Together the EU Directives aim at eliminating both juridical and economic double taxation and double non-taxation of qualifying payments. Hybrid mismatches should not lead to double taxation or to double non-taxation.

[2] The P-S Directive and the Elimination of Double Taxation

The P-S Directive, may limit the possibilities to tax an interest payment made between two qualifying companies in a qualifying relationship and based on a hybrid debt.[24] The purpose of the P-S Directive is to eliminate both economic and juridical double taxation with respect to profit distributions from subsidiaries to parent companies. The P-S Directive, therefore, operates as an incentive in favour of equity finance rather than debt finance. It promotes the financing of subsidiaries by parent companies with equity rather than debt. However, the P-S Directive strengthens the effect of tax revenues from

---

22. *See*, for example, Brown (2012), 31–41, International Fiscal Association (2012), Bärsch (2012), 91–240, Helminen (1999), 251–320, International Fiscal Association (2000a), Six (2007) and Eberhartinger and Six (2009), 5–6 for the classification practices of debt and equity hybrids in different countries.
23. Article 49 of the TFEU provides for the freedom of establishment and Art. 63 of the TFEU provides for the free movement of capital and payments. If interest deduction is denied based on reclassification only with respect to interest payments made to non-resident shareholders, there may be a conflict with the TFEU. *See* C-324/00 *Lankhorst-Hohorst* and, for example, Helminen (2015), 102–104.
24. *See also* Bundgaard (2010), 446–456 about the effects of the P-S Directive on the tax treatment of income form hybrid instruments.

debt and equity realizing in two different states. Tax revenues from debt are realized by the state of residence of the parent company, whereas tax revenues from equity are realized by the state of residence of the subsidiary. Therefore, even though the P-S Directive benefits would be applicable, debt finance may be used instead of equity in order to avoid taxation in the state of residence of the subsidiary.

The P-S Directive concerns the taxation of distributions of profits from a subsidiary company to a parent company by virtue of association between the companies. The term 'profit distribution' as a somewhat broader term than 'dividend' covers any payment by the subsidiary to the parent company on grounds of the shareholder relationship between the companies. Article 4 of the Directive does not clarify what is meant by the term 'association' in the Article, but read together with Article 3, the term should mean a holding in the capital of the subsidiary by the parent company. The P-S Directive, thus, covers profit distributions made by virtue of an association based on a holding in the equity capital of a subsidiary. There is, however, no reason why the term 'association' could not cover constructive equity capital. Therefore, income from hybrid debt that is actually equity by its nature, should qualify under the P-S Directive.

The P-S Directive should cover distributions from a subsidiary to a parent company on hybrid instruments classified as equity for domestic tax law purposes. If the source state taxes interest on hybrid debt as a dividend subject to withholding tax and denies an interest deduction, economic double taxation is the result. Because the purpose of the P-S Directive is to eliminate such double taxation in the relations between subsidiaries and parent companies, the P-S Directive should be applied in these situations. If the source state treats an investment as equity and the interest on it as a dividend, it should not argue that the interest is not the kind of profit distribution covered by the P-S Directive. Further, if hybrid debt is treated as equity, hybrid debt should also be taken into account in calculating the fulfilment of the holding requirement between two companies for the purposes of the P-S Directive. P-S Directive benefits should be made available even though only the constructive equity would bring the holding to the level required.[25]

It seems clear that the source state must make available the benefits provided by the P-S Directive in situations where the state treats debt as equity and, therefore, interest as a dividend for tax purposes. The question of whether the state of residence of the recipient of the interest on the hybrid debt must accept this classification and also provide the benefits of the P-S Directive is more problematic. This interpretation, after all, would mean that the state could not tax the interest in the way that it otherwise probably would.

In principle, in situations where the hybrid debt is by its economic nature actually equity, the state of residence of the interest recipient should also make available P-S

---

25. This view is taken, for example, in the Commentary on Art. 10(2) of the OECD Model with respect to the holding requirement in the article. *See* para. 15 of the Commentary on Art. 10 of the OECD Model. *See also* for this view Sommerhalder (1996), 94 with respect to thin capitalization situations. *See*, however, Bundgaard (2010a), 496–498, who interprets the P-S Directive narrowly as not covering hybrid instruments.

Directive benefits. The state, however, may not agree that the equity characteristics on a hybrid debt are so distinctive that the investment actually constitutes constructive equity capital for tax purposes. Therefore, the state may not accept the source state taxation and may tax the interest as interest instead. It may be suggested, however, that at least in situations where the state must accept a dividend treatment for tax treaty purposes, the state should also make available the benefits of the P-S Directive. Similarly, the state should accept a dividend treatment in situations where, in the obverse situation, the state itself would have reclassified the interest as a dividend.

Interpretative assistance, with respect to the term 'profit distribution' of the P-S Directive, may be derived from the EU Interest-Royalty Directive, which prohibits source state withholding taxes in the case of qualifying intra-group interest payments. According to Article 4 of the Interest-Royalty Directive, Member States do not need to make available the tax benefits based on the Interest-Royalty Directive in the case of payments that are by their nature profit distributions or in the case of payments from different types of hybrid financing.[26] Article 4(1) of the Interest-Royalty Directive enumerates different situations in which the source state of interest does not have to ensure the benefits based on the Interest-Royalty Directive. The list includes:

- payment that is treated as a profit distribution under the national law of the source state;
- payments from debt-claims participating in profits (profit-participating loans);
- payments from debt-claims, which entitle the creditor to convert the right to interest to the right to participate in profits of the debtor (convertible loans); and
- payments from debt-claims with no provision for repayment of the principal amount or where the repayment is due more than fifty years after the date of issue (perpetual debt).

According to Article 4(2) of the Proposal for the Interest-Royalty Directive, the P-S Directive should be applied instead of the Interest-Royalty Directive to the kinds of interest listed in Article 4(1), if paid between qualifying companies. According to the commentary on the Proposal, the taxation of interest as a profit distribution under the P-S Directive is possible, for example, if the taxation follows from a tax treaty between two Member States or is based on the domestic tax law of the source state.[27] These statements clearly indicate that during the preparations of the Interest-Royalty Directive, the Commission was of the opinion that income from hybrid instruments, if treated as a dividend in the source state, or if treated as a dividend for tax treaty purposes, qualifies as a profit distribution under the P-S Directive if paid between qualifying companies in a qualifying relationship. The Commission's opinion, thus, promotes the interpretation suggested above.

---

26. *See also* Explanatory memorandum to the proposal for a council directive COM (98) 67 final, commentary on Art. 4.
27. *See also* Explanatory memorandum to the proposal for a council directive COM (98) 67 final, commentary on Art. 4.

Chapter 9: Classification of Return on Debt-Equity Hybrids §9.02[C]

In the end, the express reference to the P-S Directive was not included in the final version of Article 4 of the Interest-Royalty Directive.[28] The preparatory works of the Interest-Royalty Directive, however, have interpretative value despite the fact that the express reference to the P-S Directive was not included in the final version the Interest-Royalty Directive. The fact that the P-S Directive is not expressly mentioned in the final version of the Interest-Royalty Directive does not suggest that payments on hybrid instruments could not qualify as profit distributions for the purposes of the P-S Directive. The fact that the express reference to the P-S Directive was dropped during the preparations can only be understood as an indication of the fact that it was taken into account that there may be situations of reclassified hybrid interest that do not fall under the scope of application of the P-S Directive even though most of the situations do. For the mentioned reason, it was probably considered to be a better alternative not to refer expressly to the P-S Directive but to leave it to a case-by-case determination whether a specific payment falls under the P-S Directive or not.

The Interest-Royalty Directive only concerns the tax treatment in the source state and does not limit in any way the tax treatment of qualifying interest payments in the state of residence of the recipient of the payment. Therefore, the Interest-Royalty Directive or the Proposal for the Directive does not give much guidance on whether the residence state should apply the P-S Directive to eliminate international juridical and economic double taxation in the case of payments on hybrids reclassified as profit distributions qualifying under the P-S Directive in the source state. The commentary of the Proposal to the Interest-Royalty Directive only states that the rules of the P-S Directive must be applied in order to avoid double taxation. It does not state whether this reference only includes international juridical double taxation or international economic double taxation as well.

Because the P-S Directive requires that both economic and juridical double taxation be eliminated, the P-S Directive's limitations should also concern taxation in the state of residence of the income recipient. It cannot, however, be required that this state would in any case accept the source state classification. Such a requirement would give the source state too much power to collect tax revenues instead of the state of residence of an income recipient. The state of residence of the income recipient should, however, accept the source state classification and make available the P-S Directive benefits, at least, if the income qualifies as a dividend for tax treaty purposes in the case of the two countries concerned and in any case where the state agrees that the investment is by its true nature equity instead of debt.

The EU Arbitration Convention does not seem to be applicable to solve classification conflicts with respect to hybrid instruments. According to Article 1 of the Convention, the Convention applies where, for taxation purposes, the same profits are included in the profits of two enterprises resident in two different states in situations

---

28. The express reference to the P-S Directive was dropped among other reasons because the scope of the Interest-Royalty Directive is different from the scope of the P-S Directive. Therefore, it is clear that all payments on hybrids that do not qualify under the Interest-Royalty Directive because of the express exclusion cannot qualify under the P-S Directive. *See also* Brokelind (2003), 165–166, Brokelind (2005), 327, Weber (2001), 15–30 and Oliver (1999), 204–206.

where the arm's length principle is not followed. The Convention, thus, strictly speaking applies only in transfer-pricing situations. Primarily, it only applies to the double taxation caused by interest that deviates from arm's length interest, but not to the double taxation caused by an inconsistent classification of a hybrid instrument.[29]

According to the Commentary on the OECD Model, Article 9 of the Model is applicable:

> [N]ot only in determining whether the rate of interest provided for in a loan contract is an arm's length rate, but also whether a *prima facie* loan may be regarded as a loan or should be regarded as some other kind of payment, in particular a contribution to equity capital.[30]

In line with this interpretation, the arm's length principle of Article 4 of the Arbitration Convention should also cover such situations. Broadly interpreted, the procedures of the Convention should also be applicable in eliminating the double taxation caused by classification conflicts with respect to hybrid debt.[31] Because this broad interpretation, however, is not generally accepted, in practice, the reference to a mutual agreement procedure provided by tax treaties is needed in order to eliminate economic double taxation in these situations.[32]

[3] The EU Directives and the Elimination of Double Non-taxation

Hybrid instruments may cause not only double taxation but also unintended double-non taxation situations. The source state may treat a payment on a hybrid as a tax-deductible interest not subject to source state withholding tax and the state of residence of the payment's recipient may treat it as a tax-exempt direct investment dividend. It is important that the P-S Directive itself does not create these unintended double non-taxation situations. Therefore in 2014 a special mismatch provision was added to Article 4(1) of the P-S Directive.[33] According to Article 4(1) the state of residence of the dividend recipient parent company[34] shall refrain from taxing the distributed profits that come under the scope of the P-S Directive only to the extent that the distributed profits are not deductible by the subsidiary and tax the profits to the

---

29. *See*, for example, Sommerhalder (1996), 94 for this strict interpretation in the case of thin capitalization situations. Also Bundgaard (2010a), 498–499 is of the opinion, that the Arbitration Convention does not apply. In 2016 the Commission made a proposal for a dispute resolution mechanism with wider scope. *See* Proposal for a Council Directive on Double Taxation Dispute Resolution Mechanism in the European Union, 25.10.2016, COM(2016) 686 final.
30. Paragraph 3(b) of the Commentary on Art. 9 of the OECD Model.
31. This interpretation is also suggested in Piltz (1996), 137 with respect to thin capitalization situations.
32. *See also* Helminen (1999), 266–270, Helminen (2004b), 60–61, Bundgaard (2010a), 490–500 and Eberhatinger and Six (2009), 12–15 for the P-S Directive from the perspective of debt-equity hybrids.
33. Council Directive 2014/86/EU of 8 Jul. 2014 amending Directive 2011/96/EU on the common system of taxation applicable in the case of parent companies and subsidiaries of different Member States.
34. Or the permanent establishment state, if dividend is taxed as income of a permanent establishment.

extent that the profits are deductible by the subsidiary. This provision does not affect the classification of payments on hybrids for domestic tax law purposes or for the P-S Directive purposes. It only eliminates the unintended double non-taxation caused by mismatches.

While the P-S Directive eliminates double non-taxation situations caused by hybrid instruments within the scope of the P-S Directive, the EU Anti-Tax Avoidance Directive requires the EU Member States to eliminate double non-taxation caused by hybrid mismatches more broadly. The Anti-Tax Avoidance Directive requires that one of the two jurisdictions in a mismatch situation denies the deduction of a payment leading to a double deduction or deduction non-inclusion situation.[35] Article 9 of the Anti-Tax Avoidance Directive includes such a hybrid mismatch neutralizing provision.

The Anti-Tax Avoidance Directive defines the hybrid mismatches covered by the Directive.[36] According to the Directive, a 'hybrid mismatch' means a situation between a taxpayer in one Member State and an associated enterprise in another Member State or a structured arrangement between parties in Member States where the following outcome is attributable to differences in the characterization of a financial instrument or entity:[37]

(a) a deduction of the same payment, expenses or losses occurs both in the Member State in which the payment has its source, the expenses are incurred or the losses are suffered and in another Member State ('double deduction'); or

(b) there is a deduction of a payment in the Member State in which the payment has its source without a corresponding inclusion for tax purposes of the same payment in the other Member State ('deduction without inclusion').

According to the Directive, to the extent that a hybrid mismatch results in a double deduction, the deduction shall be given only in the Member State where such payment has its source.[38] Instead, to the extent that a hybrid mismatch results in a deduction without inclusion, the Member State of the payer shall deny the deduction of such payment.[39]

The hybrid mismatch neutralizing rule tackles mismatch situations attributable to differences in the classification of a financial instrument or entity and is not intended to affect the general features of the tax system of a Member State.[40] The hybrid mismatch rule of the Anti-Tax Avoidance Directive, thus, does not have an impact on how payments on hybrids are classified for domestic tax law purposes or for the P-S Directive purposes. It only affects the deductibility of such payments.

---

35. Non-inclusion means a situation in which a payment is not included in the taxable income of its recipient.
36. Article 2(9) Anti-Tax Avoidance Directive.
37. Article 2(9) Anti-Tax Avoidance Directive.
38. Article 9(1) Anti-Tax Avoidance Directive.
39. Article 9(2) Anti-Tax Avoidance Directive.
40. Point 13 Preamble to the Anti-Tax Avoidance Directive.

[D] Tax Treaties

[1] The Model Conventions

The Model Conventions, in general, do not hinder the contracting states from reclassifying debt as equity and interest as a dividend for domestic law purposes. Domestic law classification is independent from tax treaty classification. The discrimination articles of the Models, however, generally require that as long as interest would be deductible in purely domestic relations, it is also deductible in cross-border situations. Therefore, even though cross-border interest would be reclassified and treated as a dividend under domestic tax law, it must be deductible to the same extent that it would be deductible if the interest were domestic.[41]

With respect to tax treaties, it must be determined whether interest on hybrid debt or a dividend on hybrid equity qualifies for treaty purposes as a dividend or as interest. The fact that the applicability of the dividend articles may be quite broad leads to the problem that the same payment may seem to qualify both under the dividend definition of Article 10(3) and the interest definition of Article 11(3) of the OECD Model. The same problem applies with respect to the UN or US Models. According to the Commentary on the OECD Model, such an overlap should be solved in favour of the dividend article, because '...the term "interest" as used in Article 11 does not include items of income which are dealt with under Article 10...'.[42] This principle of the precedence of Article 10 over Article 11 also applies with respect to the US Model, which expressly mentions the principle in Article 11. Therefore, as long as income on hybrid instruments qualifies under Article 10 of the Models, it qualifies as a dividend instead of as interest for treaty purposes.[43]

Only income from *corporate rights* constitutes a dividend within the meaning of Article 10 of the OECD Model and the US Model.[44] The autonomous parts of the dividend definitions of both of the Models require that a dividend be income from shares or other corporate rights. In the OECD Model, the requirement of corporate rights follows directly from the wording of the definition, whereas with respect to the US Model, the requirement is derived from the interpretation in the Technical Explanations of the 2006 Model.[45]

The part of the dividend definitions referring to source state classification also requires that a dividend be income from corporate rights. The term 'corporate right' is

---

41. Articles 24(4) and 24(5) of the OECD Model and Arts 24(3) and 24(4) of the US Model generally require that to the extent that income paid by a domestic company to a resident be deductible in taxation of the company, the income is also deductible if paid to a non-resident.
42. Paragraph 19 of the Commentary on Art. 11 of the OECD Model. *See*, however, Avery Jones et al. (2009), 36 who consider that originally it might have been intended that the interest article has priority over the dividend article. *See* about the history of the dividend and interest articles of the OECD Model also e.g., Pijl (2011), 483–502.
43. *See* Avery Jones et al. (2009), 41–44 for examples on how the overlap of the dividend article and the interest article is solved in different actual treaties.
44. *See* Ch. 5 s. §5.07. *See* Avery Jones et al. (2009), 14–19 for examples of corporate rights in the companies of different countries.
45. Article 10, para. 166 of the Technical Explanation of the 2006 US Model.

Chapter 9: Classification of Return on Debt-Equity Hybrids §9.02[D]

expressly used in the wording of the third part of the dividend definition of the OECD Model referring to source state classification. Because the term has relevance with respect to all the parts of the dividend definition, it seems that it must be interpreted autonomously with respect to the whole definition. If the term is not interpreted in this way, there would be no point including the term at all in the third part of the definition.[46] In practice, however, it is usual for states, when they are in the position of the source state, to be of the opinion that as long as they tax income as a dividend, the income also qualifies as a dividend under the tax treaty definitions following the OECD Model.[47]

At least the wording '...as well as income...' in the US Model seems to include any income that is taxed in the same manner as income from shares in the source state. From the Technical Explanation of the 2006 US Model, it follows, however, that only income from corporate rights also qualifies under the third part of the definition of the US Model. For the purposes of the US Model, it is, however, enough that the source state views the income as '...a return on an equity investment in a corporation...'.[48] The OECD Model should, instead, require autonomous classification.

It follows from the wording of Article 10 of both Models that in order to qualify under the autonomous parts of the definitions, *a corporate right must also participate in profits and must not be a debt-claim*. This express requirement seems only to be a clarification because the term 'corporate right' in itself should mean that it is not a debt-claim and that it must participate in profits.[49] Therefore, even though the express reference does not refer to the third part of the dividend definition, the same requirement also actually concerns the third part.

According to the Commentary on Article 10 of the OECD Model, 'dividend' generally means a distribution of profits to the shareholders as a return on the capital that the shareholders have made available to the company as its shareholders.[50] Generally, income qualifies as a dividend only if it is received by a shareholder because of the recipient's position as a shareholder or because of a comparable position in a company.[51] Income paid by a company by virtue of a debtor-creditor relationship does not qualify as a dividend. A debt instrument may qualify as a dividend-generating right only if the instrument is by its substance actually equity rather than debt and if it participates in profits. The holder of a corporate right must have the right to benefit from a possible increment in the value of the company's assets. The holder of corporate

---

46. For example, Vogel et al. (1997), 650 suggests autonomous interpretation, even though the term is used in the part of the definition referring to source state classification. *See* for this narrow interpretation also Vogel and Lehner (2008), 201.
47. *See* Avery Jones et al. (2009), 22, who mention that most states consider that the third part of the dividend definition covers income from any financial relationship which is treated as constituting corporate right under national law.
48. Article 10, paras 165 and 166 of the Technical Explanation of the 2006 US Model.
49. *See also* for this opinion Vogel et al. (1997), 655.
50. The Commentary on Art. 10 of the OECD Model, paras 1 and 3.
51. For example, Vogel et al. (1997), 650, interprets this requirement to include that the income is paid because of the shareholder relationship.

rights must be entitled *to participate both in the current profits of the company and in the liquidation proceeds.*[52]

According to the Commentary, '...debt-claims, and bonds and debentures in particular, which carry a right to participate in the debtor's profits are, nonetheless, regarded as loans if the contract by its general character clearly evidences a loan at interest...'.[53] Furthermore, '...debt-claims participating in profits do not come...' into the category of rights assimilated to shares. '...Likewise interest on convertible debentures is not a dividend...'.[54] According to the Commentary, '...interest on participating bonds should not normally be considered as a dividend, and neither should a convertible bond until such time as the bonds are actually converted into shares...'.[55] However, interest on such bonds may '...be considered as a dividend if the loan effectively shares the risks run by the debtor company...'.[56] '...Article 10 deals not only with a dividend as such but also with interest on loans insofar as the lender effectively shares the risks run by the company, i.e., when the repayment depends largely on the success or otherwise of the enterprise's business...'.[57]

The conclusion may be drawn from the Commentary that a profit-participating or conversion right does not alone change the nature of debt to equity. Profit participation is an essential characteristic for equity classification, but it alone is not enough. However, if the equity features of a profit-participating loan as a whole indicate that the loan effectively shares the risk run by the company, then the loan is equity rather than debt. The loan will, therefore, also qualify as a dividend-generating right under Article 10 of the OECD Model. The term 'corporate rights' interpreted in accordance with the Commentary, clearly means not only rights in the form of equity, but also rights in the form of debt-claims that, by their true nature, are actually equity. This interpretation also receives support by the statement in paragraph 15d of the Commentary on Article 10(2). Accordingly, a loan may be taken as capital for the purposes of Article 10(2) in a situation where income from the loan is treated as a dividend under Article 10 because of the income's domestic law treatment in a situation where a loan is reclassified as share capital.

Debt claims qualify as dividend-generating rights only in situations where the nature of a debt-claim is closer to equity because it effectively shares the risk run by the company. According to the Commentary, the question of:

> [W]hether the contributor of loan shares the risk run by the enterprise must be determined in each individual case in the light of all the circumstances, as for

---

52. Vogel et al. (1997), 651, interprets the term corporate right to require '...not only to a share in (current) profits, but also to at least a share in the liquidation proceeds, i.e. in the company's hidden reserves...'. Hattingh (2009), 519, however, considers that '...the absence of a right to share in future liquidation proceeds would not be fatal to treat a person as holding the necessary profit-participating corporate rights'. Pijl (2011) 493, 496, 501 and 502 seems to accept a very broad meaning to the term corporate right including '... instruments where a company is the 'counterparty', whether contractually or based in company law, of the holder.'
53. Paragraph 18 of the Commentary on Art. 11 of the OECD Model.
54. Paragraph 24 of the Commentary on Art. 10 of the OECD Model.
55. Paragraph 19 of the Commentary on Art. 11 of the OECD Model.
56. *Ibid.*
57. Paragraph 25 of the Commentary on Art. 10 of the OECD Model.

example the following: the loan very heavily outweighs any other contribution to the enterprise's capital (or was taken out to replace a substantial proportion of capital which has been lost) and is substantially unmatched by redeemable assets; the creditor will share in any profits of the company; repayment of the loan is subordinated to claims of other creditors or to the payment of dividends; the level or payment of interest would depend on the profits of the company; the loan contract contains no fixed provisions for repayment by a definite date.[58]

Both debt and equity investments include certain risk. The entrepreneurial risk involved in equity finance in a company is generally higher and also different from the risk involved in debt finance in the same company. The entrepreneurial risk meant here cannot mean any creditor's general risk of not being able to enforce the debt-claim because of the borrower company's insolvency or because of the debt being irrecoverable. In order to qualify as a corporate right for the purposes of Article 10 of the Models, the investor must accept such entrepreneurial risk as corresponds to the risk of a shareholder.[59]

Limitations in the control rights of a shareholder do not directly increase or decrease the risk component. Article 10 must, thus, also cover, in addition to regular shares, rights that do not carry full membership rights, like the right to vote at a shareholders' meeting and other rights relating to the control of the company. As long as a shareholder participates in both the current profits and any eventual liquidation proceeds of a corporation, the lack of control rights does not change the character of equity to debt.[60] The holder of the right must, however, face entrepreneurial risk. The investment in a corporate right must include the possibility of a total loss of the capital invested.[61]

In conclusion, a hybrid investment either in the form of debt or equity, may qualify as a dividend-generating investment under Article 10 of the OECD Model only if it entitles the investor to the right to participate both in the current profits and in any liquidation proceeds of the debtor corporation. Even though an investment would be profit participating, it qualifies as a dividend-generating investment only if the investor must accept the possible risk of the loss of the investment in a way comparable to the risk assumed by a shareholder. Whether or not such risk is involved must be evaluated in light of all the characteristics of the investment.

It is, of course, possible that two states do not agree on whether such characteristics are present. Under the US Model, the fact that the source state deems such characteristics to exist, and, therefore, taxes income on a hybrid instrument as a dividend also requires that the state of residence of the recipient of the income accept the dividend classification. In any other case, it is unclear whether the other state has to accept the classification of the source state.

Even though Article 10(3) of the OECD Model refers to source state classification, the source state classification is decisive only if a corporate right exists from the perspective of an autonomous interpretation. Because Article 3(2) refers to the law of

---

58. Paragraph 25 of the Commentary on Art. 10 of the OECD Model.
59. *See also* Vogel et al. (1997), 651.
60. *See also ibid.*, 653.
61. *See also ibid.*, 651.

the state applying the treaty, the state of residence of the income recipient may apply its own law to determine whether the income is from a corporate right in an unclear situation. If the state of residence of the recipient does not agree that a hybrid investment is a corporate right, it may not be required to accept the dividend treatment of the source state. Such a classification conflict may require resolution by means of a mutual agreement procedure.

Especially problematic, with respect to tax treaty classification, are domestic law rules that do not classify debt as equity but only interest as a dividend. If the source state does not take the view that the income is from a corporate right, it may be difficult for the country to argue that the income is from corporate rights from the perspective of an autonomous interpretation. Income that is not from a corporate right does not qualify as a dividend under the Models.[62]

[2] Actual Tax Treaties

The dividend definition of actual tax treaties may be slightly different from the perspective of hybrid instruments. Many treaties, however, follow the OECD Model and provide that income from shares or other rights, not being debt-claims, participating in profits, qualifies as a dividend. Income from other corporate rights qualifies if it is treated in the same way as income from shares in the source state. Under these treaties, only income from a corporate right qualifies as a dividend.

The dividend definition of some other treaties covers income from shares or other rights, not being debt-claims, participating in profits. Other income derived from other rights qualifies as a dividend if it is subjected to the same taxation treatment as income from shares by the laws of the contracting state of which the company making the distribution is a resident. Corporate rights that are not debt-claims and that participate in profits, thus, already qualify under the autonomous part of the definition. Under these treaties, income from hybrid instruments qualifies as a dividend if the source state treats the income as a dividend. In such a situation, it is not required that the instrument qualifies as a corporate right, but may also be a debt-claim. The other state must accept the classification of the source state. Because of the broad reference to source state classification, actual classification conflicts with respect to these treaties should be rare.

The dividend definition of some other treaties also covers income from shares or other rights, not being debt-claims, participating in profits. Income from other corporate rights qualifies if it is subjected to the same tax treatment as income from shares by the laws of the source state. Income from arrangements, including debt obligations, carrying the right to participate in profits to the extent so characterized under the laws of the state in which the income arises, is also included. The starting point under these treaties is that a dividend is income from corporate rights. However, income from rights

---

62. Countries with such a system may have to expressly reserve the right to apply the system in tax treaties. *See* Portner (1996a), 268. *See also* Helminen (1999), 270–276, Helminen (2004b), 58–60 and Eberhartinger and Six (2009), 6–11 about tax treaty classification of payments on hybrid instruments.

that do not qualify as corporate rights but are debt-claims may also qualify as a dividend. Income from debt-claims qualifies only if the debt investment is profit participating and if the income is treated in the same way as a dividend in the source state. It is not a requirement that the investor otherwise takes part in the entrepreneurial risk. Thus, under these treaties, the other state must largely accept the dividend classification of the source state.

The dividend definition of some treaties covers in addition to income from shares also income from other corporate rights if the source state treats the income in the same way as income from shares. In addition, any income that is treated in the source state in the same way as income from shares qualifies as a dividend. Besides the expressly enumerated items, these treaties are based on source state classification. So long as the source state treats income from a hybrid as a dividend the other state must accept the dividend treatment and eliminate double taxation accordingly.

Finally, some treaties dictate that income from shares or other rights, not being debt-claims, participating in profits, qualifies as a dividend. Other income from a company qualifies if it is treated in the source state the same way as income from shares. Thus, income from corporate rights qualifies under the autonomous part of the definition. However, income from any other hybrid instruments qualifies if the source state treats such income the same way as income from shares. The other state must largely accept the dividend classification of the source state and eliminate double taxation accordingly.

In conclusion, actual classification conflicts with respect to hybrid instruments are largely avoided only by some treaties. Under some treaties, the source state classification is largely decisive. Other treaties provide that source state classification is decisive to the extent that a hybrid involves the right to participate in profits. The most limited definition is the one that follows the OECD Model. The treaties following the wording of the OECD Model, therefore, may most easily lead to an actual classification conflict.

Some treaties provide for the possibility of the reference to mutual agreement procedure in the case of inconsistent domestic tax law classification of a hybrid instrument in a cross-border situation. The use of the mutual agreement procedure, of course, limits the danger of double taxation or double non-taxation. Some treaties expressly require a switch from the exemption method to the credit method in a classification conflict situation in order to eliminate the possibility to double tax benefits by the use of hybrid instruments.[63] Article 5 of the Multilateral Convention to Implement Tax Treaty Related Measures to Prevent Base Erosion and Profit Shifting will increase the number of such tax treaties considerably that deny an exemption in hybrid mismatch situations.[64]

---

63. *See also* Helminen (2004b), 61 about debt-equity hybrids and the elimination of double taxation.
64. The text of the Convention was published on 24 Nov. 2016 and it will have to be signed and ratified before it will enter into force.

§9.03 INTEREST ON LONG-TERM OR PERPETUAL DEBT

[A] Introduction

One basic difference between debt and equity is that a creditor has a right to a refund at the end of a fixed time, whereas a shareholder generally is not entitled to any refund during the lifetime of the company, that is, before the winding up of the company. Equity is a perpetual investment intended for the continuing use by a company, whereas debt is a temporary investment.[65] In distinguishing debt from equity, the period of the investment and the conditions of the termination of the investment may, therefore, be used as one meaningful characteristic.

In hybrid investments, the line between debt and equity with respect to terms concerning the repayment of the capital invested may be unclear. In practice, loan contracts may include no fixed provisions for repayment by a definite date or the loan period may be very long. It is possible to agree, for example, that a loan matures only upon the liquidation of the debtor company. Similarly, it is possible for a corporation to issue shares that may be redeemable before the liquidation of the corporation. The permanency of a debt investment may, therefore, in practice be even stronger than that of an equity investment. The question arises on how perpetual debt should be treated for tax purposes.

Perpetual debt means any debt investment with an undetermined period of duration or with no fixed provisions of termination, without the right of the debtor to terminate the loan. Perpetual debt is, by its economic substance, very close to equity. In a perpetual debt investment, the primary right of the creditor to recover the contribution is postponed indefinitely. Therefore, the creditor may actually be subjected to the risks of the underlying enterprise in the same way that a shareholder would be. It may be argued that if it is not intended to repay the loan, the investment is not debt at all but is actually hidden equity in the form of debt. Therefore, it may be argued that interest paid on perpetual debt may also be regarded as a dividend for tax purposes because it is a return on equity.[66]

In the same way that it is usual for a shareholder to make a debt investment in a corporation, it is also usual for a corporation to lend money or other assets to shareholders. Such loans, however, do not raise the question of the line between debt and equity. The granting of loans from corporations to their shareholders, however, is a form in which corporate assets may be transferred from a corporation to its shareholders or at least be made available for the use of the shareholder. Loans may be used to transfer company assets to shareholders in order to avoid dividend taxation. Therefore, it is possible that such loan capital, in and of itself, is actually a dividend by its economic nature.

The starting point with respect to loans from a corporation to its shareholders is that a loan does not constitute a profit distribution because the shareholder is expected

---

65. For example, Kilpi (1973), 190 and 194 distinguishes debt from equity by reference to the terms of repayment.
66. This observation is made, for example, by Ryynänen (1996), 388.

Chapter 9: Classification of Return on Debt-Equity Hybrids   §9.03[B]

to pay the principal back on the maturity date. The situation, however, is not clear with respect to perpetual loans, that is, loans that lack a fixed date of termination or that have a fixed date of termination but, for all intents and purposes, will not be paid back. With respect to perpetual debt from a company to one of its shareholders, it may be asked whether the loan actually constitutes a profit distribution and, therefore, a dividend for tax purposes.

[B]   **Domestic Tax Laws**

The importance of a fixed maturity date as a characteristic of debt depends on the country concerned. In many countries, a fixed maturity date is probably regarded as the most important characteristic of debt. Instead, some other countries do not give the maturity date any relevance when classifying a hybrid for tax purposes.

Many countries consider that because perpetual debt lacks a fixed maturity date, it may be reclassified as equity and interest on it as a dividend for tax purposes. The reclassification may be based on a specific provision on hybrids, on general anti-avoidance provisions or on general principles of tax law and case law. A fixed maturity date alone, however, does not necessarily guarantee debt classification and the lack of a fixed maturity date does not necessarily guarantee equity classification.

If no other equity characteristics are present, the long-term nature of an investment alone does not necessarily make the investment treatable as equity for tax purposes. It is seldom that domestic tax laws would set a time limit on the duration of a loan in order for it to be regarded as debt. The further into the future the maturity date is, the closer is the risk of the creditor to the risk of a shareholder. In many countries, the determination of debt or equity treatment is made on a case-by-case basis, evaluating all the other debt or equity characteristics involved. A reasonable maturity date depends on all the circumstances, such as the nature of the enterprise. However, the maturity date should not be too far in the future.

In the case of loans from a company to its shareholder, reclassification is more probable because of the lack of fixed maturity date or because of an abnormally long loan period. In many countries, reclassification is possible in these situations even though, in the country concerned, reclassification would never concern third-party loans. With respect to loans from a corporation to its shareholders, the actual intention of the parties to create a debtor-creditor relationship may be examined. If, in the light of all the facts, such an intention is not present, the loans may be treated as a constructive distribution from the corporation to the shareholders. Especially if there are no interest payments on the loan and if there is no fixed maturity date, the loan may be treated as a constructive distribution. Alternatively, a perpetual loan from a shareholder may be reclassified as hidden equity and the interest on the loan as a dividend. The likelihood of reclassification may increase if an open dividend is not distributed, if a loan would not have been granted to a third party under the same conditions or if the loan is clearly based only on the shareholder relationship.

[C] The EU Parent-Subsidiary Directive

The P-S Directive covers income from hybrid debt that, by its nature, is actually equity and is, therefore, taxed as a dividend in the Member States. According to Article 4 of the Interest-Royalty Directive and according to the commentary on the Proposal for the Directive, the source state does not have to apply the Interest-Royalty Directive to payments, which are treated as profit distributions in the source state or to payments from certain types of hybrid financing. Article 4(1) of the Interest-Royalty Directive expressly mentions payments from debt-claims that do not contain terms for the repayment of the principal amount or where the repayment is due more than fifty years after the date of issue as such income.

According to Article 4(2) of the Proposal for the Interest-Royalty Directive, the P-S Directive applies with respect to such interest if paid between qualifying companies. Even though this requirement was not expressly included in the final version of the Interest-Royalty Directive, it is clear that in many situations, interest on perpetual debt may qualify as a profit distribution for the purposes of the P-S Directive.

On the basis of the preparatory materials of the Interest-Royalty Directive, the opinion of the Commission clearly was that if income from perpetual debt is treated as a dividend in the Member States, it qualifies as a profit distribution under the P-S Directive if paid between qualifying companies in a qualifying relationship. If a Member State chooses to tax interest on perpetual debt as a dividend, the benefits of the P-S Directive should be made available if the payment is made between qualifying companies in a qualifying relationship.

The P-S Directive concerns the tax treatment of distributions of profits from a subsidiary company to a parent company by virtue of the association between the companies. The term 'profit distribution' as a somewhat broader term than dividend covers any payment by the subsidiary to the parent company on the grounds of the shareholder relationship between the companies. A perpetual loan from a corporation to its shareholder may constitute a distribution of profits from a subsidiary to the parent company made by virtue of the association between the companies. Therefore, if such a loan is classified as a dividend for domestic tax law purposes, the P-S Directive benefits should also be made available if the other requirements of application of the Directive are met.

[D] Tax Treaties

In order for income to qualify as a dividend under the dividend article of the Model Conventions, it must be from corporate rights. The income must be from a right that entitles the investor to participate in profits and that subjects the investor to a risk comparable to that of a shareholder. Therefore, it is clear that the lack of a fixed date of maturity alone does not make a debt-claim a dividend-generating right. A pure perpetual debt does not entitle the investor to participate in profits.

However, under the third part of the dividend definition of the US Model, any income that is treated as income from corporate rights qualifies as a dividend if it is taxed the same way as income from shares is taxed in the source state. Under the treaties that follow the US Model, interest on perpetual debt, therefore, qualifies as a dividend if the source state treats the debt as equity and the interest on it as a dividend. Profit participation is not required for this treatment.

The Commentary includes a list of characteristics that may be evaluated in determining whether a contributor of a loan shares the risk run by the enterprise. This list includes the fact that the loan contract contains no fixed provisions for repayment by a definite date.[67] Therefore, even though the lack of fixed provisions for repayment by a definite date alone may not make a debt investment qualify as a corporate right, such treatment is possible if other equity characteristics are also involved. Interest on a perpetual debt may be treated as a dividend, for example, if the investor is also entitled to participate in company profits and in any liquidation proceeds.

A perpetual debt from a company to its shareholders may constitute a constructive distribution. The transfer of assets from a company to its shareholders in the form of perpetual debt by virtue of the shareholder relationship is income from shares. A perpetual loan from a company to its shareholders, thus, generally qualifies as a dividend under the Models to the same extent as a constructive dividend.

The dividend definitions of actual treaties may differ slightly from each other. The dividend definition of many actual treaties covers income from shares or other rights not being debt-claims participating in profits in the same way as the Models do. The third part of the dividend definition of some treaties, however does not require that dividend be income from a corporate right. Some treaties cover any other income derived from other rights if it is subjected to the same taxation treatment as income from shares by the laws of the contracting state of which the company making the distribution is a resident. The dividend definition of some other treaties covers any income that is treated in the source state in the same way as income from shares is treated. Despite the differences, these treaties lead to the same consequence as regards the classification of perpetual debt.

Under these treaties, as long as the source state treats income from perpetual debt as a dividend, the other state must accept the dividend treatment for tax treaty purposes and must eliminate double taxation accordingly. If the source state does not treat income from perpetual debt as a dividend, then it does not qualify as a dividend for the purposes of the treaties because it is not income from a corporate right. Perpetual debt from a company to one of its shareholders granted to a shareholder by virtue of the shareholder relationship also qualifies as a dividend under the treaties.

The dividend article of some treaties covers, in addition to income from shares or other rights, not being debt-claims and participating in profits also, income from other corporate rights, if it is subjected to the same tax treatment as income from shares by the laws of the source state. Because perpetual debt is not a corporate right, income from perpetual debt does not qualify as a dividend under these treaties no matter how the income is treated under domestic law. The same treatment applies with respect to the treaties, the dividend definition of which is similar to the dividend definition of the

---

67. Paragraph 25 of the Commentary on Art. 10 of the OECD Model.

OECD Model. Instead, perpetual debt from a company to its shareholders granted by virtue of the shareholder relationship may qualify as a dividend also under these treaties.

In conclusion, income from perpetual debt, with no other equity characteristics, does not qualify as a dividend under the autonomous parts of the tax treaty dividend definitions. Under some treaties, income from perpetual debt qualifies as a dividend if the source state treats the income as a dividend but under some other treaties, income from pure perpetual debt does not qualify as a dividend. The fact that a loan is perpetual does not, in itself, make it a corporate right. Under the treaties that require that dividend is income for a corporate right, income from perpetual debt may qualify as a dividend only if the investment may be regarded as constituting a corporate right because of other equity characteristics involved. Perpetual debt from a company to its shareholders, instead, may qualify as dividend under all of the different types of treaties in the situations in which constructive dividend would qualify as a dividend under the treaties.[68]

The difference between the treaties that require dividend to be income from a corporate right and the treaties that do not contain this requirement is that under the latter, the other state has to accept the dividend classification of the source state for treaty purposes. With respect to the former, the other state may not agree that the instrument is a corporate right, and, therefore, may not accept the source state dividend treatment.

Classification conflicts are satisfactorily solved in favour of the classification in the source state only in the case of the treaties that do not include the requirement of dividend being income from a corporate right. Under the treaties that follow the OECD Model, classification conflicts are not prevented. Under the treaties following the OECD Model, one of the states may view an instrument as qualifying as a corporate right whereas the other may not. The states may disagree on whether an investor shares the risks assumed by a company in the way required for a corporate right to exist. Such a disagreement is not solved even by a reference to the Commentary on the OECD Model, because the Commentary only provides for a case-by-case analysis in determining the status of an instrument as a corporate right. Reference to a mutual agreement procedure may be needed in order for double taxation to be avoided.

§9.04 INTEREST ON PROFIT-PARTICIPATING DEBT INSTRUMENTS

[A] Introduction

A typical characteristic of debt is that the investor is entitled to fixed interest whether or not the debtor company is profitable. Interest on straight debt is unconditional or contingent upon adequate corporate earnings. The return on debt is, therefore, not as risky as the return on equity the amount of which depends on company profits. A dividend may be paid only if there are corporate earnings or surplus left after all other

---

68. *See*, for the treatment of a constructive dividend, Ch. 8 of this study.

rights have been satisfied, and only if the company decides to make a distribution rather than to retain the profits. An equity investor enjoys unlimited return potential, whereas a debt investor does not enjoy the positive development in a company's profitability.

The riskier the investment, the higher the return that an investor requires on the investment. To compensate for the higher risk, in addition to offering higher interest rates, a debtor company may also make interest partly or wholly dependent on the debtor company's profits or dividend distributions. A debt investor may, in this way, enjoy the unlimited return potential, normally enjoyed only by an equity investor.[69] Loans that have been structured so that their interest is partly or wholly dependent on the profits or dividend distributions of the debtor company are referred to as profit-participating loans.[70] Profit-participating loans are contractual claims with a profit-related remuneration. The profit-participating clauses may confer some or all of the property rights of a shareholder-like participation in the profits and in the proceeds of a liquidation or a right of subscription to shares, but does not confer any membership rights, such as the right to vote at shareholder meetings.

The most important difference between an investment in company shares and a profit-participating loan is that the latter is a contractual claim that creates a debtor-creditor relationship and not a shareholder relationship. The difference between a dividend as a return on equity and interest as a return on a profit-participating loan is that a dividend is based on a decision of a shareholders' meeting whereas profit or dividend-related interest is based on the loan contract. A profit-dependent interest clause is only a special rule of calculating interest and it does not make an interest payment a profit distribution. The claims of a profit-participating loan holder always have priority in the liquidation of a company in contrast to the claims of an equity holder.[71]

Profit participation makes a debt investment economically very close to equity because the returns on it vary depending on the profits or dividend distributions of the issuer. It may be asked whether the interest paid on the instrument is actually a dividend because the creditor in a way assumes part of the risks of the enterprise, and may be entitled to unlimited return potential.

[B] Domestic Tax Laws

In most countries, the sole fact that interest is determined by reference to the corporate profits or a dividend of the debtor does not make debt treatable as equity and the interest therefrom treatable as a dividend for tax purposes. Many countries, instead, consider profit participation as an essential characteristic for equity classification. As a consequence, many countries consider that profit participation does not necessarily

---

69. *See*, for the difference in return potential in debt and equity investment, for example, Villa (1995), 236, Mähönen and Villa (1996), 615 and Villa (1997), 261.
70. *See*, for different profit-participating clauses, Villa (1995), 239–242.
71. *See* Villa (1997), 262 for these differences.

make a debt reclassifiable as equity, but an instrument may be treated as equity only if it participates in profits.

Many countries consider that profit-related interest as opposed to fixed interest is one strong equity characteristic. Profit-participating loans with other equity characteristics may, therefore, be treated as equity. For example, if the debt investor participates not only in company profits but also in company losses and the liquidation proceeds, the investment may be regarded as equity for tax purposes. The more equity characteristics that exist, for example, a very long maturity or the possibility of conversion in addition to profit-related interest, the bigger the risk that the instrument will be reclassified as hidden equity and the interest on it treated as dividend. Dividend treatment may apply also in the case of non-arm's length interest or in the case of thin capitalization.

In some countries, a bifurcation approach is also possible. A debt instrument containing both fixed and profit-related interest may be bifurcated for tax purposes into its debt and equity components. The profit-based part of interest may be regarded as a return on equity, whereas the fixed part of interest is treated as interest on debt. Typically, however, an instrument is treated in total as either debt or equity.

[C] The EU Parent-Subsidiary Directive

The P-S Directive covers income from hybrid debt that is, by its nature, actually equity, and therefore, is taxed as a dividend in EU Member States. According to Article 4 of the Interest-Royalty Directive and according to the commentary on the Proposal for the Directive, Member States do not have to apply the Interest-Royalty Directive to payments, which are by their nature profit distributions, or to income from certain hybrid financing. Article 4(1) of the Interest-Royalty Directive expressly mentions income from debt-claims holding the right to participate in the profits of the payer as the kind of income to which the Member States do not have to apply the Directive.

According to Article 4(2) of the Proposal for the Interest-Royalty Directive, the P-S Directive applies to interest on profit-participating loans such interest as is paid between qualifying companies. On the basis of the Proposal, the Commission was clearly of the opinion that income from profit-participating debt in most situations qualifies as a profit distribution under the P-S Directive if treated as a dividend in the Member States and if paid in a qualifying relationship between two qualifying companies.

Even though there may be situations in which interest paid on a profit-participating loan does not qualify as dividend for the purposes of the P-S Directive, the Member States should apply the P-S Directive when they treat the interest as dividend for domestic tax purposes and when the interest is paid between two qualifying companies in a qualifying relationship.

[D] Tax Treaties

In order for income to qualify as a dividend under the dividend definitions of the Model Conventions, the income must be from corporate rights. A dividend-generating right must entitle the investor to participate in profits and subject the investor to risk comparable to that of a shareholder. Under the third part of the dividend definition of the US Model, however, any income also qualifies if it is treated as income from corporate rights and taxed the same way as income from shares in the source state. Under the treaties that follow the US Model, interest on profit-participating loans, therefore, always qualifies as a dividend if the source state treats the interest as a dividend because it treats the investment as equity.

Interest qualifies as interest under the Models, '...whether or not carrying a right to participate in the debtor's profits...'.[72] According to the Commentary on the OECD Model, '...debt-claims, and bonds and debentures in particular, which carry a right to participate in the debtor's profits are nonetheless regarded as loans, if the contract by its general character clearly evidences a loan at interest...'.[73] Further, according to the Commentary, '...Interest on participating bonds should not normally be considered as a dividend...'.[74] According to the Commentary, debt-claims do not qualify as dividend-generating securities even though participating in profits.[75] It is clear that the sole fact that a debt investment is a profit-participating one does not make it a corporate right. A dividend on a pure profit-participating loan must be treated as interest and not as a dividend under the OECD Model.

However, according to the Commentary, interest on participating bonds should be treated as a dividend if the loan '...effectively shares the risks run by the debtor company...'.[76] As discussed above, the Commentary includes a list of characteristics that may be evaluated in determining whether a contributor of loan shares the risk run by the enterprise. This list includes the fact that the creditor will share in any profits of the company and that the level of payment of interest would depend on the profits of the company.[77] It is clear that even though profit participation alone does not make a debt investment qualify as a corporate right, if other equity characteristics are present, dividend treatment is possible, for example, if a profit-participating loan is structured in such a way that the investor also participates in the company's losses and liquidation proceeds in addition to the current profits.

The US Model includes a specific rule concerning the taxation of profit-participating interest. According to Article 11(2), interest that is determined by reference to:

> [T]he receipts, sales, income, profits, or other cash flow of the debtor or a connected person with respect to the debtor, to any change in the value of any

---

72. Articles 11(3) of the OECD and UN Models and Art. 11(2) of the US Model.
73. Paragraph 18 of the Commentary on Art. 11 of the OECD Model.
74. Paragraph 19 of the Commentary on Art. 11 of the OECD Model.
75. Paragraph 24 of the Commentary on Art. 10 of the OECD Model.
76. Paragraph 19 of the Commentary on Art. 10 of the OECD Model and para. 19 of the Commentary on Art. 11 of the OECD Model.
77. Paragraph 25 of the Commentary on Art. 10 of the OECD Model.

property of the debtor or related person, or to any dividend, partnership distribution, or similar payment made by the debtor to a connected person with respect to the debtor

may also be taxed in the source state according to the laws of the source state at a rate not to exceed 15% of the gross amount of the interest. This rate is the same as applies to portfolio dividends.[78] The fact that the taxation of profit-participating interest in the source state is limited to the same tax rate applied to a dividend, does not, by itself, make a profit-based interest qualify as a dividend under the Model.

It follows from Article 11(2) that profit-participating interest does not automatically qualify as a dividend under Article 10, but qualifies as interest under Article 11, even though in the source state it may be taxed at the same rate applicable to dividends. Because Article 11(2) refers to the source state's tax laws, profit-participating interest qualifies as a dividend under the Model only if the source state classifies such interest as a dividend. This outcome follows from Article 10(7) of the Model. Article 11(2) actually only broadens the taxing right of profit-participating interest in the source state from the rate that applies to regular interest to the same rate that applies to a dividend. But whether such interest is classified as a dividend depends on the dividend definition of Article 10(7).

The autonomous part of the dividend definition of Article 10(3) of the OECD Model expressly mentions, in addition to shares, *jouissance* shares and *jouissance* rights. Because under domestic law, such rights may cover a very wide range of rights,[79] not all *jouissance* rights under domestic law necessarily are covered by the tax treaty terms of *jouissance* shares and *jouissance* rights. In fact, from the construction of the wording of Article 10(3), it also follows that shares and *jouissance* rights and *jouissance* shares must be corporate rights. Therefore, even though *jouissance* rights are expressly mentioned, they actually are covered only if the legal characteristics attached to such instruments under domestic law involve profit participation and risks comparable to a shareholding.[80] Under the US Model, however, income from *jouissance* rights qualifies in any case as a dividend if it is treated as a dividend in the source state.

Many actual treaties mention certain profit participation arrangements expressly in the dividend definition in the same way as the OECD Model. The list of the expressly mentioned arrangements, however, varies treaty by treaty. In the case of many treaties, the payments on the expressly mentioned arrangements are considered to constitute dividend for treaty purposes no matter what the domestic law treatment is. For the purposes of other treaties, however, the classification also in the case of expressly mentioned arrangement depends on the classification of one of the treaty partners.

---

78. *See also* Raineri and Engle (1996), 1730.
79. *See* for examples of different rights referred to as *jouissance* rights or *jouissance* shares Vogel et al. (1997), 653.
80. The fact that *jouissance* rights and *jouissance* shares are expressly mentioned in a dividend article of a tax treaty, does not make a substantial difference compared to such treaties where such shares and rights are not expressly enumerated. Vogel et al. (1997), 654, interprets the wording of the OECD Model to require that *jouissance* rights are corporate rights. *See also* Laule (1997), 579 and Theisen and Wenz (1996), 167.

Under many treaties, dividend classification requires also, in the case of the expressly mentioned arrangements, that the arrangement constitutes a corporate right.

The dividend definition of many actual treaties follow the OECD Model and cover, in addition to the expressly mentioned arrangements, income from shares or other rights, not being debt-claims and participating in profits. Income from other corporate rights qualifies to the extent that it is treated the same way as income from shares is treated in the source state.

The dividend definitions of some treaties differ from the OECD Model and also cover income from other arrangements, including debt obligations, carrying the right to participate in profits, if so characterized under the laws of the state in which the income arises. Under some other treaties, other income from a company qualifies if it is treated in the source state in the same way as income from shares. Income from profit-participating loans qualifies as a dividend for the purposes of these treaties either because other equity characteristics are present so that the loan constitutes a corporate right, or because the income from the loan is treated as a dividend in the source state.

Some treaties provide that income from shares or other rights, not being debt-claims and participating in profits, qualifies as a dividend. Other income derived from other rights also qualifies if it is subjected to the same taxation treatment as income from shares by the laws of the contracting state of which the company making the distribution is a resident. Corporate rights qualify under the autonomous part of the definition. Income from rights not qualifying as corporate rights qualifies as a dividend only if the source state treats the income as a dividend. Under the autonomous part of the definition, profit participation loans only qualify if they also contain other equity characteristics. Income from pure profit-participating loans qualifies if the source state treats it as a dividend, under the third part of the definition.

Some treaties provide that income from shares qualifies as a dividend. Income from other corporate shares qualifies if the income is treated in the same way as income from shares is treated in the source state. In addition, any income qualifies if it is treated in the source state in the same way as income from shares.

In conclusion, many actual tax treaties satisfactorily solve classification conflicts with respect to profit-participating loans in favour of the classification of the source state. As long as the source state classifies interest on a profit-participating loan as a dividend, the other state must accept the classification and must eliminate double taxation accordingly. There are, however, many treaties that follow the OECD Model and require that income from a profit-participating loan be income from a corporate right.[81] Under these treaties, the state of residence of the income recipient may not accept the dividend classification of the source state because it does not agree that the instrument is a corporate right. As a result, double taxation may not be eliminated unless the conflict is solved by means of a mutual agreement procedure.

---

81. *See also* Bundgaard – Dyppel (2010), 657–662 for the classification of interest on profit-participating loans for tax treaty purposes.

§9.05 INTEREST ON CONVERTIBLE DEBT INSTRUMENTS

[A] Introduction

Convertible loans are interest-bearing debt instruments containing either the right or the obligation to convert the loan into shares of the issuer company, usually at a predetermined price and within a specified time period. Convertible loans entitle the investor to exchange its right to interest for a right to a share in corporate profits.[82]

A convertible loan is debt that creates a debtor-creditor relationship. A convertible bond investor may, however, by using the conversion right, change from a creditor into a shareholder. The conversion right allows the investor to benefit from a rise in the value of the shares into which the loan may be converted, while avoiding the risk of a reduction in the value of the shares. A right to convert a bond to stock, thus, allows the creditor to enjoy unlimited return potential.

The possibility of unlimited return potential is a typical characteristic of equity, and not of debt. An equity investment entitles the investor to a share of the company assets but may also be used to cover company losses. In a way, a convertible bond, in the form of a conversion right, includes the potential of enjoying a share of the company's profits, while at the same time, if the conversion is not compulsory, avoiding participation in the company's losses. If an issuer corporation has the right to decide whether the debt is converted into equity or if the conversion is obligatory, the instrument is even closer to equity because an investor may not choose whether the invested amount is paid back.[83]

In reality, a convertible loan includes two investments. It consists of a regular loan and an option to acquire the common stock of the issuer. In taxation, it is, therefore, possible to treat these components either separately or to treat the instrument as a unit.[84] However, neither the loan part nor the option part is equity that generates a dividend. Therefore, it is usual to treat pure convertible loans as debt in taxation until the moment that it is actually converted into share capital.

Option loans are close to convertible debt in their nature, that is, loans with equity warrants issued by corporations over their own shares. Share warrants are contractual arrangements that confer on the holder an option to subscribe for a designated number of shares of the corporation at a fixed or variable price at a later date or at any time during the term of the contract. Option loans grant the creditor not only the right to receive interest, but also the right to buy new shares of the issuing corporation. Debt instruments, which contain equity warrants in the same way as convertible loans do, offer the investor the possibility of participating in an increase of

---

82. *See*, for the basic characteristics of a convertible bond, Pike and Neale (1993), 283, Fabozzi et al. (1994), 426 and 541–546 and Van Horne (1995), 594–615.
83. *See*, for the advantages and disadvantages of convertible loans, generally, Koski (1972), 19 and 24–28 and McCormick and Creamer (1987), 40–42.
84. *See* Hariton (1988), 781 for the separation approach.

the debtor corporation's value. Generally, the option holder is able to take advantage of the rise in the value of corporate shares without bearing the risk of a shareholder.[85]

An option loan actually includes two components: the loan, the interest rate of which is often lower than the market rate for regular loans, and the share warrant, the value of which depends on the value of the shares that it entitles the investor to subscribe for. However, neither the loan portion nor the option portion may be seen as equity. Neither a regular loan nor an option, as such, creates a dividend. Therefore, it is usual to treat an option loan as debt in taxation until the moment that it is actually converted into share capital.[86]

The difference between option loans and convertible loans is that in a warrant bond, the loan remains as a loan and it only entitles the investor to make an additional investment in share capital, whereas the loan part of a convertible loan does not remain when the loan is converted into shares. The difference is also that the conversion right may not be separated from the loan and sold separately, but the option to buy corporate shares in a warrant bond may usually be separated and sold separately from the loan part of the option loan.

[B] Domestic Tax Laws

In most countries, convertible debt is treated as debt for tax purposes until it is actually converted into equity. Usually, the right to convert a debt instrument into corporate shares does not, in itself, change the classification of a debt instrument into equity for tax purposes. Also, a debt instrument containing a stock purchase right is often treated as debt instead of equity. Some countries, however, bifurcate such an instrument to its debt and option components.

Although convertibility alone does not lead to an equity classification, convertibility is usually considered to be a characteristic that is taken into account in debt/equity classification. Both convertible loans and option loans may be classified as equity if they also contain other equity characteristics. Too many equity characteristics together with a conversion right included in the terms may cause an equity classification. A convertible loan will be more easily classified as equity if the creditor is simultaneously a shareholder. The higher the probability of conversion, the greater is the likelihood of reclassification as equity.

Convertible loans or stock warrants may be assimilated to equity in taxation also for stock dividend purposes. For example, if the exercise price of the right to purchase stock is decreased periodically corresponding to the dividend payments to shareholders, the resulting increase in the corporate earnings and profits may be taxed as a dividend to the warrant holder.

---

85. *See* for the advantages of convertible loans and debt instruments with equity warrants, for example, Keinonen (1987), 268.
86. *See* for the basic characteristics of warrants Pike and Neale (1993), 283-284, Fabozzi et al. (1994), 426 and Van Horne (1995), 591-594.

[C] The Parent-Subsidiary Directive

The P-S Directive covers income from hybrid debt that by its nature is actually equity and, therefore, is taxed as a dividend in the Member States. According to Article 4 of the Interest-Royalty Directive and according to the commentary on the Proposal for the Directive, Member States do not have to apply the Interest-Royalty Directive to payments, which are treated as profit distributions in the source state or to payments from hybrid financing, which entitles the creditor to exchange the right to interest for a right to participate in the debtor's profits.

According to Article 4(2) of the Proposal for the Interest-Royalty Directive, the P-S Directive applies with respect to such interest on hybrid debt, which is not treated as interest and which is paid between qualifying companies. Even though this express reference to the P-S Directive was not included in the final version of the Interest-Royalty Directive, it is clear that during the preparation of the Directive the Commission was of the opinion that income from convertible debt, if treated as a dividend in the source state, usually qualifies as a profit distribution under the P-S Directive.

Even though there may be situation in which interest paid on a convertible loan does not qualify as dividend for the purposes of the P-S Directive, the Member States should apply the P-S Directive when they treat the interest as dividend for domestic tax purposes and when the interest is paid between two qualifying companies in a qualifying relationship.

[D] Tax Treaties

In order for income to qualify as a dividend under the dividend definitions of the Model Conventions, the income must be from corporate rights. A dividend-generating right must entitle the investor to participate in profits and the investor must be subject to risk comparable to that assumed by a shareholder. Under the third part of the dividend definition of the US Model, however, any income that is treated as income from corporate rights also qualifies as a dividend if it is taxed in the source state the same way as income from shares. Under the treaties following the US Model, interest on convertible loans, therefore, always qualifies as a dividend if the source state treats the instrument as a corporate right and the interest on it as a dividend.

According to the Commentary, the interest on convertible debentures is not a dividend.[87] Further, the interest on convertible bonds should not normally be considered to be a dividend until such time as the bonds are actually converted into shares.[88] However, the Commentary recognizes that '...the interest on such bonds should be considered as a dividend if the loan effectively shares the risk run by the debtor company...'.[89] The interest on a convertible loan, thus, qualifies generally as interest under the Models because a convertible loan is not a corporate right. If the investor

---

87. Paragraph 24 of the Commentary on Art. 10 of the OECD Model.
88. Paragraph 19 of the Commentary on Art. 11 of the OECD Model.
89. Ibid.

effectively shares in the risks assumed by the company, then the interest on convertible loan qualifies as a dividend.

The fact that a debt-claim carries a right that entitles the holder to claim an exchange or purchase of shares does not, alone, constitute the kind of entrepreneurial risk required of dividend-generating corporate rights. Such risk does not exist especially if the conversion is not obligatory and when the investor may use the claim for conversion only if the value of shares has increased. A straight convertible loan does not participate in current company profits or in the liquidation proceeds of the company until the time of the actual conversion. Therefore, a convertible loan qualifies as a dividend-generating corporate right only after the actual conversion or if the investor, in addition to possessing the conversion right, also participates in the profits, liquidation proceeds and losses of the corporation.

The dividend article of many actual treaties covers income from shares or other rights, not being debt-claims, participating in profits. Other income derived from other rights also qualifies if it is subjected to the same taxation treatment as income from shares by the laws of the contracting state of which the company making the distribution is a resident. Some other treaties provide that the income from shares or other rights, not being debt-claims, participating in profits, qualifies as a dividend. Other income from a company qualifies if the income is treated in the source state in the same way as income from shares. Similarly, under some other treaties, income from shares qualifies as a dividend. Income from other corporate rights also qualifies if the income is treated in the same way as income from shares in the source state. In addition, any income qualifies as a dividend if it is treated in the source state in the same way as income from shares. The treaties with these slightly different wordings are substantially similar as regards convertible loans.

Only corporate rights qualify under the autonomous part of the definitions. Income from rights not qualifying as corporate rights qualifies as a dividend only if the source state treats the income the same way as a dividend. The income from convertible loans, thus, qualifies under the treaties as a dividend if treated as a dividend in the source state or if the loan contains other equity characteristics.

Many other treaties provide that income from shares or other rights, not being debt-claims, participating in profits, qualifies as a dividend. Also, income from other corporate rights qualifies if it is subjected by the laws of the source state to the same tax treatment as income from shares is subjected to. In addition, income from arrangements, including debt obligations, carrying the right to participate in profits, qualifies as a dividend if so characterized under the laws of the state in which the income arises. Under the autonomous part of the dividend definition of these treaties, thus, only income from corporate rights qualifies. Under the autonomous part, the income from convertible loans, thus, qualifies only if the loan contains other equity characteristics. Under the treaties, income from a debt-claim, which is not a corporate right, qualifies as a dividend if the debt-claim entitles the holder to participate in profits and if the income is treated as a dividend in the source state. The requirement of profit participation, cannot, however, be interpreted as meaning the possibility of participating in profits only in an indirect way in the form of a conversion right. Therefore, convertible loans qualify as dividend-generating investments only if they constitute corporate rights due to the presence of other equity characteristics, or if, in addition to a conversion right, a profit participation right is also included, and the source state taxes the interest as a dividend.

Finally, some treaties follow the wording of the OECD Model. Under these treaties, income from shares or other rights, not being debt-claims, participating in profits, qualifies as a dividend. Income from other corporate rights also qualifies if it is treated the same way as income from shares in the source state. Because convertible loans do not constitute corporate rights, the income from convertible loans may qualify as a dividend only if the loan contains other equity characteristics.

In conclusion, classification conflicts may emerge, especially when more than one such equity characteristic is involved. The states may disagree whether the instrument concerned qualifies as a corporate right for treaty purposes. Under the treaties, where source state classification is decisive, the other state, however, has to accept the source state classification for treaty purposes. Classification conflicts are, thus, satisfactorily solved in favour of the classification of the source state under the treaties that differ from the OECD Model. In the case of the treaties following the OECD Model, classification conflicts may lead to double taxation unless they are solved by means of a mutual agreement procedure.

§9.06 INTEREST ON SUBORDINATED DEBT INSTRUMENTS

[A] Introduction

One basic characteristic of debt is that the claims of the debt investors have priority over any of the claims of the equity holders in company liquidation. All creditors must be satisfied before the equity holders may get their share. The principal amount of all debt must be repaid before an equity investment may be repaid, and any return on debt must be paid before any dividend may be distributed. The priority ranking of debt and interest to equity and a dividend correlates to the risks involved with each type of investment.[90]

A loan may, however, be subordinated to all other loans, either obligatorily or voluntarily.[91] Subordination means the arrangement whereby one or more creditors of a common debtor agree to postpone or subordinate payment on their debt until another creditor or group of creditors of the same debtor has been paid.[92] A subordination clause signifies that the creditor becomes last on the list of the company's creditors in the event of liquidation. The subordinated or junior creditor agrees not to be paid by the debtor until another or all other creditors of the company have been satisfied.[93] In

---

90. *See* for this correlation, for example, Villa (1995), 236.
91. Sometimes subordination of shareholder loans may be based on law. In such a situation, usually in company liquidation, a shareholder creditor is subordinated to other loan creditors even though there was no subordination clause included in the loan contract. *See*, for example, Piltz (1996), 90.
92. *See* Wood (1995), 37–43.
93. Subordinated loans may also be referred to as junior or inferior debt. *See* Henn and Aleksander (1993), 389 and Wood (1995), 37.

the event of the insolvency of the debtor company, subordinated loans are repaid after all other creditors have been satisfied but before the shareholders receive any repayment.[94]

Because a subordinated loan creditor is entitled to payment only after all other creditors' claims have been satisfied, the risks involved in the investment are very close to the risks of shareholders. A subordinated loan is, thus, in its economic nature, very close to equity. However, it is a debt obligation. It is a loan that is supposed to be repaid, and is not a perpetual investment. Because a share investment is also subordinated compared to a subordinated loan, the risk of share investment is higher. Debt, generally, may also be secured, but equity may not. A subordinated loan does not entitle the holder to control or to other shareholder rights and the loan only involves a limited return potential.[95] Because of these similarities and differences between subordinated loans and equity investments, it may be asked whether the interest on subordinated loans should be treated as interest or be reclassified as a dividend for tax purposes.

[B] Domestic Tax Laws

In many countries, the subordination of an instrument compared to all other creditors' claims in the case of the liquidation of the issuing corporation is regarded as a factor indicating equity status for tax purposes. Subordination is often referred to as a characteristic indicating that the creditor is sharing in the risks of the business in the way that a shareholder would. In most countries, subordination alone, however, does not cause the reclassification of an instrument as equity. Usually, subordination does not endanger debt classification for tax purposes so long as the debt has priority over equity and other characteristics present indicate debt rather than equity. Taken together with other equity characteristics, subordination may, however, lead to a reclassification of debt as equity. Equity treatment is possible especially if a subordinated loan is given to a corporation by all of its shareholders in proportion to their shareholding.

[C] The EU Parent-Subsidiary Directive

The P-S Directive covers income from hybrid debt that is, by its nature, actually equity, and, therefore, is taxed as a dividend in the Member States. According to Article 4 of the Interest-Royalty Directive and according to the commentary on the Proposal for the Directive, Member States do not have to apply the Directive to payments, which are, by their nature, profit distributions, or to income from hybrid financing. Article 4(1) of

---

94. *See* McCormick and Creamer (1987), 51 and Villa (1997), 33 for different types of subordination clauses.
95. Because subordinated loans are in many states regarded as equity for company law purposes, subordination is often used in company insolvency situations to improve the debt-to-equity ratio without changing the control in the company. *See*, for the advantages of subordination, McCormick and Creamer (1987), 51–52 and Wood (1995), 38–41.

Interest-Royalty Directive expressly mentions examples of situations where the source state of interest does not have to apply the Directive. The list includes the situation in which the source state treats the payment as a distribution of profits under its domestic law. The tax benefits based on the Interest-Royalty Directive, thus, do not need to be made available in the source state of a payment on a subordinated loan, if the source state treats the payment as a distribution of profits under its domestic tax law. Such payments, instead, should qualify for the benefits of the P-S Directive provided that the payment was made in a qualifying relationship between two qualifying companies.

[D] Tax Treaties

In order for income to qualify as a dividend under the dividend definitions of the Model Conventions, the income must be from corporate rights. A dividend-generating right must entitle the investor to participate in profits and the investor must be subject to the risks comparable to those assumed by a shareholder. Therefore, it is clear that solely the fact that a loan is subordinated to other loans does not make a debt-claim a dividend-generating right. A subordination clause does not entitle the investor to participate in profits. Under the third part of the dividend definition of the US Model, however, any income qualifies as a dividend if it is treated as income from corporate rights and taxed in the source state the same way as income from shares. Under the treaties following the US Model, the interest on subordinated loans, therefore, qualifies as a dividend if the source state treats the instrument as a corporate right and interest on it as a dividend.

The Commentary includes a list of characteristics that may be evaluated in determining whether a contributor of a loan shares the risks run by the enterprise. This list includes the fact that the repayment of the loan is subordinated to the claims of other creditors or to the payment of a dividend.[96] Therefore, even though subordination alone may not make a debt investment a dividend-generating right, dividend treatment is possible if other equity characteristics are also involved. The interest on subordinated loans may be treated as a dividend, for example, if the investor is also entitled to participate in company profits and in liquidation proceeds.

Under many actual treaties, income from shares or other rights, not being debt-claims, participating in profits, qualifies as a dividend. Other income derived from other rights also qualifies if it is subjected to the same taxation treatment as income from shares by the laws of the contracting state of which the company making the distribution is a resident. Instead, under some other treaties, income from shares or other rights, not being debt-claims, participating in profits, qualifies as a dividend. Other income from a company qualifies as a dividend if it is treated in the source state in the same way as income from shares. The dividend definition of certain other treaties is formulated as covering income from shares and income from other corporate rights if the income is treated the same way as income from shares is treated in the source state. In addition, any income qualifies if it is treated in the source state in the

---

96. Paragraph 25 of the Commentary on Art. 10 of the OECD Model.

same way as income from shares is treated. Despite the slightly different wordings, all these treaties are substantially similar as regards subordinated loans.

Because the feature of subordination alone does not make a loan a corporate right, a subordinated loan with no other equity characteristics does not qualify as a dividend-generating right under the autonomous parts of the dividend definitions of the treaties. However, if the source state treats interest from subordinated loans as a dividend, the interest qualifies as a dividend also for treaty purposes and the other state must accept the classification of the source state.

Under many treaties, income from shares or other rights, not being debt-claims, participating in profits, qualifies as a dividend. Income from other corporate rights also qualifies if it is subjected to the same tax treatment as income from shares is subjected to by the laws of the source state. The dividend article of some other treaties, instead, follows the wording of the OECD Model. Because a subordinated loan with no other equity characteristics is not a corporate right, income from it does not qualify as a dividend under these treaties no matter how the income is treated under domestic law. The interest on a subordinated loan qualifies as a dividend under these treaties only if the instrument contains other equity characteristics so that it constitutes a corporate right.

In conclusion, a subordination clause alone does not make income from a loan qualify as a dividend under the autonomous parts of the dividend definitions. Under many treaties, income from subordinated loans, however, qualifies as a dividend if the source state treats the income as a dividend. Under many other treaties, the income from subordinated loans may, instead, qualify only if the investment may be regarded as constituting a corporate right because of other equity characteristics involved.

Not all of the tax treaties solve classification conflicts. One of the contracting states may view an instrument as qualifying as a corporate right whereas the other may not. The Commentary on the OECD Model only provides for a case-by-case analysis in determining whether or not an instrument qualifies as a corporate right. Reference to a mutual agreement procedure may be needed in order for double taxation to be eliminated. Only the treaties that differ from the OECD Model solve classification conflicts satisfactorily in favour of the source state. Under these treaties, the other state should accept the source state classification and eliminate double taxation accordingly.

§9.07   CLASSIFICATION OF THE RETURN ON PREFERRED SHARES

[A]   Introduction

The principle of the freedom of contract makes it possible to issue shares with only limited equity characteristics and with certain debt characteristics. Preferred shares or preference shares are shares that carry certain preferential rights over ordinary shares, usually with respect to either a dividend or the repayment of capital or both.[97] Usually, the holders of preferred shares are either totally barred from voting or are entitled to

---

97. *See* for the commonness of preferred shares, McCormick and Creamer (1987), 11.

vote only in circumstances directly affecting the holders of the preferred shares. Preferred stock is often used in situations where companies need equity investors with entrepreneurial risk, but where the companies do not want to give the investors control in the company.[98]

Preferred shares entitle the holder to a fixed dividend calculated as a percentage of the principal invested in the preferred shares. Often, the claims of preferred shareholders have priority over claims of common shareholders. Preferred shares may entitle the holder to a preferential repayment of nominal value in the winding up of the corporation ahead of ordinary shareholders. Preferred shareholders are usually not entitled to participate in any surplus assets in excess of the return of nominal capital and cumulated dividends. Preferred shares may also be redeemable or convertible into ordinary shares.[99]

In general, only an equity investor, and not a debt investor, is allowed to take part in the decision-making processes of a corporation in the form of voting rights.[100] Because of the lack of or limitation in voting rights, non-voting preferred stock is very close to debt in its economic nature. Preferred shares also entitle the holder to a fixed return that does not depend on the corporation's profitability in a way that is normally possible only for debt investors.

Preferred shares do not, however, totally correspond to debt investments. Preferred shares do not contain a fixed date of termination. The payment of return on preferred shares depends on the company's decision to distribute a dividend and it may only be paid if there are profits that may be distributed as a dividend in the company. In liquidation, the rights of preferred shareholders are subordinated to all debt creditors. If preferred non-voting shares are redeemable, that is, if the company has agreed to repurchase them on a fixed date or at a date decided upon by the preferred shareholder, they are even closer to debt from an economic perspective. From an economic point of view, there is not much reason for distinguishing between the tax treatment of debt and such redeemable preferred shares.[101]

An equity investment has generally been characterized as a long-term investment that may be repaid only by company liquidation, whereas debt, in general, is a temporary investment with a fixed date or terms of maturity. The relative nature of the duration of an investment[102] makes the length of an investment ineffective in distinguishing debt from equity. The length of the investment period may not be decisive, but rather the fact whether the date or the conditions of the maturity are fixed beforehand. A characteristic of debt is that the creditor unlike a shareholder, knows the date of maturity beforehand or it is, at least, in the control of the creditor when the

---

98. *See* for different reasons for the use of preferred shares, McCormick and Creamer (1987), 11–13.
99. *See* Gower et al. (1979), 412, McCormick and Creamer (1987), 11, Lang (1990), 170, Pike and Neale (1993), 276–277, Fabozzi et al. (1994), 452–435, Villa (1994a), 331–332 and Villa (1997), 2, for the typical characteristics of preferred shares.
100. The fact that a debt investment does not legally entitle a creditor to voting rights in the debtor corporation does not mean that a creditor could not have factual influence on the decisions of the debtor corporation.
101. *See* Gower et al. (1979), 418, Villa (1994a), 334 and Villa (1995), 235.
102. *See* Ryynänen (1996), 389.

investment is to be redeemed. The feature of redeemability present in a capital investment is strong evidence of debt rather than equity. Redeemable preference shares are, therefore, largely comparable to profit-participating loans.[103] With respect to redeemable preferred shares, it may be questioned whether the dividend on them should be taxed as interest.

In taxation, debt in most situations is favoured over equity. The need for reclassifying equity as debt for taxation purposes is not as great as the need for reclassifying debt as equity. But because interest is taxed, in general, only in the state of residence of the investor, whereas a direct investment dividend may be taxed only in the source state, equity may be used to avoid tax in the state of residence of the investor. The tax authorities of the state of residence of the investor may question the form of an investment as hybrid equity and reclassify the investment as debt for tax purposes. In practice, however, reclassification of equity as debt is rather rare.

[B]   Domestic Tax Laws

In most countries, preferred shares are classified as equity for tax purposes. If the instrument is labelled as equity by the issuer, it is not likely that the instrument will be classified as debt for tax purposes. If a third party does not guarantee dividend or redemption payments, debt classification is especially unlikely.

Especially, redeemable preference shares may fall into either the category of debt or the category of equity, depending on the exact conditions involved. A mandatory redemption provision increases the risk of a debt classification. Other key factors determining the classification may include, for example, the existence of voting rights, a redemption price, the likelihood of redemption, a preference position in liquidation, a regular fixed return and whether or not the dividend is cumulative.

In the classification of redeemable preferred shares, the actual characteristics of debt or equity are decisive for tax law purposes in many countries. For example, if the actual characteristics of an investment made in the form of redeemable preference shares without voting rights are closer to profit-participating perpetual debt than to a share investment, reclassification may be possible. In such a situation, a dividend on the shares may also be treated as interest.

[C]   The EU Parent-Subsidiary Directive

The P-S Directive concerns the taxation of distributions of profits by a subsidiary to its parent company made by virtue of the parent company's association with the subsidiary. Preference shares that form part of the subsidiary's share capital should be comparable to any other shares. The parent-subsidiary relationship requires that the parent company has a minimum holding of 10% in the capital of the subsidiary. The P-S Directive does not distinguish between different types of capital. Generally, the

---

103. *See* Gower et al. (1979), 418, Andersson (1987), 339, Mähönen and Villa (1996), 616, Ryynänen (1996), 389 and Villa (1997), 113.

term 'capital' is understood to include not only actual shareholding, but also hidden equity capital.

From the fact that even hidden equity capital is considered to be included in the P-S Directive's ambit, then a holding of preference shares must be included, at the least. After all, preference shares form a part of the share capital of the company. However, the P-S Directive also allows the holding requirement to be calculated on the basis of voting rights. If this approach is selected, non-voting preference shares do not qualify as shares for the purposes of calculating the 10% holding requirement. However, if the requirement is fulfilled based on the voting rights of ordinary shares, distributions on non-voting preference shares must also qualify for the benefits of the P-S Directive.

The P-S Directive only concerns distributions of profits. Therefore, if the actual nature of a payment is not a distribution of profit but rather a payment of interest, the application of the P-S Directive should not be required. The form of hybrid equity may be used instead of debt in order to take advantage of the benefits of the P-S Directive. By the use of equity instead of debt, taxation in the state of residence of the parent company may be avoided. The use of debt is more advantageous with respect to taxation in the state of residence of the subsidiary. The most advantageous situation for a taxpayer would be where the state of residence of the subsidiary treats income on hybrid equity as deductible interest whereas the state of residence of the parent company treats it as an exempted direct investment dividend.

In practice, however, the state of residence of the subsidiary will hardly reclassify a dividend paid on hybrid equity as interest because it is more advantageous for the state to treat the payment as a non-deductible dividend. Even the fact that the state then must refrain from subjecting the dividend to withholding tax in accordance with the P-S Directive does not change the attractiveness of the dividend treatment because interest paid to a non-resident is often exempt anyway.[104] The state of residence of the parent company may argue that the nature of the payment is actually interest despite it being in the form of a dividend because dividend treatment would require the state to refrain from taxing the income.

Article 1(2) of the P-S Directive includes a general anti-avoidance provision. According to this provision the Member States shall not grant the directive benefits to an arrangement or a series of arrangements which, having been put into place for the main purpose or one of the main purposes of obtaining a tax advantage that defeats the object of the directive, are not genuine having regard to all relevant facts and circumstances.[105] An arrangement or a series of arrangements are not regarded as genuine to the extent that they are not put into place for valid commercial reasons which reflect economic reality.[106] The Member States are not allowed to grant the directive benefits in situations covered by the anti-avoidance provision. It may be said

---

104. For example, the Interest-Royalty Directive prevents source state withholding taxes in the case of interest payments that come under the scope of the directive.
105. Article 1(2) of the P-S Directive.
106. Article 1(3) of the P-S Directive. Weber (1996), 65 suggested that P-S Directive concept of abuse should be interpreted based on this kind of 'commercial-purpose-test' even before the 2015 amendment of Art. 1 making this test more evident. For the amendment, see Council Directive

that the object of the P-S Directive is not to exempt a distribution which is a part of a wholly artificial tax avoidance arrangement. Article 1(4) of the P-S Directive allows expressly also 'the application of domestic or agreement-based provisions required for the prevention of tax evasion, tax fraud or abuse'.[107]

Hybrid equity may be used instead of debt in order to benefit abusively from the P-S Directive. In order to prevent tax avoidance, the state of residence of the parent company may not be required to make available the P-S Directive benefits to income from a hybrid equity investment in a subsidiary. The P-S Directive benefits should not be made available in the case of a wholly artificial tax avoidance arrangement where tax avoidance is the only or main motive for the use of preferred shares and where there are no valid commercial reasons for the arrangement.

In conclusion, the P-S Directive benefits must be made available in the case of a dividend on preferred shares in the same way as with respect to any profit distributions. However, in the case of wholly artificial tax avoidance arrangements where there are no valid commercial reasons for the use of preferred shares, the benefits must not be made available.

[D]   Tax Treaties

According to Article 10(3) of the OECD Model, '…income from shares,…or other rights, not being debt-claims, participating in profits, as well as income from other corporate rights…' qualifies as a dividend. Different classes of company shares qualify for the purposes of Article 10 as shares so long as they may be regarded as being corporate rights. In other words, the investor must participate in entrepreneurial risk. As discussed above, the restrictions on control rights such as restrictions on voting rights or even the total lack of voting rights are irrelevant for the purposes of Article 10(3). An important feature is the participation of the investor in the profits, liquidation proceeds and losses of the company.[108]

Preferred shares are clearly the kind of corporate rights mentioned in Article 10(3) of the OECD Model even though they carry no voting rights.[109] The fact that preferred shares have better rights to company profits than ordinary shares does not change the fact that preferred shares are indeed shares. Only if the rights of the investor to participate in the company's profits or liquidation proceeds are limited may a share

---

(EU) 2015/121 of 27 Jan. 2015 amending Directive 2011/96/EU on the Common System of Taxation Applicable in the Case of Parent Companies and Subsidiaries of Different Member States).

107. It has not been not perfectly clear what is meant by '…provisions required for the prevention of…fraud or abuse…'. *See* for the uncertainty, for example, Farmer (1994), 314 and Weber (1996), 63–69. It is sometimes argued that because the article uses the term 'provision', it would not include general domestic law anti-avoidance principles. *See* for this opinion Raby (1992), 220 and de Hosson (1990), 426–427. *See*, for example, Helminen (2015), 178–180 about the application of the P-S Directive in a tax avoidance situation and about the possibility to deny any EU law benefits in the case of tax avoidance situations Helminen (2015), 138–145.
108. *See* Vogel et al. (1997), 653 for how only the proprietary rights of a shareholder are relevant with respect to Art. 10(3) of the OECD Model.
109. *See also* Vogel et al. (1997), 650 and 653 and Giuliani (2002), 14 for this opinion.

not qualify as a dividend-generating investment. Income from preferred shares, thus, qualifies as income from shares under the autonomous part of the dividend definition and must be treated as a dividend despite the treatment under the domestic tax law of the states involved.

Preferred shares qualify as corporate rights even though they are redeemable, because under the company law of different states, a company may redeem any of its shares and not only preferred shares. However, it is true that an investment that contains a mandatory redemption provision shares the risk run by the company only until the redemption. The risk, with respect to the investment, is therefore comparable to the risk of a debt investment. If the shares are not redeemed before liquidation, the claims of the preferred share investor are subordinated to the debt investors. In liquidation, the investment is comparable to share investments and not debt investments. The only situation where a preferred share may not qualify as a corporate right is when it contains both a mandatory redemption provision that requires redemption within a relatively short period of time and a provision that grants liquidation preference. The states involved may, however, disagree whether a corporate right exists even in this type of situation.

In practice, it is in the interest of the state of residence of the income recipient to classify income as interest, whereas it is in interest of the source state to classify income as a dividend. Therefore, classification conflicts with respect to preferred shares are relevant in situations where the state of residence of the income recipient treats a dividend on preferred shares as interest. As discussed above, the state of residence of the income recipient is not required to follow the source state dividend treatment under the OECD Model unless it agrees that the income is from a corporate right. The conflict may, therefore, be left unsolved. Under the treaties following the US Model, this problem should not emerge because any income qualifies as a dividend under the treaty if it is treated in the source state as a return on an equity investment. The state of residence of the income recipient has to accept the dividend treatment in the source state and eliminate double taxation accordingly.

Also under actual treaties, income from shares that are corporate rights qualifies as a dividend under the autonomous parts of the dividend definitions. Income from preferred shares must normally be treated as a dividend under the treaties no matter what the classification under domestic law is.

Classification conflicts, however, are possible if one of the contracting states reclassifies a dividend on redeemable preferred shares as interest and holds the view that a redeemable preferred share is not a corporate right.

Under many treaties, however, any income from any rights qualifies as a dividend if it is treated as a dividend in the source state. For the purposes of these treaties, the state of residence of the dividend recipient must accept the source state dividend classification. Also, many other treaties solve classification conflicts in favour of the dividend classification of the source state. Under some treaties, income from any arrangements, including debt obligations, carrying the right to participate in profits, qualifies as a dividend if the source state treats such income as a dividend. Under some other treaties, any income qualifies as a dividend if it is treated in the source state as a dividend. The treaties that follow the wording of the OECD Model, however, require that a dividend be income from a corporate right no matter what the treatment in the source state is.

Because it is generally for the benefit of the state of residence of income recipient to treat income as interest instead of as a dividend, the treaties that do not follow the OECD Model wording solve possible classification conflicts more satisfactorily with respect to preferred shares. Under the treaties based on the wording of the OECD Model, unsolved classification conflicts with respect to a dividend on redeemable preferred shares are possible. In practice, such conflicts, however, do not emerge very often because it is not very usual that countries treat a dividend on redeemable preference shares as interest.

§9.08   CONCLUSIONS

In most countries, the classification of hybrid instruments and income on hybrid instruments for tax purposes is based on a case-by-case approach. The domestic tax law of many countries does not include special provisions concerning the classification of income on certain specific hybrid instruments. In many countries, the classification of hybrid instruments and the income on them is based on evaluating the different equity and debt characteristics on the instrument concerned. Usually, distinguishing between interest and a dividend is based on distinguishing between debt and equity. Income on debt is interest whereas income on equity is a dividend. In distinguishing debt from equity, the form used is not decisive. Decisive is whether the actual substance of an instrument is either debt or equity.

The case-by-case approach applied in different states is understandable because it would be impossible to cover each possible hybrid instrument in tax law expressly. Hybrid instruments usually do not contain only one hybrid characteristic but rather several. With respect to situations where only one hybrid characteristic is involved, different states are usually in agreement about the classification. In most situations, the form of a hybrid instrument with only one hybrid characteristic is respected for tax purposes. With respect to such hybrids, classification conflicts are therefore not usual. However, most states seem to be prepared to reclassify hybrid instruments in situations where more than one hybrid characteristic is involved. Primarily, these situations, however, concern the reclassification of hybrid debt as equity, but not the reclassification of hybrid equity as debt.

Classification conflicts emerge very easily in the case of hybrids with more than one equity characteristic. The case-by-case approach may lead to a situation where one of the states treats an instrument as interest-generating debt and the other as a dividend-generating equity. Such inconsistent domestic law classification may lead to actual classification conflicts and international double taxation. The tax treaties completed between the states do not necessarily prevent such classification conflicts.

The treaties that do not follow the wording of the OECD Model function better in the solving of classification conflicts. These are the treaties that do not require that dividend be income from a corporate right. Under these treaties, any income qualifies as a dividend if it is treated as a dividend for tax purposes in the source state. Actual classification conflicts are satisfactorily solved in favour of the dividend classification in the source state. Classification conflicts remain unsolved under these treaties only in situations where the source state treats an item of income as interest while the other state treats the same item as a dividend. Because interest treatment generally leads to higher tax revenues in the state of residence of the income recipient, in practice, unsolved classification conflicts should be rare. In any case, such classification conflicts would not lead to double taxation if the cross-border interest is not taxed in the source state in any case.

The treaties that follow the wording of the OECD Model do not prevent actual classification conflicts. Under these treaties, only income from corporate rights qualifies as a dividend no matter what the domestic law classification is. If the states interpret different hybrid instruments as constituting corporate rights, they may treat income from the instruments according to different articles of the treaties. International double taxation may not be eliminated unless the conflict is solved by means of a mutual agreement procedure. For this reason, there would be good reason to amend the OECD Model in this respect.

CHAPTER 10
Classification of Interest in Thin Capitalization Situations

§10.01 INTRODUCTION

Parent companies or shareholders, in general, often make debt investments in addition to equity investments in their subsidiaries or in the corporation in which they hold shares. An investor may simultaneously be in the position of a shareholder and a creditor, and receive both dividend and interest in return. In such a mixed position, the form used for an investment does not necessarily correspond to the actual economic nature of the investment because debt and equity investments are largely substitutable for each other. Many times tax considerations may be decisive in selecting the form of finance either as debt or as equity.

Tax revenue from debt generally is realized primarily by the state of residence of the investor whereas the tax revenue from direct investment equity, in particular, is realized by the state of residence of the financed corporation.[1] The use of debt finance instead of equity, thus, distributes tax revenues from the source state to the state of residence of the recipient of the return on an investment. In order to avoid taxation in the source state, a corporation may be financed excessively with debt.[2] This kind of tax planning through excessive use of debt finance compared to the use of equity finance is referred to as *thin capitalization*. Thin capitalization means an abnormally high debt-to-equity ratio of a corporation in a situation where the debt finance comes from an affiliated contributor of capital.[3]

---

1. *See*, for example, Rohatgi (2007), 215 about the tax and non-tax advantages related to the use of debt instead of equity.
2. For example, Zielke (2010), 62 mentions shareholder debt financing as the most important instrument of international tax planning. *See* OECD (2015e), 15–18 for the use of interest for base erosion and profit shifting.
3. The contributor of debt capital is often simultaneously a direct shareholder. Thin capitalization may, however, occur also in the form of the so-called back-to-back financing, where the visible

In order to protect tax revenues, many states have adopted *special anti-thin capitalization regimes* in their tax legislation. Alternatively, the problem may be tackled by means of specific interest deduction limitation provisions, general arm's length rules or general rules aimed against tax avoidance.[4] In a thin capitalization situation, a shareholder loan may be considered as equity under domestic law despite the form used because, from an economic point of view, it is more like equity in its substance. The fact that unrelated persons would not have granted a loan under similar circumstances may be regarded as an indication that the loan is not arm's length, and was granted only because of the shareholder relationship.[5] Because thin capitalization reduces the tax revenue of the source state, thin capitalization may also be seen as a misuse of the legal options available to reduce the tax burden, and, therefore, as an abuse of law. Therefore, general anti-avoidance rules may be applied to thin capitalization situations.

Under special anti-thin capitalization regimes, debt may be reclassified as equity if the actual debt-to-equity ratio either exceeds a fixed limit or exceeds the arm's length ratio considering all the circumstances.[6] Whether or not the debt is reclassified as equity, the interest deduction may be denied under such regimes. Sometimes, the interest paid on the excessive part of the debt is also reclassified as dividend for withholding tax purposes.[7] Interesting from the perspective of this study are especially such domestic law rules that actually reclassify interest as dividend. The number of the states that actually reclassify a thin capitalization interest as dividend, however, has

---

capital contributor is directly not a shareholder but actually is an affiliate of the multinational group. The term 'thin capitalization' is not an exact legal term but is used loosely covering different situations. In this study, the term 'thin capitalization' is used narrowly to refer solely to cases with an excessive use of debt finance compared to equity finance. See for similar usage, Alaluusua and Niskakangas (1984), 11, Tikka (1989), 202, Collado and Rey (1993), 111, Arnold (1994), 512, Sommerhalder (1996), 82 and Piltz (1996), 89. Sometimes the term is, however, used more broadly to refer to situations of hybrid finance as well. See Lüthi (1991), 447, United Nations (1988), 24 and Raineri and Engle (1996), 1722.

4. Tax revenue may be protected also, for example, by rules allowing taxing controlled foreign company profits or withholding taxes on dividend interest and royalties. See Jackson (1990), 319. See also OECD (2015e), 19–22 for different means to protect tax base against thin capitalization and excessive interest deductions.
5. The problem of thin capitalization does not concern the question of whether interest paid on loans in a thinly capitalized company is excessive or not. Excessive part of interest may be reclassified as dividend whether or not the company is thinly capitalized.
6. *See* for examples of debt-to-equity ratios in different countries' thin capitalization legislation Zielke (2010), 70–72, Eicke (2009), 245–264, Rohatgi (2007), 217–239 and IBFD (2005), 367–451.
7. *See* International Fiscal Association (1996a), 4. *See* more about the different approaches in tackling thin capitalization, for example, OECD (1979), 15–16 and 191, OECD (1987), 72, Collado and Rey (1993), 112, Vapaavuori (1996a), 528, Rohatgi (2007), 214–239 and Hinny (2008), 23–28 and 37–40. A new tendency has been to make the traditional thin capitalization rules more restrictive or to introduce new rules that may not be limited only to related parties and that limit interest deduction generally to a percentage of the EBIT or a similar business figure. *See*, for example, Zielke (2010), 70–72, Äimä (2009), 355–402 and Hinny (2008), 23–28 about the new tendencies and for country examples of the new type of rules.

decreased over the past decade.[8] Many states consider that it is sufficient to limit interest deduction without questioning the proper classification of the payment.[9]

The domestic thin capitalization regimes are often applied, disregarding the tax consequences in the state of residence of the recipient of the interest. The state of residence of the shareholder receiving the interest does not, however, necessarily respect the source state classification, but makes its own classification.[10] Anti-thin capitalization regimes may, thus, lead to classification conflicts and international double taxation.

This study does not try to determine when a company is considered or should be considered to be thinly capitalized, and should, therefore, trigger thin capitalization regimes. This problem is a difficult one that is in its nature strongly economic in addition to legal. This study does not seek to explain the situations in which the ratio of debt to equity is considered excessive in different states or what components are ascribed to debt and equity with respect to thin capitalization calculations in different states.

§10.02 NON-DISCRIMINATION

[A] Tax Treaties

The domestic law provisions reclassifying tax-deductible interest as non-deductible dividend in thin capitalization situations may be questionable from the perspective of the tax treaty non-discrimination articles. It may be questioned whether denial of interest deduction is in accordance with Article 24(4) and 24(5) of the OECD Model and similar articles of the other Models.[11] In most situations the application of such domestic law thin capitalization regimes, which reclassify interest as dividend only in non-arm's length situations, however, complies with tax treaties.

---

8. The number of such provision that reclassify interest as dividend has decreased especially in Europe, because of the EU P-S Directive. See Zielke (2010), 80–81 for examples of countries that reclassify interest as dividend under domestic thin capitalization rules.
9. For example, the OECD BEPS Action 4 report recommendation is based on an interest deduction limitation provision not dealing with the classification of the payment. See OECD (2015e).
10. Often countries feel free to classify interest according to their own domestic legislation also in a tax treaty situation. See the General rapport of thin capitalization in 1996 International Fiscal Association Congress in Piltz (1996), 122.
11. See paras 56 and 58 of the Commentary on Art. 24 of the OECD Model, Brandt (1997), 261 and 262, Adonnino (1993), 64, van Raad (1986), 178, International Fiscal Association (1996a), 2, Fernández (1996), 952, Piltz (1996), 133–134, Engle and Raineri (1996), 793–794, McCarthy (1997), 239, Michielse (1997), 571, de Hosson and Michielse (1989), 483, Avery Jones et al. (1996), 343–344, Carrero (1996), 296–297, Raineri and Engle (1996), 1729 and 1731, Doernberg and van Raad (1990), 203, Doernberg and van Raad (1997), 207, Teixeira (1996), 477, Müller-Seils (1994), 191, Menck (1994), 71, Herzig (1994), 114, Theisen and Wenz (1996), 126, Prinz (1995), 44, Andersson (1995), 205, VM 1995:10 72, Vapaavuori (1996), 414 and Vapaavuori (1996a), 534, VM 1995:10, 72, Andersson and Vapaavuori (1994), 231, Hinnekens and Hinnekens (2008), 35–38, Helminen (2016a), 362–363 and Sieker (1997), 220–222.

In situations where both Article 24(4) and 24(5) are included in a tax treaty, the application of thin capitalization regimes that follow the arm's length principle are not prohibited. This interpretation is based on the fact that Article 9(1) of the OECD Model is applicable to tackle thin capitalization, and the reference to Article 9 in Article 24(4) would be meaningless if Article 25(5) would limit situations based on the application of Article 9(1).

Also, according to the Commentary on Article 24 of the OECD Model:

> Paragraph 4 does not prohibit the country of the borrower from applying its domestic rules on thin capitalization insofar as these are compatible with paragraph 1 of Article 9 or paragraph 6 of Article 11.[12]

Domestic law thin capitalization rules are also in accordance with paragraph 5 of Article 24 '...provided that the treatment would be the same if the interest had been paid to a non-resident associated enterprise that did not itself own or control any of the capital of the payer'.[13] Because Articles 9 and 11 form part of the context of Article 24, adjustments that are compatible with these provisions could not be considered to violate Article 24(5).[14]

In this study, the starting point is that the domestic law thin capitalization regime concerned does not constitute discrimination prohibited by tax treaties, and discussed here is only the treaty classification in a situation where a state applies its domestic law regime.

[B] The TFEU

Because of the EU law limitations, many EU Member States have been forced to amend their thin capitalization provisions and to adopt new approaches to limit interest deductions. In case C-324/00, *Lankhorst-Hohorst*, the EU Court found the German thin capitalization provision to be in conflict with the freedom of establishment principle of the TFEU.[15] The provision was considered to be in conflict with the TFEU irrespective of the fact that the application of the provision was based on the fact whether the dividend imputation system applied to a company or not, and not directly on the nationality or residence of a company. In practice, loans between a German company and a foreign company and not between two German companies, however, particularly came under the scope of application of the provision. The German thin capitalization provision denying tax deductibility of an interest payment, therefore, was considered to create a restriction on the freedom of establishment.[16]

The conclusion from the EU Court's judgments on the cases on national thin capitalization provisions is that a thin capitalization provision that does not expressly

---

12. *See* para. 74 of the Commentary on Art. 24 of the OECD Model.
13. *See* para. 79 of the Commentary on Art. 24 of the OECD Model.
14. *Ibid.*
15. *See also* C-524/04 *Test Claimants in the Thin Cap Group Litigation* concerning the British system.
16. The EU Court followed its earlier judgments in C-105/07 *Lammers & van Cleeff* on the thin capitalization provision of Belgium and held that the provision was in conflict with the freedom of establishment principle of the TFEU (Art. 49).

exclude EU Member States from its scope of application can be in accordance with the TFEU only if it applies both formally and effectively in the same way to loans between domestic companies and to loans between a domestic company and a company from another Member State.[17]

A national thin capitalization provision, however, may be applied to a completely artificial tax avoidance arrangement without the freedom of establishment principle of the TFEU prohibiting it.[18] Even in the cases involving a completely artificial tax avoidance arrangement, an interest payment may be treated as a non-deductible profit distribution primarily only if it exceeds an arm's length amount if the same is not done in the case of internal situations.[19] Even in these cases, the taxpayer must be given the right to show that there are business reasons behind the arrangement. It must be possible for the evidence of the business purpose to be made available without too high an administrative burden.[20] Solely the fact that there is an intra-group cross-border loan and that the set debt-to-equity ratio is exceeded does not mean that the arrangement is a completely artificial tax avoidance arrangement.[21]

This study does not question whether or not a certain domestic law thin capitalization regime complies with the TFEU. The starting point in this study is that the domestic law regime concerned does not constitute prohibited discrimination or restriction, and that at least one state is of the opinion that a company is thinly capitalized and, therefore, applies its special domestic law thin capitalization regime. With respect to such a situation, this study examines the extent to which thin capitalization interest may be and actually is taxed as dividend under the different legal systems of international tax law.[22]

---

17. See also Helminen (2003), 41–42, Brosens (2004), 188–213, Vinther and Werlauff (2003), 97–106, Gutmann and Hinnekens (2003), 90 97 and Andersson (2003), 464–466.
18. See, for example, C-524/04 Test Claimants in the Thin Cap Group Litigation, paras 72 and 74 and C-105/07 Lammers & van Cleeff, paras 26 and 28.
19. C-524/04 Test Claimants in the Thin Cap Group Litigation, paras 80 and 81 and C-105/07 Lammers & van Cleeff, paras 29 and 30.
20. C-524/04 Test Claimants in the Thin Cap Group Litigation.
21. See, for example, C-524/04 Test Claimants in the Thin Cap Group Litigation, para. 73 and C-105/07 Lammers & van Cleeff, paras 27 and 33. See also Helminen (2015), 102–104, Äimä (2009), 369–375 and Hinny (2008), 28–31 about the implications of the TFEU on the treatment of thin capitalization situations. For older literature, see, for example, Bachmann (1995), 241, Knobbe-Keuk (1992), 408, International Fiscal Association (1996), 2, Essers et al. (1994), 174–175 and Piltz (1996), 136.
22. Sometimes, not only thin capitalization, but also a situation of excessive equity finance, that is, the so-called *fat capitalization* is regarded to be a problem. By fat capitalization is meant situations where equity capital of a company is extensive compared to its operations. One reason for such a situation may be that direct investment dividend is largely exempted. In practice, fat capitalization is, however, seldom seen as a problem. Therefore, special fat capitalization preventing legislation is rare. The domestic laws of the states covered in this study do not include such regimes. In principle, any rules that limit the possibility for tax-free dividend, however, may be seen as fat capitalization rules. These rules, however, only limit the possibility for exemption. They do not suggest that a distribution would not be dividend and that it would be some other type of income instead. For these reasons, the problem of excessive equity finance is not discussed further here. See, for literature on fat capitalization, Gäverth (1997), 236–249, Gäverth (1998), 233, Gäverth (1999), 31–32, 34–40, 44–48, Piltz (1996), 123, Wyntin (1996), 360–362 and Pistone (2008), 847–864.

§10.03 THE EU PARENT-SUBSIDIARY DIRECTIVE

The EU Anti-tax Avoidance Directive includes an interest deduction limitation provision in Article 4.[23] All EU Member Countries must limit interest deductions in accordance with the Directive minimum requirements. The domestic laws of the Member States, however, may include also anti-thin capitalization provisions leading to reclassification of interest as dividend. As long as domestic law thin capitalization rules comply with the EU founding treaties (the TEU and the TFEU), they may be applied also in the relations between two EU Member States. The P-S Directive, however, may limit the relevance of the domestic law thin capitalization regimes.

The P-S Directive concerns the taxation of distributions of profits from a subsidiary company to a parent company by virtue of the association between the companies. Article 4 of the P-S Directive does not clarify what is meant by the term 'association' in the article, but read together with Article 3, it should mean a holding of the parent company in the capital of the subsidiary. Because Article 3 uses only the term 'capital' it must also cover constructive equity capital. Therefore, income from debt that actually is, by its nature, equity, should also qualify under the P-S Directive.

The P-S Directive should cover distributions on debt classified as equity because of thin capitalization for domestic tax law purposes. If thin capitalization indicates that the creditor assumes the risks of the debtor corporation in the same manner as an equity investor, a distribution on debt should qualify as a distribution under the P-S Directive if the source state treats it as such for tax purposes. To the extent that debt is treated as equity, the debt should also be taken into account in calculating the fulfilment of the holding requirement between two companies for the purposes of the P-S Directive. If a state reclassifies debt as equity, the state should grant the benefits of the P-S Directive also even though it is only by the addition of this reclassified debt that the holding is raised to the level required.[24]

It seems clear that the source state must grant the benefits provided by the P-S Directive in situations where the state taxes debt as equity and, therefore, interest as dividend. More problematic is the question of whether the state of residence of the recipient of the interest on the debt has to accept this classification and provide the benefits of the P-S Directive as well, and refrain from taxing the interest that it otherwise would be allowed to tax. In principle, in situations where the debt is, by its economic nature, actually equity, the other state should also grant P-S Directive benefits. There is no reason why constructive equity investments should not qualify for purposes of the P-S Directive.

The states may, however, disagree on whether thin capitalization changes the classification from debt to equity. Therefore, the other state may not accept the source state classification and may tax the interest as interest. It may be suggested, however, that the state also grant the benefits of the P-S Directive at least in situations where the

---

23. *See* e.g., Helminen (2016e), Ch. 3.4.3. for the Directive interest deduction limitation provision.
24. This interpretation is in line with the interpretation in para. 15 of the Commentary on Art. 10(2) of the OECD Model with respect to the holding requirement in Art. 10 of the Model. *See also* Sommerhalder (1996), 94.

state must accept dividend treatment for tax treaty purposes. Similarly, the state should accept dividend treatment if, in the obverse situation, it would have reclassified the interest as dividend.[25] In practice, however, there are no means to oblige the state to do so.

The Interest-Royalty Directive is interesting as regards the profit distribution definition of the P-S Directive. According to Article 5(2) of the Proposal for the Interest-Royalty Directive, the Directive would not apply to the interest paid between associated parties on the amount of debt that exceeds the amount that would have been agreed upon in the absence of such a special relationship. In this way, it was mentioned expressly in the Proposal that the Directive benefits would not have to be made available in thin capitalization situations. The Proposal for the Interest-Royalty Directive, however, did not identify the type of income that the thin capitalization interest should be taxed as and whether it would qualify under the P-S Directive.

The express reference to excessive debt was not included in the final version of the Interest-Royalty Directive. Only the idea of Article 5(1) of the Proposal for the Interest-Royalty Directive was included in the final version of the Interest-Royalty Directive. According to Article 4(2) of the Interest-Royalty Directive,[26] the Directive does not have to be applied in the source state in the case of the part of an interest payment that exceeds an arm's length amount. If this Article of the Interest-Royalty Directive is interpreted in conformity with the Commentary on Article 9(1) of the OECD Model, this article is relevant not only in determining whether the rate of interest is in arm's length but also whether a prima facie loan may be regarded as a loan or should be regarded as a contribution to equity capital.[27] As a consequence, even though thin capitalization situations were not expressly excluded from the compulsory scope of application of the Interest-Royalty Directive based on the general provision concerning excessive interest, the Member States do not have to make available the Directive benefits in thin capitalization situations.

Further, according to Article 4(1) of the Interest-Royalty Directive and according to the commentary on the Proposed Directive, Member States do not have to apply the Directive to payments that are treated as profit distribution under their domestic law.[28] The Member States, thus, do not have to make available the Interest-Royalty Directive benefits in the case of a thin capitalization interest, which they treat as a dividend under their domestic law.

According to Article 4(2) of the Proposal for the Interest-Royalty Directive, the P-S Directive instead of the Interest-Royalty Directive should be applied with respect to such interest, which is treated as a profit distribution in the source state to the extent that such interest is paid between qualifying companies. According to the commentary on the Proposed Directive, taxation as profit distribution under the P-S Directive instead of the Interest-Royalty Directive would be possible, for example, if such

---

25. Also, for example, Carrero (1996), 292 makes this suggestion.
26. This is the idea that was originally included in Art. 5(1) of the Proposal.
27. Paragraph 3 of the Commentary on Art. 9 of the OECD Model.
28. The explanatory memorandum to the Proposal for a Council Directive (COM (98) 67 final), commentary on Art. 4.

taxation ensues from a tax treaty between two Member States or is based on the domestic tax law of the source state.[29]

The express reference to the P-S Directive was not included in the final version of the Interest-Royalty Directive. The Proposed Directive, however, clearly indicates that the Commission was of the opinion that income from debt, if treated as dividend in the source state, qualifies as a profit distribution under the P-S Directive if paid between qualifying companies in a qualifying relationship. This opinion promotes the interpretation that thin capitalization interest may qualify under the P-S Directive, if the interest is reclassified as dividend in the source state. The source state, thus, must not impose any withholding tax if it reclassifies a thin capitalization interest as dividend provided that the interest payment was made between two qualifying companies in a qualifying relationship.[30]

The EU Arbitration Convention is applicable in solving classification conflicts leading to double taxation. The EU Arbitration Convention, strictly speaking, does not, however, seem to be applicable in solving classification conflicts with respect to thin capitalization situations. According to Article 1 of the Convention, it applies where, for tax purposes, the same profits are included in the profits of two enterprises resident in two different states in situations where the arm's length principle is not followed. The Convention, thus, strictly speaking, applies only in situations involving transfer-pricing problems, but not to conflicts caused by the inconsistent classification of a debt investment.[31]

The Commentary on the OECD Model, however, takes the view that Article 9 of the Model is applicable '...not only in determining whether the rate of interest provided for in a loan contract is an arm's length rate, but also whether a *prima facie* loan may be regarded as a loan or should be regarded as some other kind of payment, in particular a contribution to equity capital...'.[32] Following this interpretation, the arm's length principle of Article 4 of the Arbitration Convention should also cover such situations. Broadly interpreted, therefore, the procedures of the Convention should also be applicable in avoiding the double taxation caused by classification conflicts in thin capitalization situations.[33] Because this broad interpretation is, however, not generally accepted, in practice, the reference to the mutual agreement procedure

---

29. The explanatory memorandum to the Proposal for a Council Directive (COM (98) 67 final), commentary on Art. 4.
30. See more closely about the Interest-Royalty Directive above in Ch. 9 s. §9.04. *See also* the opinion of advocate general Jean Mischo from 26 Sep. 2002 on the C-324/00 *Lankhorst-Hohorst* in which the advocate general took the stand that the P-S Directive applied to the interest reclassified as dividend under the German thin capitalization regime. The EU Court itself did not refer to the P-S Directive, because the case was solved already on the basis of the freedom of establishment principle. *See also* Gutmann-Hinnekens (2003), 90–97 and Brokelind (2003), 160–161.
31. *See* about this strict interpretation Sommerhalder (1996), 94.
32. Paragraph 3(b) of the Commentary on Art. 9 of the OECD Model.
33. For example, Piltz (1996), 137 suggests this interpretation. The Revised Code of Conduct for the effective implementation of the Arbitration Convention of the Council of the European Union from 30 Dec. 2009 (2009/C322/01) also suggests that the Arbitration convention should be applied to eliminate double taxation caused by national thin capitalization provisions.

provided by tax treaties is needed in order to avoid economic double taxation in these situations.[34]

Because the domestic law thin capitalization regimes concern especially associated enterprises, these regimes, in fact, often apply exactly in the kinds of situations covered by the P-S Directive. Therefore, the P-S Directive often, in fact, hinders Member States from imposing withholding tax on thin capitalization interest reclassified as dividend. Because interest, instead, may be subjected to withholding tax,[35] unless prohibited by a tax treaty, states may prefer the kinds of domestic law regimes, which only deny interest deduction but which do not reclassify debt as equity and interest as dividend. In such situations, the P-S Directive is not applicable. It may rarely be required that P-S Directive benefits be granted in a situation where neither one of the states views the debt as being equity and interest on it dividend.

§10.04 TAX TREATIES

So long as domestic law thin capitalization regimes do not conflict with non-discrimination articles of tax treaties, they, in principle, are applicable in tax treaty situations. In general, it is thought that Article 9(1) of the OECD Model allows not only the denial of interest deduction with respect to excessive interest, but also the reclassification of debt as equity and the denial of interest deduction in a thin capitalization situation. According to the Commentary on Article 9(1) of the OECD Model:

> [T]he Article is relevant not only in determining whether the rate of interest provided for in a loan contract is an arm's length rate, but also whether a *prima facie* loan may be regarded as a loan or should be regarded as some other kind of payment, in particular a contribution to equity capital.[36]

Article 9(1) allows for the examining of whether the capital structure of a corporation meets the arm's length standard. If the arm's length standard is not met, Article 9(1) allows the denial of interest deduction because the interest would have been dividend in an arm's length situation.[37]

---

34. In 2016 the Commission proposed a dispute resolution mechanism with wider scope. *See* Proposal for a Council Directive on Double Taxation Dispute Resolution Mechanism in the European Union, 25.10.2016, COM(2016) 686 final.
35. The Interest-Royalty Directive does not seem to hinder such treatment because it allows the Member States not to apply the Directive to thin capitalization interest.
36. Paragraph 3 of the Commentary on Art. 9 of the OECD Model. The opinion is expressed also, for example, in OECD (1979), 21, International Fiscal Association (1996a), 3, Portner (1996), 25–26 and OECD (1987), para. 48. The same opinion with respect to the US Model is expressed, for example, in Technical Explanation, Art. 9, para. 136 and Doernberg and van Raad (1997), 77.
37. This principle is indicated also in OECD (1994a), 43–44 and referred to, for example, in Fairley and Penny (1988), 9, referring to OECD (1987). *See* about the same principle with respect to Art. 9(1) of the UN Model in United Nations (1988), 27. However, for example, Hosson and Michelse (1989), 480, Becker (1990), 52 and Michielse (1997), 568 and 572 are of the opinion, that Art. 9(1) may not be applied to reclassify debt as equity because of thin capitalization.

Instead, it is widely thought that Article 9(1) does not allow for a more extensive denial of the interest deduction than what follows from the arm's length standard.[38] According to the Commentary, Article 9(1), '...does not prevent the application of national rules on thin capitalization insofar as their effect is to assimilate the profits of the borrower to an amount corresponding to the profits which would have accrued in an arm's length situation...'. The application of rules designed to deal with thin capitalization should normally, however, '...not have the effect of increasing the taxable profits of the relevant domestic enterprise to more than the arm's length profit, and that this principle should be followed in applying existing tax treaties...'.[39]

A problem with Article 9(1), in practice, is that it is very difficult to say when a loan meets the arm's length standard.[40] Therefore, the arm's length principle leaves much room for different interpretation.[41] Article 9(1), also, does not identify which of the income type articles of the OECD Model should apply to that kind of interest for which the interest deduction has been denied. Because Article 9(1) simply states that the profits shall be 'taxed accordingly', the nature of the item must be considered in light of all the income type articles of the Model. Thin capitalization interest may, thus, qualify as dividend under the OECD Model only if it qualifies as dividend under Article 10(3).[42] According to the Commentary, '...the term "interest" as used in Article 11 does not include items of income which are dealt with under Article 10...'.[43] Therefore, if interest in a thin capitalization situation qualifies as dividend under Article 10, it is dividend, even though the interest would seem to fit also under the definition of interest of Article 11(3).

In general, only if thin capitalization interest qualifies as dividend under the tax treaty concerned, the source state may subject it to withholding tax allowed by the dividend article of the treaty. As discussed above, dividend treatment requires that, from the perspective of an autonomous interpretation, the income be from *corporate rights*. The dividend definition of the US Model, however, covers any income that is treated as income from corporate rights under the domestic law of the source state.

---

38. The answer to the question depends on whether Art. 9(1) is interpreted to be restrictive or only illustrative in its scope. If it is restrictive, interest deduction could be denied only to the extent that the interest exceeds the interest that would have been paid in an arm's length situation. If it is, instead, only illustrative, also an adjustment exceeding the arm's length adjustment would be possible. See OECD (1987), 18 and Michielse (1997), 568–569. In practice, some states view Art. 9(1) as limiting the use of their thin capitalization regimes whereas others do not. See OECD (1987), 22 and Piltz (1996), 129–130.
39. Paragraph 3 of the Commentary on Art. 9 of the OECD Model. See also de Hosson and Michielse (1989), 482 and Schauhoff (1993), 469 and 471 for argumentation for this restrictive interpretation. See also United Nations (1988), 28 with respect to Art. 9(1) of the UN Model.
40. This problem is recognized, for example, in International Fiscal Association (1996a), 2, Michielse (1997), 570 and Fernández (1996), 951–952.
41. It may even be questioned whether the theoretical arm's length debt is possible to define at all in practice. See de Hosson and Michielse (1989), 477 and International Fiscal Association (1996a), 3.
42. According to OECD (1987), 23, in practice, however, it varies from country to country whether definitions of Arts 10 and 11 are regarded to govern also with respect to other treaty articles. For example, de Hosson and Michielse (1989), 478 is of the opinion that for the purposes of Art. 9 domestic law definitions should be decisive. See also Michielse (1997), 567.
43. Paragraph 19 of the Commentary on Art. 11 of the OECD Model.

Under the US Model, thin capitalization interest must, thus, be treated as dividend if the source state reclassifies thin capitalization debt as equity and taxes the interest as dividend.[44]

As discussed above, the autonomous interpretation of the term 'corporate right' requires that the investor *effectively assume the risks run by the company*. According to the Commentary, such risk participation exists if the '...repayment depends largely on the success or otherwise of the enterprise's business...'.[45] The Commentary also expressly mentions that the Model allows the state of the borrower company, under certain conditions, to treat interest as dividend in thin capitalization situations.[46] Thin capitalization interest may be treated as dividend if the debt investor assumes the risks run by the enterprise.[47]

According to the Commentary, it must be determined case by case in light of all circumstances whether the risk component is present. The Commentary mention, among other risk-indicating factors, the fact that '...the loan very heavily outweighs any other contribution to the enterprise's capital (or was taken out to replace a substantial proportion of capital which has been lost) and is substantially unmatched by redeemable assets...'.[48] Accordingly, an abnormally high debt-to-equity ratio may indicate that the debt investor assumes the risk run by the company. According to the Commentary, a loan constitutes capital for the purposes of Article 10(2a), '...when on the basis of internal law or practice ("thin capitalization", or assimilation of a loan to share capital), the income derived in respect thereof is treated as dividend under Article 10...'.[49] Thin capitalization interest may, thus, at least sometimes qualify as dividend under the Model.[50]

Article 9(1) is also complied with when only the kind of interest that is paid on debt where the holder assumes the risks run by the company is treated as dividend. The reason why an independent third party would not have made a debt investment in a thin capitalization situation is that the investment actually would include risks comparable to those assumed by an equity investment. Therefore, actually the requirements for the application of Article 9(1) to reclassify debt as equity and the requirement of risks of a corporate right in Article 10(3) are the same. Article 9(1) does not allow the denial of interest deduction because of thin capitalization unless the

---

44. This is pointed out also in the Technical Explanation to the US 2006 Model, according to which '...a payment denominated as interest that is made by a thinly capitalized corporation may be treated as a dividend to the extent that the debt is recharacterized as equity under the laws of the source State'. The Technical Explanation to the US 2006 Model para. 167.
45. Paragraph 25 of the Commentary on Art. 10 of the OECD Model.
46. Paragraph 67 of the Commentary on Art. 23 of the OECD Model.
47. Paragraph 19 of the Commentary on Art. 11 of the OECD Model.
48. Paragraph 25 of the Commentary on Art. 10 of the OECD Model.
49. Paragraph 15d of the Commentary on Art. 10 of the OECD Model.
50. *See* Michielse (1997), 566. Also, paras 1.65 and 1.67 of the 2010 OECD Transfer Pricing Guidelines recognized that a loan may be re-characterized as equity when in an arm's length situation having regard to the economic circumstances of the borrowing company the investment would not be structured as a loan. *See*, however, Avery Jones et al. (2009), 27 for how it seems clear that originally the drafters of Art. 10 of the OECD Model did not have thin capitalization in mind. Also, Avery Jones et al. (2009), 28–29, however, agree that a thin capitalization debt may be treated as a membership right.

investment assumes risks comparable to a share investment. On the other hand, if Article 9(1) allows the denial of interest deduction, also the risks of the investment must be such that the investment is a corporate right and the income on it, thus, qualifies as dividend. Therefore, generally, if a state is of the opinion that it may deny interest deduction in thin capitalization situations, it actually should also treat the interest as dividend.

The determination must be made case by case in light of all circumstances. A high debt-to-equity ratio alone does not necessarily indicate the kind of risk required for a corporate right. In fact, in the opinion of the author of this study, a high debt-to-equity ratio without other equity characteristics that increase the risk of the creditor may seldom be viewed as making a debt-claim a corporate right. Despite the increased risks, the risk is not comparable to the risk of a shareholder investment, the return on which may be paid only if the corporation is profitable, and the principal amount of which may be paid back only after all creditors have been satisfied. Therefore, interest normally does not qualify as dividend under tax treaties solely because of thin capitalization.

The Commentary only refers to the risk run by a company with respect to the reclassification of thin capitalization interest as dividend. Therefore, it may be asked whether it still has to be required that the investment participates in profits in order to qualify as a corporate right. Profit participation, after all, seems to be an essential characteristic of a corporate right.[51] Strictly interpreted, thin capitalization interest could never qualify as dividend unless the investment is also profit participating. Dividend treatment in other situations is possible, actually, only if Article 9 is interpreted broadly, as allowing the reclassification of debt as equity solely because of thin capitalization. Because the investment in such a situation is deemed to be a share investment, it does not matter whether it is actually profit participating.

Another possible approach to taxing thin capitalization interest as dividend is to assume that because, in an arm's length situation, no debt investment would have existed, interest cannot exist. The whole interest is, thus, excessive, and is actually paid because of the recipient's holding in the shares of the payer. The income is, thus, income from the shares and not from the debt investment. With respect to this approach, it is irrelevant whether the debt investment was profit participating or not. Article 9, together with Article 10, thus, allows the taxing of interest as dividend because of thin capitalization in a situation where an independent party would not have made an investment in the company because the company is or becomes thinly capitalized. This approach does not even require that the debt investment is deemed to constitute an equity investment, but dividend treatment is possible solely because an independent party would not have made an investment at all.

The opinion of the author of this study is that, unless a debt investment is profit participating, it should not be reclassified as a share investment. Thin capitalization only includes risks of loss of the investment but does not include unlimited return potential. Therefore, the investment is not a corporate right. Thin capitalization

---

51. *See* Ch. 9 s. §9.02[D] of this study.

interest, therefore, should be taxed as dividend only if the debt investor is simultaneously a shareholder, and the interest is deemed to be income from the actual share investment by a broad application of Article 9.

According to the Commentary, '...the State of residence of the lender would be obliged to give relief for any juridical or economic double taxation of the interest as if the payment was in fact a dividend...', in situations where the source state is allowed to treat thin capitalization interest as dividend because the loan effectively shares the risks run by the company.[52] According to the Commentary, this obligation may be derived '...from the actual wording of Article 23, when it grants relief in respect of income defined as dividend in Article 10 or of items of income dealt with in Article 10...' and '...from the context of the Convention, i.e., from a combination of Articles 9, 10, 11 and 23...'.[53]

Double taxation, in practice, may, however, still not be eliminated, because there are no exact means to determine the arm's length standard and the existence of the required risk. Therefore, two contracting states may correctly treat thin capitalization interest under different articles of a tax treaty even though the states would agree on the principles when thin capitalization interest constitutes dividend. The other state must accept the source state dividend treatment and eliminate double taxation accordingly only to the extent that the state agrees that a debt investment would not have been made in an arm's length situation and the interest is actually paid on a corporate right.[54] It is, however, suggested that at least to the extent that the state would treat the interest as dividend in a reciprocal situation it should also accept the dividend treatment of the other state.[55]

Under many treaties, income from shares or other rights, not being debt-claims, participating in profits, qualifies as dividend. Also, other income from other rights qualifies if it is subjected to the same taxation treatment as income from shares in the source state. The dividend article of some other treaties covers income from shares or other corporate rights if the income is treated in the same way as income from shares in the source state. In addition, any income qualifies if it is treated in the source state in the same way as income from shares. Similarly, the dividend article of certain treaties covers income from shares or other rights, not being debt-claims, participating in profits. Also, other income from a company qualifies if it is treated in the source state in the same way as income from shares. The treaties also include an article similar to Article 9 of the OECD Model. All these treaties with slightly different dividend definitions are substantially similar with respect to the treatment of thin capitalization interest.

---

52. Paragraphs 67 and 68 of the Commentary on Art. 23 of the OECD Model.
53. Paragraph 68 of the Commentary on Art. 23 of the OECD Model. This view is expressed also, for example, by Portner (1996), 28 and Carrero (1996), 286.
54. The International Fiscal Association congress resolution of 1996, however, suggested that the countries concerned should be obliged to eliminate possible double taxation whether or not the taxation is in accordance with the provisions of the relevant tax treaty. *See* International Fiscal Association (1996b), 72.
55. This suggestion is included also in para. 68 of the Commentary on Art. 23 of the OECD Model.

Under these treaties, the source state is free to treat thin capitalization interest as dividend, if it treats the interest as dividend under domestic law. If the source state treats the interest as dividend, the other state must also accept the treatment and eliminate double taxation accordingly. Because the source state classification is determinative, dividend treatment is correct application of the treaties even if the debt investment would meet the arm's length standard. The anti-discrimination articles of the treaties may, of course, limit the denial of interest deduction. In any case, the wording used in these treaties is better than the wording used in the OECD Model, because the wording used in these treaties avoids classification conflicts better.

The dividend article of certain treaties covers income from shares or other rights, not being debt-claims, participating in profits. Also, income from other corporate rights qualifies, if it is subjected to the same tax treatment as income from shares in the source state. In addition, income from arrangements, including debt obligations, carrying the right to participate in profits, qualifies as dividend if so characterized under the laws of the state in which the income arises. The treaties also include an article corresponding to Article 9 of the OECD Model.

Unless not profit participating, thin capitalization interest, thus, qualifies as dividend under these treaties only if it is income from a corporate right. As discussed above, such treatment is possible only if Article 9 is applicable because an independent party would not have made a debt investment but an equity investment or would not have made any investment at all. The other state, however, does not have to accept the dividend treatment in the source state because it may not accept that there is a deviation from the arm's length standard. Therefore, a reference to a mutual agreement procedure may be required in order for double taxation to be eliminated. Also, the anti-discrimination articles of this treaty may limit the possibilities of denying the interest deduction in thin capitalization situations.

The dividend article of certain actual treaties covers income from shares or other rights, not being debt-claims, participating in profits, qualifies as dividend. Also, income from other corporate rights qualifies if it is treated the same way as income from shares in the source state. The treaties also include an article similar to Article 9(1) of the OECD Model. These treaties follow the OECD Model. Thin capitalization interest may, thus, be treated as dividend under the treaties only if it may be deemed to be income from corporate rights.[56] The treaties do not solve classification conflicts caused by the fact that the states disagree on whether or not a debt investment would have existed in an arm's length situation. A reference to a mutual agreement procedure may, thus, be needed in order for double taxation to be avoided.

In conclusion, actual classification conflicts with respect to thin capitalization interest are, in practice, avoided in the case of the treaties that differ from the OECD model in the way that dividend does not need to be income from a corporate right.

---

56. In practice, Germany may treat interest as dividend under domestic law in thin capitalization situations even though it may not reclassify the debt as equity. Therefore, because not even Germany in such a situation views that the income is from corporate rights, in many situations where Germany treats thin capitalization interest as dividend under domestic law it may not treat the interest as dividend under the treaty. *See* about this problem Portner (1996c), 67.

Under these treaties, classification conflicts with respect to dividend are solved in accordance with the classification in the source state. The other state must accept the source state classification and eliminate double taxation accordingly. Instead, in the case of the treaties that follow the OECD Model, actual classification conflicts are possible. For the purposes of these treaties, dividend treatment of thin capitalization interest, if no other equity characteristics are present, is possible only if the debt investment does not meet the arm's length standard. The source state may treat the interest as dividend and the other state may treat it as interest because they interpret the arm's length standard differently.[57]

§10.05 CONCLUSIONS

Only some countries apply a thin capitalization regime based on which an interest payment may be reclassified as dividend for tax purposes solely because of thin capitalization. In the other states, thin capitalization is rather only regarded as one characteristic evaluated together with other equity characteristics in determining the actual nature of an investment. Taken together with other equity characteristics, thin capitalization, thus, may lead to the reclassification of debt as equity and of interest also in the countries that do not reclassify interest as dividend solely because of thin capitalization.

In a situation where a state under domestic law reclassifies interest as dividend in thin capitalization situations, the state must also grant the benefits of the P-S Directive, if the holding requirement and other requirements of the Directive are met. The other state involved, however, may not agree that a profit distribution exists, and may, therefore, not grant P-S Directive benefits as the state of residence of the income recipient. The procedures of the Arbitration Convention should, in principle, be applicable in such situations to abolish double taxation. The mutual agreement procedures provided by tax treaties are, however, simpler and, therefore, in practice, more often referred to. The P-S Directive does not affect thin capitalization regimes or other interest deduction limitation provisions that only deny interest deduction.

Classification conflicts are avoided with respect to the tax treaties that differ from the OECD Model in respect to the fact that the dividend article does not require dividend to be income from a corporate right. In the case of these treaties, the other state must accept the dividend treatment of thin capitalization interest of the source state. Instead, actual classification conflicts with respect to thin capitalization interest may emerge in the case of treaties that follow the OECD Model in its wording.[58]

---

57. See Zielke (2010), 75–79 for country examples indicating how common it is in practice to accept the tax classification of the source state in the residence state for treaty purposes.
58. See Zielke (2010), 62–92 for the magnitude of double taxation cases caused by national thin capitalization provisions in tax treaty situations and especially 89–90 on how tax treaties and national thin capitalization rules should be developed to function better together.

CHAPTER 11
Classification of Liquidation Distributions

§11.01 INTRODUCTION

In addition to regular dividend distributions, there are many other ways in which a shareholder may benefit from corporate profits. For example, by selling shares, a shareholder may realize the increased value of the shares caused by retained corporate profits. A corporation may also be totally liquidated and its assets may be transferred to the shareholders. Further, a corporation may be partially liquidated. The share capital of a corporation may be reduced and the assets transferred in connection with the reduction from the corporation to the shareholders.

Among many other possible forms of company reorganizations, the above-mentioned three basic forms in which a shareholder may benefit from corporate profits may be used instead of regular dividend distributions to minimize taxes. By accumulating profits in a corporate entity, instead of distributing the profits as a dividend, and then disposing of its holding or liquidating the company, a shareholder gets income in the form of capital gains or liquidation proceeds instead of a dividend. These types of income are often more favourably taxed than a dividend.

By selling stock, a shareholder may get the same benefit as it would have gained if the corporation had distributed its profits in the form of a cash dividend. The amount by which the sales price exceeds the acquisition cost of the shares is actually the return on the share investment. If the company itself redeems its own shares from the shareholder, the payment made to the shareholder is especially close to a dividend. Dividend taxation may be avoided in a group of companies, for example, by selling shares of a subsidiary company from one subsidiary to another. Through such intra-group sales, accumulated company profits may be transferred in the form of capital gains from a subsidiary to the shareholder or parent company without losing control of the shares.

Upon the total liquidation of a corporation,[1] all the assets of the corporation that are left after all the liabilities of the entity are satisfied are transferred to the shareholders. In a total liquidation, the shareholders' rights to company assets are realized.[2] A corporation may also be only partially liquidated. The share capital of a corporation may be reduced. A corporation may repurchase its own shares or reduce the par value of shares. In such a partial liquidation, company assets are distributed to the shareholders if it is carried out by paying consideration to the shareholders.

Liquidation distributions generally consist of a return of the invested capital and a distribution of retained earnings. The part of assets received by the shareholders that exceeds the amount the shareholder invested in the company is comparable to a distribution of profits.[3] However, the payments made in connection with a partial or total liquidation differ from a dividend in that a dividend distribution, unlike liquidation distributions, does not change the position of the shareholders in the corporation. In a partial or total liquidation, a shareholder loses the shares or the value of the shares is reduced. If a corporation redeems the shares of all of its shareholders in proportion to their shareholding, and the company is not totally liquidated, the actual position of each shareholder remains unchanged in the company. In that situation, the payment the shareholders receive from the company is very close to a dividend.[4]

The economic similarities between liquidation distributions and a dividend raise the question of the extent to which these two types of distributions should be taxed similarly. From a tax neutrality point of view, the taxation of distributed corporate profits in the form of a dividend or in the form of an economically similar liquidation distribution should not be different. In principle, liquidation distributions should not be favoured in taxation by allowing corporations to restrain from dividend distribution and, instead, distributing company profits to shareholders in the form of liquidating distributions, or vice versa. The question to be asked is the extent to which the liquidation distributions and the dividend must be similar in order for similar tax treatment to be necessary.

The fact that liquidation distributions may be taxed in some states as capital gains and in other states as a dividend raises problems in cross-border situations.[5] The classification of liquidation distributions as a dividend or as capital gains strongly affects in which state the distribution is taxed. Under tax treaties generally, capital gains are taxed solely in the state of residence of the recipient of the gain, whereas a dividend may also be taxed in the source state. It is advantageous to the source state to

---

1. There are many reasons for which a corporation is completely liquidated, either voluntary or mandatory. One common reason for a mandatory liquidation and dissolution is the shortage of capital. See for other reasons van Fraeyenhoven (1987), 38–39.
2. See Penttilä (1991), 434 for how the latent right of shareholders to company assets becomes concrete in total liquidation.
3. For example, Rosenberg (1985), 661 is of the opinion that a liquidation distribution is in its economic nature closer to a dividend than to capital gain.
4. For example, Kilpi (1989), 383 mentions that the fact that the activities of the company are continued after share repurchase or reduction of share capital makes the economic difference to a dividend disappear.
5. See, for the problem of inconsistent classification of liquidation distributions in different states, van Fraeyenhoven (1987), 45 and Avery Jones et al. (1996), 130.

classify liquidation distributions as a non-deductible dividend and for the state of residence of the recipient of the benefit to classify liquidation distributions as capital gains. Therefore, it is relevant to determine to what extent liquidation distributions may and actually do constitute a dividend for the purposes of the different legal systems of international tax law.

§11.02 DOMESTIC TAX LAWS

The classification of liquidation distributions for domestic tax law purposes varies from country to country.[6] In many countries, the rules concerning dividend are not applicable to the amounts received by shareholders in a total liquidation. A total liquidation is often assimilated to a sale of stock, and liquidation distributions are regarded as constituting capital gains instead of a dividend. Some countries, however, treat distributions made in the course of a total liquidation of corporations as dividend.

Some countries treat liquidation distributions of any kind in excess of the repayment of paid-in nominal capital and reserve funds as a dividend. For example, distributions in connection with a reduction of share capital are regarded as a dividend to the extent that the distributions do not consist of any repayment of invested capital. It is not that usual that the whole amount of the liquidation proceeds is considered to constitute a dividend.

Many countries consider that in the case of a redemption of shares the shareholder realizes taxable gains under the same conditions that apply to a sale of shares generally. Income from a sale of shares or from the redemption of shares, thus, in many countries does not constitute a dividend if carried out at arm's length prices. Especially a pro rata redemption, instead, may be treated as a distribution taxed as a dividend. In many countries, a transaction may constitute a dividend if the shares of all shareholders of a company are redeemed in proportion to their shareholding.

In other situations, it may be decisive whether the redemption results in a meaningful reduction of the shareholder's proportionate interest in the corporation. Redemption of stock, which does not lead to a decrease in the relative interest of the shareholder in the purchasing company, is often treated as a distribution of a dividend to the extent of the earnings and profits. Capital gains treatment, instead, may apply in the case of complete redemption of all of the stock of the corporation owned by the shareholder or if the shareholder completely terminates its interest in the redeeming corporation. The taxable amount may be the whole redemption price, the price reduced by the acquisition costs of the redeemed shares or any other amount below the redemption price.

Dividend treatment may apply with respect to certain tax avoidance type situations in those countries also that normally treat liquidation distributions as capital gains. Dividend classification may apply if a liquidation distribution is made in order to avoid dividend taxation. There may be, for example, domestic tax law rules with the purpose of preventing a shareholder from avoiding dividend taxation by extracting

---

6. *See* Maisto (2013) for taxation of companies on capital gains on shares.

cash by selling shares in a related corporation to its sister corporation instead of having the sister corporation make a dividend distribution equal to the sales price. Sales of shares may constitute a dividend, for example, in situations where the seller and buyer are, in some way, related to each other and the business activities, ownership and control do not factually change and there is no adequate business reason for the sale of shares.

In conclusion, some countries assimilate liquidation distributions to any alienation of shares and see a capital gain whereas some countries classify liquidation distributions as dividends. Some countries make a difference between a total and a partial liquidation whereas other countries treat them alike. Some countries make a difference between a domestic transaction and a cross-border transaction whereas some other countries treat them alike. Most countries may apply domestic law anti-avoidance type provisions to change the classification that normally would apply.

§11.03 THE EU PARENT-SUBSIDIARY DIRECTIVE

Dividend was defined in Article 2(1) of the Proposal for a Directive of the Council concerning the Harmonization of Systems of Company and of Withholding Taxes on Dividends (the Proposal)[7] as:

> [T]hat part of the profits of any corporation of a Member State, other than a corporation in liquidation, distributed by it by virtue of a proper decision of its competent authorities and divided among its members in proportion to their rights as members of the corporation.

Liquidation distributions, at least with respect to a total liquidation, were, thus, excluded. However, according to Article 7 of the Proposal, the Directive is applicable to any distribution that is regarded as a dividend distribution under the law of the source state. To the extent that liquidation distributions were treated by the source state as a dividend, they would qualify as a dividend despite the exclusion under Article 2(1).

The Proposal is, however, not helpful in interpreting the P-S Directive because the P-S Directive uses the term 'profit distribution' instead of the term 'dividend'. The question of whether liquidation distributions qualify as profit distributions under the P-S Directive may be asked especially because the term 'profit distribution' is generally understood to be broader than the term 'dividend'.

Liquidation distributions include distributions of profits from a company to its shareholders. Sometimes, such distributions are economically very close to dividend distributions. Broadly interpreted, liquidation distributions, therefore, are profit distributions at least to the extent that they exceed any return of invested capital. In practice, however, there is no unanimity on the issue of whether liquidation distributions are covered by the P-S Directive. The only thing that seems to be clear is that the term 'profit distribution' does not cover capital gains upon the sale of the shares of a

---

7. COM (75) 392 final of 23 Jul. 1975.

subsidiary to a third party. Such a transaction clearly does not include any distribution of profits from a subsidiary to its parent company.

In situations where two companies qualify as parent and subsidiary for the purposes of P-S Directive, there is not as strong an incentive to make distributions to the parent company in the form of a liquidation distribution rather than in the form of a dividend in order to avoid dividend taxation. The P-S Directive, after all, eliminates double taxation with respect to dividend distributions. Therefore, in such relations, there is actually an incentive to make a dividend distribution. The use of a liquidation distribution instead of a non-deductible dividend may transfer tax revenues from the state of residence of the subsidiary to the state of residence of the parent company. The P-S Directive does not in any way deal with this possibility of tax avoidance in the state of residence of the subsidiary because the P-S Directive does not cover the taxation of the profits from which a distribution is made. Therefore, a tax avoidance argument may not be used to interpret whether or not liquidation distributions should qualify as profit distributions under the P-S Directive.

In 2014 a special mismatch provision was added to Article 4(1) of the P-S Directive.[8] According to Article 4(1) the state of residence of the dividend recipient parent company[9] shall refrain from taxing the distributed profits that come under the scope of the P-S Directive only to the extent that the distributed profits are not deductible by the subsidiary and tax the profits to the extent that the profits are deductible by the subsidiary. This provision, however, does not affect the classification of payments for domestic tax law purposes or for the P-S Directive purposes. It only eliminates the unintended double non-taxation caused by mismatches. The mismatch provision, thus, does not help in defining the distributions that come under the scope of the Directive.[10]

The interpretation should be derived from the purpose of the P-S Directive. The purpose of the P-S Directive clearly is the elimination of economic double taxation with respect to profit distributions from subsidiaries to parent companies. The question to be asked is whether liquidation distributions are the kinds of distributions with respect to which the elimination of economic double taxation was intended.

Article 4 of the P-S Directive requires the state of residence of the parent company to either totally exempt profit distributions received from a subsidiary or at least grant both a direct and an indirect credit for taxes paid in the state of residence of the subsidiary. The wording of Article 4 expressly excludes distributions in situations where the subsidiary is liquidated. Thus, it is at least clear that the P-S Directive does

---

8. Council Directive 2014/86/EU of 8 Jul. 2014 amending Directive 2011/96/EU on the common system of taxation applicable in the case of parent companies and subsidiaries of different Member States.
9. Or the permanent establishment state, if dividend is taxed as income of a permanent establishment.
10. Also the EU Anti-tax Avoidance Directive requires the EU Member States to eliminate double non-taxation caused by mismatches. The Anti-tax Avoidance Directive requires that one of the two jurisdictions in a mismatch situation denies the deduction of a payment leading to a double deduction or deduction non-inclusion situation. Article 9 of the *Anti-tax Avoidance Directive* includes such a mismatch neutralizing provision. *See* more about the EU Anti-tax Avoidance Directive in Ch. 9 s. §9.02[C][3].

not hinder the state of residence of the parent company from taxing liquidation distributions received from a subsidiary in connection with a total liquidation of the subsidiary. The EU Court, however, has confirmed that the liquidation distributions excluded from the scope of Art. 4 do not cover liquidation distributions made in connection with a dissolution of a company in the context of a merger by acquisition.[11]

Because Article 4 uses the wording 'except when the subsidiary is liquidated...', it is not perfectly clear whether this exception also covers situations of the partial liquidation of the subsidiary, that is, distributions in connection with the repurchase of shares or in connection with a reduction in the nominal value of shares. It may be argued that because Article 4 uses the term 'liquidation' without specifying what kinds of liquidations are included, the term must cover both total and partial liquidations. On the other hand, in a partial liquidation, a subsidiary is not actually liquidated in the way required by the wording of Article 4. It may be argued that because only the nominal capital of the company is reduced, at most, only part of the subsidiary is liquidated.

Under Article 4 of the initial proposal to the P-S Directive, profit distributions received in connection with the liquidation of a subsidiary were eligible for relief in the state of residence of the recipient.[12] The inclusion of liquidation distributions was based on the fact that the taxation of liquidation distributions was regarded as an obstacle to the liquidation of a subsidiary. Liquidation distributions were excluded only in the final text. The exclusion does not necessarily mean that liquidation distributions are not viewed as distributions with respect to which economic double taxation should be eliminated. It only means that the Member States were not unanimous about whether liquidation distributions should be included. Therefore, the exclusion may not be used as an argument for interpreting Article 4 broadly to exclude liquidation distributions with respect to different forms of partial liquidation.

The exclusion of liquidation distributions may be promoted by the fact that liquidation distributions may also include a return of invested capital and capital gains and, therefore, are not necessarily profit distributions. This interpretation may also be supported by the aims of the P-S Directive of facilitating cross-border cooperation, investment and the grouping together of corporations. The inclusion of liquidation distributions under the P-S Directive would not directly promote these aims.[13] This argument is understandable with respect to total liquidations but does not have as much relevance with respect to different forms of partial liquidations. The answer to the question of whether Article 4 excludes partial liquidations may not be derived from this argument.

---

11. C-371/11 Punch Graphix.
12. Article 4 of the Proposal for a Council Directive concerning the common system of taxation applicable in the case of parent companies and subsidiaries of different Member States submitted by the Commission to the Council on 16 Jan. 1969, COM (69) 6 final.
13. This point is mentioned also, for example, by Thömmes (1992), 47. Indirectly, exemption of liquidation distributions may promote the grouping of companies because it increases flexibility. Where it is known, in the parent company, that a subsidiary may be liquidated without tax consequences when it is not needed anymore, it may be easier to establish the subsidiary in the first place.

Another argument is that because economic double taxation is not eliminated in many Member States, in the same way, with respect to liquidation distributions, as it is eliminated with respect to a direct investment dividend, there is no reason to do so either with respect to cross-border relations. The objective of the P-S Directive is to make the taxation of cross-border situations as advantageous as in domestic relations. The objective is not to make the taxation more advantageous. Therefore, the benefits of Article 4 should not be required to be granted with respect to liquidation distributions in connection with partial liquidations, at least, if the state of residence of the parent company would not eliminate double taxation with respect to similar distributions in purely domestic relations. If the state treats liquidation distributions received in connection with a partial liquidation as a dividend with respect to which economic double taxation is eliminated in purely domestic situations, the state should also grant P-S Directive benefits in a similar cross-border situation. Because the wording of Article 4 is unclear with respect to liquidation distributions in connection with a partial liquidation, the granting of the benefits may not be required but only suggested.

With respect to a partial liquidation, where all the shares of a subsidiary owned by a parent company are repurchased by the subsidiary, it may especially be argued that the state of residence of the parent company does not have to grant the P-S Directive benefits of Article 4. Article 4 expressly requires that the profit distribution be made by virtue of the parent company's association with the subsidiary. Because the parent company in such a situation ceases to have any holding in the subsidiary, the distribution is not actually made by virtue of the association but, rather, by virtue of the abandonment of the association. This situation is, thus, very close to a total liquidation in nature.

Article 5 of the P-S Directive provides for relief from withholding tax with respect to profit distributions in the state of residence of the subsidiary. Article 5 mentions profit distributions, without any reference to liquidation distributions. Therefore, there seems to be no reason why liquidation distributions should be treated differently from actual dividend distributions under this article. Article 5 seems to include liquidation distributions of any kind, that is, both total and partial liquidation distributions.[14]

This asymmetry between the treatment in the source state and the treatment in the state of residence of the recipient of the liquidation distribution seems peculiar. If it is accepted that liquidation distributions are not distributions with respect to which economic double taxation should be eliminated in the state of residence of the recipient of such distribution, why should it be required in the source state? Of course, it may be argued, based on the tax neutrality requirements, that in situations where there is no withholding tax on a dividend, there should also be no withholding tax on liquidation distributions. It is not very useful to subject liquidation distributions to withholding tax, because the tax may easily be avoided by distributing profits in the form of a dividend prior to liquidation.[15] However, the same arguments may also be made with

---

14. This interpretation is supported, for example, by de Hosson (1990), 433 and Vanistendael (1992), 606.
15. *See* Vanistendael (1992), 605, for this argument for the inclusion of liquidation distributions under Art. 5 of the P-S Directive.

respect to the taxation in the state of residence of the recipient of a distribution and, despite this fact, liquidation distributions are excluded under Article 4 of the P-S Directive. Therefore, according to the opinion of the author of this study, these arguments neither explain nor give any reason for the asymmetry between Articles 4 and 5.

The asymmetry may only be explained by the fact that liquidation distributions often qualify under tax treaties as capital gains instead of as a dividend. It would follow from many tax treaties that only the state of residence, but not the source state, may tax the distribution. This argument questions the need for the P-S Directive to hinder source state taxation when tax treaties already hinder it. On the other hand, there is no tax treaty between all EU Member States so the asymmetry may not be properly explained by the reference to tax treaties. From the fact that liquidation distributions are expressly excluded under Article 4 but not under Article 5, the conclusion must be drawn that liquidation distributions are actually covered by Article 5. The fact that, at the time of the drafting of the P-S Directive, there was considered to be a need to exclude liquidation distributions expressly from the scope of Article 4, indicates that liquidation distributions were regarded as constituting, at least sometimes, the kinds of distributions meant by the P-S Directive. Liquidation distributions must be covered by Article 5 because the express exclusion is made in Article 4 but not in Article 5, even though the express exclusion in Article 4 suggests that liquidation distributions may qualify as profit distributions.

A liquidation distribution must meet the general requirement of being a profit distribution in order to qualify under Article 5. According to the opinion of the author of this study, the benefits of the P-S Directive do not necessarily have to be granted with respect to the whole amount of a liquidation distribution because a liquidation distribution may also include a return of invested capital in addition to a profit distribution. A state may not be required to grant the benefits of the P-S Directive with respect to the part of a liquidation distribution that represents a return of capital as it only applies to liquidation distributions in excess of the return of invested capital. In regard to many countries this distinction, however, has no relevance because a return of capital is generally not regarded as being a taxable transfer under the domestic law.

Because of the variation in the domestic law classification of different types of liquidation distribution a conflict with the P-S Directive can very easily emerge unless the problem is specifically addressed in the domestic law implementation provisions.[16]

§11.04 TAX TREATIES

[A] The Model Treaties

Article 13 of the OECD Model concerns the taxation of capital gains. According to the article, capital gains are gains from the alienation of property. The article does not

---

16. *See*, for example, Eicker (1998a), 84.

define the term 'capital gains' any better.[17] According to the Commentary, capital gains include in particular '...gains resulting from the sale or exchange of property and also from a partial alienation, the expropriation, the transfer to a company in exchange for stock, the sale of a right, the gift and even the passing of property on death...'.[18]

The OECD Model does not include any special article concerning gains from the alienation of corporate rights, therefore, proceeds from the alienation of shares and other corporate rights are taxed under Article 13 of the OECD Model concerning capital gains.[19] The starting point is that income from the alienation of corporate rights is capital gains from moveable property under Article 13(5) of the OECD Model,[20] instead of a dividend as '...income from corporate rights...' under Article 10. Capital gains treatment applies even though shareholders would realize accumulated corporate profits through the alienation.[21]

Only income from corporate rights qualifies as a dividend under Article 10(3) of the OECD Model. A dividend is generally income paid to a shareholder because of the shareholder's position as such. The proceeds from the alienation of corporate rights are not a dividend. They are not paid because of the recipient's position as a shareholder, but rather because of the shareholder's surrender of its position.[22] Therefore, a normal sale of shares that does not include a reduction in share capital falls under Article 13.

Liquidation distributions are not expressly included in any of the articles of the OECD Model and may therefore be regarded as qualifying either under Article 10 as a dividend, under Article 7 as business profits, under Article 13 as capital gains or under Article 21 as other income. There is no guidance in the Model itself or in the Commentary on whether Article 13 or Article 10 takes precedence in a situation where an item of income seems to qualify under both. Liquidation distributions are especially problematic in the sense that they may partly constitute the repayment of capital and partly a profit distribution. In order to qualify as a dividend under Article 10 of the OECD Model, liquidation distributions, however, should be income from corporate rights.

The starting point is that the repayment of capital is not income from corporate rights, but a repayment of a corporate right and, therefore, not a dividend. The repayment of capital, strictly speaking, does not include any income. Autonomously interpreted, the repayment of capital does not seem to qualify as a dividend. According to paragraph 28 of the Commentary on Article 10(3) of the OECD Model, '...normally, distributions by a company which have the effect of reducing the membership rights, for instance payments constituting a reimbursement of capital in any form whatever,

---

17. Substantially similar articles are included in the US and UN Models.
18. Paragraph 5 of the Commentary on Art. 13 of the OECD Model.
19. Article 13 of the OECD Model, however, includes a special paragraph concerning gains from the alienation of shares deriving more than 50% of their value directly or indirectly from immovable property.
20. Article 13(6) of the US Model is substantially similar. Paragraphs 4 and 5 of Art. 13 of the UN Model expressly cover alienation of shares. Gains from the alienation of shares in a real property company are assimilated to alienation of immoveable property under many treaties.
21. *See also* e.g., Li & Avella (2016) s. 6.2.2. for the relationship between Arts 10 and 13 of the OECD Model.
22. *See also* Vogel et al. (1997), 650.

are not regarded as dividend...'. Normally, the reimbursement of capital, therefore, does not constitute a dividend.[23]

It may be concluded from the fact that the Commentary uses the term, 'normally' that the view is taken that, sometimes, the repayment of capital may constitute a dividend. Many authors are of the opinion that if liquidation distributions constitute a dividend according to the domestic tax law of the source state, it may be regarded as a dividend with respect to a tax treaty.[24] In order for this interpretation to be correct with respect to the part of a liquidation distribution that is a repayment of capital, the repayment of capital should be income from corporate rights.

Article 10 of the OECD Model does not define what is meant by the term 'income' in the article. Because the term 'income' is not defined in any article of the Model, it has to be interpreted in accordance with the general rule of Article 3(2) of the Model. The fact that the term 'income' is used both in the autonomous parts of the dividend definition of Article 10(3) and in the part referring to source state classification makes the interpretation especially difficult. The wording of Article 10(3) seems to require the term 'income' to be given an autonomous interpretation for the purposes of the whole definition.[25]

However, such an interpretation does not seem reasonable with respect to the third part of the dividend definition because it would allow the state of residence to nullify the source state classification by giving the term 'income' an interpretation differing from the one of the source state. Such an interpretation cannot be in accordance with the Commentary, according to which benefits in money or money's worth, such as disguised distributions of profits and profits on a liquidation, qualify as a dividend so long as the source state treats such benefits as a dividend.[26] The context may be said to require that the term 'income' be interpreted in accordance with the law of the source state, at least for the purposes of the third part of the definition. So long as the source state treats a repayment of capital as income, it actually qualifies as income also for the purposes of the Model.

In order to qualify as a dividend for the purposes of the OECD Model, the income must be from corporate rights. This requirement is not included in the US Model, but any income qualifies as a dividend, under the third part of the dividend definition of the US Model if it is treated as a dividend in the source state. Under the US Model, liquidation distributions qualify with respect to both the part reflecting a repayment of capital and the part constituting a profit distribution if the source state treats such payments as a dividend.[27] If the source state, under such a treaty, treats a liquidation distribution as a dividend, the other state must eliminate double taxation with respect to the payment in accordance with the rules concerning a dividend.

The repayment of capital is not income from shares because the repayment of capital is not made because of the recipient's position as a shareholder, but rather

---

23. This view is expressed also in Ryynänen (1996), 471 and Vogel et al. (1997), 658.
24. See, for example, Andersson et al. (1991), 135 and Ryynänen (1996), 471 at fn. 221.
25. See, for discussion on this problem, Ch. 7 s. §7.02[D] of this study.
26. Paragraph 28 of the Commentary on Art. 10 of the OECD Model.
27. This interpretation is made also in the technical Explanation to Art. 10(5) of the US 2006 Model at para. 166.

because of its surrender of its position as a shareholder. Therefore, according to the opinion of the author of this study, the repayment of capital should not normally qualify as a dividend under the OECD Model, as is suggested by the Commentary. Only in situations where the repayment of capital is only partial and is carried out in such a way that the position of the shareholders in a company is not changed, the repayment of capital may be income from shares. The repayment of capital in connection with a total liquidation should never be treated as a dividend. The repayment of capital in connection with the repurchase of all the shares of a shareholder should not be treated as a dividend. The repayment of capital may be regarded as constituting income from shares if only part of the shares of all the shareholders is repurchased or if the nominal value of the shares of all the shareholders is reduced in such a way that the shareholders' position in the company is not changed.

The part of liquidation distributions that consists of a repayment of capital may qualify as a dividend under the OECD Model only if made in connection with a partial liquidation, but not if made in connection with a total liquidation. With respect to partial liquidations, dividend treatment should be an exception. Dividend treatment should be possible only in cases where the repayment of capital does not reduce the membership rights of a shareholder if the source state treats such a payment as dividend income.

The above interpretation is in line with the Commentary, according to which '…profits on a liquidation…' qualify as a dividend under Article 10 so long as the source state treats such benefits as a dividend.[28] Furthermore, according to the Commentary, distributions that have the effect of reducing membership rights, such as payments constituting a reimbursement of capital, are not normally regarded as a dividend.[29] The fact that the Commentary suggest that '…profits on a liquidation…' qualify as a dividend so long as the source state treats such profits as a dividend, does not mean that the part of liquidation proceeds that constitutes a repayment of capital would always qualify as a dividend if treated as a dividend in the source state. Strictly speaking, the repayment of capital is not a profit on liquidation. Only the part of a liquidation distribution that exceeds the amount of repaid capital is actually a profit on liquidation. The part of a liquidation distribution that represents a repayment of capital qualifies as a dividend only where such a repayment does not change the position of the shareholders in the company.

The fact that the part of a liquidation distribution that consists of a repayment of capital is generally not meant to be covered by Article 10 is also supported by paragraph 31 of the Commentary on Article 13(4). According to the Commentary, with respect to liquidation distributions:

> [T]he difference between the selling price and the par value of the shares may be treated in the state of which the company is a resident as a distribution of accumulated profits and not as a capital gain. The article does not prevent the state of residence of the company from taxing such distributions at the rates provided for in Article 10: such taxation is permitted because such difference is covered by

---

28. Paragraph 28 of the Commentary on Art. 10 of the OECD Model.
29. *Ibid.*

the definition of the term 'dividend' contained in paragraph 3 of Article 10 and interpreted in Article 28 of the Commentary relating thereto.

The reference to 'profits on a liquidation' also means the difference between the payment made in connection with a liquidation and the par value of the shares. The Commentary suggest that such a difference qualifies as a dividend under the Model so long as the source state treats it as a dividend. The Commentary do not suggest anywhere that the part of a liquidation distribution representing the repayment of capital should be treated as a dividend.

From paragraph 28 of the Commentary on Article 10(3) and from paragraph 31 of the Commentary on Article 13(4), it clearly follows that the part of a liquidation distribution that exceeds the part that constitutes a repayment of capital may be treated as a dividend under the Model if treated as such in the source state. The Commentary do not allow the treatment of liquidation distributions as a dividend in general, but only if the source state treats such income as a dividend. The source state may tax liquidation distributions with respect to the part exceeding the repayment of capital as a dividend only if it treats the payment under domestic law as income taxed similarly as income from shares. Otherwise, the state has to treat the payment to the extent that it is a gain from the alienation of property under Article 13 and, otherwise, under Article 21. However, generally only Article 10 accords the source state any taxing right.

It may be asked whether the part of a liquidation distribution in excess of the repayment of capital could qualify under the autonomous part of the dividend definition of Article 10(3) of the OECD Model. Then, the source state would be entitled to impose dividend withholding tax for the payments even though the state would not treat the payment as a dividend under its domestic tax law. If liquidation distributions are income from shares, they qualify as a dividend under the autonomous part of the dividend definition and must not be evaluated under the third part of the definition.[30]

With respect to liquidation distributions, paragraph 31 of the Commentary[31] refers to paragraph 28 of the Commentary. This paragraph states that liquidation distributions may be taxed as a dividend so long as the source state taxes such benefits as a dividend. It may be concluded then, that the source state may treat liquidation distributions as a dividend under tax treaties only if it taxes such benefits as a dividend under the domestic tax law of the state.

However, it may also be argued that a liquidation distribution exceeding the part of the repayment of capital is actually income from shares and, therefore, qualifies under the autonomous part of the dividend definition and not under the part of the definition referring to the law of the source state. It is clear that this part of the liquidation distribution may be regarded as being income. It may be asked whether the income is from shares or if it is only income from the alienation of shares. Especially where the membership rights of the shareholders are not changed, such income may be viewed as being income from shares. The income seems to qualify simultaneously both as a dividend under the autonomous part of the dividend definition and as capital

---

30. *See*, for this argument, Avery Jones et al. (1996), 130.
31. Paragraph 31 of the Commentary on Art. 13 of the OECD Model.

gains. Only paragraph 28 of the Commentary may be interpreted as requiring that liquidation distributions should be taxed under the dividend article only if the source state taxes such benefits as a dividend even though liquidation distributions at least sometimes qualify under the autonomous part of the dividend definition.

Although liquidation distributions may qualify under Article 10(3), and even under its autonomous part, it cannot be ignored that liquidation distributions also often clearly qualify under Article 13 as capital gains. The Commentary on Article 13 state that liquidation distributions may be taxed as a dividend, but not that they *must* be taxed as a dividend. This conclusion can be drawn from the fact that the Commentary only use such expressions as 'does not prevent' from taxing as a dividend. Even though liquidation distributions would be regarded as income from shares qualifying under the autonomous part of the dividend definition, the source state may not be required to treat liquidation distributions as a dividend instead of as capital gains. It seems that the source state may choose whether to apply either Article 10 or 13 because there is no rule granting priority to either article when a certain item of income qualifies under both.[32] However, in practice, it is irrelevant whether the state is required or allowed to treat liquidation distributions as a dividend, because it is generally in the interests of the source state to treat the benefit as a dividend.

Although tax treaties may grant the choice of dual classification, it does not seem to be in line with the purpose of tax treaties that the source state should be able to choose the classification that brings it the highest taxing right. It also seems peculiar that the source state should be able to classify the benefit as capital gains under domestic law, but treat the benefit as a dividend under a tax treaty in order to get the taxing right for the benefit. According to the opinion of the author of this study, even though liquidation distributions would qualify under the autonomous part of the dividend definition, the source state should follow its own domestic law classification of liquidation distributions in choosing the tax treaty classification.

Only if liquidation distributions are taxed as a dividend under the domestic law of the source state may the source state also tax them as a dividend under tax treaties. The source state should not treat the distribution as a dividend under a tax treaty only to gain the taxing right to the benefit instead of the state of residence of the recipient of the distribution, even though the source state actually does not believe that the payment is a dividend. This interpretation is also in line with the Commentary according to which profits on a liquidation qualify as a dividend so long as the source state taxes such benefits as a dividend.[33]

It is questionable whether the source state should be allowed to treat liquidation distributions as a dividend under tax treaties despite its domestic law classification of capital gains if the state of residence of the recipient of the distribution would, in the

---

32. *See* an example of such a case from the Netherlands 25 May 1994 HR, in which the profit was taxed as a dividend but in which it was considered that the profits could have been taxed as capital gain, analysed in Tax Treaty Interpretation (1997), 35-7–35-11.
33. Paragraph 28 of the Commentary on Art. 10 of the OECD Model. This interpretation was followed also, for example, by the Netherlands Supreme Court in its decision 38.461 from 12 Dec. 2003 in which the court considered that the Netherlands could not treat the proceeds in a buyback of a company by its own shares as dividend for tax treaty purposes.

obverse situation, treat the distribution as a dividend. This treatment would be in line with the principle of reciprocity. If one of the states as the source state treats liquidation distributions as a dividend under the tax treaty, it may be required that the state accept a dividend classification also in the obverse situation where the other state is the source state.

According to the opinion of the author of this study, if the state of residence of the recipient of the benefit taxes liquidation distributions as a dividend under its domestic law and, when it is the source state, treats such benefits as a dividend for tax treaty purposes, the other state, when it is the source state, should also be allowed to choose the dividend classification under the autonomous part of the dividend article. This treatment should be possible even though the state did not classify a liquidation distribution as a dividend under its domestic tax law, but would subject the distribution to withholding tax under its domestic tax law anyway. The source state may treat liquidation distributions as a dividend under tax treaties either if the domestic law of the state would classify such benefits as a dividend or if the state of residence of the recipient of the benefit would treat the benefit as a dividend under the treaty if it were the source state.

The taxation of a payment under the autonomous part of the dividend definition raises the question of the extent to which the state of residence of the recipient of liquidation distributions must accept the source state dividend classification. This question may be answered by referring to the principles set forth in the Commentary with respect to thin capitalization.[34] Accordingly, the state of residence of the recipient of liquidation distributions may be required to accept the dividend classification of the source state and eliminate double taxation as it eliminates double taxation with respect to a dividend. It must accept the source state classification and give credit for the withholding taxes paid in the source state if the double taxation relief article of the applicable treaty grants relief with respect to the income dealt with in Article 10, and the domestic law of the source state classifies the benefit as a dividend.

When the domestic law of the source state does not classify such income as a dividend, tax treaty dividend classification of the source state must be accepted if the state of residence of the recipient of the distribution recognizes that it was proper for the source state to tax the liquidation distributions as a dividend. For example, if the state of residence of the recipient would itself, in the obverse situation, treat liquidation distributions as a dividend, it should also accept the source state classification. It may be said that the state of residence of the income recipient must accept the source state classification, in any case, when it views that the source state has correctly applied the treaty by treating the benefit as a dividend. A reference to a mutual agreement procedure may be required in order for the conflict to be resolved.[35]

---

34. Paragraph 68 of the Commentary on Art. 23 of the OECD Model.
35. Also, Avery Jones et al. (1996), 130 is of the opinion that source state classification has to be accepted if the source state taxation is in accordance with Art. 10.

[B] Actual Treaties

The dividend definitions of many actual treaties cover income from shares or other rights. Other income derived from other rights qualifies as dividend if it is subjected to the same taxation treatment as income from shares by the laws of the contracting state of which the company making the distribution is a resident. Under some other treaties, income from shares qualifies as a dividend. Income from other corporate rights also qualifies if it is subjected to the same tax treatment as income from shares by the laws of the source state. Some treaties cover income from shares and income from other corporate rights to the extent that it is treated in the same way as income from shares in the source state.

Despite the different formulations, under all these treaties, liquidation distributions must be income from shares or other rights and not income from the alienation of shares or other rights in order to qualify as a dividend. The treaties are similar to the OECD Model in regard to the line drawn between a dividend and capital gains. The domestic tax law practice of taxing liquidation distributions as a dividend only to the extent that they exceed the part that is a repayment of capital is in line with the principles of the OECD Model.[36] To the extent that a country, as the source state, treats liquidation distributions as a dividend, such distributions also qualify as a dividend for the purposes of the treaties. The domestic law practice of treating liquidation distributions as a dividend only in exceptional cases, especially in cases where the position of the shareholders is not changed also seems to be in line with these treaties. The items that qualify as dividend for domestic law purposes in the source state qualify as dividend also for treaty purposes.

It may be questioned whether such a domestic tax law system, which imposes withholding tax on the whole amount of a liquidation distribution, is in line with tax treaties because a return of invested capital normally does not qualify as a dividend. The dividend withholding tax should normally be limited only to the part of the payment exceeding the repayment of capital. Only in exceptional situations, where the position of the shareholders is not changed, dividend withholding tax with respect to the whole amount of a dividend seems to be acceptable.

Some treaties provide that income from shares qualifies as a dividend. Income from other corporate rights qualifies, if the income is treated the same way as income from shares is treated in the source state. In addition, any income qualifies as a dividend if it is treated in the source state in the same way as income from shares. For example, under the treaty among the Nordic countries, income from shares qualifies as a dividend and other income from a company qualifies if it is treated in the source state in the same way as income from shares.[37]

Under these treaties, any income qualifies if it is treated as a dividend in the source state. The area of application of the dividend article of these treaties with respect to liquidation distributions is, therefore, broader than it is with respect to the OECD

---

36. *See also* Vogel et al. (1997), 679–680.
37. Article 10(6) of the Nordic Treaty. *See also* Helminen (2013a), 241–245 for the dividend definition of the Nordic Treaty.

Model. It is similar to the scope of application of the dividend article of the US Model. So long as the source state classifies liquidation distributions either partly or totally as a dividend, the other state must accept the dividend treatment and must eliminate double taxation accordingly.

§11.05 CONCLUSIONS

The classification of liquidation distributions for domestic tax law purposes varies from country to country. Some countries assimilate liquidation distributions to any alienation of shares and see a capital gain whereas some countries classify liquidation distributions as dividends. Some countries make a difference between a total and a partial liquidation whereas other countries treat them alike. Some countries make a difference between a domestic transaction and a cross-border transaction whereas other countries treat them alike. Most countries may apply domestic law anti-avoidance type provisions to change the classification that normally would apply. Dividend classification may apply if the purpose of the transaction was to avoid dividend taxation.

Liquidation distributions qualify for the benefits of Article 5 of the P-S Directive but, generally, not for benefits under Article 4. If a state treats liquidation distributions as a dividend, it seems reasonable, however, that the state, as the state of residence of the recipient, also applies the direct investment dividend relief provided in Article 4 with respect to such distributions. Because of the unclear wording of the P-S Directive, such treatment may, however, not be required. The benefits of Article 5 in the form of a withholding tax exemption must be granted only with respect to the part of liquidation distributions that are profit distribution, but not to the part that constitutes a return of capital.

Many actual treaties follow the OECD Model with respect to the line drawn between a dividend and capital gains. Liquidation distributions may be treated as a dividend under these treaties only if the source state treats such distributions as a dividend under domestic law. However, despite such domestic law treatment, only the part of a liquidation distribution exceeding the part that constitutes a repayment of capital may be treated as a dividend. Only in exceptional cases, when the position of shareholders is not changed, may it be regarded as acceptable to treat the part constituting a repayment of capital as a dividend if it is treated as such under domestic law. If these limitations are followed, the state of residence of the recipient of the liquidation distribution should accept the dividend treatment of the source state and should eliminate double taxation accordingly.

The scope of application of the divided article of many actual treaties is broader than under the OECD Model. For the purposes of these treaties, any income that is treated in the source state in the same way as income from shares qualifies as a dividend. So long as liquidation distributions are regarded as constituting income, the distributions qualify as a dividend under the treaties if treated as such in the source state. The term 'income' in such a situation must derive its meaning from the law of the source state. Therefore, liquidation distributions always qualify as a dividend if the source state treats liquidation distributions as a dividend under its domestic law.

CHAPTER 12
Concluding Remarks

§12.01 GENERAL

This study has examined the concept of a dividend and how it is understood under the different legal systems of international tax law. A review was made of the extent to which the domestic tax laws, EU tax law and tax treaties accord to the concept of a dividend similar or different definitions. This study has analysed the extent to which the differences in the concept of a dividend may lead to classification conflicts in cross-border situations. A discussion ensued concerning the extent to which the danger of international double taxation or non-taxation is avoided in these situations. The following remarks were made.

§12.02 DIVIDEND-DISTRIBUTING ENTITIES

Under the domestic tax laws of different states, generally, only entities classified as separately taxable entities for tax purposes qualify as dividend-distributing entities. The answer to the question of whether an entity qualifies as a dividend-distributing entity, thus, largely depends on the entity classification rules of each state's domestic tax law. Therefore, it is possible that a state regards an entity, organized under the company law of another state, as a dividend-distributing entity, whereas the other state does not. Inconsistent entity classification under the domestic tax law of two different states is possible.

Inconsistent entity classification under the domestic tax law of two contracting states may, in principle, also lead to income classification conflicts under tax treaties. Tax treaties, however, normally solve such conflicts. In general, the state of residence of an income recipient must accept the corporate treatment and, therefore, the dividend treatment of the state of residence of an entity for tax treaty purposes. Ordinarily, the state of organization is simultaneously the state of residence of the entity for tax treaty purposes, and it is largely accepted that the tax treatment in such a state determines whether the entity qualifies as a dividend-distributing company for tax treaty purposes. Under tax treaties, an entity classification conflict is normally solved in accordance with the domestic tax law classification of the state of residence of an income-paying entity.

An actual, unsolved classification conflict is possible in a situation where the state of organization of an entity is one of the contracting states and the state of residence of the entity, for tax treaty purposes, is the other contracting state. Classification conflict is, then, possible if the owners of the entity are residents in the same state where the entity is organized and if the other state taxes the entity as a resident because the effective management of the entity is in that state. With respect to such situations, the treaties are unclear about which of the contracting state's tax treatment is decisive for tax treaty purposes. The interpretation in favour of the classification of either state's classification is, thus, the correct application of the treaty. Due to inconsistent entity classification, one of the contracting states may treat the same item of income as a dividend and the other may not.

Such a conflict may lead to a situation where the state of organization of the entity that is simultaneously the state of residence of the income recipient does not eliminate double taxation with respect to the taxes paid for the distribution in the other state. Double taxation may remain uneliminated, especially because in the state of organization the taxation has generally occurred earlier than in the other state. In order for the state of organization to be able to eliminate double taxation, either it should have left the income untaxed upon its realization or it should refund at the time of an actual distribution a certain part of the taxes paid at the time of the realization. The treaties are not clear about whether, in such an income classification conflict, the other state must eliminate double taxation despite the conflict. It is suggested that double taxation be eliminated in the state of residence of the income recipient because the other state has correctly applied the treaty.

In order to avoid the potential classification conflicts described above, tax treaties should expressly state which of the contracting state's tax treatments is decisive in determining the status of an entity as a dividend-distributing entity. The clearest choice, with respect to a dividend, is that the treatment in the state of residence of an entity is decisive. The fact that the term 'company' is defined as a body corporate or entities taxed as bodies corporate is only confusing with respect to a dividend. For the purposes of a dividend, the clearest choice would be a formulation referring only to an entity taxed as a body corporate. Accordingly, it should be expressly stated that an entity may only qualify as a dividend-distributing entity, in any case, if it is treated as a separately taxable entity in the state that is the state of residence of the entity for the purposes of the treaty.

In practice, the cases are seldom in which entity classification leads to situations where international double taxation is not eliminated to the extent required by tax treaties. In fact, in many cases, inconsistent classification under the domestic tax law of two contracting states leads to a situation where the states eliminate double taxation in accordance with domestic tax law provisions more extensively than is required by a treaty. Inconsistent entity classification may lead to situations where double taxation is eliminated in the state of residence of the owners of an entity with respect to both foreign taxes paid by the foreign entity and those foreign taxes paid by its owners. Double taxation may be eliminated with respect to both of them even though the applicable treaty would require elimination only with respect to the taxes paid by the owners.

Inconsistent entity classification under the domestic tax law of two states may lead to a situation where income on a portfolio investment is actually taxed as lightly as income on a direct investment. Therefore, in a situation of inconsistent entity classification, domestic tax law should not grant a credit for the foreign taxes paid by the foreign entity. Rather, a credit should be granted only for the foreign taxes paid by the owners if the state of residence of the income recipient does not want to restrict its taxing right more extensively than that required by tax treaties.

§12.03 DIVIDEND-STRIPPING AND THE DIVIDEND-GENERATING RELATIONSHIP

[A] The Basic Relationship

Normally, domestic law dividend taxation requires the transfer of a benefit from a corporation to one of its shareholder in the shareholder's capacity as such. Benefits from a corporation to another person who is associated with the shareholder may also be taxed as a dividend for the shareholder. This treatment, however, requires that the benefit be transferred because of the shareholder relationship. The P-S Directive only concerns distributions between companies where the recipient holds a certain amount of capital or voting rights in the distributing company. The distribution must also be made by virtue of the holding in the capital or in the voting rights.

Strictly interpreted, distributions between two subsidiary companies of a common parent may not qualify for P-S Directive benefits even though they are treated as a dividend under domestic law. The P-S Directive does not seem to hinder the state of residence of the subsidiaries to tax the benefit transferred from one of the subsidiaries to the other. However, under domestic law, where such a benefit is taxed as a dividend, it is often assumed that the distribution is actually made first to the common parent company of the subsidiaries and, therefore, only the distribution is taxed as a constructive dividend. There is, thus, a fictive profit distribution from a subsidiary to its parent company made by virtue of the subsidiary's association with the parent company. From the point of view of the state that taxes such income as a dividend, there is a distribution of profits from a subsidiary to its parent company.

The wording of the P-S Directive does not expressly include or exclude fictive distributions. Despite this omission, the P-S Directive may be interpreted as applying to such situations where the domestic tax law of a Member State subjects a fictive distribution to taxation as if an actual distribution had been made. It follows logically from the fictive dividend treatment under domestic law that the state treats the fictive distribution as a distribution also for the purposes of the P-S Directive. There are no grounds for the state to tax the amount, as it deems it to be a dividend from a subsidiary to its parent company because it could not have taxed the amount if the benefit had actually been distributed as a dividend from the subsidiary to the parent company. The benefit, therefore, may not be viewed as having been transferred in order to avoid dividend taxation.

If the holding requirement is fulfilled between the distributing subsidiary and the parent company, the P-S Directive should hinder the state of residence of the distributing company from imposing a dividend withholding tax with respect to the fictive dividend. The state of residence of the parent company, if it deems that the parent company has received a constructive dividend, should also exempt the fictive income or at least eliminate economic double taxation with respect to the income in accordance with the requirements of the P-S Directive. If there is no qualifying relationship between the distributing subsidiary and the parent company, the P-S Directive does not hinder dividend taxation.

For the purposes of most tax treaties, income may constitute a dividend not only if it is paid to a shareholder, but also in cases where it is paid to any other person. Fundamentally, however, a dividend must be income on ownership interests in a company. Other income paid by a company may qualify as a dividend under the treaties only if the source state treats it as a dividend. In this respect, the narrowest dividend definition seems to be the one found in some treaties that only includes income from 'corporate rights' in addition to the expressly mentioned types of income. Many other treaties include income from any arrangements '...carrying the right to participate in profits...' or income from any rights. Some treaties include any income paid by a company, which is the broadest definition in this respect.

In conclusion, many tax treaties give rather broad latitude to the state of residence of an income-distributing company to determine, in accordance with its domestic tax law, whether the relationship between the company and the income recipient is such that the income constitutes a dividend. The state of residence of the income recipient must accept the dividend classification of the source state even though the state, under its own domestic tax law, would not regard the relationship as a dividend-generating relationship. The power of the source state classification is especially evident because the status of an entity as a company is also determined for the most part in accordance with the tax treatment of the state of residence of the entity.

[B]   Dividend-Stripping Arrangements

[1]   Transfer of Dividend Rights

Dividend stripping in the form of a transfer of dividend rights by a shareholder retaining the shares is effectively hindered under the domestic tax law of many states. Some states apply the approach of taxing the proceeds from an alienation of dividend rights as a dividend, whereas some other states apply the approach of taxing the shareholder for the dividend received by a holder of dividend rights. Under domestic tax law, the proceeds from the alienation of dividend rights, thus, may or may not be taxed as a dividend depending on the approach. Therefore, inconsistent classification under the domestic tax law of two states is possible.

The inconsistency under domestic laws does not lead to unsolved classification conflicts under tax treaties. Under most treaties, income from the alienation of property may not be taxed as a dividend no matter what the domestic law treatment is. Many tax treaties allow dividend treatment, but if the source state treats the income as a dividend, the other state must accept the treatment and eliminate double taxation accordingly.

Many tax treaties distort the domestic law approach of taxing the proceeds from an alienation of dividend rights as dividend. Because many tax treaties do not allow the source state to tax the proceeds from an alienation of dividend rights, source state taxes may be avoided by transferring dividend rights to a resident of the same state in which the corporation, in which the transferor is a shareholder, is a resident.

Because of the problem caused by the approach of treating the proceeds from an alienation of dividend rights as a dividend in tax treaty situations, such an approach should not be used. Dividend stripping in the form of the transfer of dividend rights separately from shares may best be avoided by taxing a dividend as the income of the shareholder even though the dividend rights had been transferred to another person.

[2] Equity Securities Lending Transactions

The tax classification of substitute dividend payments under securities lending transactions differs from state to state. Some states treat a substitute dividend as a dividend, at least if paid to non-residents, whereas many other states do not classify a substitute dividend as a dividend. Differing domestic law classification of a substitute dividend may lead to inconsistent classification in cross-border situations.

Actual classification conflicts concerning substitute dividend payments are rather satisfactorily avoided in tax treaties. Generally, a substitute dividend may not be treated as a dividend under tax treaties because it is not income from corporate rights. The source state is not allowed to impose withholding tax. If the state does so, it applies the treaty incorrectly. Therefore, the other state may not be required to grant a credit with respect to the tax imposed by the source state. Under some treaties, a substitute dividend paid by a company qualifies as a dividend if treated as such in the source state. Under these treaties, the state of residence of the income recipient must accept the source state classification and must eliminate double taxation accordingly.

Some other treaties are more problematic as regards a substitute dividend. Under some treaties, a substitute dividend may be classified as a dividend if it is regarded as being income from a right taxed the same way as income from shares is taxed in the source state. Because opinions differ on whether a substitute dividend is income from a right, actual classification conflicts may emerge. The source state may treat a substitute dividend as a dividend but the state of residence of the recipient of a substitute dividend may not eliminate double taxation with respect to the possible withholding tax imposed in the source state. The residence state may view that the treaty has not been properly applied in the source state. Therefore, where at least one of the contracting states treats a substitute dividend as a dividend under domestic law, it is suggested that tax treaties expressly mention if a substitute dividend is to be treated as a dividend.

[3] Derivative Financial Instruments

Neither domestic law nor tax treaties are very well equipped to address the complicated issues raised by derivative financial instruments. Non-residents may easily avoid withholding tax by the use of synthetic equity investments instead of real equity investments. Taxes may be avoided by choosing a specific form of a derivative transaction that produces the desired economic result. None of the states covered here treat dividend equivalent payments on equity derivatives as a dividend, therefore they do not qualify as a dividend under tax treaties either and classification conflicts involving the question of dividend classification do not emerge in practice.

Derivative financial instruments are essential in modern finance and the present treatment seems well argued. Because equity derivatives are used for many reasons other than tax avoidance, general treatment of income from equity derivatives as a dividend does not seem reasonable. The formation of such a specific provision only covering situations of avoidance of dividend taxation is, in practice, difficult. The general taxation of dividend equivalent payments on equity derivatives as a dividend could distort the efficient use of equity derivatives to an unreasonable extent. Therefore, there is no reason to change present domestic law approaches. Dividend equivalent payments on equity derivatives should be classified as a dividend only in exceptional cases of clear tax avoidance based on domestic law rules and principles concerning transfers deviating from the arm's length standard and tax avoidance.

§12.04 FICTIVE DISTRIBUTIONS

[A] CFC Income

The domestic tax laws of many states include a special CFC regime aimed at taxing the undistributed profits of a controlled foreign company in the hands of the shareholders of the company. In practice, however, tax treaties and EU law substantially limit the applicability of these regimes in tax treaty situations and in the case of EU Member States.

The domestic law regimes of some states are based on the fictive distribution approach and the regimes of other states are based on the look-through approach. Despite the fact that many states have a CFC regime, the taxation of CFC income always leads to a conflict situation. CFC regimes either subject a fictive distribution from a company to its owners to tax where the state of residence of the company does not recognize any distribution, or treat an entity as a more or less transparent entity even though it is treated as a separately taxable entity in the state of its organization.

CFC taxation may lead to international double taxation if an actual distribution from the company is taxed in addition to the fictive distribution or the income assigned to the owners. Because the domestic law CFC regimes refrain from taxing actual distributions to the extent covered by the fictive distribution, in practice, CFC regimes only cause undesirable double taxation with respect to the withholding tax imposed in the source state with respect to an actual distribution. In general, it is suggested that credit for the withholding tax be granted even though no tax is paid at the time of the actual distribution in the state of residence of the owners. In practice, this treatment would mean a refund of taxes or a carry forward of the unused credit.

The TFEU and tax treaties limit CFC taxation considerably. In the case of a CFC in an EU Member State, CFC taxation in another EU Member State is possible only in the case of wholly artificial tax avoidance arrangements no matter if the P-S Directive is considered to be applicable. A distribution deemed to exist under a CFC regime also qualifies as a dividend for the purposes of tax treaties. With respect to CFC regimes that are based on the fictive distribution approach, the direct investment dividend rules of tax treaties must be applied. The dividend articles of tax treaties, on the other hand, do not seem to limit taxation under the CFC regimes based on the look-through approach. Tax treaty dividend treatment may not be required with respect to such regimes.

[B]   Bonus Shares

There are different approaches to the treatment of bonus shares under the domestic tax laws of different states. Some states consider that bonus shares constitute dividend for tax purposes, whereas many other states do not consider a dividend to exist. There are some states that do not consider the issue of bonus shares to constitute any type of taxable income for the shareholders. However, where bonus shares are issued in such a way that the proportionate interests of shareholders are changed, bonus shares may also constitute a dividend in the states that in other situations do not see a dividend.

For the purposes of many tax treaties, bonus shares qualify as a dividend as long as the source state treats them as taxable dividend. To the extent that the source state does not treat bonus shares as a dividend, bonus shares do not qualify as a dividend but rather as other income under the tax treaties. Actual unsolved classification conflicts do not emerge.

In practice, the fact that some states classify bonus shares as a dividend and some do not does not lead to income classification conflicts, which would lead to double taxation. Where a state does not classify bonus shares as a dividend, it is probable that it does not treat bonus shares as taxable income at all. Therefore, bonus shares are either subject to dividend treatment in both of the states or they are treated as a dividend in one of the states and not taxed in the other state at all. In many cases, bonus shares are left totally untaxed, which is, however, not a problem because bonus shares also seem to be subject to tax in purely domestic situations only in exceptional cases.

§12.05   ECONOMIC BENEFITS IN THE FORM OF TRANSFER PRICES

Double taxation is often caused by the fact that two states have different opinions as to what the amount of the arm's length price is in transactions between related parties. Therefore, even though the states, in principle, would share an opinion with respect to a classification of economic benefits transferred from a corporation to one of its shareholders in the form of transfer prices, in practice, double taxation is often not avoided. Most states tax economic benefits transferred from a corporation to one of its shareholders in the form of transfer prices as a constructive dividend under domestic law. Such benefits also qualify for the purposes of the P-S Directive. Such benefits that are taxed as a dividend in the source state also qualify as a dividend for the purposes of tax treaties. It is not common that states would consider that a return of a constructive dividend eliminates dividend taxation.

Despite the fact that most states generally agree that a constructive dividend qualifies as a dividend under the tax treaties, in practice double taxation may not be avoided. Because it is only in the interest of the source state to argue that there is a benefit transferred from the state to the other state in the form of transfer prices, the other state does not necessarily recognize such a benefit. The state of residence of the recipient of such a benefit may not eliminate double taxation with respect to the taxes imposed in the source state even though the source state, in principle, has correctly applied the treaty.

The same problem applies with respect to the P-S Directive. Even though it is generally accepted that the P-S Directive benefits are available with respect to a constructive dividend, the state of residence of the recipient of such benefit may not exempt the benefit. This state may consider that there is no deviation from the arm's length price. The Arbitration Convention provides a useful tool to solve such a problem. In practice, however, the arbitration procedure is rarely resorted to because the mutual agreement procedures provided for by tax treaties offer simpler means for solving classification conflicts.

§12.06 RETURN ON DEBT-EQUITY HYBRIDS

The tax classification of hybrid instruments and the income on them seems to be based on a case-by-case approach in most states. In distinguishing debt from equity and interest from a dividend, the form used is not decisive but what is decisive is whether the actual substance of an instrument is either debt or equity. With respect to situations where only one hybrid characteristic is involved, the states seem to be rather unanimous about classification. Generally, one hybrid characteristic alone does not seem to change the classification of an instrument. With respect to such hybrids, classification conflicts should, therefore, be rare. Most states seem to be prepared to reclassify hybrid instruments in situations where more than one hybrid characteristic is involved.

Despite the fact that the approaches in different states are very similar, classification conflicts, especially with respect to hybrids with more than one equity characteristic, may emerge. It is possible that one of the states treats such an instrument as debt and the income on it as interest, while the other state treats it as equity and the income on it as a dividend. Such inconsistent classification under domestic tax law may also lead to actual classification conflicts and international double taxation.

Classification conflicts leading to double taxation are avoided best under the treaties that differ from the OECD Model in the respect that they do not require dividend to be income from corporate rights. Under these treaties, any income qualifies as a dividend if it is treated in the same way as a dividend is treated in the source state. Under these treaties, the other state must accept the dividend classification of the source state for tax treaty purposes, and thereby, actual classification conflicts are avoided. These treaties do not avoid classification conflicts where the source state treats an item of income as interest and the other state treats the same item as a dividend. Because interest treatment generally leads to higher tax revenues in the state of residence of the income recipient, in practice, such a classification conflict is irrelevant. Even if such a conflict emerged, international double taxation would not occur because interest generally is not taxed in the source state at all.

With respect to the treaties that follow the OECD Model, actual classification conflicts may easily emerge. Under these treaties, generally only income from corporate rights qualifies as a dividend no matter what the domestic law classification is. If the states interpret different instruments as constituting corporate rights, they may treat the income from the instruments under different articles of the treaties, and double taxation in practice may not be eliminated. The treaties do not require that double taxation be eliminated in these situations unless the state of residence of the income recipient accepts that the source state properly applied the treaty. The parties may have to resort to the mutual agreement procedures provided for by these treaties in order for double taxation to be eliminated.

§12.07 THIN CAPITALIZATION INTEREST

The sole fact that a company is thinly capitalized does not seem to cause interest to be taxed as a dividend in many countries. Thin capitalization is regarded rather only as one characteristic to be evaluated together with other equity characteristics of a debt investment.

For tax treaty treatment, classification conflicts are avoided with respect to the treaties that differ from the OECD Model in respect to the fact that they do not require dividend to be income from corporate rights. Under these treaties, the other state must accept the possible dividend treatment of thin capitalization interest of the source state.

Actual classification conflicts may emerge in the relations between such countries that have completed a tax treaty with the wording of the OECD Model. The source state may treat thin capitalization interest as a dividend where the residence state does not accept, and may not be required to accept, the dividend treatment. A reference to the mutual agreement procedure provided for by the tax treaties may be needed in these situations.

§12.08 LIQUIDATION DISTRIBUTIONS

The treatment of liquidation distributions varies under the domestic tax laws of different states. In some states, liquidation distributions may constitute a dividend only in exceptional cases of tax avoidance. In some other states, only a distribution made in connection with partial liquidations may constitute a dividend. In yet some other states, liquidation distributions constitute a dividend to the extent that the distribution exceeds a return of invested capital. In some states, liquidation distributions to shareholders in any form are treated as dividend. Inconsistent classification is, therefore, possible in cross-border situations.

Liquidation distributions qualify for the benefits of Article 5 of the P-S Directive, but generally not for the benefits of Article 4. If a state treats liquidation distributions as a dividend, it seems reasonable, however, that the state also applies the direct investment dividend relief provided in Article 4 with respect to such distributions as the state of residence of the recipient. Because of the unclear wording of the P-S Directive, such treatment, however, may not be required. The benefits of Article 5 in the form of a withholding tax exemption must be granted only with respect to the part of liquidation distributions that are profit distributions, but not to the part that constitutes a return of capital.

Many tax treaties follow the OECD Model with respect to the line drawn between a dividend and capital gains. Liquidation distributions may be treated as a dividend under the treaties only if the source state treats such distributions as a dividend under domestic law. Double taxation in such situations is avoided because the other state has to accept the source state treatment.

Classification conflicts should be avoided also under treaties that have a broader dividend definition than the OECD Model does. Any income that is treated in the source state in the same way as income from shares is taxed qualifies as a dividend for the purposes of these treaties. Liquidation distributions qualify as a dividend if the source state treats liquidation distributions as a dividend under its domestic law.

§12.09 FINAL CONCLUSIONS

In conclusion, the domestic tax law concepts of a dividend found in domestic tax laws of different states differ from each other on the points covered in this study. With respect to any of the issues covered in this study, it is possible that one of the states classifies an item of income as a dividend, whereas another classifies the same item of income as some other type of income or not as income at all. The differences in domestic law classification, however, normally do not lead to actual unsolved classification conflicts and to double taxation. Under the tax treaties, in most of the cases, one of the states involved has to accept the classification of the other state for treaty purposes. Even if a tax treaty did not solve a classification conflict, in most cases, international double taxation is satisfactorily eliminated. Generally, it follows from the applicable tax treaty or from unilateral domestic tax law that international double taxation is satisfactorily eliminated.

The fact that states do not necessarily agree on the amount of an arm's length transfer price seems to be most problematic with respect to double taxation. This problem, however, is not actually about the concept of a dividend, but a problem of transfer pricing and the arm's length principle in general. Therefore, clarification of the definitions for the concept of a dividend does not serve as a solution to the problem. The case of hybrid instruments is another situation in which inconsistent domestic law classification may lead to double taxation, which certain tax treaties are inefficient at eliminating. This problem may be alleviated by clarifying the dividend definitions of the problematic tax treaties.

Otherwise, the problem seems to be that the differences in income classification under the domestic tax law of different states may be taken advantage of in order to minimize tax or to switch taxation from one state to another. Because of the domestic law rules concerning the elimination of international double taxation, inconsistent entity classification may lead to a situation where a portfolio investment is treated as advantageously as a direct investment in the state of residence of the investor. By selecting an entity form, which is treated as a separately taxable entity in its state of organization and as a transparent entity in the state of residence of the investor, an investor may largely avoid tax in the state of residence of the investor. Because this possibility is caused by domestic tax law rules, it may be easily eliminated by unilateral domestic law rules if it is desired.

The different dividend-stripping arrangements are the most problematic with respect to the possibility of tax avoidance in one state. It follows from many tax treaties that the proceeds from an alienation of dividend rights cannot be taxed in the state of residence of the company in which the alienor is a shareholder. Most tax treaties also hinder source state withholding tax with respect to a substitute dividend and dividend equivalent payments. An investor may in many cases avoid source state dividend withholding tax by alienating dividend rights or by exploiting different securities lending transactions or derivative financial instruments. Dividend articles of the tax treaties in their present form do not cover the different payments made under the different dividend-stripping arrangements but it is technically possible to amend the dividend definitions of tax treaties to cover the items. Thus, the problem is rather to make the policy decision of whether to subject these items to source state withholding tax or not.

Finally, it must be remembered that all the problems relating to the concept of a dividend and inconsistent income classification are relevant only as long as a dividend is taxed differently to other income. Thus, sometimes it may be more reasonable to solve the problems by amending dividend taxation or by amending taxation of other items of income rather than by amending or clarifying the dividend definitions. For example, the OECD BEPS Action on hybrid mismatches[1] is based on the elimination of the double tax benefits caused by mismatches rather than on the elimination of the mismatches themselves.

---

1. *See* OECD (2015).

Bibliography

Aalto, Esa. *Koron vähennysoikeus henkilöverotuksessa.* Lakimiesliiton kustannus (1988).

Aarnio, Aulis. *Mitä lainoppi on?.* Kustannusosakeyhtiö Tammi (1978).

Aarnio, Aulis. *Oikeussäännösten tulkinnasta.* Tutkimus lainopillisen perustelun rationalisuudesta ja hyväksyttävyydestä. Helsingin Yliopiston Monistuspalvelu Painatusjaos (1982).

Aarnio, Aulis. *Laintulkinnan teoria.* Yleisen oikeustieteen oppikirja. WSOY (1988).

Adonnino, Pietro. General Report, Non-discrimination Rules in International Taxation. *Cahiers de droit fiscal international,* LXXVIIIb. Kluwer (1993), 19–71.

Äimä, Kristiina. *Sisäiset korot lähiyhtiöiden kansainvälisessä verotuksessa.* WSOYpro (2009).

Alaluusua, Seppo & Heikki Niskakangas. *Verotus kansainvälistyvän yrityksen päätöksiin vaikuttavana tekijänä.* Liiketaloustieteellisen tutki-muslaitoksen julkaisuja sarja A:45 (1984).

The American Law Institute Federal Tax Project. *International Aspects of United States Income Taxation II.* Proposals on United States Income Tax Treaties (1992).

Andersson, Edward. No. muu pääomansijoitus osakeyhtiöön verotuksen kannalta. *Verotus* (1987): 331–341.

Andersson, Edward. Miten ulkomaisia sijoituksia verotetaan?. *Verotus* (1992): 112–116.

Andersson, Edward. Subordinerade lån och andra kapitallån vid beskattningen. *Juhlajulkaisu – Festskrift Roschier-Holmberg & Waselius 60 v. år 1936–1996.* Roschier-Holmberg & Waselius (1995), 25–39.

Andersson, Edward. Förhållandet mellan Bassamfundsskattelagen och Finlands dubbelbeskattningsavtal. *JFT* (2000): 203–216.

Andersson, Edward. Alikapitalisointi ja syrjintäkielto. *Verotus* (2003): 460–468.

Andersson, E., et al. *Det nordiska skatteavtalet med kommentarer,* andra upplagan. Jurist – og Økonomiforbund, Juristförbundets Förlag, TANO, Norstedts (1991).

Andersson, Edward & Ahti Vapaavuori. IFA:n 47. kongressi. *Verotus* (1994): 228–233.

Andersson, Jan. *Om vinstutdelning från aktiebolag, En studie av aktiebolagsrättsliga skyddsregler.* Iustus Förlag (1995).

Andersson, Krister & Erik Norrman. *Capital Taxation and Neutrality – A Study of Tax Wedges with Special Reference to Sweden.* Lund Economic Studies (1987).

Bibliography

Arginelli, Paolo & Michele Gusmeroli. The 2007 Leiden Alumni Forum on Recent and Pending Direct Taxation Cases Before the European Court of Justice. *Intertax* (2008): 312-325.

Arnold, Brian J. General Report, Deductibility of Interests and Other Financing Charges in Computing Income. *Cahiers de droit fiscal international*, LXXIXa. Kluwer (1994), 491-541.

Arnold, Brian J. The Interpretation of Tax Treaties: Myth and Reality. *Bulletin for International Taxation* (2010): 2-15.

Arnold, B.J. & P. Dibout. General Report. Limits on the Use of Low-Tax Regimes by Multinational Businesses: Current Measures and Emerging Trends. *Cahiers de droit fiscal international*, LXXXVIb. Kluwer (2001), 21-89.

Arvidsson, Richard. *Dolda vinstöverförningar, En Skatterättslig studie av interprissättningen i multinationella koncerner.* Juristförlaget (1990).

Ault, Hugh & Jacques Sasseville. 2008 OECD Model: The New Arbitration Provision. *Bulletin for International Taxation* (2009): 208-15.

Auranen, Anja. Kansainvälinen kaksinkertainen verotus ja sen estäminen. *Verotus* (1979): 271-277.

Avery Jones, John F. Interpretation of Tax Treaties, *Bulletin for International Fiscal Documentation* (1986): 75-85.

Avery Jones, John F. Report of the United Kingdom. *Cahiers de droit fiscal international*, LXXVIIIa. Interpretation of Double Taxation Conventions, International Fiscal Association. Kluwer (1993), 597-614.

Avery Jones, John F. Article 3(2) of the OECD Model Convention and the Commentary to It: Treaty Interpretation. *European Taxation* (1993a): 252-257.

Avery Jones, John F. The 'One True Meaning' of a Tax Treaty. *Bulletin for International Fiscal Documentation* (2001): 220-224.

Avery Jones, John F. Treaty Interpretation. *Global Tax Treaty Commentaries*, IBFD, online (2016).

Avery Jones, John F., et al. The Interpretation of Tax Treaties with Particular Reference to Article 3(2) of the OECD Model-I. *British Tax Review* (1984a): 14-54.

Avery Jones, John F., et al. The Interpretation of Tax Treaties with Particular Reference to Article 3(2) of the OECD Model-II. *British Tax Review* (1984b): 90-108.

Avery Jones, John F., et al. Credit and Exemption under Tax Treaties in Cases of Differing Income Characterization. *European Taxation* (1996): 118-146.

Avery Jones, John F., et al. Whether the Definition of Dividend Limited to the Dividend Article Applies to the Double Taxation Relief Article Granting Underlying Credit. *Bulletin for International Fiscal Documentation* (1999): 103-108.

Avery Jones, John F., et al. Characterization of Other States' Partnerships for Income Tax. *Bulletin for International Fiscal Documentation* (2002): 288-320.

Avery Jones, John F., et al. The Definitions of Dividends and Interest in the OECD Model: Something Lost in Translation? *World Tax Journal* (2009): 5-45. The same article has been published in *the British Tax Review* 4/2005 (2009).

Avi-Yonah, Reuven S. & Linda Z. Swartz. US International Tax Treatment of Financial Derivatives. *Tax Notes International* (1997): 787-800.

Bachmann, Birgit. Prohibitions of Discrimination: EC-Treaty Rules and Direct Taxation in Germany. *EC Tax Review* (1995): 237-245.
Baranowski, Karl-Heinz. *Besteuerung von Auslandsbeziehungen*, 2. Völlig überarbeitete und erweiterte Auflage, Verlag Neue Wirtschafts-Briefe (1996).
Barnefeld, Jesper. *Taxation of Cross-Border Partnerships*. IBFD (2005).
Bärsch, Sven-Erik. *Taxation of Hybrid Financial Instruments and the Remuneration Derived Therefrom in an International and Cross-border Context: Issues and Options for Reform*. Springer (2012).
Becker, Helmut. Once Again: Thin Capitalization and Treaty Overriding. *Intertax* (1990): 52.
Becker, Helmut & Otmar Thömmes. Treaty Shopping and EC Law Critical Notes to Article 28 of the New German – US Double Taxation Convention. *European Taxation* (1991): 173-176.
Becker, Helmut & Felix Würm. Double-taxation Conventions and the Conflict Between International Agreements and Subsequent Domestic Laws. *Intertax* (1988): 257-263.
Bellingwout, Jaap. Amurta: A Tribute to (the Late) Advocate General Geelhoed. *European Taxation* (2008): 124-132.
Benson, David M. & Matthew M. McKenna. Deductibility of Interests and Other Financing Charges in Computing Income. *Bulletin for International Fiscal Documentation* (1994a): 310-314.
Benson, David M. & Matthew M. McKenna. National Report of the United States, Deductibility of Interests and Other Financing Charges in Computing Income. *Cahiers de droit fiscal international*, LXXIXa. Kluwer (1994b): 465-474.
Bergström, Sture. *Skatter och civilrätt. En studie över användningen av civilrättsliga termer i skaterättsliga sammanhang*. Liber Förlag (1978).
Bergström, Sture. Rättsliga metoder att förhindra skatteflykt. Lagtolkningsmetoder och en allmän generalklausul mot skatteflykt. *Skattenytt* (1992): 597-601.
Bergkvist, Sven-Bezzina, et al. The 2005 Leiden Forum on Recent and Pending Direct Taxation Cases Before the European Court of Justice. *Intertax* (2006): 199-226.
Bezzina, Juanita, et al. The 2005 Leiden Forum on Recent and Pending Direct Taxation Cases Before the European Court of Justice. *Intertax* (2006): 199-226.
Bieber, Thomas, et al. Taxation of Cross-Border Portfolio Dividends in Austria: The Austrian Supreme Administrative Court Interprets EC Law. *European Taxation* (2008): 583-589.
Bippus, Birgit Elsa. Dividenden-Stripping, Strategien zur Vermeidung der Besteuerung inländischer Dividendenerträge ausländischer Anteilseigner. *Recht der internationalen Wirtschaft* (1994): 945-960.
Birk, Dieter (ed.). *Handbuch des Europäischen Steuer- und Abgabenrechts*. Verlag Neue Wirtschafts-Briefe (1995).
Blumenberg, Jens. Transfer Pricing in Germany. *Tax Notes International* (1997): 1803-1808.
Bogdan, Michael. *Komparativ rätt*. Whit a Summary in English Comparative Law. Juridiska Föreningen i Lund (1978).

Bouzoraa, Dali & Pierre-Jean Douvier. Compatibility of CFC Rules with Tax Treaties: Lower Courts Reach Conflicting Conclusions. *European Taxation* (1997): 103–106.
Brandt, Peter. Inverkan av skatteavtal och EG-rätten på under-kapitaliseringsfrågor. *Skattenytt* (1997): 254–273.
Brocker, Stefan & Jan Grapatin. *Ansvarsgenombrott*. Norstedts Juridik AB (1996).
Brokelind, Cécile. Konsekvenserna av felaktigt införlivande av ett EG-directiv: medlemsstaternas ansvar?. *Svensk skattetidning* (1996): 900–903.
Brokelind, Cécile. Ten years of application of the Parent-Subsidiary Directive. *EC Tax Review* (2003): 158–167.
Brokelind, Cécilé. Swedish Supreme Administrative Court Rejects Reference to ECJ Regarding Application of EC Parent-Subsidiary Directive. *European Taxation* (2005): 323–330.
Brokelind, Cécile. The ECJ Bouanich Case: The Capital Gains and Dividend Classification of Share Buy-Backs in Swedish Tax Law. *European Taxation* (2006): 268–274.
Brosens, Linda. Thin Capitalization Rules and EU Law. *EC Tax Review* (2004): 188–213.
Brown, Patricia. The Debt-equity Conundrum. *Cahiers de droit fiscal international*, volume 97b, Sdu/IFA (2012):17–43.
Bullenm Andreas. *Arm's Length Transaction Structures: Recognising and Restructuring Controlled Transactions in Transfer Pricing*, Faculty of Law, University of Oslo (2010).
Bundgaard, Jakob. Classification and Treatment of Hybrid Financial Instruments and Income Derived Therefrom under EU Corporate Tax Directives – Part 1. *European Taxation* (2010): 442–456.
Bundgaard, Jakob. Classification and Treatment of Hybrid Financial Instruments and Income Derived Therefrom under EU Corporate Tax Directives – Part 2. *European Taxation* (2010a): 490–500.
Bundgaard, Jakob –Dyppel, Katja Joo. Profit-Participating Loans in International Tax Law. *Intertax* (2010): 643–662.
Bureau Francis Lefebvre, Loyens & Volkmaars, Oppenhoff & Rädler. *Hybrid Financing*. IBFD Publications BV and Editions Francis Lefebvre (1996).
Bühler, Ottmar. *Prinzipen des Internationalen Steuerrechts*. IBFD (1964).
Cadosch, Roger M., et al. The 2006 Leiden Alumni Forum on Taxation of Cross-Border Dividends in Europe and the Relation with Third Countries: The Cases Pending Before the European Court of Justice. *Intertax* (2006): 622–635.
Carlberg, A. Bassamfundsbeskattningens förenlighet med EG-rätt. *JFT* (2000): 217–234.
Carrero, José M. Caldeón. Spanish Thin Capitalisation in Light of the Non-Discrimination Principle: Its Compatibility with Double Tax treaties and EC Law. *Intertax* (1996): 282–309.
CFE. The Consequences of the Verkooijen Judgement. *European Taxation* (2002): 241–246.
Clayson, Murray. Eliminating Double Tax on Dividends. *International Tax Review* (1994): 43–45.

Cnossen, Sijbren (ed.). *Tax Coordination in the European Community*. Kluwer (1987).
Collado, Albert & Fernando Rey. New Thin Capitalization Regulations in a Comparative Framework. *European Taxation* (1993): 110–119.
Commission. *Communication from the Commission to the Council, the European Parliament and the Economic and Social Committee: Dividend Taxation of Individuals in the Internal Market*. 19.12.2003 COM (2003) 810.
Cordner, Richard. Growth of Securities Lending Depends on Regulations. *Securities Lending, the Taxation of International Stock Lending, International Tax Review* Supplement June (1992): 2–4.
Couzin, Robert. *Corporate Residence and International Taxation*. IBFD (2002).
Craig, Paul & Gráinne De Búrca. *EU Law – Text, Cases, and Materials*. 6th edn. Oxford University Press (2015).
Dahlberg, Mattias. *Svensk skatteavtalspolitik och utländska basbolag – mot bakgrund av svensk intern internationell skatterätt*. Iustus Förlag (2000).
Dahlberg, Mattias & Wiman. Bertil Genral Report, *The Taxation of Foreign Passive Income for Groups of Companies, Cahiers de droit fiscal international*, volume 98a, IFA/Sdu (2013): 17–56.
Daniels, Ton. Introduction and General Outline. In *Cross-Border Securities Lending*. Baker & McKenzie (1993): 1–15.
David, Cyrille. General Introduction, *Tax Treatment of Financial Instruments*, ed. Michielse Geerten. Kluwer (1996): 1–15.
Debatin, Helmut. Qualifikationsprobleme im Doppelbesteuerungs-recht. *Finanz-Rundschau* (1979), 493–499.
Debatin, Helmut. Zum Grundverständnis der Doppelbesteuerungsabkommen, Anmerkungen zu Fahldeutungen. *Recht der internationalen Wirtschaft* (1988), 727–729.
Denys, Lieven A. The ECJ Case Law on Cross Border Dividends Revisited. *European Taxation* (2007): 221–237.
Déry, Jean-Marc & David A. Ward. National Report of Canada, Interpretation of Double Taxation Conventions. *Cahiers de droit fiscal international*, LXXVIIIa. Kluwer (1993): 259–293.
Diehl, Wolfram. Qualificationskonflikte im Aussensteuerrecht. *Finanz-Rundschau* 1978 (1978): 517–526.
Doernberg, Richard L. & Kees van Raad. The Legality of the Earnings-Stripping Provision under US Income Tax Treaties. *Tax Notes International* (1990): 199–206.
Doernberg, Richard L. & Kees van Raad. *The 1996 United States Model Income Tax Convention: Analysis, Commentary and Comparison*. Kluwer (1997).
Duncan, James A. General Report, *Tax Treatment of Hybrid Financial Instruments in Cross-border Transactions, Cahiers de droit fiscal international*, LXXXVa. Kluwer (2000), 21–34.
Du Toit, Charl. *Beneficial Ownership of Royalties in Bilateral Tax Treaties*. IBFD (1999).
Du Toit, Charl. The Evolution of the Term 'Beneficial Ownership' in Relation to International Taxation over the Past 45 Years. *Bulletin for International Taxation* (2010): 500–509.

Easson, A. J. *Taxation in the European Community*. The Athlone Press (1993).
Eberhartinger, Eva & Martin Six. Taxation of Cross-Border Hybrid Finance: A Legal Analysis. *Intertax* (2009): 4–18.
Eicke, Rolf. *Tax Planning with Holding Companies – Repatriation of US Profits from Europe*. Kluwer (2009).
Eicker, Klaus. Germany, *EC Corporate Tax Law*. Looseleaf, ed. Otmar-Betten Thömmes. IBFD Publications (1998a), Germany-1–Germany-98.
Eicker, Klaus. Tax Treaties and EC Law: Comment on the *Gilly* Case. *European Taxation* (1998b): 322–327.
Eilers, Stephan. Gemeinschaftsrechtliche Anwendungsrestriktion für §42 AO. *Der Betrieb* (1993): 1156–1160.
Engelen, Frans. *Interpretation of Tax Treaties under International Law*. IBFD, Online, (2004).
Engle, Howard S. & Walter T. Raineri. National Report of the United Sates, International Aspects of Thin Capitalization. *Cahiers de droit fiscal international*, LXXXIb. Kluwer (1996): 773–799.
English, Joachim. Shareholder Relief and EC Treaty Law – Supranational 'Aims and Effects'?. *Intertax* (2005): 200–214.
Escher, Felix. *Die Methoden zur Ausschaltung der Doppelbesteuerung*. Verlag Paul Haupt (1974).
Essers, P., et al. Some Fiscal Aspects of Financing Structures within a Group of Companies and Thin Capitalization Approaches in Europe, Report of the Winter Course 1994. *EC Tax Review* (1994): 167–176.
Fabozzi, Frank J., Franco Modigliani & Michael G. Ferri. *Foundations of Financial Markets and Institutions*. Prentice Hall International (1994).
Fairley, John & Mark Penny. Thin Capitalisation. *Tax Planning International Review* (1988): 8–12.
Faria, Angelo G.A. International Capital Flows, *Tax Policy Handbook*, ed. Parthasarathi Shome (1995): 220–221, Tax Policy Division Fiscal Affairs Department International Monetary Fund.
Farmer, Paul. National Anti-Abuse Clauses and Distortion of the Single Market: Comments on Prof. Dr Rädler's Article. *European Taxation* (1994): 314.
Farmer, Paul & Richard Lyal. *EC Tax Law*. Clarendon Press (1994).
Fernández, Albertina M. Dorgan Blasts Arm's Length Transfer Pricing Method. *Tax Notes International* (1996): 2081–2083.
Fibbe, G.K. The Different Translations of the Term 'Company' in the Merger Directive and the Parent-Subsidiary Directive: A Babylonian Confusion of Tongues?. *EC Tax Review* (2006): 95–102.
Fink, Eli, Eugene Ferraro & James Mann. Financial Instruments. *United States Taxation Guide. International Tax Review* (1994): 30–38.
Fink, Eli, Eugene Ferraro & James Mann. Securities Lending. *United States Taxation Guide. International Tax Review* (1994a): 51–54.
Fontana, Renata. The Uncertain Future of CFC Regimes in the Member States of the European Union – Part 1. *European Taxation* (2006a): 259–267.

Fontana, Renata. The Uncertain Future of CFC Regimes in the Member States of the European Union – Part 2. *European Taxation* (2006b): 317–334.
Fontana, Renata. Conference Report: The EU and Third Countries: Direct Taxation. 13–14 October 2006, Vienna. *Intertax* (2007): 589–597.
Fortuin, A. The Influence of European Law on Direct Taxation – Recent and Future Developments. *European Taxation* (2007): 144–148.
Franks, Julian R., John E. Broyles & Willard T. Carleton. *Corporate Finance, Concepts and Applications.* Kent Publishing Company (1985).
van Fraeyenhoven, Guy. General Report, Tax Problems of Liquidation of Corporations. *Cahiers de droit fiscal international*, LXXIIb. Kluwer (1987): 37–56.
Förster, Jutta & Anders Schollmeier. Harmonisierung der Unternehmensbesteuerung. In *Handbuch des Europäißchen Steuer- und Abgabenrechts*, edited by Dieter Birk. Verlag Neue Wirtschafts-Briefe (1995): 813–899.
Le Gall, Jean-Pierre. General Report, Subject I, International Income Tax Problems of Partnerships. *Cahiers de droit fiscal international*, LXXXa. Kluwer (1995): 655–708.
Gareis, Robert, et al. Cross-Border Securities Lending in the United States of America. *Cross-Border Securities Lending.* Baker & McKenzie (1993): 132–157.
Gassner, W., M. Lang & E. Lechner (eds). *Doppelbesteuerungsabkommen und EU-Recht.* Linde Verlag (1996).
Giuliani, Federico M. Article 10(3) of the OECD Model and Borderline Cases of Corporate Distributions. *Bulletin for International Fiscal Documentation* (2002): 11–14.
Goode, Richard. *The Corporation Income Tax.* John Wiley & Sons, Inc. (1951).
Gower, L.C.B., et al. *Gower's Principles of Modern Company Law.* 4th edn. Stevens & Sons (1979).
Groes, Gerrit. Arbitration in Bilateral tax Treaties. *Intertax* (2002): 3–27.
Grosskopf, Göran. Olovlig vinstutdelning – bolagsrättsliga och skatterättsliga synpunkter. *Skattenytt* (1993): 109–117.
Grossmann, Klaus. *Doppelt ansässige Kapitalgesellschaften im internationalen Steuerrecht im Insbesondere im Verhältnis Deutschland-USA.* C.H. Beck'sche Verlagsbuchhandlung (1995).
Guttmann, Daniel & Luc Hinnekens. The Lankhorst-Hohorst Case. The ECJ Finds German Thin Capitalization Rules Incompatible with Freedom of Establishment. *EC Tax Review* (2003): 90–97.
Gündisch, Stephan. Solving Conflicts of Qualification by Analogous Application of Tax Treaties. *Bulletin for International Fiscal Documentation* (2005): 424–431.
Gäbel, Johannes. The End of Dividend Stripping?. *International Tax Review* (1994): 15–18.
Gäverth, Leif. Beskattning av utdelning till annan än aktieägare (eller kuponginnehavare). *Skattenytt* (1996): 587–603.
Gäverth, Leif. Skatteplanering med hjälp av överkapitaliserade bolag. *Skattenytt* (1997): 234–253.
Gäverth, Leif. Skatteflykt och kapitaliseringsfrågor. *Skattenytt* (1998): 231–264.
Gäverth, Leif. *Skatteplanering och kapitaliseringsfrågor.* Uppsala universitet (1999).

Hamaekers, Hubert. Fiscal Sovereignty and Tax Harmonization in the EC. *European Taxation* (1993): 25–27.
Hannes, Berthold. *Qualificationskonflikte im Internationalen Steuer-recht.* S + W Steuer- und Wirtschaftsverlag (1992).
Hariton, David P. The Taxation of Complex Financial Instruments. *Tax Law Review* (1988): 731–788.
Harris, Peter A. *Corporate/Shareholder Income Taxation and Allocating Taxing Rights Between Countries.* A Comparison of Imputation Systems, IBFD Publications (1996).
Harris, Peter A. Working Party Twelve and Article 10 of the 1963 OECD Model. *Australian Tax Forum* (1999/2000): 1–224.
Harris, Peter A. Article 10 – Dividend, *Global Tax Treaty Commentaries*, IBFD, online (2016).
Harvey, Ronald B., Michael S. Burke & Susan K. Shapiro. Uses of Hybrid Entities in the International Arena. *Tax Notes International* (1995): 1609–1618.
Hattingh, Johann. South Africa: The Volkswagen Case and the Secondary Tax on Companies: Part 2 – The Effect on the Taxation of Dividends with Emphasis on Deemed (Constructive) Dividends. *Bulletin for International Taxation* (2009): 509–533.
HE 218/1997. *Hallituksen esitys Eduskunnalle arvopaperien lainaussopimusten ja takaisinostosopimusten verotusta koskevaksi lainsäädännöksi* (1997).
Helminen, Marjaana. *Konserniavustus askeleena kohti lisääntyvää konserniajattelua?.* Publications of the Turku School of Economics and Business Administration, Series KR-9:1992 (1992).
Helminen, Marjaana. *Vertaileva tutkimus keskeisistä ongelmista yhtiöveron hyvitysjärjestelmässä ja osinkotulojen verovapauteen perustuvassa järjestelmässä.* Publications of the Turku School of Economics and Business Administration, Series D-2:1994 (1994).
Helminen, Marjaana. *The Dividend Concept in International Tax Law – Dividend Payments Between Corporate Entities.* Kluwer (1999).
Helminen, Marjaana. Onko sijoitusrahaston voitonjako osinkoa kansainvälisessä vero-oikeudessa?. *Verotus* (1999a): 371–385.
Helminen, Marjaana. Do Distribution From Investment Funds Constitute Dividends for International Tax Law Purposes?. *Tax Notes International* (1999b): 2155–2170.
Helminen, Marjaana. Distributions From Finnish Investment Funds and the Dividend Concept of Tax Treaties. *Tax Notes International* (1999c): 1549–1551.
Helminen, Marjaana. KHO:n ratkaisu 14.6.1999 T 1600 ja suomalaisen sijoitusrahaston voitto-osuus verosopimusten osinkoartiklojen valossa. *Verotus* (1999d): 473–476.
Helminen, Marjaana. Classification of Investment Fund Distributions. *Derivatives & Financial Instruments* (2000): 135–139.
Helminen, Marjaana. Beneficial Ownership of Dividends: Relevance of the New Netherlands Dividend-Stripping Rules in Tax Treaty Situations. *European Taxation* (2002): 454–460.

Bibliography

Helminen, Marjaana. Pending Cases Filed by Finnish Courts: The Danner Case and the Lindman Case, *Direct Taxation: Recent ECJ Developments*, ed. Michael Lang. Kluwer (2003): 103–117.

Helminen, Marjaana. National Report Finland. *CFC Legislation, Domestic Provisions, Tax Treaties and EC Law*, ed. M. Lang, H-J. Aigner, H. Scheuerle & M. Stefaner. Linde Verlag (2004): 191–219.

Helminen, Marjaana. Väliyhteisölaki aiheuttaa edelleen päänvaivaa. *Verotus* (2004a): 28–38.

Helminen, Marjaana. Classification of Cross-border Payments on Hybrid Instruments. *Bulletin for International Fiscal Documentation* (2004b): 56–61.

Helminen, Marjaana. Is There a Future for CFC-Regimes in the Future in the EU?. *Intertax* (2005): 117–123.

Helminen, Marjaana. Scope and Interpretation of the Nordic Multilateral Double Taxation Convention. *Bulletin for International Fiscal Documentation* (2007): 23–38.

Helminen, Marjaana. Dividends, Interest and Royalties under the Nordic Multilateral Double Taxation Convention. *Bulletin for International Fiscal Documentation* (2007a): 49–64.

Helminen, Marjaana. Dividends under the Nordic Multilateral Double Taxation Convention. In *Memoriam Kari S. Tikka 1944–2006*. Lakimiesyhdistys (2007b): 48–63.

Helminen, Marjaana. Non-discrimination and the Nordic Multilateral Double Taxation Convention. *Bulletin for International Fiscal Documentation* (2007c): 103–108.

Helminen, Marjaana. *EU vero-oikeus – Välitön verotus*. Talentum (2008a).

Helminen, Marjaana. Onko rajat ylittävien osinkojen lähdeverotus tullut tien päähän?. *Verotus* (2008b): 397–405.

Helminen, Marjaana. The Future of the Source State Dividend Withholding Taxes in Finland and in EU. *European Taxation* (2008c): 354–360.

Helminen, Marjaana. Finland: The Aberdeen Fininvest Alpha Case, *ECJ-Recent Developments in Direct Taxation*, ed. Michael Lang, Pasquale Pistone, Josef-Staringer Such & Linde Claus. Kluwer (2008d): 79–90.

Helminen, Marjaana.The Finnish Dividend Withholding Tax System and the Principle of the Free Movement of Capital: A Never-Ending Story? *European Taxation* (2010a): 402–408.

Helminen, Marjaana. *Kansainvälinen tuloverotus*. 2nd edn. Edita (2013).

Helminen, Marjaana. *The Nordic Multilateral Tax Traty as a Model for a Multilateral EU Tax Treaty*, IBFD (2013a).

Helminen, Marjaana. The Principle of Elimination of Double Taxation under EU Law – Does it Exist?, *Principles of Law: Function, Status and Impact in EU Tax Law*, ed. Brokelind, Cécile, IBFD (2014): 391–412.

Helminen, Marjaana. *EU Tax Law – Direct Taxation*. 2015 edn. IBFD (2015).

Helminen, Marjaana. EU Law Compatibility of BEPS Action 2: Neutralising the Effects of Hybris Mismatch Arrangements, *British Tax Review* (2015a): 325–339.

Helminen, Marjaana. *Finnish International Taxation*. 2016 edn. Forum Iuris (2016).

Helminen, Marjaana. *Kansainvälinen verotus*. Talentum (2016a).

Helminen, Marjaana. The Notion of Tax and the Elimination of International Double Taxation or Double Non-taxation, *Cahiers de droit fiscal international*, vol 101, International Fiscal Association (2016b): 153-225.

Helminen, Marjaana. Article 11: Interest, *Global Tax Treaty Commentaries*, IBFD, online (2016c).

Helminen, Marjaana. Finland, *Gaars – A Key Element of Tax Systems in the Post-BEPS World*, ed. Lang, Michael, IBFD, (2016d): 247-274.

Helminen, Marjaana. *EU Tax Law – Direct Taxation*. 2016 edn. IBFD, electronic, (2016e).

Henn, Harry G. & John R. Alexander. *Laws of Corporations and Other Business Enterprises*. 3rd edn. West Publishing Co. (1983).

Herzig, Norbert. Standortsicherungsgesetz: Gesetzliche Regelung der Gesellschafter-Fremdfinanzierung in §8a KStG (Teil I). *Der Betrieb* (1994): 110-115.

Heyvaert, Werner E.C. Transfer Pricing Planning in an Integrated Europe: The 1990 Arbitration Convention. *Tax Notes International* (1997): 15, 1859-1865.

Hilling, Maria. *Free Movement and Tax Treaties in the Internal Market*. JIBS Dissertation Series No. 026, Jönköping International Business School (2005).

Hinnekens, Luc. The Application of Anti-treaty Shopping Provisions to Belgian Coordination Centers. *Intertax* (1989): 350-361.

Hinnekens, Luc. Compatibility of Bilateral Tax Treaties with European Community Law: The Rules. *EC Tax Review* (1994): 146-166.

Hinnekens, Luc. Compatibility of Bilateral Tax Treaties with European Community Law – Application of the Rules. *EC Tax Review* (1995): 202-237.

Hinnekens, Luc & Philippe Hinnekens. General Report. *Non-discrimination at the Crossroads of International Taxation.* Cahiers de droit fiscal international, 93a. Sdu Fiscale & Financiële Uitgevers (2008): 15-54.

Hinny, Pascal. General Report. *Cahiers de droit fiscal international*, 93b. Sdu Fiscale & Financiële Uitgevers (2008): 17-50.

Hintsanen, Lari & Kennet Pettersson. The Implications of the ECJ Holding the Denial of Finnish Imputation Credits in Cross-Border Situations to Be Incompatible with the EC Treaty in the Manninen Case. *European Taxation* (2005): 130-137.

Van Horne, James C. *Financial Management and Policy*. Prentice Hall International (1995).

de Hosson, Fred C. (ed.). *The Direct Investment Tax Initiatives of the European Community*. Kluwer Law and Taxation Publishers (1990).

de Hosson, Fred C. The Parent-Subsidiary Directive. *Intertax* (1990a): 414-437.

de Hosson, Fred C. & Geerten M.M. Michielse. Treaty Aspects of the 'Thin Capitalisation' Issue – A Review of the OECD Report. *Intertax* (1989): 476-484.

Hultqvist, Anders. *Legalitetsprincipen vid inkomstbeskattningen*. Juristförlaget (1995).

Huttunen, Allan. Vastuun samaistuksesta konsernissa, osakeyhtiössä ja erityisesti vakuutusosakeyhtiöiden konsernissa. *Vastuun samaistuksesta ja muita kirjoituksia*, toim. Ari Saarnilehto, Turun yliopiston oikeustuieteellisen tiedekunnan julkaisuja, B kokoomateosten sarja nro 51 (1996): 5-76.

Höhn, Ernst. General Report. The Tax Treatment of Interests in International Economic Transactions. *Cahiers de droit fiscal international*, LXVIIa. International Fiscal Association, Kluwer (1982): 123–171.

IBFD. A Comparative Study on the Thin Capitalization Rules in the Member States of the European Union and Certain Other States. *European Taxation* (2005): 367–451.

Iihi, Uwe, et al. Dividend Taxation in the European Union. Trends in Company/Shareholder Taxation: Single or Double Taxation?. *Cahiers de international*, LXXXVIIIa. Kluwer (2003): 71–96.

Ikkala, Jarmo, et al. *Verosuunnittelun käsikirja*. Kauppakaari Oy (1997).

Inland Revenue. Entity Classification. *Tax Bulletin* (1999): 627.

Inland Revenue. Entity Classification. *Tax Bulletin* (2000): 809–812.

International Fiscal Association. The Treatment of Capital Gains for Tax Purposes. The Interpretation of Double Taxation Conventions, the Treatment of Debts and Interests thereon in International Taxation. *Cahiers de droit fiscal international*, XLII. Kluwer (1960).

International Fiscal Association. *Tax Treaties and Domestic Legislation*. Proceedings of a Seminar held in Rio de Janeiro in 1989 during the 43rd Congress of International Fiscal Association, Kluwer (1991).

International Fiscal Association. Transfer Pricing in the Absence of Comparable Market Prices. *Cahiers de droit fiscal international*, LXXVIIa. Kluwer (1992).

International Fiscal Association. Interpretation of Double Taxation Conventions. *Cahiers de droit fiscal international*, LXXVIIIa. Kluwer (1993a).

International Fiscal Association. Non-discrimination Rules in International Taxation. *Cahiers de droit fiscal international*, LXXVIIIb. Kluwer (1993b).

International Fiscal Association. Deductibility of Interests and Other Financing Charges in Computing Income. *Cahiers de droit fiscal international*, LXXIXa. Kluwer (1994).

International Fiscal Association. *How Domestic Anti-avoidance Rules Affect Double Taxation Conventions*. Kluwer (1994a).

International Fiscal Association. Tax Aspects of Derivative Financial Instruments. *Cahiers de droit fiscal international*, LXXXb. Kluwer (1995).

International Fiscal Association. *International Fiscal Association Yearbook 1995*. IFA (1995a).

International Fiscal Association. International Aspects of Thin Capitalization. *Cahiers de droit fiscal international*, LXXXIb. Kluwer (1996).

International Fiscal Association. *Draft Resolution on Subject II: International Aspects of Thin Capitalization*, with a background paper, The Congress of the International Fiscal Association, Geneve, 1–6 September 1996 (1996a).

International Fiscal Association. *International Fiscal Association Yearbook 1996*, IFA (1996b).

International Fiscal Association. *The OECD Model Convention – 1998 and Beyond. The Concept of Beneficial Ownership in Tax Treaties*. Kluwer (2000).

International Fiscal Association. Tax Treatment of Hybrid Financial Instruments in Cross-border Transactions. *Cahiers de droit fiscal international*, LXXXVa. Kluwer (2000a).
International Fiscal Association. Trends in Company/Shareholder Taxation: Single or Double Taxation?. *Cahiers de droit fiscal international*, LXXXVIIIa. Kluwer (2003).
International Fiscal Association. Double Non-taxation. *Cahiers de droit fiscal international*, 89a. Sdu (2004).
International Fiscal Association. The Debt-equity Conundrum. *Cahiers de droit fiscal international*, volume 97b, Sdu (2012).
International Fiscal Association. The Taxation of Foreign Passive Income for Groups of Companies, *Cahiers de droit fiscal international*, volume 98a, IFA/Sdu (2013).
International Fiscal Association. Qualification of Taxable Entities and Treaty Protection. *Cahiers de droit fiscal international*, volume 99b, Sdu (2014).
Isomaa-Myllymäki Anita. *Konsernin sisäisen rahoituksen markkinaehtoisuus – Markkinaehtoperiaatteen soveltamisen oikeudelliset rajoitukset etuyhteysluotonannossa, Alma Talent (2016).*
Jackson, Brian. Thin Capitalisation. *European Taxation* (1990): 319–322.
Jacobs, Otto H. The Effects of Business Taxation on Shareholder Financing of Corporations – An analysis of Taxation Concepts in France, Germany and United States. *Intertax* (1989): 464–476.
Jacobs, Otto H. Steuerliche Vorteilhaftigkeit des Einsatzes von Eigen- oder Fremdkapital bei der internationalen Konzernfinanzierung. *Steuer und Wirtschaft* (1996): 26–42.
Jann, Martin. The Court of Justice of the European Communities and Its Impact on Direct Taxation. *EC Tax Review* (1996): 160.
Jiménez, Adolfo Martin. Article 12 – Royalties, *Global Tax Traty Commentaries*, IBFD, online, (2016).
Jinyan, Li & Avella, Francesco. Article 13 – Capital Gains, *Global Tax Treaty Commentaries*, IBFD online (2016).
Juusela, Janne & Risto Walden. International Fiscal Association (IFA): n 55. kongressi San Franciscossa 30.9.–5.10.2001, *Verotus* (2002): 72–76
Kanervo, Timo. Kansallinen väliyhteisölainsäädäntö, verosopimukset ja EC-lainsäädäntö, I osa. *Verotus* (2001a): 305–314.
Kanervo, Timo. Kansallinen väliyhteisölainsäädäntö, verosopimukset ja EC-lainsäädäntö, II osa. *Verotus* (2001b): 421–428.
Kanervo, Timo. Tapaus väliyhteisötulosta ratkaistu ECT:ssa. *Verotus* (2006): 542–546.
Katz, Stanley I. National Report of United States, Interpretation of Double Taxation Conventions. *Cahiers de droit fiscal international*, LXXVIIIa. Kluwer (1993), 615–660.
Kau, Randall K.C. Carving up Assets and Liabilities – Integration or Bifurcation of Financial Products. *Taxes, The Tax Magazine* (1990): 1003–1014.
Keinonen, Markku. Standardisoidut optiosopimukset ja verotus. *Verotus* (1987): 267–278.

Keinonen, Markku. Uudet rahoitusinstrumentit verotuksessa. *Verotus* (1995a): 167–180.
Keinonen, Markku. Uudet rahoitusinstrumentit verotuksessa II. *Verotus* (1995a): 237–246.
Keinonen, Markku. Arvopapereiden lainaus- ja takaisinostosopimukset: tausta, kirjanpito ja verotus. *Verots* (1998): 153–175.
Kemmeren, Eric C.C.M. The Termination of the 'Most Favoured Nation Clause' Dispute in Tax Treaty Law and the Necessity of a Euro Model Tax Convention. *EC Tax Review* (1997): 146–152.
Kemmeren, Eric C.C.M. ECJ Should Not Unbundle Integrated Tax Systems. *EC Tax Review* (2008a): 4–11.
Kemmeren, Eric C.C.M. After Repeal of Article 293 EC Treaty under the Lisbon Treaty: The EU Objective of Eliminating Double Taxation Can Be Applied More Widely. *EC Tax Review* (2008a): 156–158.
Kempler, David I. Equity Flavoured Debt Instruments: Tax Considerations of Characterisation Conversion and Modification, United States. *Tax Management International Forum* (1996): 50–56.
Killius, Jürgen. The EC Arbitration Convention, *The Direct Investment Tax Initiatives of the European Community*, ed. Fred C. de Hosson. Kluwer (1990).
Killius, Jürgen. The EC Arbitration Convention. *Intertax* (1990a): 437–446.
Kilpi, Lassi. *Pääomavähennys. Vero-oikeudellinen tutkimus pääomavähennysten suhteesta luonnollisiin vähennyksiin tulo- ja omaisuusverolaissa*. Suomalaisen lakimiesyhdistyksen julkaisuja B-sarja No. 52 (1952).
Kilpi, Lassi. *Yhteisön ja sen jäsenen kahdenkertainen verotus*. WSOY (1962).
Kilpi, Lassi. Osake- ja osuuspääomaan verrattava pääomansijoitus ja veronalainen tulo. *Lakimies* (1973): 187–209.
Kilpi, Lassi. KHO:n oikeuskäytäntöä tulo- ja omaisuusverotuksen piiristä vuonna 1982. *Defensor Legis* (1983): 28–53.
Kilpi, Lassi. Verotuslain 56 §:n soveltaminen. *Verotus* (1987): 7–17.
Kilpi, Lassi. Verosuunnittelun sudenkuopista. *Verotus* (1989): 377–390.
King, John R. Debt and Equity Financing, *Tax Policy Handbook*, ed. Shome, Parthasarathi. Tax Policy Division Fiscal Affairs Department International Monetary Fund (1995): 158–161.
de Kleer, Maurice. Towards a European Anti-Abuse Doctrine in Direct Taxation?. *Intertax* (1996): 137–144.
KM 1992:32. *Osakeyhtiölakitoimikunta 1990:n mietintö*. Valtion painatuskeskus.
Knechtle, Arnold A. *Basic Problems in International Fiscal Law*. Kluwer (1979).
Knobbe-Keuk, Brigitte. 'Qualifikationskonflikte' im internationalen Steuerrecht der Personengesellschaften. *Recht der internationalen Wirtschaft* (1991): 306–316.
Knobbe-Keuk, Brigitte. Developments in Thin Capitalization and Some Legal Obstacles to Legislation. *European Taxation* (1992): 405–408.
Knuutinen, Reijo. *Muoto ja sisältö vero-oikeudessa*. Suomalainen lakimiesyhdistys (2009).
Korge, Thomas J. Debt or Equity Financing of Foreign Investments in the United States. *Tax Notes International* (1996): 753–769.

Koskenkylä, Heikki. *Tax Reform and the Neutrality Principle: What Is It All About?*. Bank of Finland Research Department (1987).

Koski, Pauli. *Vaihtovelkakirjat*, Suomalaisen lakimiesyhdistyksen julkaisuja B-sarja N:o 159 (1972).

Kosters, Bart. The United Nations Model Tax Convention and Its Recent Developments. *Asia-Pasific Tax Bulletin* (2004): 4–11.

Krever, Richard. General Report: GAARs, *Gaars – A Key Element of Tax Systems in the Post-BEPS World*, ed. Lang, Michael, IBFD, (2016d): 1–20.

Kuivisto, Eija. Emo-tytäryhtiödirektiivin ja yritysjärjestelydirektiivin muutoksista. *Tilintarkastus* (2005): 38–45.

Kukkonen, Matti. *Osakeyhtiön myynnin verotus, Tutkimus osakeyhtiön myynnin tuloverotuksesta erityisesti harvainomisteista yhtiötä silmällä pitäen*. Lakimiesliiton kustannus (1994).

Kuortti, Hannu. Bulvaanisuhteesta. *Verotus* (1997): 164–177.

Lamers, Suke W.G. & Ton J.A. Stevens. Classification Conflicts: The Cross-Border Tax Treatment of the Profit Share of Limited Partners. *European Taxation* (2004): 155–164.

Lang, Michael. *Hybride Finanzierungen im internationalen Steuerrecht*. Wirtschaftsverlag Anton Orac (1991).

Lang, Michael. Die Bindung der Doppelbesteuerungsabkommen an die Grundfreiheiten des EU-Rechts. In *Doppelbesteuerungsabkommen und EU-Recht*, edited by Wolfgang Gassner, Michael Lang & Eduard Lechner. Linde Verlag (1996): 25–43.

Lang, Michael (ed.). *Tax Treaty Interpretation*. Kluwer (2000).

Lang, Michael. *The Application of the OECD Model Tax Convention to Partnerships – A Critical Analysis of the Report Prepared by the OECD Comity on Fiscal Affairs*. Kluwer and Linde Verlag (2000a).

Lang, Michael. CFC Legislation and Community Law. *European Taxation* (2002): 374–379.

Lang, Michael. General Report. Double Non-taxation. *Cahiers de droit fiscal international*, 89a. Sdu Fiscale & Financiële Uitgevers (2004): 73–119.

Lang, Michael. ECJ Case Law on Cross-Border Dividend Taxation – Recent Developments. *EC Tax Review* (2008): 67–77.

Lang, Michael & Mario Züger (ed.). *Settlement of Disputes in Tax Treaty Law*. Kluwer (2002).

Lang, Michael et al. (ed.). *CFC Legislation, Tax Treaties and EC Law*. Kluwer (2004).

Lang, Michael et al. (ed.) *Beneficial Ownership: Recent Trends*, IBFD, online, (2013).

Lang, Michael & Staringer, Claus. General Report, Qualification of Taxabe Entities and Treaty Protection, *Cahiers de droit fiscal international*, volume 99b, IFA/Sdu (2014): 17–82.

Langer, Marshall J. Override of Tax Treaties by Ordinary Legislation. *Bulletin for International Fiscal Documentation* (1980): 552–553.

Larking, Barry. Fokus Bank: the End of Withholding Tax as We Know It?. *EC Tax Review* (2005): 69–77.

Laule, Gerhard. Genußschein, Doppelbesteuerungsabkommen und die Praxis der deutscen Finanzgerichte. *Internationales Steuerrecht* (1997): 577–582.
Lawrence, Brian. Government Restrictions on International Corporate Finance (Thin Capitalisation). *Bulletin for International Fiscal Documentation* (1990): 118–129.
Li, Jinyan & Avella, Francesco. Article 13: Capital Gains, *Global Tax Treaty Commentaries*, IBFD, online (2016).
Liede, Hannele & Antero Joutsi. Osinkojen lähdeverotus Suomessa Eurooppa-oikeuden näkökulmasta. *Tilintarkastus* (2005): 93–97.
Liede, Hannele & Eija Kuivisto. Euroopan yhteisöjen tuomioistuimen ajankohtaista yritysverotukseen liittyvää oikeuskäytäntöä. *Tilintarkastus* (2006): 86–95.
Lindencrona, Gustaf. *Skatter och kapitalflykt. Beskattningens inverkan på det financiella kapitalets och dess ägares rörlighet över Sveriges gränser mot bakgrund av den pågående ekonomiska integrationen i Västeuropa*. Jurist- och samhällsvetareförbundets Förlag AB (1972).
Lindencrona, Gustaf. Generalrapport angående kringgående av skattelag, *Kringgående av skattelag*. Rapporter och inlägg vid Nordiska skattevetenskapliga forskningsrådets seminarium om kringgåendeproblemen I nordisk skattelagstiftning I Södertälje I oktober 1975. Nordiska skattevetenskapliga forskningsrådets skriftserie Nr 3, LiberFörlag (1976): 105–122.
Lindencrona, Gustaf. *Dubbelbeskattningsavtalsrätt*. Juristförlaget JF AB (1994).
Lodin, Sven-Olof. *Koncernbeskattningen i USA*. Nordedts förlag (1973).
Lüthi, D. Thin Capitalisation of Companies in International Tax Law. *Intertax* (1991): 446–453.
Lyons, Susan M. Officials Discuss Challenges Posed by Financial Instruments. *Tax Notes International* (1996): 1195–1197.
Maisto, Guglielmo. The EC Court's Interpretation of the Parent-Subsidiary Directive under the Denkavit Case. *Intertax* (1997): 180–189.
Maisto, Guglielmo. The 2003 Amendments to the EC Parent-Subsidiary Directive: What's Next?. *EC Tax Review* (2004): 164–181.
Maisto, Guglielmo & Carola van den Bruinhorst. Taxation of Cross-Border Dividends. *European Taxation* (1993): 286–297.
Maisto, Guglielmo & Pasquale Pistone. A European Model for Member States' Legislation on the Taxation of Controlled Foreign Subsidiaries (CFCs) – Part 1. *European Taxation* (2008): 503–513.
Maisto, Guglielmo & Pasquale Pistone. A European Model for Member States' Legislation on the Taxation of Controlled Foreign Subsidiaries (CFCs) – Part 2. *European Taxation* (2008a): 554–570.
Maisto, Guglielmo. *Taxation of Companies on Capital Gains on Shares under Domestic Law, EU Law and Tax Treaties*. IBFD (2013).
Malherbe, Jacques & Olivier Delattre. Compatibility of Limitation on Benefits Provisions with EC Law. *European Taxation* (1996): 12–20.
Malmgrén, Marianne. Tuloverosopimusten ja eurooppaoikeuden suhteesta. *Verotus* (2006): 356–366.
Malmgrén, Marianne. *Oikeushenkilön asuinvaltio verotuksessa ja yrityksen kansainvälistyminen*. Edita (2009).

Mannio, Lauri. *Korko vero-oikeudessa*. Kauppakaari (1997).

Matikkala, Timo. EY:n siirtohinnoittelun vastaoikaisut mahdollistavan verosopimuksen sisältö ja vaikutus kansainvälisen yrityksen verotukseen. *Verotus* (1992): 164-175.

Mattsson, Nils. Gränsgångare i Norden. Några synpunkter på skatteavtal och EG-rätt. *In memoriam Kari S. Tikka 1944-2006*. Suomalainen lakimiesyhdistys (2007): 221-234.

May, Gregory. Flying on Instruments: Synthetic Investment and the Avoidance of Withholding Tax. *Tax Notes International* (1996): 1625-1635.

May, Gregory. Flying on Instruments: Synthetic Investment and the Avoidance of Withholding Tax. *Derivatives Quarterly* (1997): 23-34.

McCarthy, Constance M. Thin Capitalization and Transfer Pricing. *International Transfer Pricing Journal* (1997): 232-239.

McCormick, Roger & Harriet Creamer (eds). *Hybrid Corporate Securities: International Legal Aspects*. Sweet & Maxwell (1987).

McLure, Charles E. *Must Corporate Income Be Taxed Twice?*. Studies of Government Finance, The Brookings Institution (1979).

Menck, Thomas. Unterkapitalisierung und DBA Zu §8a KStG und zum OECD-Musterabkommen. *Finanz-Rundschau* (1994): 69-76.

Metzger, Dieter. 'Pacta sunt servanda'- A Level Playing Field for International Fiscal Law. *Archiv für Scweizerisches Abgaberecht* (1996): 215-224.

Meussen, Gerald. Cadbury Schweppes: The ECJ Significantly Limits the Application of CFC Rules in the Member States. *European Taxation* (2007): 13-18.

Michielse, Geerten M.M. Treaty Aspects of Thin Capitalization. *Bulletin for International Fiscal Documentation* (1997): 565-573.

Mittelstadt, David & Robert Corrigan. Corporate Debt and Equity in the United States. *Tax Planning International Review* (1990): 3-8.

Murray, Rebecca. *Tax Avoidance*. Sweet & Maxwell (2013).

Musgrave, Peggy B. Interjurisdictional Coordination of Taxes on Capital Income, *Tax Coordination in the European Community*, ed. Cnossen, Sijbren. Kluwer (1987): 197-225.

Musgrave, Richard & Musgrave Peggy. *Public Finance in Theory and Practice*. 5th edn. McGraw-Hill (1989).

Müller-Seils, Hans-Jürgen. National report of Germany, Deductibility of Interests and Other Financing Charges in Computing Income. *Cahiers de droit fiscal international*, LXXIXa. Kluwer (1994): 185-199.

Myrsky, Matti. *Osakeyhtiön ja sen osakkeenomistajan kahdenkertaisesta verotuksesta*. Suomen lakimiesliiton kustannus Oy (1988).

Myrsky, Matti. Vero-oikeustutkimuksen vaihtoehdoista ja mahdollisuuksista. *Verotus* (1997): 529-534.

Mähönen, Jukka & Seppo Villa. Taloudellisesta etuoikeusjärjestyksestä osakeyhtiön varojen jaossa de lege ferenda. *Defensor Legis* (1996): 602-623.

Neighbour, John. Innovative Financial Instruments challenge the Global Tax System. *Tax Notes International* (1997): 931-936.

Newey, Robert. Hoechst Decision: Interest as Compensation for Discriminatory Tax Charge. *European Taxation* (2001): 287–292.

Niskakangas, Heikki. *Rojaltit ja palvelumaksut kansainvälisessä verooikeudessa.* Suomen lakimiesliiton kustannus Oy (1983).

Niskakangas, Heikki. Kansainvälisen yrityksen tuloksenohjauksen uudet tuulet. *Verotus* (1991): 33–46.

Norr, Martin. *The Taxation of Corporations and Shareholders.* Kluwer (1982).

Nykänen, Pekka. Täyttääkö ETA-alueelta saaduista osingoista suoritetun veron palauttamisesta annettu laki EY-oikeuden vaatimukset?. *Verotus* (2006a): 149–165.

Nykänen, Pekka. Rajoitetusti verovelvollisen luonnollisen henkilön saamien osinkotulojen verotus EY-oikeuden näkökulmasta. In *Oikeus- ja vakuutustiedettä*, edited by Jukka Kultalahti & Seppo Penttilä. Tampereen yliopisto, oikeustieteiden laitos (2006a): 545–574.

OECD. *Transfer Pricing and Multinational Enterprises.* Report of the OECD Committee of Fiscal Affairs. OECD (1979).

OECD. *Transfer Pricing and Multinational Enterprises. Three Taxation Issues.* OECD (1984).

OECD. *Thin Capitalisation Taxation of Entertainers, Artistes and Sportsmen.* Issues in International Taxation. OECD (1987a).

OECD. *International Tax Avoidance and Evasion, Four Related Studies.* Issues in International Taxation No. 1, OECD (1987b).

OECD. *Taxing Profits in a Global Economy – Domestic and International Issues.* OECD (1991).

OECD. *Taxation of New Financial Instruments.* OECD (1994a).

OECD. *Transfer Pricing Guidelines for Multinational Enterprises and Tax Administration.* Discussion Draft of part I. OECD (1994b).

OECD. Taxation of Global Trading of Financial Instruments: A discussion Draft, full text of the OECD's discussion draft, released on 14 February 1997, on taxation of global trading of financial instruments, prepared by the Special Session on Innovative Financial Transactions. *Tax Notes International* (1997): 597–623.

OECD. The Application of the OECD Model Tax Convention to Partnerships. *Issues in International Taxation*, No. 6, OECD (1999).

OECD. *Transfer Pricing Guidelines for Multinational Enterprises and Tax Administrations.* OECD (2010).

OECD Model. *Model Tax Convention on Income and on Capital*, condensed version 15 July 2014, OECD.

OECD. *Neutralising the Effects of Hybrid Mismatch Arrangements, Action 2 – 2015 Final Report*, OECD Publishing (2015).

OECD.*Preventing the Granting of Treaty Benefits in Inappropriate Circumstances, Action 6 - 2015 Final Report*, OECD Publishing (2015a).

OECD. *Designing Effective Controlled Foreign Company Rules, Action 3 - 2015 Final Report*, OECD Publishing (2015b).

OECD. *Aligning Transfer Pricing Outcomes with Value Creation, Actions 8-10 - 2015 Final Reports*, OECD Publishing (2015c).

OECD. *Transfer Pricing Documentation and Country-by-Country Reporting, Action 13 - 2015 Final Report*, OECD Publishing (2015d).

OECD. *Limiting Base Erosion Involving Interest Deductions and Other Financial Payments, Action 4 - 2015 Final Report*, OECD Publishing (2015e).

Oliver, J. & B. David. The OECD Model and Controlled Foreign Company Regimes. *Intertax* (1995): 556–557.

Oliver, J. & B. David. The Proposed EU Interest and Royalties Directive. *EC Tax Review* (1999): 204–206.

O'Shea, Tom. The UK's CFC Rules and the Freedom of Establishment: Cadbury Schweppes Plc and Its IFSC Subsidiaries – Tax Avoidance or Tax Mitigation?. *EC Tax Review* (2007): 13–33.

O'Shea, Tom. *EU Tax Law and Double Tax Conventions*. Avoir Fiscal Limited (2008).

Panayia, Christiana H.J.I. The Effect of Community Law on Pre-accession Tax Treaties. *EC Tax Review* (2007): 121–132.

Park, William W. & David R. Tillinghast. *Income Tax Treaty Arbitration*. International Fiscal Association (2004).

Pato, António Calisto. Cross-Border Direct Tax Issues of Investment Funds from the Perspective of European Law. *EC Tax Review* (2008): 197–220.

Peeters, Bruno & Anne Van de Vijver. ECJ Rules on Compatibility of Belgian Participation Exemption Regime with EC Parent-Subsidiary Directive. *EC Tax Review* (2009): 146–156.

Penn, Oren S. Withholding Tax Issues in Cross-Border Equity Swaps: The Dividend Problem. *Tax Notes International* (1993): 917–933.

Penttilä, Seppo. *Osakkeen arvo verotuksessa, Tutkimus arvostusongelmasta tulo- ja varallisuusverotuksessa erityisesti osakkeen arvoa silmällä pitäen*. Suomalaisen lakimiesyhdistyksen julkaisuja B-sarja N:o 201. Finnpublishers Oy (1991).

Penttilä, Seppo. Euroopan yhteisöjen tuomioistuimen ratkaisujen vaikutus Suomen tuloverotukseen. *International Fiscal Association:n kansainvälisen verotuksen päivä Uudistuva kansainvälinen verotus*. Helsinki, 13 March 1996 (1996a).

Penttilä, Seppo. Eurooppavero-oikeus Suomen tuloverotuksessa. *Verotus* (1996b): 235–246.

Penttilä, Seppo. EY-oikeus tuloverotuksessa – soveltaminen ja ongelmakohtia. *Vero-opintopäivät* (2005a): 15–33.

Penttilä, Seppo. Ajankohtaista EC-tuomioistuimen oikeuskäytännöstä. *Keskuskauppakamarin suuri veropäivä* (2005b): 1–26.

Petruzzi Raffaele. *Transfer Pricing Aspects of Intra-Group Financing*, Kluwer (2016).

Pieper, Stefan Ulrich. Das Gemeinschaftsrecht. *Handbuch des Europäisschen Steuer- und Abgabenrechts*, edited by Dieter Birk. Verlag Neue Wirtschafts-Briefe (1995): 73–91.

Pijl, Hans. Interest from Hybrid Debts in Tax Treatie, *Bulletin for International Taxation* (2011): 482–502.

Pike, Richard & Bill Neale. *Corporate Finance and Investment Decisions and Strategies*. Prentice Hall (1993).

Piltz, Detlev. Qualificationskonflikte in internationalen Steuerrecht unter besonderer Berücksichtigung von Personengesellschaften. In *Besteuerung internationaler Konzerne*, edited by Fischer, Lutz. Verlag Dr Otto Schmidt KG (1993): 21-47.

Piltz, Detlev J. Besteuerung umqualifizierten Zinsen im Empfängerstaat. In *Unternehmensfinanzierung im Internationalen Steuerrecht*, edited by Detlev J. Pilz & Harald Schaumburg. Verlag Dr Otto Schmidt KG (1995a): 116-124.

Piltz, Detlev J. Hybride Finanzierungen in Doppelbesteuerungsabkommen. In *Unternehmensfinanzierung im Internationalen Steuerrecht*, edited by Detlev J. Pilz & Harald Schaumburg. Verlag Dr Otto Schmidt KG (1995b): 125-144.

Piltz, Detlev J. General Report. International aspects of Thin Capitalization. *Cahiers de droit fiscal internationa*, LXXXIb. Kluwer (1996): 83-139.

Pires, Manuel. *International Juridical Double Taxation of Income*. Kluwer (1989).

Pistone, Pasquale. *The Impact of Community Law on Tax Treaties*. Kluwer (2002).

Pistone, Pasquale. Towards European International Tax Law. *EC Tax Review* (2005): 4-9.

Pistone, Pasquale. The Impact of European Law on the Relations with Third Countries in the Field of Direct Taxation. *Intertax* (2006): 234-244.

Pistone, Pasquale. Tax Treaties and the Internal Market in the New European Scenario. *Intertax* (2007): 75-81.

Pistone, Pasquale. Outbound Investments and Interest Deduction: An Era of Fat Cap in European International Tax Law?, *Common Consolidated Corporate Tax Base*, ed. Michael Lang, Pasquale Pistone, Josef Schuch & Claus Staringer. Linde (2008): 847-864.

Pizzoni, Barbara Emma. Conflicts of Qualification of Share Buy-Backs. *Intertax* (2006): 10-25.

Plambeck, Charles T., David H. Rosenbloom & Diane M. Ring. General Report, Subject II. Tax Aspects of Derivative Financial Instruments. *Cahiers de droit fiscal international*, LXXXb. Kluwer (1995): 653-690.

Portner, Rosemarie. National Report of Germany, Subject II. Tax Aspects of Derivative Financial Instruments. *Cahiers de droit fiscal international*, LXXXb. Kluwer (1995): 229-249.

Portner, Rosmarie. Verainbarkeit des §8 a KStG mit den Doppelbesteuerungsabkommen (Teil I). *Internationales Steuerrecht* (1996a): 23-30.

Portner, Rosemarie. Thin Capitalization and Tax Treaties: Unlimited Right to Tax Dividends and Interests at Source?. *European Taxation* (1996b): 267-269.

Portner, Rosemarie. Doppelbesteuerungsabkommen – Uneingeschränktes Quellenbesteuerungsrecht bei Abzugsfähigkeit von Vergütungen auf gewinnabhängige Finanzierungsinstrumente. *Internationales Steuerrecht* (1996b): 409-411.

Portner, Rosemarie. Vereinbarkeit des §8a KStG mit den Doppelbesteuerungsabkommen (Teil II). *Internationales Steuerrecht* (1996c): 66-70.

von Poser, Arwed and Gross-Naedlitz. *Der Qualifikationskonflikt bei Doppelbesteuerungsabkommen*. Universität München (1972).

Prinz, Ulrich. Ausgewählte Problemfälle zu §8a KStG aus der Beratungspraxis. In *Gesellschafterfremdfinanzierung und Beteiligung an ausländischen Gesellschaften im Körperschaftsteuerrecht*, edited by Nobert Herzig. Verlag Dr Otto Schmidt (1995): 41–106.

Pöllath, Reinhard. National Report of Germany, Interpretation of Double Taxation Conventions. *Cahiers de droit fiscal international*, LXXVIIIa. Kluwer (1993): 327–348.

van Raad, C. Interpretation and Application of Tax Treaties by Tax Courts. *European Taxation* (1996): 3–7.

van Raad, Kees. *Nondiscrimination in International Tax Law*. Kluwer (1986).

van Raad, Kees. General Report, Recognition of Foreign Enterprises as Taxable Entities. *Cahiers de droit fiscal international*, LXXIIIa. Kluwer (1988): 19–66.

Raby, Nick. National Implementation of the Parent-Subsidiary Directive: Some Problems and Opportunities Identified. *EC Tax Review* (1992): 216–223.

Raedel, John R. & Mark H. French. Going International – Initial Tax Considerations in Establishing Partnering Arrangements: An Overview. *Tax Notes International* (1995): 1591–1608.

Rainer, A., et al. ECJ Restricts Scope of CFC Legislation. *Intertax* (2006): 636–638.

Raineri, Walter T. & Howard S. Engle. Thin Capitalization Issues in the United States. *Tax Notes International* (1996): 1715–1732.

Rapakko, Annamaria. *Base Company Taxation*. Kluwer (1989).

Reimer, Ekkehart & Rust, Alexander. *Klaus Vogel on Double Taxation Conventions*, fourth edition, volume 1, Kluwer (2015).

Reimer, Ekkehart & Rust, Alexander. *Klaus Vogel on Double Taxation Conventions*, fourth edition, volume 2, Kluwer (2015a).

Reinhold, Richard L. Tax Issues in Equity Swap Transactions. *Tax Notes* (1992): 1185–1203.

Resch, Richard. Tax Treatment of US S-Corporations Under the Germany-US Tax Treaty. *European Taxation* (2009): 122–128.

Richman, Peggy Brewer. *Taxation of Foreign Investment Income*. The Johns Hopkins Press (1963).

Robertson, Pau & Daryl V. Burckel. When Is Debt Synonymous 2ith Equity? Recent Developments in the Classification of Hybrid Securities. *Taxes, The Tax Magazine* (1988): 784–790.

Rodhe, Knut. Moderbolags ansvar för dotterbolags skulder. *Balans* (1984): 14–17.

Rodhe, Knut. Moderbolags ansvar för dotterbolags skulder. In *Festskrift till Jan Hellner*, edited by Pa Norstedt & Söners Förlag. Malmö (1984a): 481–499.

Rohatgi, Roy. *Basic International Taxation*. Kluwer (2002).

Rohatgi, Roy. *Basic International Taxation, Volume 1: Principles*. 2nd edn. BNA International (2005).

Rohatgi, Roy. *Basic International Taxation, Volume 2: Practice*. 2nd edn. BNA International (2007).

Ronfeld, T. CFC Rules Go Up in Smoke – With Retroactive Effect. *Intertax* (2007): 45–48.

Rosenberg, Tuure. Hallinnasta ja bulvaanisuhteesta verotuksessa. *Verotus* (1980): 175-188.
Rosenberg, Tuure. Osakeyhtiön jako-osan in natura arvostuksesta ja verotuksesta. *Lakimies* (1985): 660-672.
RSV 1996:1 RSV Rapport 1996:1. *Redovisning och beskattning av financiella instrument inom företagssektorn.* Riksskatteverket (1996).
Ruding Report. *Report of the Committee of Independent Experts on Company Taxation.* Commission of the European Communities, Office for Official Publications of the European Communities (1992).
de Ruiter, Marlies. Supplementary Dispute Resolution. *European Taxation* (2008): 493-499.
Russo, Raffaelle. Partnerships and Other Hybrid Entities and the EC Corporate Direct Tax Directives. *European Taxation* (2006): 478-486.
Rust, Alexander. The New Approach to Qualification Conflicts Has Its Limits. *Bulletin for International fiscal Documentation* (2003): 45-50.
Rust, Alexander. CFC Legislation and EC Law. *Intertax* (2008): 492-501.
Ryynänen, Olli. *Förtäckt dividend I beskattningen.* Skrifter utgivna vid Svenska handelshögskolan Nr 64 (1996).
Ryynänen, Olli. Förtäckt dividend i beskattningen. *Tidskrift utgiven av juridiska föreningen i Finland* (1996a): 351-359.
Ryynänen, Olli. Skattesynpunkter på internationella företagsomstruktureringar. *Tidskrift utgiven av juridiska föreningen i Finland* (1996b): 463-491.
Ryynänen, Olli. Commentary on the Implementation of the EC Direct Tax Measures In Finland. In *EC Corporate Tax Law.* Looseleaf, edited by Otmar-Betten Thömmes. Rijkele, IBFD Publications (1997).
Ryynänen, Olli. The Concept of a Beneficial Owner in the Application of Finnish Tax Treaties. *Scandinavian Studies in Law*, ed. Peter Wahlgren, volume 44 Tax Law. Stockholm Institute for Scandinavian Law (2003): 345-366.
Rädler, Albert J. Do National Anti-Abuse Clauses Distort the Internal Market?. *European Taxation* (1994): 311-313.
Rädler, Albert J., Martin Lauster & Jens Blumenberg. Tax Abuse and EC Law. *EC Tax Review* (1997): 86-101.
Saarikivi, Maj-Lis. *Ulkomailta saatujen tytäryhtiöosinkijen verotus.* Helsingin kauppakorkeakoulun julkaisuja B-146 (1994).
Sacchetto, Claudio & Marco Barassi (ed.). *Introduction to Comparative Tax Law.* Rubbettino (2008).
Sainio, Olli J. *Verosopimusten vaikutus elinkeinotulon verotukseen.* Suomen lakimiesliiton kustannus Oy (1976).
Sandler, Daniel. *Pushing the Boundaries: The Interaction Between Tax Treaties and Controlled Foreign Company Legislation.* The Institute of Taxation (1994).
Sandström, K.G.A. *Svenska dubbelbeskattningsavtal i vad de avse skatt på inkomst eller förmögenhet.* Norstedts (1949).
Sandström, K.G.A. *Beskattningen vid aktieutdelning samt utdelning från ekonomisk förening, Inkomstbeskattning av det utdelande företaget samt av utdelningsmottagare.* Norstedts (1962).

Sasseville, Jaques & Vann, Richard J. Article 7: Business Profis, *Global Tax Treaty Commentaries*, IBFD, online (2016).
Sato, Mitsuo & Richard Bird. International Aspects of Taxation of Corporations and Shareholders. *International Monetary Fund Staff Papers* (1975): 384–455.
Saunders, Roy. Transfer Pricing and the Multinational Enterprise. *European Taxation* (1989): 251–262.
Schaffner, Jean. The OECD Report on the Application of Tax Treaties to Partnerships. *Bulletin for International Fiscal Documentation* (2000): 218–226.
Schauhoff, Stephan. Tax Planning under Germany's New 'Thin Capitalization' Rules. *Intertax* (1993): 466–473.
Schaumburg, Harald. *Internationales Steuerrecht*, 2. Völlig überarbeitete und erweiterte Auflage. Verlag Dr Otto Schmidt (1998).
Schelpe, Dirk. The Arbitration Convention: Its Origin, Its Opportunities and Its Weaknesses. *EC Tax Review* (1995): 68–77.
Schenk, Deborah H. Taxation of Equity Derivatives: A Partial Integration Proposal. *Tax Law Review* (1995): 571–641.
Scherer, Thomas B. *Doppelbesteuerung und Europäisches Gemeinschaftsrecht*. Verlag C.H. Beck (1995).
Schnitger, Arne. German CFC Legislation Pending Before the European Court of Justice – Abuse of the Law and Revival of the Most-Favoured-Nation-Clause?. *EC Tax Review* (2006): 151–160.
Schlütter, Egon. Personengesellschaft oder Körperschaft? – Aktuelle Qualificationsfragen. In *Grundfragen des Internationalen Steuerrechts*, edited by Klaus Vogel. Verlag Dr Otto Schmidt KG (1985): 215–234.
af Schultén, Gerhard. Moderbolags ansvar för dotterbolags förpliktelser (ansvarsgenombrott). *Det 30. nordiske juristmötet, Oslo 15.–17. august 1984* (1984).
Schusch, Josef. 'Most Favoured Nation Clause' in Tax Treaty Law. *EC Tax Review* (1996): 161–165.
Schwarz, Hubertus & Justus Fischer-Zernin. Deutsches 'Treaty Overriding' im Entwurf zum Steueränderungsgesetz 1992. *Recht der internationalen Wirtschaft* (1992): 49–53.
Schön, Wolfgang. The Distinct Equity of the Debt-Equity Distinction, *Bulletin for International Taxation* (2012): 490–502.
Schönfeld, Jens. The Cadbury Schweppes Case: Are the Days of the United Kingdom's CFC Legislation Numbered?. *European Taxation* (2004): 441–452.
Schönfeld, J. & B. Lieber. Swedish CFC Rules under Scrutiny of EC Law: Harmful Tax Competition and the Free Movement of Capital in Relation to Third Countries. *Intertax* (2006): 96–100.
Selig, Matthias E. Characterisation of Foreign Entities for Tax Purposes, thesis submitted for the degree of Doctor of Juridical Science at Deaking University Melbourne (Australia) (2003).
Shannon, Harry A. United States Income Tax Treaties: Reference to Domestic Law for the Meaning of Undefined Terms. *Intertax* (1989): 453–463.
Sheppard, Lee A. Derivative Financial Products, To Withhold or Not to Withhold on Equity Swaps?. *Tax Notes International* (1992): 119–121.

Sheppard, Lee A. The Debt/Equity Distinction Shall Rise Again. *Tax Notes International* (1998): 143–146.
Shome, Parthasarathi (ed.). *Tax Policy Handbook*. Tax Policy Division Fiscal Affairs Depatment International Monetary Fund (1995): 3–21.
Sieker, Klaus. Thin Capitalization and Transfer Pricing. *International Transfer Pricing Journal* (1997): 214–222.
Sivonen, Jaakko. Väliyhteisölainsäädännön EC-oikeuden mukaisuus Euroopan yhteisöjen tuomioistuimen punnittavana. *Tilintarkastus* (2005): 76–81.
Six, Martin. *Hybride Finanzierung im Internationalen Steuerrecht am Beispiel von Genussrechten*. Linde (2007).
Sjöholm, Markus. Treaty shopping – en utmaning för dubbelbeskattningsavtalen. *Tidskrift utgiven av juridiska föreningen i Finland* (1996): 360–389.
Skaar, Arvid A. *Permanent Establishment Erosion of a Tax Treaty Principle*. Series of International Taxation. Kluwer (1991).
Snel, Freek P.J. & Lucas C. Mas. The Classification of Partnerships for Tax Purposes: A Comparative Analysis. *European Taxation* (2003): 367–377.
Solway, Richard J. & Paul J.R. Bothamley. Treasury Centers, Hybrid Instruments, and Foreign Currency Strategies. *Tax Notes International* (1995): 1679–1688.
Sommerhalder, Ruud A. Approaches to Thin Capitalization. *European Taxation* (1996): 82–95.
Stobbe, Ludwig. Qualificationsprobleme und -konflicte bei der internationalen Einkommenbesteuerung. *Deutsche Steuerzeitung* (1989): 241–245.
Stohlmeier, Thomas. German Limited Liability Company – Unlimited Liability of Parent Company?. *International Business Lawyer* (1993): 135–137.
Strand, Jeff. Commentary Taxing New Financial Products in a Second-Best World: Bifurcation and Integration. *Tax Law Review* (1995): 545–569.
Ståhl, Kristina. *Aktiebeskattning och fria kapitalrörelser*. Iustus Förlag (1996a).
Ståhl, Kristina. Sweden: New Act on the Effects of Tax Treaty Provisions on Domestic Law. *Intertax* (1996a): 434–435.
Ståhl, Kristina. Dividend Taxation in a Free Capital Market. *EC Tax Review* (1997): 227–236.
Ståhl, Kristina, Österman, Roger Persson, Hilling, Maria and Öberg Jesper. *EU Skatterätt*. 3nd edn. Iustus Förlag (2011).
Sundgren, Peter. Förhållandet mellan dubbelbeskattningsavtal och intern skatterätt. *Svensk skattetidning* (1992): 284–295.
Suurnäkki, Matti. *Suomesta ulkomaille maksettavien tytäryhtiöosinkojen verotus*. Helsingin kauppakorkeakoulun julkaisuja B-121 (1992).
Sörensen, Peter Brich. *Issues in the Theory of International Tax Coordination*. Bank of Finland (1990).
Tax Treaty Interpretation. The International Tax Treaties Service, edited by Michael Edwardes-Ker. In-Depth Publishing, last update December 1997 (1997).
Teixeira, Gloria. Thin Capitalization in the Portuguese Tax System. *Intertax* (1996): 472–479.
Taixeira, Renata R. Tax Treaty Consequences of Secondary Transfer Pricing Adjustments. *Intertax* (2009): 449–472.

Tenore, Mario. The Scope for 'Consistent Interpretation' in the Area of Dividend Taxation. *Legal Remedies in European Tax Law*, ed P. Pistone. IBFD (2009): 27-44.
Tenore, Mario. Taxation of Dividends: A Comparison of Selected Issues Ynder Article 10 OECD MC and the Parent-Subsidiary Directive. *Intertax* (2010): 222-238.
Tenore, Mario. Taxation of Cross-Border Dividends in the European Union from Past to Future, *EC Tax Review* (2010a): 74-84.
Terra, Ben J. M. & Peter J. Wattel. *European Tax Law*. 6th edn. Kluwer (2012).
Theisen, Manuel René & Martin Wenz. Federal Republic of Germany, *Tax Treatment of Financial Instruments*, ed. Michielse Geerten. Kluwer (1996): 81-229.
Thuronyi, Victor. *Comparative Tax Law*. Kluwer (2003).
Thömmes, Otmar. The European Dimension in International Tax Law, *The Direct Investment Tax Initiatives of the European Community*, ed. Fred C. de Hosson. Kluwer (1990): 97-117.
Thömmes, Otmar. Commentary on the Parent/Subsidiaries Directive. *EC Corporate Tax Law*. Commentary to the EC Direct Tax Measures and Member States Implementation, Chapter 6, ed. Otmar-Betten Thömmes, Rijkele, looseleaf, International Bureau of Fiscal Documentation Publications (1992).
Tikka, Kari S. *Veron minimoinnista*. Tutkimus tulo- tai omaisuusverosta vapautumisen tarkoituksesssa tehdysistä toimista lainsoveltamisongelmana erityisesti silmällä pitäen verotuslain 56 §:ää, Suomalaisen lakimiesyhdistyksen julkaisuja B-sarja N:o 165, Förlagsbolaget Judex Kustannusyhtiö (1972).
Tikka, Kari S. Oikeustieteen tehtävistä verotutkimuksessa. *Lakimies* (1983): 1079-1093.
Tikka, Kari S. Yhtiöveron hyvitysjärjestelmä III. *Verotus* (1989): 201-210.
Tikka, Kari S. *Veropolitiikka*. Lakimiesliiton kustannus (1990).
Tikka, Kari S. Om kringgåendeproblemet och skatteflyktsklausulen i den finska inkomstbeskattningen. *Skattenytt* (1992): 583-590.
Tobin, James J. & William R. Seto. Hybrid Entities. *Bulletin for International Fiscal Documentation* (1994): 315-320.
Toivanen, Heikki. Osakeyhtiön johtajan ja tilintarkastajan vastuu. *Lakimies* (1995): 261-291.
Tumpel, Michael. Die Bedeutung der abkommensrechtlichen Ansässgkeit für die Mutter-Tochter-Richtlinie und die Fusionsrichtlinie. In *Doppelbesteuerungsabkommen und EU-Recht*, edited by Wolfgang Gassner, Michael Lang & Eduard Lechner. Linde Verlag (1996): 181-199.
Turner, G. The Legitimacy of CFC Legislation within the Community. *EC Tax Journal* (2007): 23-47.
UN 2003. *Manual for Negotiation of Bilateral Tax Treaties Between Developed and Developing Countries* (2003).
UN Model. *United Nations Model Double Taxation Convention Between Developed and Developing Countries*. UN (2011).
United Nations. *Contributions to International Co-operation in Tax Matters*. United Nations Department of International Economic and Social Affairs, United Nations Publications (1988).

Van Unnik, Dirk & Maarten Boudesteijn. The New US – Dutch Tax Treaty and the Treaty of Rome. *EC Tax Review* (1993): 106–115.
US Model. *United States Model Income Tax Convention of February 17, 2016.*
Utz, Stephen G. *Tax Policy: An Introduction and Survey of the Principal Debates.* West Publishing Co. (1993).
Van den Hurk, H. Is the Ability of the Member States to Conclude Tax Treaties Chained Up?. *EC Tax Review* (2004): 17–30.
Vanistendael, Frans. The Implementation of the Parent/Subsidiary Directive in the EC-Comments on Some Unresolved Questions. *Tax Notes International* (1992): 599–619.
Vanistendael, Frans. Impact of European Tax Law on Tax Treaties with Third Countries. *EC Tax Review* (1999): 163–170.
Vanistendael, Frans. Is Tax Avoidance the Same Thung under the OECD Base Erosion and Profit Shifting Action Plan, National Tax Law and EU Law, *Bulletin for International Taxation* (2016): 163–172.
Van Sprundel, D.E. An Analysis of the Netherlands Dividend Withholding Tax on Shares – No Need to Abolish This Tax Yet?. *European Taxation* (2008): 607–618.
Vann, Richard J. General Report, Trends in Company/Shareholder Taxation: Single or Double Taxation?. *Cahiers de droit fiscal international*, LXXXVIIIa. Kluwer (2003), 21–70.
Vann, Richard J. *Global Tax Treaty Commentaries*, IBFD, online (2016).
Vapaavuori, Ahti. *Suomeen suuntautuvien portfoliosijoitusten verokohtelu.* Vammalan kirjapaino Oy (1991).
Vapaavuori, Ahti. National Report of Finland, International Aspects of Thin Capitalization. *Cahiers de droit fiscal international*, LXXXIb. Kluwer (1996): 411–418.
Vapaavuori, Ahti. IFA:n 50. Kongressi Genevessä 1.-6.9.1996: Kiinteän toimipaikan tulon ja varallisuuden määrittämisen periaatteet ja niiden soveltaminen ra hoitusinstituutioiden verotuksessa sekä kainsainvälisiä näkökohtia alikapitalisoinnista. *Verotus* (1996a): 525–537.
Vapaavuori, Ahti. Trends in Finnish International Taxation, *International Market Change and the Law*, ed. Jukka Mähönen. Publications of Turku Law School (1996b).
Vapaavuori, Ahti. Eurooppavero-oikeuden vaikutuksesta ulkomaisten väliyhteisöjen verotukseen. *Verotus* (1998): 47–58.
Vapaavuori, Ahti. Eurooppavero-oikeuden vaikutuksista kansainvälisen kahdenkertaisen verotuksen lieventämisen alalla. *Verotus* (2001): 460–471.
Vapaavuori, Ahti. Väliyhteisölainsäädännön soveltamisesta verosopimus-tilanteessa. *Verotus* (2002): 360–371.
Vapaavuori, Ahti. *Eurooppaoikeus ja kansainvälinen verotus*, Talentum (2003).
Verdoner, Louan –Offermanns, René – Huibregtse, Steef. A Cross-Country Perspective on Beneficial Ownership – Part 1, *European Taxation* (2010): 419–429.
Vesanen, Tauno. *Arvopaperiverotuksesta.* Lakimiesliiton kustannus (1981).
Vetter, Tobias. Zum Begriff des 'Qualifikationskonflikts' im DBA Deutschland-USA. *Internationales Steuerrecht* (1997): 649–652.

Bibliography

Viherkenttä, Timo. *Tax Incentives in Developing Countries and International Taxation.* Kluwer (1991).
Viitala, Tomi. *Taxation of Investment Funds in the European Union.* IBFD (2005).
Villa, Seppo. Vakautettu laina vai pääomalaina. *Defensor Legis* (1994): 65–81.
Villa, Seppo. Äänioikeudeltaan rajoitettu osake de lege ferenda. *Defensor Legis* (1994a): 328–340.
Villa, Seppo. Voitto-osuuslainasta. *Defensor Legis* (1995): 233–242.
Villa, Seppo. *Pääomalaina.* Lakimiesliiton Kustannus (1997).
Vinther, Nikolaij & Erik Werlauff. The Need for Fresh Thinking About Tax Rules on Thin Capitalization: The Consequences of the Judgement of the ECJ in Lankhorst-Hohors. *EC Tax Review* (2003): 97–106.
VM 1994:13 *Kansainvälisen verotuksen uudistamistyöryhmän väliraportti*, Valtiovarainministeriön työryhmämuistio 1994:13. Valtiovarainministeriö vero-osasto.
VM 1995:10 *Kansainvälisen verotuksen uudistamistyöryhmän muistio*, Valtiovarainministeriön työryhmämuistioita 1995:10. Valtiovarainministeriö vero-osasto.
Vogel, Klaus. Doppelbesteuerungsabkommen und ihre Auslegung (I). *Steuer und Wirtschaft* (1982a): 111–124.
Vogel, Klaus. Doppelbesteuerungsabkommen und ihre Auslegung (II). *Steuer und Wirtschaft* (1982b): 286–301.
Vogel, Klaus. Conflicts of Qualification: The Discussion is not Finished. *Bulletin for International Fiscal Documentation* (2003): 41–44.
Vogel, K., et al. *Klaus Vogel on Double Taxation Conventions – A Commentary to the OECD, UN and US Model Conventions for the Avoidance of Double Taxation of Income and Capital With Particular Reference to German Treaty Practice.* 3rd edn. Translation of Klaus Vogel, Doppelbesteuerungsabkommen, 1996, Kluwer (1997).
Vogel, Kalaus & Rainer Prokisch. General Report. Interpretation of Double Taxation Conventions. *Cahiers de droit fiscal international*, LXXVIIIa. Kluwer (1993): 55–85.
Vogel, Klaus, Daniel Gutmann & Ana Paula Dourado. Tax Treaties Between Member States and Third States: 'Reciprocity' in Bilateral Tax Treaties and Non-discrimination in EC Law. *EC Tax Review* (2006): 83–94.
Vogel, Klaus & Morris Lehner. *DBA Doppelbesteuerungsabkommen.* Kommentar, 5., völlig neubearbeitete Auflage, C. H. Beck (2008).
Voipio, Jaakko. *Verotuksen kiertämisestä. Luovutustoimien vero-oikeudellisista vaikutuksista erityisesti silmällä pitäen näennäisluovutuksia sekä verovelvollisen yrityksiä määrätä oikeusvaikutusten syntymisestä.* WSOY (1968).
Voipio, Jaakko. *Peitelty voitonsiirto ja kunnallisverotus.* Suomen kunnallisliitto (1971).
Wahlroos, Heikki & Eija Kuivisto. Euroopan yhteisöjen oikeus asettaa muutospaineita lähdeverotukseen. *Tilintarkastus* (2008): 60–66.
Warren, Alvin C., Jr. Financial Contract Innovation and Income Tax Policy. *Harvard Law Review* (1993): 460–492.
Wattel, Peter J. & Otto Marres. Characterization of Fictitious Income under OECD-Patterned Tax Treaties. *European Taxation* (2003): 66–79.

Weber, Dennis. A Closer Look at the General Anti-abuse Clause in the Parent-Subsidiary Directive and the Merger Directive. *EC Tax Review* (1996): 63-69.
Weber, Dennis. The Proposed EU Interest and Royalty Directive. *EC Tax Review* (2001): 15-30.
Weber, Dennis. The New Common Minimum Anti-Abuse Rule in the EU Parent-Subsidiary Directive: Background, Impact, Applicability, Purpose and Effect. *Intertax* (2016): 98-129.
Weidman, Oktavia. *Taxation of Derivatives*, Kluwer (2015).
Weisbach, David A. Tax Responses to Financial Contract Innovation. *Tax Law Review* (1995): 491-544.
Weisbach, David. A. The Use of Neutralities in International Tax Policy. *National Tax Journal* (2015): 635-652.
Wenehed, Lars-Erik. *CFC-Lagstiftning*. Juristförlaget (2000).
Whitehead, S. CFC Legislation and Abuse of Law in the Community, *The Influence of European Law on Direct Taxation – Recent and Future Developments*, ed. Weber Dennis. Kluwer (2007): 1-16.
Wheeler, Joanna C. General Report. Conflicts in the Attribution of Income to a Person. *Cahiers de droit fiscal international*, 92b. Kluwer (2007): 17-58.
Whitehead, S. Practical Implications Arising from the European Court's Recent Decisions Concerning CFC legislation and Dividend Taxation. *EC Tax Review* (2007a): 176-183.
Wheeler, Joanna. The Attribution of Income to a Person for Tax Treaty Purposes. *Bulletin for International Fiscal Documentation* (2005): 477-488.
Widmann, Siegfried. Zurechnungen und Umqualificationen durch das nationale Recht in ihrem Verhältnis zum DBA-Recht. In *Grundfragen des Internationalen Steuerrechts*, edited by Klaus Vogel. Verlag Dr Otto Schmidt KG (1985): 235-257.
Widmer, Max. Verosopimuksen tulkinta. *Verotus* (1970). 21-24.
Wikström, Kauko. Konserniavustuksesta. *Juhlajulkaisu P.J. Muukkonen*. Turun Yliopisto (1987): 161-169.
Wikström, Kauko. *Oikeus ja talous*. Lakimiesliiton kustannus (1994).
Wikström, Kauko. *Yleiset opit verotuksessa*. Turun yliopisto oikeustieteellinen tiedekunta (2008).
Wiman, Bertil. *Prissättning inom multinationella koncerner*. Iustus förlag (1987).
Wiman, Bertil. Über die Vermeidung und Beseitigung von Merfachbesteuerung bei Ausschüttungen zwichen Gesellschaften nach schwedischem recht. *Internationales SteuerRecht* (1995): 566-570.
Wittendorff, Jens. *Transfer Pricing*. Karnov (2016).
Wood, Philip R. *Project Finance, Subordinated Debt and State Loans*. Sweet & Maxwell (1995).
Wyntin, Dag. National Report of Belgium, International Aspects of Thin Capitalization. *Cahiers de droit fiscal international*, LXXXIb. Kluwer (1996): 341-366.
Ylä-Liedepohja, Jouko. Monikäsitteinen verotuksen neutraalisuus. *Verotus* (1992): 342-347.

Bibliography

Zee, Howell H. Taxation and Efficiency, *Tax Policy Handbook*, ed. Parthasarathi Shome. Tax Policy Division Fiscal Affairs Department International Monetary Fund (1995): 25–29.

Zielke, Rainer. Shareholder Debt Financing and Double Taxation in the OECD: An Empirical Survey with Recommendations for the Further Development of the OECD Model and International Tax Planning. *Intertax* (2010): 62–92.

Zimmer, Frederik. General Report. Form and Substance in Tax Law. *Cahiers de droit fiscal international*, LXXXVIIa. Kluwer (2002): 19–67.

Züger, Mario. *Arbitration under Tax Treaties. Improving Legal Protection in International Tax Law.* IBFD (2001).

Züger, Mario. General Report. *Settlement of Disputes in Tax Treaty Law*, ed. Michael Lang & Züger Mario. Kluwer (2004): 15–47.

Index

A

Arbitration Convention, 152, 157, 164, 175, 176, 216, 223, 248
Arm's length principle, 152, 155, 158, 159, 176, 212, 216, 218, 250
Assignment rules, 44
Autonomous classification, 46–48, 98, 179

B

Base company, 130
Basic instruments, 117
Beneficial owner, 25, 26, 104, 159
Bonus shares, 5, 64, 142–149, 161, 247
Business purpose doctrine, 213

C

Call option, 118, 119
Capital Directive, 63, 64
Capital export neutrality, 130
Capital import neutrality, 11
Caps, 118
CFC. *See* controlled foreign corporations (CFC)
'Check-the-box', 77
Classical system, 17
Classification conflict, 2, 13–14, 16, 40–57, 71, 76, 78, 79, 87, 90–92, 107, 114, 116, 126–128, 131, 141, 149, 175, 176, 182, 183, 188, 193, 198, 201, 206–208, 211, 216, 222, 223, 241, 242, 245–250

Classification problem, 2, 42–49, 89
Collars, 118, 119
Compensatory tax, 19
Complex financial instruments, 166
Conditional additional shareholder contribution, 5
Conduit company, 130
Constitutive norms, 59, 60
Controlled foreign corporations (CFC), 5, 129–142, 246–247
Convertible debt/convertible loan, 174, 194–198
Correlative adjustment, 153
Credit method, 19, 21, 22, 24, 26, 45, 53, 55, 140, 183

D

Debt-equity hybrids, 165–208, 248–249
Derivative financial instruments, 5, 15, 94, 117–128, 246, 251
Derivatives, 117–128, 246
Direct credit, 26, 30
Direct investment dividend, 7, 14, 18, 19, 25–28, 31, 51, 55, 115, 134, 135, 139, 140, 142, 176, 203, 204, 231, 240, 247, 250
Directive shopping, 134
Distributive rules, 44
Dividend equivalent payments, 5, 15, 94, 109, 110, 117–128, 246, 251
Dividend received deduction, 17
Dividend right, 5, 94, 101–108, 244–245, 251

Index

Dividend-stripping, 93–128, 243–246, 251

E

Earnings and profits, 124, 144, 195, 227
Entity classification, 75–79, 87, 89, 91, 92, 131, 141, 162, 241–243, 251
Equalization tax, 47
Equity derivatives, 119–121, 124–128, 246
Equity securities lending, 5, 15, 94, 108–118, 245–246
Exemption method, 18, 21, 22, 45, 53, 55, 139, 140, 183

F

Fat capitalization, 213
Fictive distribution, 5, 15, 97, 101, 114, 129–149, 158, 243, 246–247
Fictive dividend, 97, 132, 137–141, 158, 243, 244
Floors, 118, 119
Forward, 118–122, 141, 247
Full repurchase transaction, 110
Future, 94, 101, 108, 117, 118, 130, 185

H

Hidden profit distribution, 5, 152
Hybrid entities, 75, 80, 135
Hybrid instruments, 5, 6, 15, 63, 166–168, 170–173, 175–178, 181–183, 207, 208, 248, 251

I

Imputation system, 19, 212
Indirect credit, 26, 30, 229
Innovative financial instruments, 166
Integrated system, 17
Intermediary entity, 136
International double taxation, 2, 9, 16, 23, 24, 26, 34, 43–46, 51, 55, 56, 78, 79, 92, 142, 159, 207, 208, 211, 241, 242, 246, 248–251

Interpretation, 10, 12, 35, 37, 42, 43, 46–51, 53–55, 57, 59, 63, 65, 71, 85–87, 89–91, 105, 106, 113, 116, 125, 135, 138, 139, 146, 147, 156, 161, 162, 173–176, 178, 180–182, 212, 216, 218, 219, 229, 230, 234, 235, 237, 242

J

Jouissance **rights,** 67, 70, 192

Jouissance shares, 67, 70, 192

L

Lex fori, 46, 47

Limited repurchase transaction, 110
Linked approach, 110, 122
Liquidation, 6, 16, 64, 103, 121, 144, 167, 168, 180, 181, 184, 187, 189–191, 197–200, 202, 203, 205, 206, 225, 226, 230, 231, 235–237, 240, 250
Liquidation distributions, 63, 225–240, 249–250
Look-through approach, 110, 131, 132, 135, 141, 142, 246, 247

M

Mezzanine financing, 166

N

Negative classification conflict, 42, 54
Negative classification problem, 45
Neutrality, 10–12, 18, 61, 62, 130, 166, 170, 226, 231
New financial instruments, 121
Non-transparent entity, 75, 77, 79
Notional principal contract, 118, 119

Index

O
Option, 79, 80, 118, 119, 194, 195, 210

P
Partial liquidation, 226, 228, 230, 231, 235, 240, 250
Pass-through entity, 75
Perpetual debt, 174, 184–188, 203
Portfolio dividend, 7, 14, 18, 19, 25, 26, 30, 192
Positive classification conflict, 42, 54
Preference shares, 201, 203, 204, 207
Preferred shares, 144, 201–207
Primary instruments, 117
Primary sheltering, 130
Profit debentures, 180
Profit-participating loans, 174, 180, 189–191, 193, 203
Put option, 118, 119

R
Redeemable preferred shares, 202, 203, 206, 207
Regulative norms, 59

S
Secondary sheltering, 130
Securities loan, 109, 120
Securities repurchase transaction, 109
Separate entity approach, 151
Separate tax subject, 13, 75, 82–90, 131, 135
Separate transaction approach, 110, 122, 123
Share repurchase, 109, 226, 230, 235
Share warrant, 194, 195
Silent partnership, 76
Source state classification, 35, 46, 47, 51–55, 69, 70, 72, 100, 103, 105, 138, 146–148, 162, 175, 178, 179, 181–183, 192, 193, 198, 201, 214, 222, 223, 234, 238, 240, 244, 245
Split-rate system, 122
Stock dividend, 142, 143, 195
Stripped dividend, 93–128, 243–246, 251
Subject classification, 75
Subject-to-tax clauses, 45
Subordinated loan, 199–201
Substance over form doctrine, 170
Substitute payments, 5, 15, 108–117
Substitution problem, 41
Swaps, 117–121
Synthetic equity, 94, 117, 119, 121, 122, 124–127, 246

T
Tax planning, 1, 10, 28, 166, 167, 209
Thin capitalization, 6, 14, 117, 171, 190, 209–223, 238, 249
Total liquidation, 6, 16, 226–228, 230, 231, 235
Transfer prices, 151–164, 247–248, 250
Transfer pricing, 4, 151–157, 161, 162, 176, 216, 250
Transparent, 4, 7, 13, 75, 77–80, 82, 86–89, 91, 131, 135, 141, 142, 246, 251
Treaty shopping, 26

SERIES ON INTERNATIONAL TAXATION

1. Alberto Xavier, *The Taxation of Foreign Investment in Brazil*, 1980 (ISBN 90-200-0582-0).
2. Hugh J. Ault & Albert J. Rädler, *The German Corporation Tax Law with 1980 Amendments*, 1981 (ISBN 90-200-0642-8).
3. Paul R. McDaniel & Hugh J. Ault, *Introduction to United States International Taxation*, 1981 (ISBN 90-6544-004-6).
4. Albert J. Rädler, *German Transfer Pricing/Prix de Transfer en Allemagne*, 1984 (ISBN 90-6544-143-3).
5. Paul R. McDaniel & Stanley S. Surrey, *International Aspects of Tax Expenditures: A Comparative Study*, 1985 (ISBN 90-654-4163-8).
6. Kees van Raad, *Nondiscrimination in International Tax Law*, 1986 (ISBN 90-6544-266-9).
7. Sijbren Cnossen (ed.), *Tax Coordination in the European Community*, 1987 (ISBN 90-6544-272-3).
8. Ben Terra, *Sales Taxation. The Case of Value Added Tax in the European Community*, 1989 (ISBN 90-6544-381-9).
9. Rutsel S.J. Martha, *The Jurisdiction to Tax in International Law: Theory and Practice of Legislative Fiscal Jurisdiction*, 1989 (ISBN 90-654-4416-5).
10. Paul R. McDaniel & Hugh J. Ault, *Introduction to United States International Taxation* (3rd revised edition), 1989 (ISBN 90-6544-423-8).
11. Manuel Pires, *International Juridicial Double Taxation of Income*, 1989 (ISBN 90-6544-426-2).
12. A.H.M. Daniels, *Issues in International Partnership Taxation*, 1991 (ISBN 90-654-4577-3).
13. Arvid A. Skaar, *Permanent Establishment: Erosion of a Tax Treaty Principle*, 1992 (ISBN 90-6544-594-3).
14. Cyrille David & Geerten M.M. Michielse (eds), *Tax Treatment of Financial Instruments*, 1996 (ISBN 90-654-4666-4).
15. Herbert H. Alpert & Kees van Raad (eds), *Essays on International Taxation*, 1993 (ISBN 90-654-4781-4).
16. Wolfgang Gassner, Michael Lang & Eduard Lechner (eds), *Tax Treaties and EC Law*, 1997 (ISBN 90-411-0680-4).
17. Glória Teixeira, *Taxing Corporate Profits in the EU*, 1997 (ISBN 90-411-0703-7).
18. Michael Lang et al. (eds), *Multilateral Tax Treaties*, 1998 (ISBN 90-411-0704-5).
19. Stef van Weeghel, *The Improper Use of Tax Treaties*, 1998 (ISBN 90-411-0737-1).
20. Klaus Vogel (ed.), *Interpretation of Tax Law and Treaties and Transfer Pricing in Japan and Germany*, 1998 (ISBN 90-411-9655-2).
21. Bertil Wiman (ed.), *International Studies in Taxation: Law and Economics; Liber Amicorum Leif Mutén*, 1999 (ISBN 90-411-9692-7).
22. Alfonso J. Martín Jiménez, *Towards Corporate Tax Harmonization in the European Community*, 1999 (ISBN 90-411-9690-0).

23. Ramon J. Jeffery, *The Impact of State Sovereignty on Global Trade and International Taxation*, 1999 (ISBN 90-411-9703-6).
24. A.J. Easson, *Taxation of Foreign Direct Investment*, 1999 (ISBN 90-411-9741-9).
25. Marjaana Helminen, *The Dividend Concept in International Tax Law: Dividend Payments Between Corporate Entities*, 1999 (ISBN 90-411-9765-6).
26. Paul Kirchhof, Moris Lehner, Kees van Raad, Arndt Raupach & Michael-Rodi (eds), *International and Comparative Taxation: Essays in Honour of Klaus Vogel*, 2002 (ISBN 90-411-9841-5).
27. Krister Andersson, Peter Melz & Christer Silfverberg (eds), *Liber Amicorum Sven-Olof Lodin*, 2001 (ISBN 90-411-9850-4).
28. Juan Martín Jovanovich, *Customs Valuation and Transfer Pricing: Is It Possible to Harmonize Customs and Tax Rules?*, 2002 (ISBN 90-411-9888-1).
29. Stefano Simontacchi, *Taxation of Capital Gains under the OECD Model Convention: With Special Regard to Immovable Property*, 2007 (ISBN 978-90-411-2549-1).
30. Michael Lang, Josef Schuch, & Claus Staringer (eds), *Tax Treaty Law and EC Law*, 2007 (ISBN 978-90-411-2629-0).
31. Duncan Bentley, *Taxpayers' Rights: Theory Origin and Implementation*, 2007 (ISBN 978-90-411-2650-4).
32. Sergio André Rocha, *Interpretation of Double Taxation Conventions: General Theory and Brazilian Perspective*, 2008 (ISBN 978-90-411-2822-5).
33. Robert F. van Brederode, *Systems of General Sales Taxation: Theory, Policy and Practice*, 2009 (ISBN 978-90-411-2832-4).
34. John G. Head & Richard Krever (eds), *Tax Reform in the 21st Century: A Volume in Memory of Richard Musgrave*, 2009 (ISBN 978-90-411-2829-4).
35. Jens Wittendorff, *Transfer Pricing and the Arm's Length Principle in International Tax Law*, 2010 (ISBN 978-90-411-3270-3).
36. Marjaana Helminen, *The International Tax Law Concept of Dividend*, Second Edition, 2017 (ISBN 978-90-411-8394-1).
37. Robert F. van Brederode (ed.), *Immovable Property under VAT: A Comparative Global Analysis*, 2011 (ISBN 978-90-411-3126-3).
38. Dennis Weber & Stef van Weeghel, *The 2010 OECD Updates: Model Tax Convention & Transfer Pricing Guidelines - A Critical Review*, 2011 (ISBN 978-90-411-3812-5).
39. Yariv Brauner & Martin James McMahon, Jr. (eds), *The Proper Tax Base: Structural Fairness from an International and Comparative Perspective— Essays in Honour of Paul McDaniel*, 2012 (ISBN 978-90-411-3286-4).
40. Robert F. van Brederode (ed.), *Science, Technology and Taxation*, 2012 (ISBN 978-90-411-3125-6).
41. Oskar Henkow, *The VAT/GST Treatment of Public Bodies*, 2013 (ISBN 978-90-411-4663-2).
42. Jean Schaffner, *How Fixed Is a Permanent Establishment?*, 2013 (ISBN 978-90-411-4662-5).

43. Miguel Correia, *Taxation of Corporate Groups*, 2013 (ISBN 978-90-411-4841-4).
44. Veronika Daurer, *Tax Treaties and Developing Countries*, 2014 (ISBN 978-90-411-4982-4).
45. Claire Micheau, *State Aid, Subsidy and Tax Incentives under EU and WTO Law*, 2014 (ISBN 978-90-411-4555-0).
46. Robert F. van Brederode & Richard Krever (eds), *Legal Interpretation of Tax Law*, 2014 (ISBN 978-90-411-4945-9).
47. Radhakishan Rawal, *Taxation of Cross-border Services*, 2014 (ISBN 978-90-411-4947-3).
48. João Dácio Rolim, *Proportionality and Fair Taxation*, 2014 (ISBN 978-90-411-5838-3).
49. Paulo Rosenblatt, *General Anti-avoidance Rules for Major Developing Countries*, 2015 (ISBN 978-90-411-5839-0).
50. Gaspar Lopes Dias V.S., *Tax Arbitrage through Cross-Border Financial Engineering*, 2015 (ISBN 978-90-411-5875-8).
51. Geerten M.M. Michielse & Victor Thuronyi (eds), *Tax Design Issues Worldwide*, 2015 (ISBN 978-90-411-5610-5).
52. Oktavia Weidmann, *Taxation of Derivatives*, 2015 (ISBN 978-90-411-5977-9).
53. Chris Evans, Richard Krever & Peter Mellor (eds), *Tax Simplification*, 2015 (ISBN 978-90-411-5976-2).
54. Reuven Avi-Yonah & Joel Slemrod (eds), *Taxation and Migration*, 2015 (ISBN 978-90-411-6136-9).
55. Alexander Bosman, *Other Income under Tax Treaties: An Analysis of Article 21 of the OECD Model Convention*, 2015 (ISBN 978-90-411-6610-4).
56. John Abrahamson, *International Taxation of Manufacturing and Distribution*, 2016 (ISBN 978-90-411-6664-7).
57. Frederik Boulogne, *Shortcomings in the EU Merger Directive*, 2016 (ISBN 978-90-411-6713-2).
58. Angelika Meindl-Ringler, *Beneficial Ownership in International Tax Law*, 2016 (ISBN 978-90-411-6833-7).
59. Andreas Waltrich, *Cross-Border Taxation of Permanent Establishments: An International Comparison*, 2016 (ISBN 978-90-411-6832-0).